Historical Dictionaries of Literature and the Arts
Jon Woronoff, Series Editor

1. *Science Fiction Literature*, by Brian Stableford, 2004.
2. *Hong Kong Cinema*, by Lisa Odham Stokes, 2007.
3. *American Radio Soap Operas*, by Jim Cox, 2005.
4. *Japanese Traditional Theatre*, by Samuel L. Leiter, 2006.
5. *Fantasy Literature*, by Brian Stableford, 2005.
6. *Australian and New Zealand Cinema*, by Albert Moran and Errol Vieth, 2006.
7. *African-American Television*, by Kathleen Fearn-Banks, 2006.
8. *Lesbian Literature*, by Meredith Miller, 2006.
9. *Scandinavian Literature and Theater*, by Jan Sjåvik, 2006.
10. *British Radio*, by Seán Street, 2006.
11. *German Theater*, by William Grange, 2006.
12. *African American Cinema*, by S. Torriano Berry and Venise Berry, 2006.
13. *Sacred Music*, by Joseph P. Swain, 2006.
14. *Russian Theater*, by Laurence Senelick, 2007.
15. *French Cinema*, by Dayna Oscherwitz and MaryEllen Higgins, 2007.
16. *Postmodernist Literature and Theater*, by Fran Mason, 2007.
17. *Irish Cinema*, by Roderick Flynn and Pat Brereton, 2007.
18. *Australian Radio and Television*, by Albert Moran and Chris Keating, 2007.
19. *Polish Cinema*, by Marek Haltof, 2007.
20. *Old Time Radio*, by Robert C. Reinehr and Jon D. Swartz, 2008.
21. *Renaissance Art*, by Lilian H. Zirpolo, 2008.
22. *Broadway Musical*, by William A. Everett and Paul R. Laird, 2008.
23. *American Theater: Modernism*, by James Fisher and Felicia Hardison Londré, 2008.
24. *German Cinema*, by Robert C. Reimer and Carol J. Reimer, 2008.
25. *Horror Cinema*, by Peter Hutchings, 2008.
26. *Westerns in Cinema*, by Paul Varner, 2008.
27. *Chinese Theater*, by Tan Ye, 2008.
28. *Italian Cinema*, by Gino Moliterno, 2008.
29. *Architecture*, by Allison Lee Palmer, 2008.
30. *Russian and Soviet Cinema*, by Peter Rollberg, 2008.

31. *African American Theater*, by Anthony D. Hill, 2009.
32. *Postwar German Literature*, by William Grange, 2009.
33. *Modern Japanese Literature and Theater*, by J. Scott Miller, 2009.
34. *Animation and Cartoons*, by Nichola Dobson, 2009.
35. *Modern Chinese Literature*, by Li-hua Ying, 2010.
36. *Middle Eastern Cinema*, by Terri Ginsberg and Chris Lippard, 2010.
37. *Spanish Cinema*, by Alberto Mira, 2010.
38. *Film Noir*, by Andrew Spicer, 2010.
39. *French Theater*, by Edward Forman, 2010.
40. *Choral Music*, by Melvin P. Unger, 2010.
41. *Westerns in Literature*, by Paul Varner, 2010.
42. *Baroque Art and Architecture*, by Lilian H. Zirpolo, 2010.
43. *Surrealism*, by Keith Aspley, 2010.
44. *Science Fiction Cinema*, by M. Keith Booker, 2010.
45. *Latin American Literature and Theater*, by Richard A. Young and Odile Cisneros, 2010.
46. *Children's Literature*, by Emer O'Sullivan, 2010.

Historical Dictionary of Children's Literature

Emer O'Sullivan

Historical Dictionaries of Literature and the Arts, No. 46

The Scarecrow Press, Inc.
Lanham • Toronto • Plymouth, UK
2010

Published by Scarecrow Press, Inc.
A wholly owned subsidiary of The Rowman & Littlefield Publishing Group, Inc.
4501 Forbes Boulevard, Suite 200, Lanham, Maryland 20706
http://www.scarecrowpress.com

Estover Road, Plymouth PL6 7PY, United Kingdom

British Library Cataloguing in Publication Information Available

Library of Congress Cataloging-in-Publication Data

O'Sullivan, Emer.
Historical dictionary of children's literature / Emer O'Sullivan.
p. cm. — (Historical dictionaries of literature and the arts ; no. 46)
Includes bibliographical references.
ISBN 978-0-8108-6080-3 (cloth : alk. paper) — ISBN 978-0-8108-7496-1 (ebook)
1. Children's literature—History and criticism—Dictionaries. 2. Children's literature—Bio-bibliography—Dictionaries. I. Title.
PN1009.A1O775 2010
809'.89282—dc22 2010020555

∞™ The paper used in this publication meets the minimum requirements of American National Standard for Information Sciences—Permanence of Paper for Printed Library Materials, ANSI/NISO Z39.48-1992.

Printed in the United States of America

Contents

Editor's Foreword

Once upon a time it would have been simple to describe children's literature. They were straightforward books using unsophisticated language, dealing with few and mostly congenial or uplifting topics, and helping children adjust to what grown-ups thought should be their proper status and conduct. Over the centuries, and especially in recent decades, however, this has changed enormously. The language for younger children is still relatively simple, but it grows rapidly in sophistication for older audiences and engages in wordplay that, although easily received by readers, many adults cannot grasp. There is no end to the number of themes—not just being good boys and girls, but being inventive or innovative ones who can cope with very serious issues (illness, brutality, warfare, death) and who may eventually decide what they want to become. And this literature no longer comes solely from the West (mainly the United States, Great Britain, and Europe) but from around the world, with some works in foreign languages translated into English. These books (or translations) are then often adapted for television, film, and other media.

This *Historical Dictionary of Children's Literature* impressively covers all the bases, providing concise and informative entries in the dictionary section on a variety of topics: some of the better authors and their works, as well as their illustrators, from earliest to most recent times; their craft, including the different forms literature can assume—from picture books to poetry to lengthy and involved novels—and the variety of genres, such as adventure, fantasy, mystery, and science fiction; and finally the growing range of themes, such as animals in the wild or pets, family life, affection and love, sex and sexism, intolerance, and racism. The history is summarized in the chronology and then put into context in the introduction. Naturally, since this book cannot address all aspects of a vast and rapidly expanding universe, one of its most helpful components is a bibliography, which points toward other sources for reading and research.

The author is Emer O'Sullivan, from Ireland, who is a professor of English literature at Leuphana University in Lüneburg, Germany, and formerly worked at the Institute for Children's Literature Research at Frankfurt University. She is therefore well equipped to specialize in comparative children's literature and image studies, on which she wrote two scholarly publications (one in German and one in English), winning the biennial International Research Society for Children's Literature Award for outstanding research for an additional German publication in 2001. O'Sullivan also won the Children's Literature Association Book Award in 2007 for another publication, *Comparative Children's Literature*. To top it all off, aside from her scholarly writing and teaching, she has coauthored eight bilingual (English-German) children's novels. That is clearly a very solid foundation on which to write this encyclopedia, one that will guide readers gently yet firmly through what we now know is a deceptively simple field.

Jon Woronoff
Series Editor

Acknowledgments

Every encyclopedia profits from its predecessors. I owe a special debt of gratitude to the four-volume *Oxford Encyclopedia of Children's Literature*, edited by Jack Zipes, the most important, comprehensive reference work and an essential guide for anyone seriously engaged with the subject. *The Cambridge Guide to Children's Books in English*, edited by Victor Watson, was also a useful companion.

A number of students assisted me at different phases during this project. Birte Gloy, Friederike Dittmer, and Nina Schulze all deserve a mention; and I owe a special thanks to Linda Dütsch, who saw the manuscript through to completion. A warm thank-you goes to my husband, Dietmar Rösler, for his unfailing support, and to my editor Jon Woronoff for his patience.

Acronyms and Abbreviations

ALA	American Library Association (U.S.)
ALSC	Association for Library Service to Children, a division of the ALA
ASSITEJ	Association Internationale du Théâtre pour l'Enfance et la Jeunesse / International Association of Theatre for Children and Young People
BBC	British Broadcasting Corporation
BIB	Biennial of Illustrations Bratislava
CBC	Children's Book Council (U.S.)
CBE	Commander of the Most Excellent Order of the British Empire
ChLA	Children's Literature Association
CIBC	Council on Interracial Books for Children
CILIP	The Chartered Institute of Library and Information Professionals (UK)
DBE	Dame Commander of the Order of the British Empire
IBBY	International Board on Books for Young People
IRSCL	International Research Society for Children's Literature
IYL	International Youth Library
KBE	Knight Commander of the Order of the British Empire
LA	Library Association (UK)
MBE	Member of the Most Excellent Order of the British Empire
OBE	Officer of the Most Excellent Order of the British Empire
UNESCO	United Nations Educational, Scientific, and Cultural Organization
UNICEF	United Nations International Children's Emergency Fund
YALSA	Young Adult Library Services Association, a division of the ALA

Chronology

ca. 990 Aelfric's *Colloquy*, Latin text for pupils at monastery schools.

ca. 1475 *The Babees Book*, book of manners for the young.

1484 *Subtyl Historyes and Fables of Esop*, first English collection of Aesop's fables, published by William Caxton.

1485 Sir Thomas Malory's *Morte d'Arthur*, English version of the Arthurian stories and source of many later adaptations.

ca. 1553 *A New Interlude for Children to Play Named Jack Juggler, Both Witty and Very Pleasant*, first play in English specifically for children.

1563 John Foxe's *Actes and Monuments*, known as *The Book of Martyrs*. Anti-Catholic work with scenes of violent death used as a source in many later books for Protestant children.

1570 John Hart's *A Methode; or, Comfortable Beginning for All Unlearned*, arguably the first English textbook.

1605 Miguel de Cervantes' *Don Quixote*, picaresque novel subsequently adapted for children.

1658 John Amos Comenius's *Orbis Sensualium Pictus* (*The Visible World in Pictures*) uses illustrations to aid children's understanding of an informational text. Generally regarded as the first picture book for children.

1672 James Janeway's *A Token for Children: Being an Exact Account of the Conversion, Holy and Exemplary Lives, and Joyful Deaths of Several Young Children*, one of the most widely read Puritan children's books.

1678 John Bunyan's *The Pilgrim's Progress from This World to That Which Is to Come*, popular spiritual allegory.

ca. 1690 *The New England Primer*, Puritan publication that introduces young children to the alphabet through rhymes.

1693 John Locke's *Some Thoughts Concerning Education*, a founding philosophical text of modern education.

1697 Charles Perrault's *Histoires, ou Contes du temps passé*, major collection of fairy tales. English version, *Histories, or Tales of Past Times*, published in 1729, sometimes mistakenly referred to as *Tales of Mother Goose.*

1715 Isaac Watts's *Divine Songs, Attempted in Easy Language for the Use of Children*, didactic hymns. Remains popular for at least 150 years.

1717 Benjamin Harris's *The Holy Bible in Verse*, rhyming version of the Bible and first known children's book with illustrations in the future United States.

1719 Daniel Defoe's *Robinson Crusoe*, early novel of shipwreck and survival later widely adapted for children.

1726 Jonathan Swift's *Gulliver's Travels*, adult satire and source of subsequent adaptations for children.

1744 John Newbery's *A Little Pretty Pocket-Book, Intended for the Instruction and Amusement of Little Master Tommy and Pretty Miss Polly*, first children's book marketed as pleasure reading. Mary Cooper's *Tommy Thumb's Song Book*, earliest printed collection of nursery rhymes.

1745 *The History of the Holy Jesus* published in Boston, the first entirely American product for children.

1749 Sarah Fielding's *The Governess; or, The Little Female Academy*, one of the first books written specifically for girls.

1762 Jean-Jacques Rousseau's *Émile; ou, De l'éducation*, highly influential educational text which introduces the concept of the uncorrupted child and natural education. English translation *Emile* published the same year.

1765 *The History of Little Goody Two-Shoes*, the most popular children's story of the period, and *Mother Goose's Melody, or Sonnets for the Cradle*, collection of nursery rhymes, both published by Newbery.

1780 Sunday School Movement initiated by evangelists in England to teach working-class children discipline, catechism, and reading. Sunday schools first appear in the United States in the 1790s.

1781 Anna Laetitia Barbauld's *Hymns in Prose for Children*. Remains popular in Great Britain and the United States into the early years of the 20th century.

1783 Thomas Day's *The History of Sanford and Merton*, Rousseauian novel of education.

1786 Sarah Trimmer's *Economy of Charity*, written to promote Sunday-school education, and her early animal story *Fabulous Histories*, later known as *The History of the Robins*.

1789 William Blake's *Songs of Innocence* published for children.

ca. 1791 *The Oriental Moralist, or The Beauties of the Arabian Nights Entertainments*, first English selection of *The Arabian Nights* specifically for children.

1796 Maria Edgeworth's *The Parent's Assistant*, entertaining moral tales.

1799 The Religious Tract Society, publishers of books for children from 1812 on, founded in London.

1804 Jane and Ann Taylor's *Original Poems for Infant Minds*, an influential collection in the development of child-centered poetry.

1807 Charles and Mary Lamb's *Tales from Shakespeare,* prose adaptation for children.

1812–1815 Jacob and Wilhelm Grimm's *Kinder- und Hausmärchen* [Children's and Household Tales], seminal collection of fairy tales; a selection in English, *German Popular Stories*, published in 1823.

1819 Sir Walter Scott's *Ivanhoe*, a source of popular images of the Middle Ages.

1823 Clement Clarke Moore's "A Visit from St. Nicholas" ("'Twas the Night Before Christmas"), poem largely responsible for the contemporary conception of Santa Claus.

1825 The American Tract Society is founded. Begins publishing for children in 1827.

1826 James Fenimore Cooper's *The Last of the Mohicans*, famed frontier adventure novel set during the French and Indian War in 1757.

1827 *Tales of Peter Parley about America.* First of over a hundred best-selling information books by Samuel Griswold Goodrich.

1835 First collection of tales by Hans Christian Andersen, *Eventyr, fortalte for born*, appears in Denmark; a selection in English, *Wonderful Stories for Children*, published in 1846. First two books about the young American "scholar" *Rollo* by Jacob Abbott.

1839 Catherine Sinclair's *Holiday House* flouts the conventions of the moral tale.

1841 Captain Frederick Marryat's *Masterman Ready*, early sea adventure story. Charlotte Barton's *A Mother's Offering to Her Children: By a Lady, Long Resident in New South Wales*, Australia's first known children's book.

1844 Alexandre Dumas' *Les trois mousquetaires* (*The Three Musketeers*), hugely successful swashbuckling adventure story for adults, later a children's classic.

1845 Heinrich Hoffmann's *Struwwelpeter*, humorous German picture book of cautionary tales. English translation published in 1848.

1846 Edward Lear's *A Book of Nonsense* popularizes both literary nonsense and the limerick form.

1852 Nathaniel Hawthorne's *A Wonder Book for Girls and Boys*, retelling of classical myths for children; a second collection, *Tanglewood Tales*, follows a year later. Compulsory education law passed in Massachusetts; by 1918, all U.S. states have passed similar school-attendance laws. Catherine Parr Traill's survival story *Canadian Crusoe: A Tale of the Rice Lake Plains*, Canada's first children's novel.

1855 William M. Thackeray's *The Rose and the Ring*, fairy story with satirical and nonsensical elements.

1856 Charlotte Yonge's *The Daisy Chain* establishes the family story as a distinct genre.

1857 Thomas Hughes's *Tom Brown's School Days*, realistic portrayal of English boarding-school life.

1858 R. M. Ballantyne's *The Coral Island*, adventure story and juvenile robinsonade.

1862 First special reading room for boys opens in Manchester Public Library.

1863 Jules Verne's *Cinq semaines en ballon* (*Five Weeks in a Balloon*), first major science-fiction novel. Charles Kingsley's *The Water-Babies*, early classic fantasy.

1865 Lewis Carroll's *Alice's Adventures in Wonderland*, nonsense classic. Wilhelm Busch's *Max und Moritz*, a precursor of the modern comic strip. Mary Mapes Dodge's *Hans Brinker, or The Silver Skates* launches the icon of the courageous Dutch boy with his community-saving finger in the dike. Walter Crane's first toy book, *The House That Jack Built*.

1867 Hesba Stretton's *Jessica's First Prayer*, evangelical "street arab" book that starts a fashion for waif stories.

1868 Louisa May Alcott's *Little Women* establishes a distinctively American domestic realism in literature for children. Horatio Alger's *Ragged Dick*, the first of his many "rags to riches" novels.

1870 The Elementary Education Act, also known as Forster's Education Act, sets the framework for a national system of state education in Great Britain.

1871 George MacDonald's *At the Back of the North Wind*, spiritual fantasy.

1872 Susan Coolidge's *What Katy Did*, the first in the series of girls' stories about the Carr family.

1873 *St. Nicholas Magazine* for young people founded in the United States, with Mary Mapes Dodge as its first editor.

1874 *Funny Folks*, one of the first comic papers, appears in England.

1876 American Library Association founded in Philadelphia. Mark Twain's *The Adventures of Tom Sawyer*, the most famous "bad boy" novel.

1877 Anna Sewell's *Black Beauty*, popular animal "autobiography."

1878 The first pair of Randolph Caldecott's toy books are published, *The House That Jack Built* and *The Diverting History of John Gilpin.* Kate Greenaway's *Under the Window* establishes new fashions in children's wear.

1879 *Boy's Own Paper* published by the Religious Tract Society in Great Britain to combat "penny dreadfuls." *Harper's Young People* periodical launched in the United States.

1880 *Uncle Remus, His Songs and Sayings, the Folk-Lore of the Old Plantation*, black folktales adapted and compiled by Joel Chandler Harris, praised for his ability to capture plantation Negro dialect. First volume of Johanna Spyri's Swiss classic, *Heidi.*

1881–1882 Robert Louis Stevenson's *Treasure Island* is serialized in *Young Folks* magazine and sets new standards in the adventure genre. Carlo Collodi's *Pinocchio*, international classic about a puppet that comes to life, appears in serial form in an Italian children's magazine.

1883 Howard Pyle's lavishly illustrated *The Merry Adventures of Robin Hood*, one of the first retellings specifically for children.

1884 Mark Twain's *Adventures of Huckleberry Finn*, coming-of-age quest of an uneducated outcast. National Society for the Prevention of Cruelty to Children founded in England (60 years after the Royal Society for the Prevention of Cruelty to Animals).

1885 Robert Louis Stevenson's *A Child's Garden of Verses*, notable collection of poems.

1886 Frances Hodgson Burnett's *Little Lord Fauntleroy*, about an American boy heir to a British earldom, creates a fashion for boys' suits of velvet with lace collars. Kate Greenaway's *A Apple Pie*, Victorian alphabet book.

1888 Oscar Wilde's *The Happy Prince, and Other Tales*, literary fairy tales.

1889 Andrew Lang's *The Blue Fairy Book,* the first of an influential 12-book collection of fairy tales for children.

1890 Joseph Jacobs's *English Fairy Tales* aims to bring together native tales in a standard edition.

1894 Ethel Turner's *Seven Little Australians*, domestic adventures of natural, mischievous children in an urban Australian setting. Rudyard Kipling's *The Jungle Book*, short stories set in India, some centered on the orphan Mowgli who is fostered by wolves.

1895 The golliwog(g) makes its premier appearance in Bertha and Florence Upton's *The Adventures of Two Dutch Dolls—and a "Golliwogg."* The children's room opens in the Boston Public Library, the first library space specially designed for children in the United States.

1897 Rudolph Dirks's *Katzenjammer Kids*, the first newspaper comic strip.

1899 E. Nesbit's *The Story of the Treasure Seekers*, the first set of adventures of the Bastable children. Helen Bannerman's picture book *Little Black Sambo* appears in small illustrated format, heralding a change in children's publishing. Ethel Pedley's Australian-bush fantasy, *Dot and the Kangaroo. The Rover Boys at School*, the first title in the first series created by the Stratemeyer Syndicate, is published under the pseudonym Arthur M. Winfield.

1900 *The Century of the Child* is published in Swedish by children's-rights advocate Ellen Key. L. Frank Baum's *The Wonderful Wizard of Oz*, modern American fairy tale.

1901 Seymour Hicks's musical play *Bluebell in Fairyland*, one of the first commercial theatrical productions for children in London.

1902 Beatrix Potter's *The Tale of Peter Rabbit*, the first of 23 small-format animal picture books. E. Nesbit's *Five Children and It*, the first fantasy in the Psammead series. *Just So Stories*, collection of fables by Rudyard Kipling.

1903 Kate Douglas Wiggin's *Rebecca of Sunnybrook Farm*, coming-of-age story about a girl who changes the world around her through her goodness. Howard Pyle's *The Story of King Arthur and His Knights* in four volumes. Children's Educational Theater founded on New York's Lower East Side.

1904 J. M. Barrie's *Peter Pan, or The Boy Who Wouldn't Grow Up* premieres in London, the first stage play with real children as central characters. First of 72 volumes of the Stratemeyer Syndicate's Bobbsey Twins series, which runs until 1979, penned under the pseudonym Laura Lee Hope.

1905 Frances Hodgson Burnett's *A Little Princess*, Cinderella story about a wealthy girl forced to work as a servant in her boarding school.

1908 L. M. Montgomery's *Anne of Green Gables*, Canadian icon and one of the most popular girls' stories of all time. Kenneth Grahame's *The Wind in the Willows*, classic animal fantasy.

1910 Mary Grant Bruce's patriotic *A Little Bush Maid* is published in serial form and influences concepts of Australian national identity.

1913 Eleanor H. Porter's bestselling novel *Pollyanna*, about a cheerful orphan, introduces "the glad game."

1914 Brownsville Children's Library is founded in New York City, the first library devoted exclusively to children's books.

1915 The first children's library opens in Adelaide, Australia.

1918 Norman Lindsay's *The Magic Pudding* establishes a nonsense tradition in Australia. The tie-in between Johnny Gruelle's *Raggedy Ann Stories* and the doll of the same name is a marketing success in the United States.

1920 *The Brownies' Book*, a periodical for African American children from 6 to 16, is published by W. E. B. Du Bois and Augustus Granville Dill. Hugh Lofting's *The Story of Doctor Dolittle*, the first of his popular series about a vet who can speak to animals.

1922 Newbery Medal established in the United States to honor the author of the most distinguished contribution to American literature for children. *The Velveteen Rabbit* by Margery Williams, about the transformation of a toy rabbit. Carl Sandburg's *The Rootabaga Stories*, nonsense stories set in the American Midwest.

1923 Felix Salten's *Bambi*, tale of forest life later popularized by Disney, is published in German.

1924 *Horn Book Magazine*, the first periodical about literature for children and young adults, is founded in Boston.

1925 Elinor M. Brent-Dyer's *The School at the Chalet,* first of a series of almost 60 novels set in a girls' boarding school, initially in the Austrian Alps.

1926 A. A. Milne's *Winnie-the-Pooh*, illustrated by E. H. Sheperd, the classic adventures of a toy bear and other inhabitants of the Hundred Acre Wood.

1928 Wanda Gág's *Millions of Cats*, humorous original fairy tale with double-spread, black-and-white illustrations and hand-lettered text, considered the first true modern American picture book. Mickey Mouse appears for the first time in a Disney cartoon.

1929 Erich Kästner's *Emil und die Detektive* (*Emil and the Detectives*), popular and influential child-detective novel published in Germany. *Les aventures de Tintin* (*The Adventures of Tintin*), first of the popular series of comic strips created by Belgian artist Hergé.

1930 *The Hidden Staircase* by "Carolyn Keene," first of countless novels about the female amateur detective Nancy Drew published by the Stratemeyer Syndicate. Arthur Ransome's *Swallows and Amazons,* first of a 12-novel adventure series.

1931 Jean de Brunhoff's *Histoire de Babar le petit éléphant* (*The Story of Babar the Little Elephant*) heads a revival of high-quality illustrated children's books in 1930s France.

1932 Laura Ingalls Wilder's *The Little House in the Big Woods*, first of the popular series of eight Little House novels. *Popo and Fifina: Children of Haiti*, an early African American children's classic by Harlem Renaissance authors Langston Hughes and Arna Bontemps.

Mélanie Klein's *The Psychoanalysis of Children* presents techniques of child analysis.

1934 P. L. Travers's *Mary Poppins*, about a mysterious English nanny with magical powers. Geoffrey Trease's *Bows against the Barons* emphasizes Robin Hood's proletarian origin and revolutionary character in the fight against injustice.

1936 Munro Leaf and Robert Lawson's *The Story of Ferdinand*, pacifist tale about a bull who refuses to fight. Edward Ardizzone's *Little Tim and the Brave Sea Captain*, first of the popular Tim series. Carnegie Medal established in Great Britain for the writer of an outstanding children's book.

1937 J. R. R. Tolkien's *The Hobbit*, fantasy quest and prelude to The Lord of the Rings trilogy addressed to young readers. *Adventures of the Wishing Chair*, Enid Blyton's first book for children. Eve Garnett's *The Family from One-End Street* and its sequels about British working-class life. *Snow White and the Seven Dwarfs*, Disney's first animated feature film. *And to Think That I Saw It on Mulberry Street*, the first picture book by Dr. Seuss.

1938 Caldecott Medal established in the United States for the illustrator of a distinguished picture book. *The Yearling*, Marjorie Kinnan Rawlings's Pulitzer Prize–winning story of a Florida childhood.

1939 Ludwig Bemelmans's *Madeline*, picture-book adventures of a brave and precocious little girl in a convent school in Paris.

1940 Maud Hart Lovelace's *Betsy-Tacy*, the first volume of the Minnesota girl's adventures. Dorothy Kunhardt's *Pat the Bunny*, first interactive book for babies.

1941 H. A. Rey and Margret Rey's *Curious George*, picture book about a mischievous monkey. Robert McCloskey's *Make Way for Ducklings* features a pair of ducks who raise their family in a central Boston park. Mary Treadgold's *We Couldn't Leave Dinah,* pony story and one of the first children's books written about World War II.

1942 Margaret Wise Brown's *The Runaway Bunny*, illustrated by Clement Hurd. *The Poky Little Puppy*, by Janette Sebring Lowrey and

Gustaf Tenggren, in the Little Golden Books series, one of the all-time best-selling hardcover children's books in the United States.

1943 Esther Forbes's *Johnny Tremain*, historical novel set in Boston during the start of the American Revolution.

1945 Astrid Lindgren's Swedish *Pippi Långstrump* (*Pippi Longstocking*), about a parentless, financially independent girl rebel with superhuman strength, flaunts conventions in children's books. E. B. White's *Stuart Little* has a mouse as hero. Lois Lenski's *Strawberry Girl*, about migrant laborers in Florida.

1946 The United Nations International Children's Emergency Fund (UNICEF) is founded to bring relief to war-affected children.

1947 *Goodnight Moon*, by Margaret Wise Brown and Clement Hurd, depicts in rhyme the ritual of a child saying goodnight to everything around. Robert Heinlein's *Rocket Ship Galileo*, first important juvenile science-fiction novel. Unicorn Theatre for Children founded in London by Caryl Jenner.

1949 The International Youth Library (IYL), the largest library for international children's and youth literature in the world, opens in Munich.

1950 C. S. Lewis's *The Lion, the Witch, and the Wardrobe*, the first of the seven *Narnia Chronicles*.

1951 J. D. Salinger's *The Catcher in the Rye*, modern adolescent bildungsroman written for adults, whose protagonist Holden Caulfield becomes an icon of teenage rebellion.

1952 Mary Norton's *The Borrowers*, first of a series of fantasy novels about the adventures of miniature people. E. B. White's *Charlotte's Web* celebrates the friendship between a barn spider and a pig. First publication in English of Anne Frank's *Diary of a Young Girl*.

1953 International Board on Books for Young People (IBBY) founded in Zurich, Switzerland.

1954 Lucy M. Boston's *The Children of Green Knowe*, time-shift fantasy. Rosemary Sutcliff's *The Eagle of the Ninth*, first in the historical saga of the British Aquila family.

1955 Kate Greenaway Medal established in Great Britain for distinguished illustration in a children's book. Crockett Johnson's picture book *Harold and the Purple Crayon* features a four-year-old boy who has the power to create a world of his own simply by drawing it.

1956 The international Hans Christian Andersen Award is established and presented every 2nd year to an author and, since 1966, an illustrator for their entire body of work. Ian Serraillier's *The Silver Sword*, displacement adventure in war-torn Europe.

1957 Dr. Seuss's *The Cat in the Hat*, wildly imaginative and humorous story that uses only 236 distinct words, changes the face of easy readers and shows how entertaining reduced-vocabulary books can be.

1958 Philippa Pearce's *Tom's Midnight Garden*, acclaimed time-shift fantasy that draws on the notion that different times can coexist and blend.

1959 Barbie, the world's most popular doll, created by the cofounder of Mattel toy company, Ruth Handler. Ken follows in 1961, the African American doll Christie in 1969.

1960 Scott O'Dell's *Island of the Blue Dolphins*, female robinsonade.

1961 Roald Dahl's *James and the Giant Peach*, first of his humorous, fantastic, and grotesque novels for children. Norton Juster's *The Phantom Tollbooth*, an original, *Alice in Wonderland*–type adventure.

1962 Madeleine L'Engle's *A Wrinkle in Time* blends science fantasy and religious themes. Ezra Jack Keats's *The Snowy Day*, the first picture book with an African American protagonist.

1963 Maurice Sendak's *Where the Wild Things Are* uses visual symbolism to explore the child's interior world. Colin Thiele's *Storm Boy*, acclaimed Australian environmental novel.

1964 Lloyd Alexander's *The Book of Three*, first of *The Chronicles of Prydain* based on Welsh mythology. Roald Dahl's *Charlie and the Chocolate Factory*. Louise Fitzhugh's satirical *Harriet the Spy*. Anne Holm's *David* (*I Am David*), about a boy damaged by a prison camp, is published in Denmark.

1965 Susan Cooper's *Over Sea, Under Stone*, the first of five novels in *The Dark Is Rising* fantasy sequence.

1966 Mildred L. Batchelder Award established in the United States for translated children's books.

1967 Alan Garner's multilayered fantasy *The Owl Service*. Russell Hoban's *The Mouse and His Child*, philosophical fable about clockwork toys with human longings. Jill Paton Walsh's *The Dolphin Crossing,* dramatic World War II adventure of two boys' rescue mission to Dunkirk.

1968 Ursula Le Guin's *A Wizard of Earthsea*, the first fantasy in the Earthsea series, whose quest is more interested in balance than in good versus evil. Paul Zindel's *The Pigman* about the relationship between two teenagers and a lonely old man. K. M. Peyton's *Flambards*, first of a series of novels set on an English estate before, during, and after World War I. Ted Hughes's modern myth, *The Iron Man*.

1969 Eric Carle's *The Very Hungry Caterpillar*, global long-selling picture book with cutout holes that invites preschool readers to learn about the life cycle of butterflies, different foods, and the days of the week. *Sesame Street*, the educational television program for preschool children featuring Jim Henson's Muppets, starts its broadcast.

1970 Judy Blume's *Are You There, God? It's Me, Margaret*, candid depiction of teenage life. Tana Hoban's *Look Again!* one of the first picture books to feature photographs as the medium. The International Research Society for Children's Literature (IRSCL) is founded in Frankfurt, Germany.

1971 Robert C. O'Brien's *Mrs. Frisby and the Rats of NIMH*, featuring laboratory rats, addresses the moral problems of technological advance. Judith Kerr's *When Hitler Stole Pink Rabbit*, autobiographical novel about a Jewish family's exile from Nazi Germany.

1972 Richard Adams's *Watership Down*, heroic fantasy about a group of rabbits. Norma Klein's *Mom, the Wolfman, and Me*, an early account of a nontraditional family.

1973 David Macaulay's *Cathedral* recreates the building of a French Gothic cathedral. Nina Bawden's *Carrie's War*, morally complex novel about British evacuees during World War II. Bette Green's *The Summer of My German Soldier*, tragic story of an American Jewish girl who befriends an escaped German prisoner of war. The Children's Literature Association (ChLA) is founded.

1974 Virginia Hamilton's *M. C. Higgins, the Great*, an African American young adult novel that links the ancestral past with the present. Robert Cormier's *The Chocolate War*, young adult novel about a corrupt school administration. Hello Kitty, white cat character that becomes one of the most successful marketing brands in the world, created by the Japanese Sanrio company.

1975 Natalie Babbitt's *Tuck Everlasting* explores the place of death in human life. Judy Blume's *Forever*, first children's book to openly feature teenage sex. Robert Westall's *The Machine Gunners* about a group of children in wartime Tyneside who retrieve a German machine gun.

1976 Bruno Bettelheim's *The Uses of Enchantment: The Meaning and Importance of Fairytales* looks at the psychology behind fairy tales. Margaret Musgrove (text) and Leo and Diane Dillon (illustrations) feature 26 African cultures in the alphabet book *Ashanti to Zulu*. Mildred D. Taylor's *Roll of Thunder, Hear My Cry*. Alan Garner's *The Stone Book*, first of four novellas that pay tribute to the working-class artisan tradition of his family.

1977 Patricia Wrightson's *The Ice Is Coming*, first volume of the Wirrun fantasy trilogy, incorporates elements of Aboriginal culture. Katherine Paterson's *Bridge to Terabithia* features a child's response to a close friend's death. John Burningham's *Come Away from the Water, Shirley*, innovative picture book featuring different adult and child narratives on facing pages.

1978 Raymond Briggs's *The Snowman*, wordless picture book in comic-strip form.

1981 *On Market Street*, alphabet book by Anita and Arnold Lobel.

1982 Toshi Maruki's *Hiroshima no Pika*, picture-book depiction of the bombing of Hiroshima. David McKee's *I Hate My Teddy Bear* contrasts the mundane conversation of two children with mysterious and exciting activities in the pictures.

1983 Cynthia Voigt's *Homecoming*, first of a seven-book series about the Tillerman family. Anthony Browne's surreal *Gorilla* features a fantasy, anthropomorphic great ape as a surrogate father. Susanne Bösche's *Jenny Lives with Eric and Martin* (Danish original 1981), first English-language picture book on homosexuality.

1985 Virginia Hamilton's *The People Could Fly: American Black Folktales*, retold in a modern idiom. Chris Van Allsburg's *The Polar Express*, an artistic, otherworldly classic of the Christmas season.

1986 Janet and Allan Ahlberg's intertextual picture book *The Jolly Postman* playfully explores the book's physical structure. The American Girls, a brand name that issues short books featuring characters from American history, marketed with matching dolls, accessories, and activities.

1988 David Macaulay's *The Way Things Work*, monumental, at times humorous information book.

1989 Jon Scieszka and Lane Smith's *The True Story of the Three Little Pigs! by A. Wolf*, slyly humorous revised fairy tale in which the wolf gets to tell his version. *The Simpsons*, animated television show created by Matt Groening.

1990 Jerry Spinelli's *Maniac Magee* features a homeless boy with extraordinary athletic talent. Gillian Cross's *Wolf*, intertextual novel about a girl and her murderous terrorist father. United Nations Convention on the Rights of the Child comes into force after ratification by all member states of the UN except Somalia and the United States.

1991 Jostein Gaarder's *Sophie's World: A Novel about the History of Philosophy*, international crossover bestseller, is published in Norwegian.

1992 Jon Scieszka and Lane Smith's *The Stinky Cheese Man* deconstructs fairy tales by playing with the materiality of the book itself. R. L. Stine's *Welcome to Dead House*, first book in the Goosebumps horror series.

1993 Lois Lowry's *The Giver* presents a dystopian view of a future society. Zlata Filipovic's *Zlata's Diary: A Child's Life in Sarajevo*, gives an account of the war from the perspective of a 10- to 13-year-old girl. Eve Bunting and David Diaz's *Smoky Night*, picture-book response to the Los Angeles riots of 1992.

1995 Philip Pullman's *Northern Lights*, the first book of the His Dark Materials philosophical fantasy trilogy.

1996 Dear America, a highly marketed historical-fiction series set during important periods in American history and written in the form of fictional young women's diaries.

1997 *Teletubbies*, children's television program, developed by Anne Wood and Andrew Davenport for preschoolers in Great Britain. J. K. Rowling's *Harry Potter and the Philosopher's Stone* (U.S. *Harry Potter and the Sorcerer's Stone*), the first of a seven-volume cycle about a boy wizard that becomes a worldwide publishing phenomenon and one of the most widely translated book series of all time.

1998 Louis Sachar's *Holes*, cleverly constructed novel about justice, family folklore, and redemption.

1999 Lemony Snicket's *A Series of Unfortunate Events*, black-humored, gothic 13-book series. The Children's Laureate is established in Great Britain for an eminent writer or illustrator of children's books.

2000 Lauren Child's *I Will Not Ever Never Eat a Tomato*, witty, mixed-media picture book about a picky eater.

2001 Terry Pratchett's *The Amazing Maurice and His Educated Rodents*, dark and irreverent take on the Pied Piper story and the first novel in his Discworld series intended for children.

2002 Philip Pullman's *The Amber Spyglass*, the final volume in the His Dark Materials fantasy trilogy, is the first children's book ever to win the prestigious overall Whitbread Book of the Year Award. The Astrid Lindgren Memorial Award is founded to increase interest in children's literature around the world.

2003 Melvyn Burgess's *Doing It* creates a stir upon publication due to its uncompromising treatment of teenage sex. Cornelia Funke's *Tintenherz* (*Inkheart*), the first in a trilogy of fantasy novels about fiction and reading, is published in Germany.

2005 Seven Stories, the British center for children's literature near Newcastle, opens to the public. Stephenie Meyer's *Twilight*, the first in the popular series of young adult vampire novels.

2007 Prepublication sales send J. K. Rowling's *Harry Potter and the Deathly Hallows*, the final volume of the Harry Potter series, to the top of the bestseller lists six months before its actual publication in July.

2008 Brian Selznick's 532-page *The Invention of Hugo Cabret,* about an orphan and a toy maker in Paris around 1900, artfully blends narrative, illustration, and cinematic technique. Neil Gaiman's *The Graveyard Book*, about a young boy adopted and raised by the occupants of an old graveyard, is released in separate editions for the adult and children's markets.

Introduction

What is children's literature? Is it literature written by children, for children, or about children? Are there specific stylistic or thematic features common to all children's books by which they can be identified? These and related questions have been asked by scholars in their search for a definition. This section will address these questions, first looking at key differences between children's literature and its counterpart for adults. This will be followed by a brief look at the rise and development of children's literature and a reflection on the currently relevant issues of internationalism and globalization.

The singular term *children's literature* denotes a broad and diverse range of texts with different addressees, forms, genres, degrees of linguistic and aesthetic elaborateness, and functions. The material comes from a number of different sources—folklore (folktales and fairy tales), books meant originally for adults and subsequently adapted for children, and material written specifically for them. Its addressees range from infants through middle-graders to young adults. (Material for readers from about 12 to 18 years old is referred to as "young adult," or YA, literature.) Its forms include picture books, pop-up books, anthologies, novels, merchandising tie-ins, novelizations, and multimedia texts. Among its genres are adventure stories, drama, science fiction, poetry, and information books. Its degrees of linguistic complexity range from concept books with a single noun per page through beginner readers to sophisticated adolescent novels. Its functions and notions of artistry vary, from texts defined by their degree of linguistic difficulty and function of promoting literacy (children's first reading books), through texts in which content is more important than form (information books and openly educational or didactic stories), through material whose sole purpose is to amuse and entertain, to intellectually and aesthetically stimulating and challenging texts—such as the elaborate, often experimental, "literary" children's literature that has become widespread in northwestern European countries and the United States over the past 40 to 50 years. *Children's literature*, therefore, denotes a plurality of coexisting textual manifestations to which the entries in this dictionary bear witness. To privilege any of these manifestations at the expense of the others, or to define the domain of children's literature with reference to only one of them, is to ignore the rich and necessary diversity of this branch of literature.

Can any single definition of children's literature cover this wide range of addressees, forms, levels of artistry, and functions? Can whatever distinguishes it from other types of literature be found on the level of textual features in terms of quality, themes, content, or structure? Perry Nodelman lists 45 "qualities" or features he believes identify texts of children's literature across time.[1] However, many of these, such as "clearly established binary oppositions," also legitimately apply to literature for adults, even if some specific binaries identified by Nodelman (such as child/adult, knowledge/innocence, and home/away) are more prominent in children's than adult literature.

Is there a difference in quality between children's and adult literature? In the same way literature for adults consists of "great books" as well as airport bestsellers and pulp fiction, children's literature is made up of "jewels of children's books," "mediocrity," and "trash."[2] Alongside its mass-market consumables, it produces proportionately as many quality titles that stand the test of time and critical opinion as its adult counterpart. But critics tend to turn up their noses at children's literature as being a lesser form, and it is excluded from the adult canon. Taken in its entirety, it does lack the degree of complexity valued by certain literary critics, but this cannot be a damning criticism when we bear in mind its various functions and how it must accommodate beginner readers. But it is precisely this "applied" component that provokes the disdain of literary critics for whom aesthetic autonomy is the prime criterion. Some critics belittle the domain of children's literature because they take one type of textual manifestation as representative of the whole, because they use the wrong tools, or because they simply ask the wrong questions. In his study of Enid Blyton, David Rudd argues that, instead of analyzing her texts as they would canonical literature, critics should, instead, consider them with the categories of oral transmission.[3] This is the tradition into which the tales of the storyteller Blyton, with their elements of formulaic language and schematic and derivative characters, more readily fit. On the other hand, we have novels for older children and young adults that have, during the past few decades, adopted sophisticated techniques of literary modernism, including abandonment of overt and controlling narrative voices in favor of single and multiple focalizations, montage effects, stream-of-consciousness, and other forms of psychonarration. And there has been an increase in the number of experimental and playful postmodern picture books that defy linear organization and incorporate intertextuality, metafiction, and other characteristics of a distinctly and self-consciously artistic form of literature that goes beyond what used to be thought the limits of the expected or acceptable in children's books. Both of these instances stand up to and respond to the most careful and critical literary analysis.

Is there a difference between the emotional themes dealt with in children's literature and adult literature? The author Natalie Babbit reminds us that "there is no such thing as an exclusively adult emotion," and children's literature deals with them all—love, pride, grief, envy, violence, the quest for immortality, and the yearning for success.[4] Is there a difference on the level of content or structure? While children's literature privileges talking animals and fantastic creatures, and tends not to present adult preoccupations and only rarely depicts graphic sex (food is commonly seen as taking the place of sex for younger readers), it features the happiest and harshest aspects of life, as does its counterpart for adults—including war, disability, and poverty. What Babbitt claims to be the essence of the best children's literature is the "Happy Ending," which she sees not as a "happily ever after" but as a quality "which turns a story ultimately towards hope rather than resignation." Again, this affirmative quality is certainly widespread in children's literature, and it takes the difference between youth and age into consideration, but it is not one that applies to all texts for children, from early concept books to young adult novels.

While the features named above—quality, sophistication, content, emotion, and happy end—can indicate some of the differences between material for children and for adults, they do not serve to satisfyingly define the whole domain of children's literature; there are too many buts, too many exceptions. Children's literature is too broad to be satisfactorily characterized by the presence or absence of any single one of them. We have to look beyond textual features if we want to find what it is that defines children's literature in its entirety.

At the outset was the question of whether children's literature is a literature written by children, for children, or about children. Children write but are—with a few exceptions—rarely published. Literature about children abounds, but most of it is literature of childhood (sometimes but not always autobiographical) for adult rather than child readers. The true defining feature of children's literature is therefore its audience: children's literature is indeed literature for children. It is a body of texts either written specifically for, or otherwise deemed suitable or appropriate for, children. Adults act on behalf of children at every stage of literary communication: they write, edit, translate, publish, promote, review, sell, buy, recommend, lend, and teach children's books. It is adults who create, produce, and disseminate literature for children. That should not be seen as a purely negative factor, since without adult authors, publishers, intermediaries, and so on there would be no literary communication. Children cannot act independently in the literary market. But the communication between adult and child in children's literature is fundamentally asymmetrical, and many of the essential differences between children's and adult literature derive from this inequality. The principles of communication between real adult authors and real child readers are unequal in terms of command of language, experience of the world, and positions in society, although this inequality decreases in the course of the young reader's development. Children's literature tries to bridge the distance between the unequal partners involved by adapting language, subject matter, and formal and thematic features to correspond to the children's stage of development and repertory of literary skills, and by considering the supposed interests and needs of the intended child readers.

By assigning texts to children, adults also determine their functions and uses. These were, at the outset, primarily didactic or doctrinal; and, even if it has in many areas liberated itself from its didactic beginnings, a part of children's literature will always have the practical pedagogical function of promoting basic literacy. It therefore belongs to both the literary and educational realms. As it is also part of "the domain of cultural practices which exist for the purpose of socializing their target audience,"[5] it transmits dominant social and educational norms, values, and ideals of its time and culture. Because it is produced in relation to mediational structures under the aegis of publishing houses, school syllabi, literary awards, and ethical or moral gatekeepers (who in the United States today, for instance, range from advocates of critical literacy to conservative churches), children's literature may be caught in a plethora of competing ideologies. An overt form of mediational overseeing is the potential impact on children's literature of the U.S. "challenged books" phenomenon. Children's literature presents to young readers their earliest images of a world into which they are gradually venturing, and it provides them with the vocabularies they need to read the world, as well as the maps they need to negotiate the specific culture(s) of which they are a part. Children's literature was the dominant medium of enculturation for children in many developed countries up until the 20th century. Today young people access the same mass audio, visual, and digital media as adults, so children's books are now only one of several sources of socializing material, of education, information, commentary, and entertainment—albeit an important one.

The place of the adult in children's literature and his or her investment in it has been increasingly discussed since British psychoanalyst Jacqueline Rose's acclaimed study *The Case of Peter Pan, or The Impossibility of Children's Fiction* claimed that children's literature exists only to gratify adult desire for an ideal childhood, with the child in children's literature nothing more than an adult construct.[6] According to Rose, adults write for and about children in order to be able to control the children outside the book; and by rendering the child in the book innocent of all the contradictions that flaw adults' interactions with the world, adults use the child's image to address and placate difficulties in relation to themselves. This is served by an essentialist notion of the child as a singular entity with no specific class, gender, or ethnicity. While Rose's study has been criticized for its highly selective sample of books and for overlooking the ambivalent nature of many images of childhood in children's literature, she introduced a new and vital perspective, and her findings have been highly influential in children's literature scholarship.[7]

Adults may, in different capacities, belong to the audience for children's literature. In their capacity as intermediaries who buy, give, and recommend books, they read with the child in mind. Adults read aloud to and with children, and a number of them (currently increasing) read children's books for their own pleasure. Some of the adult readers' roles are actually inscribed in the texts. Remarks on covers, puffs that emphasize how suited the topic, style, level of language, and so on are for young readers, and even informational blurbs about prizes, for instance, are usually addressed to adult intermediaries rather than the children themselves. And in certain children's narratives or poems that address both child and adult readers, more than one implied reader can be discerned.

In her study *The Narrator's Voice: The Dilemma of Children's Fiction*, Barbara Wall traces the development from the early 19th century, when adults were addressed in children's fiction, to the simple address to children that has been dominant in English-language children's literature since the early 20th century.[8] She applies the term "double address" to works like J. M. Barrie's *Peter Pan*, in which narrators address children and also—either overtly or covertly—adults. They sometimes even exploit the ignorance of the implied child reader to entertain the adult, by making jokes that are funny primarily because children will not understand them. As Wall sees it, the time when children's books were written almost as much for adults as they were for children ended in the early 20th century, giving way to the era of "single address," in which children are addressed straightforwardly, with the implied author showing no consciousness that adults too might read the work.

In the early 21st century we are witnessing a publishing phenomenon in which popular children's books are marketed for both the juvenile and the adult markets, sometimes in simultaneous editions for adults and for children with identical texts but different jackets (and prices). The *Harry Potter* novels are the most striking example, and they paved the way for many others. Also, an increasing number of texts are branded "all-ages literature." Few of these are characterized by separate forms of address for two different audiences of adults and children; rather, they typically contain elements that may appeal to a variety of readers at different ages and developmental stages. The positions of addressees of these texts should be imagined on a sliding scale rather than at one of two poles that denote the constructs "adult" or "child," and it would be more appropriate to speak of literature with multiple rather than double address.

THE RISE AND EARLY DEVELOPMENT OF CHILDREN'S LITERATURE

Texts have been read by children from the earliest periods of history. Most of these were not especially written for them, but a few—possibly even going back as early as Roman times, but certainly during the Middle Ages and the Renaissance—actually were.[9] But it is not until around the early 18th century that we can talk of a body of literature produced on a broader scale specifically for a child audience. Its rise and development is closely linked with the development of a bourgeois society from the late 17th century, with England leading the way, followed by France and Germany. These three countries can be regarded as the cradles of children's literature. (While the United States was abreast of the social changes, the market there was mainly served by British books and magazines until the 19th century, when British ties were gradually severed and an indigenous children's literature started to emerge.) The rise of specific children's literature in these northwest European countries went hand in hand with the far-reaching social, economic, political, and cultural changes that accompanied the formation of the middle classes. These were, very briefly, the evolution of the middle-class, nuclear family, with the separation of family and work and the liberation of children from working life; the perception of childhood as a phase of life differing fundamentally from adult existence (a key influence here was Jean-Jacques Rousseau); the definition of children as objects of serious responsibility in need of protection and education; the emergence of a class of parents who could afford to invest in their children; the development of a school system and an increased demand for educational books for children; and changes in the literary market that later led to the production of purely commercial children's literature.

A crucial factor in the development was the educational ideology of intellectual movements such as the Puritans in England or the Enlightenment philanthropists in Germany, who believed that children needed books that differed from those for adults principally through their attachment to the educational system. However, they also realized that the pious or educational books they wanted children to read would only be effective if children actually enjoyed reading them. This encouraged the emergence of works of imaginative literature rather than ones that were exclusively didactic or devotional. In the course of time, as commercial publishers recognized the potential for a new market for attractive and entertaining children's books, educators had to further adapt their forms of reading material to appeal.

Any serious attempt to provide an account of the history of children's literature is beyond the scope of this brief introduction: readers are invited to look at the chronology and the entries in the dictionary section. But from this very brief account of the factors that aided the rise of children's literature in Europe and the United States, it should be clear that there can be no "universal" model of development that applies to all countries. If we look at the Arab world, for instance, where storytelling and the oral tradition have always played a strong role, we will see that there was no tradition of writing specifically for children before the 20th century, and that the publishing industry there was beset from the outset with difficulties having to do with the market, distribution problems, illiteracy rates, political instability, and the status of the Arabic language in postcolonial culture.[10] Similar factors have had a decisive influence on the development of children's literature in some African countries—such as the effect and legacy of colonialism; or concepts of family, childhood, education, and leisure that differ greatly from those in Europe or the United States; or the (negative) influence of the global-market players on the development of an indigenous publishing industry.[11] In many of these countries reading is not seen as a hobby but is generally confined to a school or study context, with schools as the most important buyer of children's books. These circumstances diverge significantly from those prevalent in Europe or the United States, and they have to be taken into account when asking how children's literature can develop and flourish under conditions so different from those in the countries in which it first emerged.

The emphasis of this historical dictionary is on Anglo-American children's literature, with some attention paid to significant contributions from other countries. The original plan to include dictionary entries on different countries and regions, to provide a greater international balance, could not, unfortunately, be realized within the scope of a single-volume dictionary.

INTERNATIONALISM, GLOBALIZATION, AND THE FUTURE OF CHILDREN'S LITERATURE

The notion of children everywhere perceiving the world as a place without borders, with their books freely transcending all linguistic and political boundaries, is an attractive one in many quarters of children's literature discourse. Its most eloquent exponent was the French scholar Paul Hazard, with his concept of a Universal Republic of Childhood. After World War II the notion that books could promote international understanding became a credo: children's literature, crossing all borders with ease, was expected to give rise to a utopian "universal republic of childhood." One of the most visible commercial manifestations of a "United Nations of childhood" today can be found in the "United Colors of Benetton" advertisements that exhibit children of every race and color coexisting peacefully under the banner of the international clothing manufacturer. This projects and sentimentalizes adult desires for universal peace and understanding. Children's literature is one of the major areas in which the utopia of internationalism has prospered. But it is also part of a marketplace that is global in its reach; and, since the late 20th century, a different type of internationalism has prevailed in children's literature, this time not as an idealistic postulate but rather as the result of global market forces. It is generated by multinational media companies that manufacture products for children all over the world.

Great Britain and the United States are the countries that "export" most children's literature today. In other words, their literatures are the ones most translated; but they also import the least, with translations into English accounting for only around 3 percent of books published annually in Britain, and only between 1 and 2 percent in the United States. The exclusion of works translated from other languages is generally regarded as a form of cultural poverty, as it is through translations that children become acquainted with other cultures. A lack of exposure to foreign-language books gives Anglo-American readers the false notion that all that is worth knowing is written in English.[12] Most European countries are more welcoming to literature written in languages other than their own, with translations making up between 30 percent (Germany) and 80 percent (Finland) of their respective children's literatures.

While children's literature from so-called developing countries hardly ever reaches European and American readers, a recent survey revealed that 80 percent of books for children set in non-European and non-American cultures are written by European and American authors,[13] and the discussion of colonial and neocolonial writing has increased the awareness of issues involving those "more written about than writing, more spoken about than speaking."[14] In stark contrast to this, 70 to 90 percent of books available to reading children in non-European/American cultures are by European or American authors. While these countries provide a market for multinational corporations, their own books rarely cross the linguistic, political, or cultural divide to partake in the Western market. A few organizations and individual publishers actively address this situation and undertake to distribute books from distant countries, among them the Swiss Baobab children's book foundation.

The economics of production and distribution on a global scale is a major factor in children's publishing today. Children's literature—predominantly in English—has become an international commodity in an increasingly global market. It is an extraordinary indication of the dominance of English-language publishing that today a number of German editions of the children's literature classic *Heidi*, by Johanna Spyri, are actually translations from English. The novel, written in German and hailed as Switzerland's envoy, has been adapted countless times for the English market, and global players such as Dorling Kindersley have sold the rights to their versions to be (re)translated into German.

The most striking changes in children's culture in the Western countries over the last few decades have been its commercialization and internationalization. The conditions of literature for children have changed; the children's book industry in the leading market of the United States is increasingly dominated by a handful of large media conglomerates for whom publishing is a small section of their entertainment business. This leads, for instance, to backlists being mined for highly recognizable characters and stories that offer strong merchandising possibilities. More than 200 companies worldwide currently license Beatrix Potter merchandise from Pearson PLC, making it the largest international literary licensed-merchandise program. Pearson also sells licenses for Spot (Eric Hill) and for Madeline (Ludwig Bemelmans). Noddy (Enid Blyton), Thomas the Tank Engine (Rev. W. Awdry), and Curious George (H. A. and Margret Rey) can also be experienced through a wide range of nonbook products. As Daniel Hade observes, "the mass marketplace selects which books will survive, and thus the children's book becomes less a cultural and intellectual object and more an entertainment looking for mass appeal."[15] The international influence of these multimedia giants is immense: manufacturing mass-produced goods for children, they coordinate their strategies beyond the borders of individual countries, further changing and globalizing what were once regionally contained children's cultures.

Has Harry Potter, too, changed the conditions of children's literature today? Some children's authors complain that now, in the aftermath of the phenomenally successful novels by J. K. Rowling, the goalposts in terms of sales have shifted, which is influencing the production of a wide variety of books. This polarization of the book market into an "all or nothing" situation where everyone is chasing the next big global seller means the pressure is on for huge commercial success and that the middle titles are squeezed out. On the other hand we can find, in some places, increased, small-scale production of literature specifically produced for a local market. Examples include children's literature in regional languages, like Galician in Spain, which is produced with government support and is seen as one of the best ways to introduce children to their native culture and language. Other examples are the boom in Irish children's literature in English, which was produced for the first time on a wide scale during the 1980s and 1990s thanks to the development of an indigenous market and state support; or the small, indigenous markets in Scandinavian countries such as Norway and Denmark, where government support through subsidies and purchases for school libraries ensures the flourishing of local and national literatures that do not have to look toward the global marketplace for survival. Today it looks as if the future of children's literature may lie in a two-tiered children's culture consisting of a dominant, global-market-driven tier and a parallel, weaker, local tier that will flourish in societies that can afford to cultivate it.

In the meantime, children's literature is currently enjoying a general increase in cultural prestige and attention in the wake of the Harry Potter books and films crossing over into the mainstream and into the reading and viewing lives of adults. This success has been followed—if not exactly replicated—by Stephenie Meyer's Twilight novels, with their cult following, and Cornelia Funke's Inkworld trilogy. In July 2000 a separate children's literature section was created for the *New York Times* Best Seller List, as many publishers from the "adult" sector complained that the Harry Potter books and other successful children's titles were not leaving enough room for their books. An increasing new development is the phenomenon of books that are released in separate editions for the adult and children's markets—see, for instance, the 2009 Newbery Medal winner *The Graveyard Book*, by Neil Gaiman. The commercial success and increased status of children's literature, as well as its gradual acceptance in the academy as a subject meriting serious critical attention, bode well for the future of this vibrant and varied branch of literature.

NOTES

1. Perry Nodelman, *The Hidden Adult: Defining Children's Literature* (Baltimore: Johns Hopkins University Press, 2008), 76–81.

2. These terms are used in Sheila Egoff and Wendy Sutton's "Epilogue: Some Thoughts on Connecting," in *Only connect: Readings on Children's Literature*, ed. Sheila Egoff et al., 3rd ed. (Toronto: Oxford University Press, 1996), 392–93.

3. David Rudd, *Enid Blyton and the Mystery of Children's Literature* (Basingstoke, UK: Macmillan, 2000).

4. Natalie Babbit, "Happy Endings? Of Course, and Also Joy," in *Considering Children's Literature: A Reader*, ed. Andrea Schwenke Wyile and Teya Rosenberg (Guelph, ON: Broadview Press, 2008), 5.

5. John Stephens, *Language and Ideology in Children's Fiction* (London: Longman, 1992), 8.

6. Jacqueline Rose, *The Case of Peter Pan, or The Impossibility of Children's Fiction*, rev. ed. (Basingstoke, UK: Macmillan, 1994; 1st ed. 1984).

7. See, for instance, Kimberley Reynolds, *Radical Children's Literature: Future Visions and Aesthetic Transformations in Juvenile Fiction* (London: Palgrave Macmillan, 2007).

8. Barbara Wall, *The Narrator's Voice: The Dilemma of Children's Fiction* (London: Macmillan, 1991).

9. See M. O. Grenby, *Children's Literature* (Edinburgh: Edinburgh University Press, 2008), 2.

10. See Taghreed Alqudsi-Ghabra, "Arabic Children's Literature," in *International Companion Encyclopedia of Children's Literature*, ed. Peter Hunt, 2nd ed. (London: Routledge, 2004), 954–59.

11. See Marie Laurentin, "French-Speaking Africa," in *International Companion Encyclopedia of Children's Literature*, ed. Peter Hunt, 2nd ed. (London: Routledge, 2004), 935–45; or Jay Heale, "English-Speaking Africa," in *International Companion Encyclopedia of Children's Literature*, ed. Peter Hunt, 2nd ed. (London: Routledge, 2004), 945–53.

12. See Carl Tomlinson, *Children's Books from Other Countries* (Lanham, Md.: Scarecrow Press, 1998), 4.

13. Fremde Welten, *Kinder- und Jugendbücher zu den Themen: Afrika, Asien, Lateinamerika, ethnische Minderheiten und Rassismus, empfohlen von den Lesegruppen des Kinderbuchfonds Baobab*, 17th ed. (Basel, Switzerland: Kinderbuchfonds Baobab, 2007).

14. Roderick McGillis, "Introduction," in *Voices of the Other: Children's Literature and the Postcolonial Context*, ed. Roderick McGillis (New York: Garland, 1999), xxi.

15. Daniel Hade, "Storytelling: Are Publishers Changing the Way Children Read?" *Horn Book Magazine* 78 (2002): 511.

The Dictionary

– A –

AARDEMA, VERNA (1911–2000). U.S. reteller of African and Mexican **folktales** for children known for her meticulous attention to detail and, although she was of neither African nor Mexican descent, her familiarity with both oral traditions. Onomatopoeia, rhythm, repetition, and humor characterize her retellings, and she worked with several respected illustrators of children's books. *Why Mosquitoes Buzz in People's Ears: A West African Tale*, illustrated by **Leo** and **Diane Dillon**, regarded by many as Aardema's best work, won the **Caldecott Medal** in 1976.

ABBOTT, JACOB (1803–1879). New England educator, Congregationalist minister, and author of over 200 books, including the best seller *The Young Christian, or A Familiar Illustration of the Principles of Christian Duty* (1832), published by the **American Tract Society**. Abbott wrote the first significant children's series in the United States, the 28-volume Rollo series (1835–1858), which develops in difficulty and sophistication as the child protagonist matures. In the **picture book** *Rollo Learning to Talk* he is three years old. *Rollo Learning to Read* includes stories about the five-year-old as well as instructions in reading. Episodic narratives about Rollo's daily activities at work, at school, and at play follow in subsequent books, and, as Rollo grows up and learns about the world, readers follow him on a 10-volume trip through Europe. This **nonfiction** series, hugely popular in the 19th century although largely forgotten today, stresses moral development, but it also taught the readers practical skills. Other series by Abbott include his Frankonia stories (10 volumes) and the Lucy series for girls.

ABC BOOKS OR ALPHABET BOOKS. Designed specifically to teach children the letters of the alphabet, illustrated ABC books naming and picturing common objects in alphabetical order, sometimes with rhyming couplets or small verses, developed into a separate form of publication during the early 19th century. Until the 18th century, teaching the alphabet was associated with religious instruction, and the alphabet was printed as part of a **primer**. Woodcut illustrations were introduced to aid children's learning from around the late 16th century, and the idea of instruction through play informs the picture alphabet in **John Amos Comenius**'s *Orbis Sensualium Pictus* (1658), in which letters are identified with the sounds of various animals. The bookseller **John Newbery** is credited with making the connection between picture, theme, and letter when he organized pictures and descriptions of children's games according to the alphabet in his *Little Pretty Pocket Book* (1744). The illustrations improved in quality during the 19th century, and the themes extended to ABCs of animals, birds, names, nations of the world, and so on. Some were produced by leading **picture-book** artists such as **Walter Crane**, who created a number of thematic alphabet books, including *The Railroad Alphabet* (1865) and *The Farmyard Alphabet* (1865). **Kate Greenaway** created a version of the popular *A Apple Pie* (1886). Comic and **nonsense** alphabets became popular during the 19th century; **Edward Lear** included a few of these in his *Book of Nonsense* (1846), and Crane illustrated an *Absurd ABC* (1874).

The tradition of ABC books, which, rather than teaching children how to read or explaining new vocabulary, aim to entertain them with pictures and rhymes, has been carried on, although some ABC books are still addressed to younger readers and use humor to get their attention. Examples include ***Dr. Seuss's ABC: An Amazing Alphabet Book!*** (1960), which uses zany drawings to illustrate situations like "Lazy lion licks a lollipop," or Sandra Boynton's *A Is for Angry* (1987), with animals and adjectives such as "Big Bashful Bear." ABC books challenge the imagination of **illustrators** and picture-book makers today, and many, including **Mitsumasa Anno**, **Quentin Blake**, **Anita Lobel**, **Arnold Lobel**, and **Helen Oxenbury**, have produced them. **Brian Wildsmith**'s wordless *ABC* won the **Kate Greenaway Medal** in 1962. The development of new paper technology has resulted in a proliferation of pop-up ABC books. In a recent one, the wordless *ABC3D* (2008) by Marion Bataille, each of the 26 three-dimensional letters moves and changes before the reader's eyes, although it seems unlikely that this work of art and wonder of paper engineering will find its way into children's hands. While most English-language authors traditionally had problems finding appropriate words for the letters *X* and *Z*, Dr. Seuss, in *On beyond Zebra* (1955), decided that 26 letters were not enough and extended the alphabet beyond the letter *Z* with some new ones of his own. *See also* FEELINGS, TOM; GOREY, EDWARD ST. JOHN; PACOVSKÁ, KVĚTA; VAN ALLSBURG, CHRIS.

ACHEBE, CHINUA (1930–). Nigerian poet, novelist, and essayist, regarded as one of the most important contemporary African writers. He made his name with the novel *Things Fall Apart* (1958) about his native Igbo society in the late 19th century. In 1967, he founded the Citadel Press, one aim being to publish children's stories with an African perspective. In his novel *Chike and the River* (1966), he recounts the adventures of an 11-year-old boy who leaves his home village to live with his uncle in the city of Onitsha. *How the Leopard Got His Claws* (with John Iroaganchi; 1972), *The Flute* (1977), and *The Drum* (1977) are based on Igbo **folktales** and were also published in the Igbo language.

ADAMS, RICHARD (1920–). British novelist who achieved worldwide fame with his **Carnegie Medal**–winning debut novel *Watership Down* (1972). Chronicling the adventures of a group of rabbits searching for a safe place to establish a new warren where they can live in peace, it was based on a story he told his children at bedtime. Initially rejected by many publishers, it was issued for adults by Rex Collings in 1972, reprinted by Puffin for children in 1974, and released as an animated film in 1978. This **animal story** described rabbits with a degree of biological realism hitherto unheard of in children's fiction, transforming them from cuddly bunnies into savagely fighting warriors. The book was hugely popular because of its environmental concerns and sympathy for animal rights, and it enabled Adams to give up his job as a civil servant and become a full-time writer. His later works—*Shardik* (1974), concerning a religious cult focused on a huge bear, and *The Plague Dogs* (1977), about two dogs who escape from an experimental laboratory—were not as positively received by critics.

ADAPTATION. The recasting of a work in a new form or medium, adaptation has been a central element of children's literature since children were discovered as a literary audience. Among the first books adapted with the young reader in mind was the **Bible**, issued in miniature, versified, alphabetized, or pictorial forms. Greek and Latin texts were adapted "*ad usum Delphini*" ("for the use of the Dauphin") under the orders of the French royal family, in order to give the heir a proper education in the classics. From the second half of the 18th century on, abridgments of popular adult novels of the day, such as ***Robinson Crusoe*** and ***Gulliver's Travels*** appeared, later to become part of the children's literature canon. While such adaptation was driven by the desire to adapt more complex works to the cognitive, linguistic, and interest levels of young readers, adaptations for children can frequently be driven by moral concerns. Thomas Bowdler famously expurgated Shakespeare for children in his *Family Shakespeare* (1818), giving rise to the eponym *bowdlerize*, meaning to censor prudishly.

The three most widespread forms of adaptation are *abridgment*, which usually involves shortening and simplifying works originally for adults that are regarded as at least partially suitable for or attractive to children (like novels by **Sir Walter Scott** or **Charles Dickens**); *expurgation*, which entails the removal of material deemed objectionable for young readers; and *retelling*, predominantly of **myths**, **legends**, and **fairy tales**. Books originally written for children have also been the object of adaptation; among the most notorious examples are **Beatrix Potter**'s tales in simplified language, published by Ladybird. Most editions of older classics for children in today's bookshops, such as ***The Adventures of Pinocchio*** or ***Alice in Wonderland***, are adaptations. These include pictorial versions, retellings in which the quality of the illustration is of primary importance (this is particularly the case with the fairy tales of **Hans Christian Andersen**), and other forms of medial adaptation, such as novel into film or comic. One of the great adaptors of modern times was, of course, **Walt Disney**. Many **translations** for children are rewritten for a readership in a different culture and domesticate or adapt the text to this target group in the process, for instance by localizing settings and names. *See also* BAUM, L. FRANK; BERQUIN, ARNAUD; BUNYAN, JOHN; CHAPBOOKS; LANG, ANDREW; VERNE, JULES.

ADVENTURE STORIES. The earliest adventure stories read by children were the medieval romances available in **chapbook** form. The first modern adventure story that combined the extraordinary with the realistic was **Daniel Defoe**'s *Robinson Crusoe* (1719), a survival story that spawned a genre of its own, the **robinsonades**. Though neither *Robinson Crusoe* itself nor other early representatives of various strands in the genre were written specifically for children, they were widely read by them. Examples include **James Fenimore Cooper**'s frontier adventures in the *Leatherstocking Tales* (1823–1841), **Sir Walter Scott**'s historical adventures like *Ivanhoe* (1819), **Jules Verne**'s **science-fiction** adventures such as *Twenty Thousand Leagues under the Sea* (French original 1870), and **Anna Sewell**'s animal adventure *Black Beauty* (1877). The first authors of adventure stories specifically for a young audience were **Captain Frederick Marryat**, who wrote survival narratives, accounts of life on the frontier, and historical novels for children, and **Robert Louis Stevenson**, who, with his adventure tales *Treasure Island* (1881–1882) and *Kidnapped* (1886), set new standards in the genre. **Mark Twain**'s *The Adventures of Tom Sawyer* (1876) offered a "bad boy" adventure novel in a specifically U.S. literary tradition initiated by T. B. Aldrich.

Parallel to the expansion of the British Empire in the 19th century grew the popularity of adventure stories with exotic settings. From midcentury on, numerous adventure tales loosely based on a heroic-quest narrative structure, in which a young English man is molded and strengthened by his escapades in the wild and his adventures with the natives, can be found in the form of novels by authors such as Captain Mayne Reid and **R. M. Ballantyne**. The widely read **G. A. Henty** and his contemporaries and successors, such as Captain F. S. Brereton, introduced an element of class arrogance and **racism**, and their books are seen as openly serving the imperial project. At the same time in Europe, the German Karl May was a hugely successful author of westerns and adventure novels in exotic settings. The **penny dreadfuls** in Great Britain and the **dime novels** in the United States issued crime adventures and westerns in the popular reading tradition, and from the beginning of the 20th century the Stratemeyer Syndicate produced adventure-book series such as Tom Swift, and a little later **The Hardy Boys** and the **Nancy Drew** series. With *Emil and the Detectives* (German original 1929), **Erich Kästner** authored an early, enduringly popular and highly influential child **detective novel**, and the subsequent success of **Arthur Ransome**'s Swallows and Amazons series (1930–1947) also showed that small-scale adventures of children in a domestic setting involving a **mystery** or crime could be as exciting as swashbucklers. The most prominent 20th-century mass-producer of such adventures in the mystery and detection mode was **Enid Blyton**, while the naval adventures of the 19th century found their modern equivalent in the mid-1950s with **Captain W. E. Johns**'s popular novels about Flight Commander *Biggles*.

Since the 1960s, questions of psychology and moral development have become predominant in many branches of adventure fiction. These include the science-fiction adventures of **Robert Heinlein**, **Madeleine L'Engle**, **Patricia Wrightson**, and **Gillian Rubinstein**; the survival stories of **Jean Craighead George**; the **historical** adventures of **Rosemary Sutcliff**, **Joan Aiken**, **Philip Pullman**, and **Mildred Taylor**; the ecological adventures by **Colin Thiele**; and adventures set during times of war, such as **Robert Westall**'s *The Machine Gunners* (1975). The adventure story, with its scenarios of (young) protagonists overcoming natural and man-made disasters and its themes of trials, survival, and having to develop personal strength to overcome all manners of difficulties, remains popular among young readers today. *See also* BARRIE, SIR J. M.; COLFER, EOIN; PAULSEN, GARY; SOUTHALL, IVAN; SWIFT, JONATHAN.

AESOP. Author of the most important body of **fables** in Western literature, reputedly a Greek slave, possibly of African descent, who lived from about 620 to 560 BC. The first publication of Aesop's fables was a Latin **translation** of *100 Fabulae Aesopicae* by an Italian scholar named Renutius, published in Rome in 1476. The first English collection of the fables, *Subtyl Historyes and Fables of Esop*, was printed by **William Caxton** in 1484, based on a French text taken from the German of Heinrich Steinhöwel. Most of Aesop's fables concern animals, especially the fox, the wolf, and the lion. Each points to a moral or has a moral interpretation attached. Rather than recommending high ideals of conduct, the fables usually demonstrate the plainer virtues of common sense, moderation, and worldly wisdom. They are very sharp-eyed about relationships between the powerful and apparently powerless in the natural world, and frequent themes include how to save one's own skin and how to remain on good terms with those who are in power. There are several hundred of these fables; among the best known are "The Tortoise and the Hare," "The Boy Who Cried Wolf," "The Fox and the Grapes," and "The Wolf in Sheep's Clothing."

Aesop's fables were absorbed into the body of literature deemed suitable for children at a relatively early stage, with the fable recommended as an exemplar in the study of grammar and rhetoric in the first century AD, and Aesop appearing on curricula for the young from the 11th century on. Aesop's fables are still used as moral lessons today and feature as subjects in various entertainment media, especially children's plays and cartoons.

AGARD, JOHN (1949–). Guyanese poet, playwright, performer, and anthologist for adults and children who moved to Great Britain in 1977. One of the leading Caribbean poets, Agard writes in both Standard English and Guyanese Creole. To his **poetry** for children, mainly written in lyrical Guyanese, he brings a keen feeling for the rhythms of language and a sophisticated understanding of the advantages and limitations of different varieties of English. Collections include *I Din Do Nuttin* (1983) and *Say It Again, Granny* (1986). Together with his partner, **Grace Nichols**, he coauthored a collection of Caribbean **nursery rhymes**, *No Hickory, No Dickory, No Dock* (1991). He was the BBC's first poet-in-residence in 1997.

AHLBERG, ALLAN (1938–) AND JANET (1944–1994). British husband-and-wife team who wrote and illustrated **picture books**. Janet was primarily the **illustrator** and Allan the writer in this highly successful collaboration, but they considered themselves above all bookmakers, deciding together on all aspects of production, from the book size and typeface to the endpapers, cover, and jacket copy. The Ahlberg picture books are acclaimed for their humor, their amusing pictures, and the skillful union of text and illustrations. Their innovative books invite children to indulge in playful intertextual and metafictional games. For instance, their *Each Peach, Pear, Plum* (1978), winner of the **Kate Greenaway Medal**, incorporates **nursery-rhyme** and **fairy-tale** characters into a cumulative rhyme, with an "I spy" game format that encourages children to spot hidden characters in the illustrations. *The Baby's Catalogue* (1982) followed the discovery that their baby Jessica's favorite first-reading material consisted of mail-order catalogs. In *The Jolly Postman, or Other People's Letters* (1986), which enjoyed great critical acclaim and sold more than one million copies, a bicycling postman delivers letters and postcards to fairy-tale characters. Goldilocks writes an apology to the three bears, the giant gets a holiday postcard from Jack of beanstalk fame (thanking him for the gold that paid for his break in the sun), and so on. The book contains actual letters and cards inside little envelopes to be opened and read.

In its sequels, *The Jolly Christmas Postman* (1991) and *The Jolly Pocket Postman* (1995), the Ahlbergs continued to make use of this interactive device that combines fantasy play and everyday reading and writing. Their intuitive understanding of the child's world of story is also evident in *Funnybones* (1980), *Peepo* (1981), and *It Was a Dark and Stormy Night* (1993). Allan Ahlberg had collaborated with other **illustrators**, for instance in creating the best-selling Happy Families series (from 1980), and since Janet's death he has continued to write picture books and has worked with a number of other illustrators. *Half a Pig*, illustrated by his daughter Jessica, was published in 2004.

AIKEN, JOAN (1924–2004). British author of gothic **fantasy, horror**, and suspense for adults and for children, daughter of the American poet Conrad Aiken. Author of more than 50 works for children and more than 20 for adults, Aiken is probably best known for her sequence of six novels known as the James III series of what she called her "alternate-history fantasies." The underlying idea is that the Hanoverian succession of 1714 never happened in Great Britain;

instead King James III is on the throne, followed later by Richard IV. The first of the series, *The Wolves of Willoughby Chase* (1962), in which a Channel tunnel has just been opened and wolves have migrated through it to Britain, has a swift-moving, melodramatic plot involving two young girls who endure hardship and face many dangers. *Blackhearts in Battersea* (1964), the second, introduces the theme of Hanoverian plotting and is a tale of wild action and amazing escapes from extraordinary perils. These first two books are the best known and have been made into major films. Many of Aiken's other works have been **adapted** for film and television; this included a BBC version of one of her most popular characters, Mortimer the talking raven, who, quoting Poe, cries "Nevermore!" when upset. She has also produced several collections of what she called "storytales," as well as horror stories for young readers. Aiken has been praised for her humor and her sense of suspense, her extraordinary imagination, and her colorful characters with inventive names reminiscent of **Charles Dickens**. Her plots are often predictable, with happy endings for innocent heroes and heroines, and villains receiving their just rewards. Her horror stories, on the other hand, reveal the more sinister edges of her fantasy.

ALADDIN. *See THE ARABIAN NIGHTS.*

ALCOTT, LOUISA MAY (1832–1888). U.S. novelist for adults and children best known today for the four novels about the March family, beginning with *Little Women* (1868). Raised in poverty as one of four daughters of Bronson Alcott, the transcendentalist philosopher and avant-garde educator, Alcott wrote to provide for her family and relieve them from debt; she authored, under a pseudonym, a number of sensational short stories and **dime novels**. She also wrote two serious novels for adults, *Moods* (1864) and *Work* (1873), which addresses the experiences of women who provide for themselves. An active suffragist and believer in educational reform and **feminist** ideals, Alcott emphasized in life and fiction the importance of education for women as well as the belief that having both marriage and a career was possible for women. *Little Women* is the first and most overtly autobiographical of the quartet of novels that chart the progress of the March family over a period of 30 years, from difficult times during the Civil War years to affluence and success. Covering a year in time, it relates the everyday life of a loving family of four intelligent and very different adolescent sisters (Amy, Jo, Beth, and Meg) and their mother (Marmee) in straitened circumstances, after the father has joined the Union army as a chaplain. It portrays the March girls as real people rather than mere examples, as in the moral tales of the 18th and 19th centuries from which it descends. *Little Women* was an immediate popular success and readers clamored for a sequel. In response, Alcott wrote *Little Women Part Two* (1869), known in Great Britain as *Good Wives*, which picks up three years after the end of the first part and follows the lives of the girls into womanhood and their decisions about careers and marriage; it does not shy away from issues such as ensuing disappointment and compromise. In 1880 both parts were combined into one volume called *Little Women*, and they have been published as such in the United States ever since.

Little Women is regarded as an outstanding 19th-century American children's novel and the first family story to have become an enduring classic. It established a distinctively American domestic realism for children and provided a model for subsequent family stories such as **Susan Coolidge**'s *What Katy Did* (1872). *Little Women* has been **adapted** to play, musical, opera, film, and animated-feature versions. The March sisters are reprised in two subsequent novels. *Little Men* (1871) is set in the progressive school set up by Jo and her husband Professor Bhaer (based, in fact, on Bronson Alcott's theories of education), which is attended by Meg's and Jo's children as well as the older boys Nat and Dan. *Jo's Boys* (1886) follows the lives of the girl's children in their teenage years, with an additional focus on the fortunes of Nat and Dan. Alcott wrote *Little Women* because she was encouraged to write a book for girls, not because she felt the desire to do so; her ambition lay in the realm of literature for adults. While she enjoyed the wide popular and critical success of these books and the financial freedom they provided for her family, it is likely that she, like her character Jo, had higher literary ambitions but felt she ended up having to settle for less. *See also* GENDER.

ALEXANDER, LLOYD CHUDLEY (1924–2007). U.S. author, principally of **fantasy** novels for children and young adults. As a member of the army during World War II, Alexander spent some time in Wales, which reawakened his boyhood enthusiasm for Arthurian **legend**, and in France. After the war, he studied at the Sorbonne and later translated Jean-Paul Sartre and other French authors. Most of Alexander's books are in the fantasy mode and, apart from single novels such as *The Remarkable Journey of Prince Jen* (1991), he is best known for his Prydain Chronicles, inspired by the stories of the medieval Welsh *The Mabinogion*. The five-volume series comprises *The Book of Three* (1964), *The Black Cauldron* (1965), *The Castle of Llyr* (1966), *Taran Wanderer* (1967), and *The High King* (1968), for which Alexander received the **Newbery Medal**. In The Westmark Trilogy, written in the 1980s, the theme is also that of the establishment of a new order, although here politics, rather than the magic in The Prydian Chronicles, dominates. A female protagonist, Vesper Holly, experiences international adventures during the 1870s in Alexander's third series, which is made up of *The Illyrian Adventure* (1986), *The El Dorado Adventure* (1987), *The Drackenberg Adventure* (1988), *The Jedera Adventure* (1989), and *The Philadelphia Adventure* (1990). Alexander is admired for accuracy of detail based on his research of time and place, and for offering young readers access to issues of moral significance through the medium of fantasy, by engaging them in ethical considerations raised by the characters and their actions. His books have been translated into several languages, and he was the recipient of numerous U.S. and European children's-literature awards.

ALICE IN WONDERLAND. *See* CARROLL, LEWIS.

ALL-AGES LITERATURE. *See* CROSSOVER BOOKS.

ALMOND, DAVID (1951–). British novelist and playwright from North East England, the setting of much of his work. His first children's novel, *Skellig* (1998), in which a young boy finds a mysterious creature in his garage who is both a down-and-out and an angel of hope and joy, won the **Carnegie Medal** and the Whitbread Children's Book **Award**. Subsequent novels, such as *Kit's Wilderness* (1999), *Heaven Eyes* (2001), *The Fire-Eaters* (2003; also a Whitbread winner), *Clay* (2005), and *Jackdaw Summer* (2008) have received great critical acclaim. In his work, Almond successfully employs a bold combination of realism and mystical elements; he celebrates the power of the imagination, storytelling, and friendship in a language apparently simple but profoundly poetic.

ALPHABET BOOKS. *See* ABC BOOKS OR ALPHABET BOOKS.

AMERICAN LIBRARY ASSOCIATION (ALA). The American Library Association, founded in 1876, is the oldest and largest library association in the world, with more than 64,000 members. Representing all types of libraries—public, school, academic, and so on—its mission is to promote the highest-quality library and information services and public access to information. Two of its 11 divisions are dedicated to promoting children's and young adult literature, the Association for Library Services to Children (ALSC) and the Young Adult Library Services Association (YALSA). The ALSC presents numerous **awards**, among them the **Newbery Medal**, the **Caldecott Medal**, and the **Mildred L. Batchelder Award**.

AMERICAN TRACT SOCIETY. *See* RELIGIOUS TRACT SOCIETY.

ANDERSEN, HANS CHRISTIAN (1805–1875). Danish poet and author, most famous for his fairy tales, many of which have become international classics of children's literature. Unlike the Brothers **Grimm**, who collected their tales, Andersen was a storyteller who occasionally adapted folk motifs in his 156 literary fairy tales, *Eventyr, fortalte for børn* [Wonderful Stories for Children] (1835–1848), which, written for a dual audience of children and adults, extended the boundaries of the genre. The story of his life, as he and others have described it, strongly resembles his own tales: the son of a cobbler and a washerwoman, an awkward, ugly child of ambiguous sexuality, longs for love and recognition, and finally overcomes his outsider status to become an internationally famous and best-selling author. Among his most famous tales are *The Little Matchgirl*, *The Ugly Duckling*, *The Steadfast Tin Soldier*, *The Nightingale*, *The Little Mermaid*, and *The Emperor's New Clothes*.

A common plot in Andersen's fairy tales involves a person of low origin who falls in love with somebody of higher status—the little mermaid with the prince, the tin soldier with the ballerina—and the theme of rejection occurs repeatedly. Characteristic traits include an explicit narrative voice that addresses the reader/listener and comments on events; irony; a combination of the ordinary and the fantastic; animation of the material world; everyday objects featuring as protagonists; a lack of a conventional moral; tragic endings; and, in the Danish original, linguistic freshness and experimental literary qualities. With his literary fairy tales Andersen carried on the heritage of German Romanticism in the field of children's literature initiated by **E. T. A. Hoffmann** with his story *Nussknacker und Mausekönig* (1816; *Nutcracker and Mouse King*, 1853).

Andersen's influence both on English fairy stories of the later 19th century and on the development of **fantasy** for children was immense. A selection of his tales was translated into English by Mary Howitt in 1846 and was followed in the two subsequent years by nine selections from six different translators; these helped to reestablish the fairy-tale genre in Great Britain. Andersen's fairy tales have been **translated** into numerous languages, and many of the translations have **adapted** the tales to already-existing models of children's literature, making them more moralistic and didactic than the source texts, and aligning them with traditional formats of known tales, for instance those by the Brothers Grimm. The language in many of these is overexplicit, for children to be able to understand everything easily; elements regarded as "inappropriate," such as irony or sexual overtones, are removed; and bowdlerized versions make happy endings out of tragic ones. The blurb of a 1944 translation of *The Little Matchgirl* proclaims, "Children will read with delight this new version of the famous old Hans Christian Andersen tale. For in it the little matchgirl on that long ago Christmas Eve does not perish from the bitter cold, but finds warmth and cheer in a lovely home where she lives happily ever after."

Many of Andersen's tales have now become part of a written oral tradition, with editions carrying the name of the illustrator or reteller rather than his. Andersen was regarded by **Paul Hazard** as the king of children's literature, and when the **International Board on Books**

for Young People (IBBY) set up a major **award** for children's literature in 1956, it was named in his honor: the **Hans Christian Andersen Award**. His birthday, April 2, is celebrated as International Children's Book Day.

ANIMAL FICTION. Heterogeneous group of stories that feature animals in more or less **anthropomorphic** form. The earliest animal stories available to children were **fables** and **fairy tales** with their talking animals. From the mid-18th century on, animals have featured in books written specifically for children as friends of the (human) protagonists or as subjects of fictional (auto)biographies such as *The Life and Perambulations of a Mouse* (1783), by Dorothy Killner. Today animals play a key role in **fantasy** for children and feature widely in **picture books**. In these, tension between animals and humans can represent that between children and adults, or the Romantic notion of the child's unity with nature may surface in the form of a special relationship between animals and children.

There are several different types of animal stories. Moral or (later) developmental tales that explore purely human behavior or emotions with animals standing in for human beings represent one common type. These include stories such as *Charlotte's Web* (1952), by **E. B. White**. Another group consists of narratives in which an animal protagonist or narrator observes or comments upon human conduct. These can have a critical or even a satirical slant, or they may aim to convince readers not to be cruel to animals, as in **Anna Sewell**'s *Black Beauty* (1877). Stories that describe the behavior of animals in their natural habitat feature strongly in children's literature in the United States and Canada, and include the pioneering *Wild Animals I Have Known* (1898) by Ernest Thompson Seton and novels by the notable contemporary **Jean Craighead George**. Animals can feature to great comic effect in stories that range from animals getting up to funny antics through social comedy with animals representing types of human characters. This is especially strong in the British tradition, with such famous examples as **Kenneth Grahame**'s *The Wind in the Willows* (1908) and the stories of **Beatrix Potter**. Popular comic and inventive animal stories for young children are produced today by **Dick King-Smith**, author of the modern classic *Sheep-Pig* (1983; U.S. title *Babe the Gallant Pig*), which was **adapted** for the screen as the 1995 film *Babe*. *See also* ADAMS, RICHARD; DICAMILLO, KATE; HORSE AND PONY STORIES; INKPEN, MICK; LAWSON, ROBERT; NAYLOR, PHYLLIS REYNOLDS; PAULSEN, GARY; SALTEN, FELIX.

ANNO, MITSUMASA (1926–). Japanese **illustrator** and creator of **picture books** who worked as a math teacher before bringing out his first book, *Fushigi na E* (1968; *Topsy-Turvies*, 1970). Since then he has produced a highly original body of work enjoyed by readers of all ages in many countries. It includes pedagogic, literary, and wordless picture books that delight in optical illusion, for which he has been compared with the Dutch artist M. C. Escher. Among his most acclaimed are the wordless picture books in which the artist journeys through recognizable landscapes inhabited by known historical figures and characters from popular and high culture. In *Anno's Journey* (Japanese 1977, English 1978), set in Europe, we see a bathing woman straight out of a Renoir painting on one page, and Don Quijote on another. Beethoven and characters from *Sesame Street* make appearances in landscapes or cityscapes full of otherwise authentic everyday elements. Anno delights in playing with literary and graphic conventions, and with math, science, and paradox. He received the **Hans Christian Andersen Award** in 1984.

ANNUAL. A yearly publication usually associated with a weekly or monthly magazine, story paper, or comic, or, later, with a radio or television program. The earliest annuals appeared in the 1820s; the Victorians' favorite, *Peter Parley's Annual*, ran from 1840 to 1892, drawing originally on the works of the American writer **Samuel Goodrich**. Annuals are traditionally characterized by their varied contents: stories, features, rhymes, puzzles, competitions, black-and-white illustrations, and color plates. Popular late-19th-century annuals, which usually appeared in time for Christmas, included the *Boy's Own* (1879ff.), the *Girl's Own* (1880ff.), *Little Folks* (1875ff.), and *Chatterbox* (1866ff.). Popular post–World War II annuals included *Eagle* (1951ff.) and *Girl* (1953ff.), as well as annuals based on popular television characters, such as the *Doctor Who Annual* (1966ff.). Annuals have always provided a good forum for young writers and illustrators to have their earliest work published. To keep up with the times, they have had to respond to changing tastes. However, the three most enduring British annuals, *Dandy* (1939ff.), *Beano* (1940ff.), and *Rupert Bear* (1936ff.), have remained popular through generations, despite minimal changes to format and characterization.

ANTHROPOMORPHISM. The technique of attributing uniquely human characteristics and qualities, speech, and psychology to nonhuman beings, inanimate objects, or natural or supernatural phenomena. Anthropomorphism in children's literature features primarily in **animal fiction** and in **doll and toy stories**. The Romantic belief in the child's unity with nature is a major impetus behind the production of animal stories for a young audience; and the child's capacity to endow things with life in pretense play, blurring the boundaries between animate and inanimate objects, is a further element that inspires writers to do likewise in children's books. Many famous children's television characters are anthropomorphic: funny animals such as Mickey Mouse or Bugs Bunny, the figures of letters, numbers, or shapes used in educational programs such as *Sesame Street*, and the popular steam locomotives with humanlike faces and personalities in ***Thomas the Tank Engine***. Anthropomorphism can vary in degree. The gorillas in **Anthony Browne**'s **picture books** are essentially humans with animal heads; the animal characters in **Kenneth Grahame**'s *The Wind in the Willows* (1908) wear clothes, possess technology, and pursue human activities, but are guided by animal instincts; while **Richard Adams**'s *Watership Down* (1972) presents a limited form of anthropomorphism in which the animals have the physical attributes and instincts of their real-life counterparts, only deviating from these in their capacity to speak and reason. The functions of anthropomorphism in literature range from using animals to illustrate simple moral lessons, as in **fables**, to generating greater sympathy for the animal and natural world; it can also be used for the purposes of social criticism. *See also* BANKS, LYNNE REID; BROWN, MARC; BRUNHOFF, JEAN DE AND LAURENT DE; COLFER, EOIN; DICAMILLO, KATE; GODDEN, MARGARET RUMER; GRUELLE, JOHNNY; JANOSCH; KERR, JUDITH; KING-SMITH, DICK; KIPLING, RUDYARD; KREIDOLF, ERNST; LE GUIN, URSULA; LEAF, MUNRO; MILNE,

A. A.; PADDINGTON BEAR; POTTER, BEATRIX; SIMMONDS, POSY; WELLS, ROSEMARY; WHITE, E. B.

THE ARABIAN NIGHTS. Collection of tales in Arabic also referred to as *The Thousand and One Nights*, for which there is neither an original text nor an author. One of the most famous literary products of classical Islamic civilization, it represents a merging of Arabic culture with origins that can be traced to a Persian book of **fairy tales** from the 10th century, as well as to stories from Baghdad and Cairo from between the 10th and 14th centuries. The stories are bracketed by a frame story about a king who vows to marry a virgin every night and to execute her the following morning. A vizier's daughter, Scheherazade, escapes execution by telling the king a story each night that she leaves unfinished at dawn, to be finished the following night. The stories told by Scheherazade cover a vast range: **fantasy**, heroic epics, love stories, didactic stories, and erotic and devotional tales.

The first European version of the tales, in 12 volumes (1701–1717), was by the French scholar Antoine Galland. Richard Francis Burton produced a well-respected English version in 16 volumes (1885–1888). The first, bowdlerized, version for children was *The Oriental Moralist, or Beauties of the Arabian Nights Entertainments* (1791), published by Elizabeth Newbery. The stories most popular among young readers are the **adventure stories**, which often include quests for fabulous treasure and usually involve the characters Sinbad, Aladdin, and Ali Baba. Notable collections for children are the *Dalziels' Illustrated Arabian Nights' Entertainments* (1863–1865), which includes more than 200 illustrations by eminent artists such as John Tenniel and John Everett Millais, and *The Arabian Nights Entertainments* edited by **Andrew Lang** (1898). There have been many **adaptations** of the *Arabian Nights* for both television and film, with **Walt Disney**'s animated movie *Aladdin* (1992) the most commercially successful. Aladdin is also a popular figure in British **pantomime**.

ARDAGH, PHILIP (1961–). British author best known for the best-selling Eddie Dickens series, which has been described as a cross between **Charles Dickens** and Monty Python. Starting with *Awful*

End (2002; U.S. title *A House Called Awful End*), the series is set in Victorian England and centers on young Eddie Dickens, the only member of his family not afflicted by insanity or a serious physical ailment, who is in the care of Mad Uncle Jack and Even Madder Aunt Maud. The absurd events are narrated with a strong authorial voice, and the novels are full of digressions, vocabulary lessons, and history lessons. Initially planned as a trilogy by Ardagh, volumes 4, 5, and 6 followed after the first three had enjoyed much critical and popular acclaim. It has been translated into more than 30 languages. Ardagh is also the author of several **nonfiction** titles for adults and children.

ARDIZZONE, EDWARD (1900–1979). British author and **illustrator**, born in French Indo-China (now Vietnam). Ardizzone wrote and illustrated 20 books for children and illustrated more than 100 more for other authors of adult and children's literature, including **Walter de la Mare**, **Philippa Pearce**, and **Eleanor Farjeon**. Ardizzone and Farjeon's joint production, *The Little Bookroom* (1955), won the **Carnegie Medal**. He is best known as author and illustrator of the very popular Tim series. The first title, *Little Tim and the Brave Sea Captain* (1936), was followed by *Lucy Brown and Mister Grime* the following year, and in 1938 the characters from the first two books were brought together in *Tim and Lucy Go to Sea*. The series continued after the war with *Tim All Alone* (1956), which won the first **Kate Greenaway Medal**, and the final volume was *Tim's Last Voyage* (1972). Ardizzone believed that illustrators should not draw down for children but rather up. His pen-and-ink and watercolor illustrations have been described as full of movement, conveying the richness and pleasure of everyday life while not ignoring elements that may threaten a child. The stories in the Tim series seem very simple to adult readers, but the pictures are understated and leave plenty of room for the viewer's imagination. Ardizzone, regarded by many as a quintessentially English illustrator, enjoyed an equally high reputation in the United States.

ASBJØRNSEN, PETER CHRISTEN (1812–1885). Norwegian writer and scientist who, together with **Jørgen Engebretsen Moe**, collected Norwegian **folktales**. Their life's work is so closely united that their collections are usually referred to only as "Asbjørnsen and Moe."

Asbjørnsen, a student of the natural sciences, and Moe, who studied theology, met at the University of Christiania, where, inspired by the Brothers **Grimm**, they decided to collect Norwegian folktales. The tales were partly remembered from their own childhoods, but they also spent much time gathering stories from country people. In 1841 the first of four volumes of *Norske folkeeventyr* (*Popular Tales from the Norse*, 1859) appeared. In 1851 a revised and enlarged edition was published, which adopted the unaffected style of the Grimms as its model, giving the stories a uniform style. This in turn affected the development of a Norwegian literary language. Asbjørnsen and Moe's folktales have been translated into many languages; well-known single tales include "East o' the Sun and West o' the Moon" and "Three Billy Goats Gruff."

ASIMOV, ISAAC (1920–1992). Russian-born U.S. author and biochemist, best known for his works of **science fiction** and for his popular-science books. Asimov wrote more than 350 short stories and 400 books, most of them science fiction for adults, but he was also the author of hundreds of **information books** for children; he had an exceptional ability to explain complex scientific ideas in a way that was both comprehensible to and entertaining for young readers. The series Isaac Asimov's 21st Century Library of the Universe includes, among others, volumes that explain microwaves, the universe, dinosaurs, outer space, solar power, and how electricity works.

ASSOCIATION INTERNATIONALE DU THÉÂTRE POUR L'ENFANCE ET LA JEUNESSE / INTERNATIONAL ASSOCIATION OF THEATER FOR CHILDREN AND YOUNG PEOPLE (ASSITEJ). Established in 1965 by representatives of professional theater for children and young people from 12 countries, ASSITEJ is now an international network with headquarters in Zagreb, Croatia, and national centers in more than 70 countries. The group sponsors international festivals and supports a network of thousands of individual and organizational members.

ASTRID LINDGREN MEMORIAL AWARD. The Astrid Lindgren Memorial Award, the second-highest-endowed literary prize after the Nobel Prize, was founded by the Swedish government in 2002 to increase interest in children's and youth literature around the world and, in the spirit of **Astrid Lindgren**, to strengthen children's rights on a global level. The annual award, which is administered by the Swedish National Council for Cultural Affairs, is for an entire body of work, and it is granted to authors, **illustrators**, storytellers, and promoters of reading regardless of language or nationality. (See appendix for list of recipients).

AVERY, GILLIAN (1926–). British novelist, editor, historian of children's literature, and author of a number of **historical novels** set in the 19th century that reflect her interest in the Victorian period. The first, *The Warden's Niece* (1957), tells the story of an intelligent, **orphaned** girl who escapes from a boarding school and, in the midst of adventures, pursues her interest in historical research. The last one to date, *A Likely Lad* (1971), televised by the BBC, is an astute account of class distinction and family rivalry in late-Victorian Manchester. Avery's novels have been praised for their complexity, accuracy of historical research, and sense of humor. Her *Childhood's Pattern: A Study of the Heroes and Heroines of Children's Fiction, 1770–1950* (1975) was one of the earliest full-length studies of children's literature in Great Britain. *Behold the Child: American Children and Their Books, 1621–1922* (1994) is a comprehensive study of American children's literature.

AVI (1937–). Pseudonym of Edward Irving Wortis, U.S. librarian, playwright, and storyteller who overcame dysgraphia and failure at school to become a writer. Since his first children's book, *Things That Sometimes Happen* (1970), Avi has written more than 50 books for children and young adults in a wide number of genres that include **fantasy**, **animal stories**, **historical fiction**, **mystery**, and **adventure**. Examples of his historical fiction include *The Fighting Ground* (1984), *The True Confessions of Charlotte Doyle* (1990), and *Crispin: The Cross of Lead* (2002), an adolescent identity quest of a nameless boy in 14th-century England, which won the **Newbery Medal**. Experimental young adult titles include *Nothing But the Truth* (1991), subtitled *A Documentary Novel*, which is told through the media of diaries, letters, and newspaper clippings; and the comic-book novel *City of Light, City of Dark* (1993).

AWARDS. Two major international children's literature awards, the **Hans Christian Andersen Award** and the **Astrid Lindgren Memorial Award**, honor authors and illustrators from all over the world. The NSK Neustadt Prize for Children's Literature, established in 2003 as an offshoot of the Neustadt International Prize for Literature, is awarded in alternating years to a living writer with significant achievement. The principal U.S. awards are the **Caldecott Medal** for illustrators and the **Newbery Medal** for authors. The Boston Globe–Horn Book Awards in the three categories **Picture Book**, Fiction and **Poetry**, and **Nonfiction** are also prestigious U.S. honors, as are the Coretta Scott King Award (for African American authors and illustrators) and the Phoenix Award (which honors a book originally published 20 years previously that did not receive a major award at that time).

In Great Britain, the **Carnegie Medal** is awarded to authors and the **Kate Greenaway Medal** to illustrators; the title of **children's laureate** is also awarded every two years. The Costa Children's Book Award (the Whitbread Children's Book Award until 2006) and the Guardian Children's Fiction Prize are further prominent British awards, as was the Nestlé Smarties Book Prize (which was discontinued in 2008). The Children's Book Award (since 2001 the Red House Children's Book Award) is a British national prize awarded entirely on the basis of children's votes. Other important national prizes include the Children's Books Ireland Bisto Book Award, the Canadian Library Association Book of the Year for Children Award, the Children's Book Council of Australia Book of the Year Award, and the New Zealand Post Children's Book Award.

Prizes for children's literature in languages other than English include the German Deutscher Jugendliteraturpreis; the Austrian Kinder- und Jugendliteraturpreis; the French Prix Basbab, Prix Tam-Tams, and Prix de la Presse des Jeunes; and the New Zealand Te Kura Pounamu Maori Book Award for a book written in Maori. Awards for **translations** of children's literature into English are the U.S. **Mildred L. Batchelder Award** and the biennial Marsh Award for Children's Literature in Translation, established in Great Britain in 1996. The Astrid Lindgren Translation Prize is awarded triennially by the International Federation of Translators for a single translation or for the entire body of work of a translator of books for children into any language. (See appendix for lists of recipients of the major awards). *See also* INFORMATION BOOKS.

AWDRY, REVEREND W. (WILBERT) (1911–1997). *See* THOMAS THE TANK ENGINE.

AYMÉ, MARCEL (1902–1967). French playwright and author of fiction for both adults and children, best known for *Les contes du chat perché* (1934; *The Wonderful Farm*, 1951). A children's **fantasy** classic in France, the collection of **fable**-like stories relates the adventures of two girls, Delphine and Marinette, on an enchanted farm where animals can speak. Aymé published a sequel in 1950 that was translated as *Return to the Wonderful Farm* in 1954. The 1951 American edition of *The Wonderful Farm* was the first children's book illustrated by **Maurice Sendak**.

– B –

BABAR. *See* BRUNHOFF, JEAN DE AND LAURENT DE.

BABBITT, NATALIE (1932–). U.S. author and **illustrator** best known for her novel *Tuck Everlasting* (1975) about an 11-year-old girl, Winnie, who meets the Tuck family, immortal because they once drank from a spring of everlasting life. She is kidnapped by the family, who convince her not to reveal the secret of the spring, as immortality is not the blessing that it seems. Acceptance of death as a natural part of life is a central theme in this vivid story. Babbitt has written a number of **fantasy** novels employing **folktale** elements, such as a trickster story in *The Devil's Storybook* (1974). Her narratives are entertaining and humorous, while at the same time addressing serious subjects such as how to gain love and acceptance and how to overcome fears. Babbitt has illustrated her own and others' work and has produced some **picture books**, including *Phoebe's Revolt* (1968), told in rhyming verse.

BALLANTYNE, R. M. (ROBERT MICHAEL) (1825–1894). Scottish author regarded as one of the most accomplished 19th-century writers of **adventure stories**. His most famous novel, *The Coral Island* (1857), recounts the adventures of three boys shipwrecked on a South Sea island; initially concerned with their attempts to make themselves comfortable there, it subsequently addresses the dangers encountered in the form of sharks, pirates, and cannibals. They are ultimately freed through the intervention of missionaries. Ballantyne was one of the first to portray boys enjoying real adventures away from home and free from the guidance of adults. His heroes embody the ideals of muscular Christianity; they find themselves spiritually uplifted by their period of independence, thrive on physical challenges, and, like "true Englishmen," never falter in their determination to do right. Ballantyne upholds the ideology of empire throughout; his white, British boys represent the pinnacle of civilization, and the fiendish behavior of the natives justifies the necessity of the missionary movement. **Robert Louis Stevenson** and **Sir J. M. Barrie** were fervent boy readers of the novel, and its influence is evident in *Treasure Island* and *Peter Pan*. William Golding's *Lord of the Flies* (1954) can be read as a pessimistic response to *The Coral Island*. *See also* ETHNOCENTRISM.

BANKS, LYNNE REID (1929–). British author for children and adults best known for her **fantasy** *The Indian in the Cupboard* (1980), in which the young protagonist Omri has the power to make his plastic toys, including Little Bear, the Indian of the title, come to life. Four sequels (1985–1998) followed the best-selling novel, and it was filmed in 1995 by Frank Oz. Banks, who spent a number of years teaching in a kibbutz in Israel, also wrote two novels for teenagers based on her experience there: *One More River* (1973), set in the days before, during, and after the 1967 Six-Day War, and its sequel *Broken Bridge* (1994).

BANNERMAN, HELEN (1862–1946). Scottish author who spent much of her adult life in India, where her husband worked as a medical doctor. She is most famous for her **picture book** *The Story of Little Black Sambo* (1899), a story narrated in simple text, with brightly colored pictures, and issued in a small format that heralded a change in children's publishing. In it, a little black boy encounters tigers in the jungle who take his clothes and his umbrella, but he manages to outwit them in the end and returns safely home to eat 169 pancakes for his supper. The setting is ambiguous. The location is clearly India, as there are tigers in the jungle and Indian ghee (clarified butter) is referred to; but Sambo and his parents are portrayed using iconography usually associated with African characters, and the names of Little Sambo, his mother Black Mambo, and his father Black Jumbo utilize the "mb" sound, commonly heard in African languages.

In the 1970s, *Little Black Sambo* came under fire for **racism** because of the hero's exaggerated "negroid" features and the fact that the name "Sambo" was often used for racial insults. Observing that the story itself did not contain any racist overtones, the illustrator Fred Marcellino produced a version with new pictures in 1996 called *The Story of Little Babaji*, which changes the characters' names but otherwise leaves the text unchanged. Another modern version, *Sam and the Tigers* (1996) by **Julius Lester** and **Jerry Pinkney,** reclaimed the story for African Americans by moving the setting to the American South. Bannerman never profited from the huge popularity of *Little Black Sambo* as the publisher, Richard Grant, purchased the rights for five pounds. *See also* ETHNOCENTRISM.

BARBAULD, ANNA LAETITIA (1743–1825). British poet, essayist, and children's author whose **poetry** was instrumental to the development of Romanticism in England. Her key works for children were *Lessons for Children* (1778–1779), four reading **primers** based on the educational theories of **John Locke** that seek to educate the imagination. She uses the conceit of a mother conversing with her son, and the typography of the texts progresses in difficulty as the child advances. *Lessons for Children* was reprinted for over a century and had a profound effect on the development of children's literature. Her collection *Hymns in Prose for Children* (1781) influenced the poetry of **William Blake** and William Wordsworth through its celebration of freedom in nature.

BARRIE, SIR J. M. (JAMES MATTHEW) (1860–1937). Scottish journalist, playwright, and author of the Peter Pan texts. These concern a boy who does not want to grow up, and their complex evolution is connected to the very close relationship that Barrie had with the five sons of the Llewelyn-Davies family, to whom the stories were originally told. The character of Peter Pan first appears in *The Little White Bird* (1902), a novel for adults, in a story about a baby, half bird and half boy, who lives in Kensington Gardens in London. It was later published as a book of its own, *Peter Pan in Kensington Gardens* (1906), with illustrations by **Arthur Rackham**. The play *Peter Pan, or The Boy Who Would Not Grow Up*, which had its premiere on December 27, 1904, was a huge success and has been performed every year but one since then. The novel version of the play, *Peter and Wendy* (now usually called *Peter Pan*), was published in 1911; the play itself was published, strongly annotated, in 1928.

In the play Peter Pan flies one night into the Darling's home in London, looking for his lost shadow. There he meets Wendy and her brothers Michael and John, and he takes them to Never Land, a place, inaccessible to adults, where children never get older. Wendy takes on the role of mother for Peter and the Lost Boys, children mislaid by their parents or nannies. The laws of time, growth, and parental authority do not apply on this fantastic island of palms and lagoons populated with fairies, pirates, "Red Indians," and mermaids. The only law is the law of the imagination: if someone really believes in something, it will happen. Never Land is a metaphor for children's imagination, a paradise made up of motifs taken from **fairy tales** and **adventure stories**. Peter's enemy is the one-armed pirate Captain Hook, whose lost arm, fed by Peter to a crocodile in whose stomach the owner's watch continues to tick, is replaced by an iron hook. When Wendy and her brothers are homesick, Peter returns them to their parents, who also adopt the Lost Boys. Peter refuses to be adopted but makes Mrs. Darling promise that Wendy can return to Never Land every spring to help with the cleaning. The end of the play shows Peter alone outside, looking in through a window at a happy family scene, forever excluded; the price for eternal childhood is not to be a human child.

Peter Pan is one of the figures of children's literature who have an existence beyond the text(s) in which they first appeared, and he has become a universally recognized symbol of eternal childhood. Barrie presented the copyright to *Peter Pan* to London's Great Ormond Street Hospital for Children in 1929; just before it expired on the 70th anniversary of his death, an authorized sequel, *Peter Pan in Scarlet* (2006) by **Geraldine McCaughrean**, was issued simultaneously in

31 languages. There are several film versions of *Peter Pan*; one of the best known is the **Walt Disney** cartoon version (1953). Steven Spielberg's *Hook* (1991) is a sequel about the grown-up Peter, played by Robin Williams. *Finding Never Land* (2004) is a semifictional film about Barrie as he wrote *Peter Pan.*

BAUM, L. FRANK (1856–1919). Actor, entrepreneur, filmmaker, and author of some 55 novels and numerous short stories, poems, and scripts, many under pseudonyms. He is best known for his **fantasy** novel *The Wonderful Wizard of Oz* (1900), usually referred to simply as *The Wizard of Oz*, and its 13 sequels. The success of his first two books for children in which he retold **nursery rhymes**—*Mother Goose in Prose* (1897), illustrated by Maxfield Parrish, and *Father Goose: His Book* (1899), illustrated by William Wallace Denslow—encouraged him to make a children's novel out of a bedtime story told to his four sons. *The Wonderful Wizard of Oz*, which appeared in 1900 with illustrations by Denslow, was the first full-length original fantasy that drew on American themes and sources. Indeed, in his introduction to the novel, Baum demanded the liberation of American children's literature from the dominance of European traditions, and his "modernized" **fairy tale** became a milestone in the development of American children's literature. Baum told a compelling story and created characters such as the Tin Woodman, the Cowardly Lion, the Scarecrow, and the humbug Wizard of Oz, and images such as the Yellow Brick Road, that would become ingrained in the American psyche. The fearless and optimistic Dorothy can be taken to represent the spirit of frontier America.

The novel and a stage production in 1902 were so popular that Baum started to produce sequels. The 1939 MGM film version starring Judy Garland added to their popularity, and the Oz series was continued after Baum's death, with his prior permission, by Ruth Plumlay Thompson. The novels have been translated into several languages, and other authors have presented their versions of Oz, as in **Gregory Maguire**'s revisionist novels *Wicked: The Life and Times of the Wicked Witch of the West* (1995; also made into a successful musical) and *Son of a Witch* (2005). The Russian author Alexander Melentyevich Volkov produced *The Wizard of the Emerald City*

(Russian original in 1939), a very free translation of Baum's *The Wonderful Wizard of Oz*; it was revised in 1959, and its popularity in the 1960s led to five sequels by Volkov himself that were not based on Baum's novels. Called the Magic Land series, they enjoyed huge popularity throughout Eastern Europe. In many communist and former communist countries, Volkov's version of Oz is better known than Baum's.

BAWDEN, NINA (1925–). British author of more than 40 novels for adults and children. Her widely acclaimed and morally complex novel *Carrie's War* (1973) involves two English children evacuated to Wales during World War II. One of them, Carrie, does a terrible thing when she tries to heal the breach between the very strict Mr. Evans, with whom they have been sent to live, and his estranged sister. It won the Phoenix Award in 1993 and has been adapted for the stage and television by the BBC. *The Peppermint Pig* (1975), a historical novel set during the early years of the 20th century, describes the consequences for a family after the father loses his job for a crime he did not commit; it, too, focuses on uprooted children. Bawden's interest in the way the present can become a victim of the past informs her novel *The Real Plato Jones* (1993), in which a conflict of loyalties in wartime Greece continues to have repercussions 50 years later. Most of Bawden's books have realistic settings and are addressed to older children.

BEGINNER BOOKS. *See* EASY READERS.

BELLOC, JOSEPH HILAIRE PIERRE RENÉ (1870–1953). Author of mixed French and English descent who wrote comic verse for children, starting with *The Bad Child's Book of Beasts* (1896) and its sequel *More Beasts for Worse Children* (1897). His *Cautionary Tales for Children* (1907) parodies the 19th-century genre of **cautionary tales** with comic-macabre tales of "Matilda, who told Lies, and was Burned to Death" and "Henry King, who chewed bits of String, and was early cut off in Dreadful Agonies." Regarded as among the funniest texts written for children, Belloc's poems have inspired many imitations. Authors who have continued in his tradition include Harry Graham and **Roald Dahl**.

BEMELMANS, LUDWIG (1898–1962). Austrian-born U.S. author and illustrator famous for his literary creation Madeline, the smallest, bravest, and naughtiest of 12 little girls in a convent school in Paris. The Madeline series of **picture books** (1939–1961), household favorites in Great Britain, France, and the United States, are written in rhyming couplets and illustrated in a deceptively simple style; *Madeline's Rescue* (1953) won the **Caldecott Medal**. The first book was made into an award-winning short animated cartoon in 1952, and an animated television series was produced between 1990 and 1995; a live-action film of the Madeline stories was released in 1998.

BERQUIN, ARNAUD (1747–1791). French poet, and author and editor of the periodical publication *L'ami des enfants* [The Children's Friend] (1782–1783). The plays and stories contained in the magazine were mostly translated and freely **adapted** from the work of German (**Christian Felix Weisse**), English (**Thomas Day**), and Dutch authors. Berquin's versions proved so popular that they were retranslated back into German and English.

BERRY, JAMES (1925–). Jamaican poet, novelist, and short-story writer who immigrated to Great Britain in 1948. Berry celebrates humanity and diversity in poems about children's experience in Britain and the Caribbean that reveal his musical ear for language. His collection *When I Dance* (1988) won the Signal Poetry Award in 1989. His Anancy stories and other **folktales** are linked to the African oral tradition. His first **picture book**, *Celebration Song* (1994) with pictures by Louise Brierly, puts the story of Jesus' birth in a Caribbean setting. Berry was appointed OBE in 1990.

BETTELHEIM, BRUNO (1903–1990). Controversial Austrian-born writer and child psychologist who was deported with other Austrian Jews to Dachau and Buchenwald concentration camps from 1938 to 1939; after his release he immigrated to the United States. His *Uses of Enchantment: The Meaning and Importance of Fairytales* (1976) was particularly influential. In it Bettelheim argues that the struggle between good and evil in the tales creates a catharsis for children, through which they can control their own fear and fantasies.

BEWICK, THOMAS (1753–1828). English wood engraver whose apprentice work was published in **chapbooks** for children. His love of the countryside, animals, and birds inspired both his *General History of Quadrupeds* (1790) and the great achievement with which his name is most closely associated, the two-volume *History of British Birds* (1797–1804). He also illustrated an edition of Samuel Croxall's **translation** of **Aesop**'s **fables** (1818). His delicate images, with their sense of three-dimensional depth, resulted from his innovative technique of "white-line" engraving, which paid as much attention to what was cut away from the block of hardwood as to what was left behind. Bewick, considered the finest of all English practitioners of wood engraving, was the first to make the work of the **illustrator** as important as the text in books for children.

THE BIBLE IN CHILDREN'S LITERATURE. The Bible was among the first books adapted with the child reader in mind. The earliest **adaptations** were in Latin, and the first vernacular versions written in simplified language appeared in 16th-century Germany: Martin Luther's *Passional* (1529) described the life of Christ for an audience of children and uneducated adults. The most influential Bible-story collection for Catholic children was Nicolas Fontaine's *L'Histoire du Vieux et du Nouveau Testament* (1670; *History of the Old and New Testament*, 1690), which, in translation, remained in use among Catholics in the United States until the early 20th century. Versions of the Bible in the vernacular for Jewish children only started to become available at the beginning of the 19th century, when a number appeared in German. The early 19th century also saw a number of illustrated **chapbook** versions of the best-known passages from the Bible. Children's Bibles, as other adaptations for children, often exclude material that is regarded as unsuitable for a young readership, either because it is too sexually explicit, too complex, or too frightening. Extraneous material such as commentary and moralistic interpretation may also be added, as well as extra information about characters and events to make the narratives more interesting for the child reader—a goal that has also motivated retellings through the eyes of a child or an animal (as in **Nick Butterworth** and **Mick Inkpen**'s *Animal Tales*, 1999).

Several children's authors have turned to the Bible-story genre to produce collections of stories, as opposed to a version that follows the basic structure of the Old and/or New Testaments. These include **Sarah Trimmer**, **Samuel Goodrich**, the poet **Walter de la Mare**, and **Peter Dickinson**, whose *City of Gold, and Other Stories from the Old Testament* (1980) is narrated by contemporary observers. Children's Bibles have appeared in miniature, versified, alphabetized, **illustrated**, and hieroglyphic form; as dramas; and, since the 1940s, as comic strips.

BIENNIAL OF ILLUSTRATIONS BRATISLAVA (BIB). An international competitive exhibition of **illustrations** for books for children and young adults that has been held in Slovakia since 1967 under the patronage of the United Nations Educational, Scientific and Cultural Organization (UNESCO) and the **International Board on Books for Young People (IBBY)**. Awards given at BIB are the Grand Prix, Zlaté jablko (Golden Apple), plaques, and honorable mentions.

BIERHORST, JOHN (1936–). U.S. folklorist, author, and editor of books that focus on the traditions and stories of the native peoples of North, South, and Central America. Bierhorst sees himself primarily as a translator rather than an author. Collections particularly attractive to children are *The Naked Bear: Folktales of Iroquois* (1987) and the trickster tales in *The Dancing Fox: Arctic Folktales* (1997).

BIGGLES. *See* JOHNS, CAPTAIN W. E.

BIOGRAPHY. *See* D'AULAIRE, EDGAR PARIN AND INGRI; FREEDMAN, RUSSELL; FRITZ, JEAN; HAMILTON, VIRGINIA; INFORMATION BOOKS; LAWRENCE, JACOB; LAWSON, ROBERT; PRESSLER, MIRJAM; SÍS, PETER; THIELE, COLIN.

BLACK BEAUTY. *See* SEWELL, ANNA.

BLAKE, QUENTIN (1932–). British cartoonist, **illustrator**, and author who has illustrated more than 250 books by 80 different writers including **Joan Aiken**, **Russell Hoban**, and **Michael Rosen**. The author with whom he is predominantly associated is **Roald Dahl**. Blake's spindly and spontaneous-looking pen-and-ink line drawings, usually both **fantastic** and humorous, are instantly recognizable. Primarily celebrated for his funny and anarchic illustrations for Dahl's books, his illustration of *Michael Rosen's Sad Book* (2004), which addresses Rosen's bereavement after the death of his son, shows Blake working with great poignancy in a serious emotional register. Blake has also written and illustrated **picture books** of his own, such as *Mister Magnolia* (1980), which won the **Kate Greenaway Medal**, and *Quentin Blake's ABC* (1989). He was the first **children's laureate** in Great Britain in 1999, an experience he recorded in his book *Laureate's Progress* (2002). He received the **Hans Christian Andersen Award** in 2002 and was appointed CBE for his services to children's literature in 2005.

BLAKE, WILLIAM (1757–1827). English **poet**, painter, and engraver who wrote, **illustrated**, and published his own texts. His *Songs of Innocence* were published for children in 1789 and reissued as part of the larger collection *Songs of Innocence and Experience: Shewing the Two Contrary States of the Human Soul* (1794). Few children knew the *Songs of Innocence* in Blake's lifetime; because he printed and bound his books himself, very few copies were actually made. He was one of the first major British poets to turn his attention to children, and he addressed them in ways radically new, departing completely from the moralistic conventions of his predecessors and from the poetic fashions of his day. Some of the poems are expressions of a young child's developing sense of goodness; in others, children take on the language of adults, addressing creatures smaller than themselves; while in some, mothers converse with small children. Blake uses the imagery and diction of traditional rhymes and addresses moral issues, such as race and slavery in "The Little Black Boy," in a manner that can be comforting for the child but troubling for the adult reader. Blake's work anticipates the Romantic movement that developed after his death.

BLOCK, FRANCESCA LIA (1962–). U.S. author for young adult readers. Her six Dangerous Angels novels began with the postmodern **fairy tale** *Weetzie Bat* (1989), about a punk princess with spiky bleached hair, a pink 1950s prom dress, and cowboy boots, who is granted three wishes by a genie. Since then Block has written more than a dozen further young adult novels, as well as a number of short-story collections; many of them feature assertive young women in big-city settings, often Los Angeles, her home city. Her focus is generally on characters growing up in a problematic world. Block's novels have been translated into a number of languages, and she was the recipient of the 2005 Margaret A. Edwards Lifetime Achievement Award from the **American Library Association (ALA).**

BLUME, JUDY (1938–). U.S. author of some 22 books for children and young adults, and 3 best-selling novels for adults. Since the appearance in 1970 of *Are You There, God? It's Me, Margaret*, one of the first novels to deal openly with such issues of early adolescence as menstruation, bras, and boyfriends, Blume's books have made publishing history. Hugely popular with her young readers, these novels deal effectively with issues that interest and concern them, but from which educators and parents often shy away. Her novels are written in an informal, chatty style, with a good ear for adolescent dialogue; critics have called them simplistic and some have criticized their narrow social background. *Then Again, Maybe I Won't* (1971) is about a boy receiving psychiatric help; *Blubber* (1974) describes the bullying of an overweight girl; and *Forever* (1975) was the first children's story that featured teenage sex openly and in some technical detail. It is still banned in a number of U.S. states, and it was a long time before a paperback edition appeared in Great Britain. This did nothing to diminish its popularity, with Blume becoming something of a guru for teenagers. Thousands of young readers have written letters to her describing problems in their own lives, some of which were published in *Letters to Judy: What Your Kids Wish They Could Tell You* (1986). More than 70 million copies of her books have been sold worldwide, and they have been translated into 26 languages. Herself a target for censors, Blume has become an active spokesperson for intellectual freedom and works with organizations such as the National Coalition Against Censorship.

BLYTON, ENID (1897–1968). British novelist and educational writer, and one of the best-selling children's writers of all time. Blyton's output was prodigious: writing some 10,000 words a day, she produced an estimated 700 books and 4,500 short stories from the end of the 1930s until her death 30 years later. She is best known for her series, based on recurring characters and addressed to different age groups, from toddlers to young teenagers. Blyton's books fall roughly into three types. One involves ordinary children in extraordinary situations, having **adventures**, solving crimes, and generally displaying self-sufficiency in unusual circumstances and without adult interference. Examples of this type include The Famous Five series, The Secret Seven series, The Adventure series, and The Mystery series. The second type is the boarding **school story** with more emphasis on the day-to-day life at school, including midnight feasts, practical jokes, and the social interaction of various types of characters. Examples of this type are The Malory Towers series, The St. Clare series, and The Naughtiest Girl series. In the third type, which includes The Wishing-Chair series and The Magic Faraway Tree series, children are transported into a magical world in which they meet fairies, goblins, and elves.

Blyton's enduring, worldwide popularity (with the notable exception of the United States) has been matched by adult disdain for her works. In the 1950s and 1960s the criticism was leveled at Blyton's restricted use of language, short sentences, simple vocabulary, and use of clichés; from the 1960s on the accusations were of sexism for her use of **gender** stereotypes and **racism**, especially in her portrayal of **Golliwogs**. Many supposedly offensive elements were altered in modern reprints of her books. Blyton's name and works have seen great exposure through spin offs in other media since the sale of her copyright to the entertainment company Trocadero in 1996. *See also* ETHNOCENTRISM.

BOJUNGA (NUNES), LYGIA (1932–). Brazilian actress and author of some 20 novels for children. She was the first non-European, non-U.S. author to receive the **Hans Christian Andersen Award** (1982); in 2004 she received the prestigious **Astrid Lindgren Memorial Award**. Her books combine magical realism and acute psychological observation with a passion for democracy and social justice. In them the child's point of view is always paramount. Her novels have been translated into several languages, but only two are available in

English. *Os Colegas* (1972; *The Companions*, 1989) is a parable about freedom that tells of the friendship between a scared, abandoned young rabbit and a bear and a dog who have escaped from captivity. In *O Mio Amigo Pintor* (1987; *My Friend the Painter*, 1991), a boy deals with his grief over the painter's death with the help of colors.

BOND, MICHAEL (1926–). *See* PADDINGTON BEAR.

BOND, RUSKIN (1934–). Anglo-Indian writer, author of numerous stories for children describing life in the Himalayan foothills. *A Room on the Roof* (1956), the story of a teenage boy torn between his English and his Indian cultural heritages, won the John Llewellyn Rhys Memorial Prize in 1957. Other children's books include *The Blue Umbrella* (1974) and *Getting Granny's Glasses* (1985). He also wrote a children's **biography** of India's first prime minister, Jawaharlal Nehru (1976).

BOSTON, LUCY M. (1892–1990). British author best known for her Green Knowe series of six **fantasy** novels, which starts with *The Children of Green Knowe* (1954) and concludes with *The Stones of Green Knowe* (1976). These time-shift novels are set in a 12th-century manor house near Cambridge, based on Boston's own home, in which children of the Oldknow family from different historical periods and generations can perceive and speak with each other. Many of the young protagonists are **orphans**, and the themes of displacement and abandoned children are present in most of the novels. The author's son, Peter Boston, illustrated the series.

BOUTET DE MONVEL, LOUIS MAURICE (1851–1913). French painter and **illustrator** renowned for his decorative illustrations of children's books, collections of songs, and an edition of the **fables** of **Jean de La Fontaine**. His modern style, with its use of clean lines and pale colors, was influenced by Japanese aesthetics. *La vie de Jeanne d'Arc* (1896; *Joan of Arc*, 1918) is regarded as his finest work.

BOYCE, FRANK COTTRELL (1961–). British screenwriter and novelist whose first novel for children, *Millions* (2004), was based on his screenplay for the film of the same name. The story centers on the kind-hearted, seven-year-old Damian and his brother, who find a bag containing a huge quantity of banknotes. In the end, after the money has caused all sorts of problems, Damian decides to burn it. After exploring how money changes people in *Millions*, Boyce addressed the effect of art in his second novel for children, *Framed* (2005). The same quirkiness and lightness of touch are evident in this novel about what happens to the inhabitants of the Welsh village Manod when the National Gallery in London moves all of its paintings there, to be stored in an abandoned mine for protection from flooding in London.

BRAZIL, ANGELA (1868–1947). British author of **school stories** for girls who rescued the genre from the moralistic grip of earlier writers to create a new breed of jolly, hockey-playing, slang-using schoolgirls. Although her output was extensive, she did not write any series; each novel stands on its own, with different characters. A common feature is romantic friendships between girls. The unself-conscious snobbery, the schoolgirl pride in "Britishness," and the strong anti-German sentiment (especially in the books produced during the war period) all underline the datedness of her books today.

BRIGGS, RAYMOND (1934–). British author and **illustrator** best known for his **picture books** in comic-strip form that address a wide range of readerships and subject matter. Briggs started out illustrating books by other authors; for the *Mother Goose Treasury* (1966), with **Iona and Peter Opie**'s text, he received his first **Kate Greenaway Medal**. He received his second for *Father Christmas* (1973), the book with which his distinctive comic-strip style became established. His Father Christmas, who hates wintry weather, is, like *Fungus the Bogeyman* (1977), one of Briggs's characteristically grumpy old men who also enjoy the simple pleasures of life—working-class characters who make do with what life has thrown at them. This recurrent theme in Briggs's work culminates in *Ethel and Ernest: A True Story* (1998), a moving, unsentimental account of his parents' marriage in graphic novel form, which addresses themes of class and social aspiration. Power and class are addressed in his satirical work *When the Wind Blows* (1982), in which an elderly couple naively follow the government's hopelessly inadequate procedures after a nuclear bomb has dropped. *The Tin-Pot Foreign General and the Old Iron Woman* (1984) is a condemnation of the Falklands War between the United Kingdom and Argentina. *The Snowman* (1978), a wordless picture book that tells the story of a snowman who comes to life to play with the little boy who made him, is one of Briggs's most popular works; the highly successful animated film version is shown on British television every Christmas. A special friendship between a magical being and a young child are also at the center of *The Man* (1992) and *The Bear* (1994).

BROOKS, RON (1948–). Australian **illustrator** and maker of **picture books**. Two of Brooks's early books, *The Bunyip of Berkeley's Creek* (1973) and *John Brown, Rose and the Midnight Cat* (1977), both with text by Jenny Wagner, won the Children's Book Council of Australia Picture Book of the Year Award. They are now considered classics and are widely recognized as having introduced Australian picture books onto the world scene. While not aggressively Australian, they do present local icons such as a kookaburra perched in a tree and a bunyip, an amphibious animal from Aboriginal folklore. Renowned for his vast range of artistic styles, Brooks applies whichever one he feels empathizes best with the text in hand. He is particularly skillful at lending a human expression to an animal face, as shown in his recent illustrations of two books written by **Margaret Wild**, *Old Pig* (1996) and the international-award-winning *Fox* (2001). The imaginative life of children is explored in two books cowritten with his wife Margaret Perversi, *Henry's Bed* (1997) and *Henry's Bath* (1997).

BROWN, MARC (1946–). U.S. author and **illustrator** best known for the humorous series of books involving an **anthropomorphic** aardvark called Arthur, beginning with *Arthur's Nose* (1976). Arthur attends third grade and lives with his parents and five-year-old sister, D.W. The stories are firmly rooted in contemporary middle-class American suburbia and describe situations with which children can easily identify, such as losing a tooth or having to wear glasses. Arthur's younger sister features in several titles of her own, including *D.W. Rides Again!* (1993). The animated television series *Arthur*, developed in 1996, has proved exceptionally popular and has won several **awards**. An industry has developed around the character, which includes Arthur-based toys, computer software, and curriculum-support material. Brown has also edited and illustrated collections of finger rhymes and other **poetry** for very young listeners.

BROWN, MARCIA (1918–). U.S author and **illustrator**, and the first artist to receive the **Caldecott Medal** three times. Brown is interested in the folklore of other cultures, has traveled extensively, and enjoys experimenting with different forms of illustration. She worked as a storyteller at the New York Public Library, and many of her publications are retellings of stories from different cultures and periods. She received the Caldecott Honor award for her retelling of the traditional folktale *Stone Soup* in 1947, and won the Caldecott Medal in 1955 for her pen-and-ink drawings with pastel color overwashes for **Charles Perrault**'s *Cinderella*, which she translated herself. The second medal was for the woodcut illustrations for her version of an Indian tale, *Once a Mouse . . .* (1961), and the third was for her book *Shadow* (1982), an African tale based on a poem by Blaise Cendrars. Her collage illustrations for this book attracted some negative criticism of alleged **racial** stereotyping, but this story about what Africa has to offer humanity is generally considered a fine achievement.

BROWN, MARGARET WISE (1910–1952). U.S. author of more than 100 **picture books** for young children. Among her best known are *The Runaway Bunny* (1942) and *Goodnight Moon* (1947), both illustrated by Clement Hurd. Sometimes referred to in the United States as the "laureate of the nursery," Brown had a talent for amusing, delighting, and comforting small children. She was particularly sensitive to sound, as shown by *The Noisy Book* (1939) and its sequels, in which she encouraged children to listen to the sounds and rhythms of their own everyday surroundings. She published under a number of pseudonyms, including Golden MacDonald, the name that appeared on *The Little Island* (1946), a **Caldecott Medal** winner illustrated by **Leonard Weisgard**. As an editor at William R. Scott, Brown published innovative books for children and contracted established authors to write for children; one result was Gertrude Stein's *The World Is Round* (1939).

BROWNE, ANTHONY (1946–). British author and **illustrator** of **picture books**, many of which feature **anthropomorphic** great apes. *Gorilla* (1983), a surreal story in which a **fantasy** gorilla becomes a surrogate father for a lonely young girl, won the **Kate Greenaway Medal**, and his books featuring Willy, the vulnerable and imaginative chimpanzee—from *Willy the Wimp* (1985) to *Willy the Dreamer* (1997)—are particularly popular. Browne received his second Kate Greenaway Medal for *Zoo* (1992), which contrasts primitive human visitors with dignified wild animals. His work is remarkable for its use of surreal imagery and pictorial quotation. This generates pictures layered with meaning, as in *Voices in the Park* (1998), the story of an afternoon visit to the park from four different perspectives. This complexity has earned him criticism from some quarters. Browne has also illustrated the work of other writers, including Annalena McAfee, **Janni Howker**, and **Michael Rosen**, and **fairy tales** such as *Hansel and Gretel* (1981); and he produced an acclaimed interpretation of **Lewis Carroll**'s *Alice's Adventures in Wonderland* (1988). Browne received the **Hans Christian Andersen Award** for his body of work in 2000.

BRUCE, MARY GRANT (1878–1958). Australian children's author and journalist whose writing was influential in forming concepts of Australian national identity, especially in relation to visions of the bush. Although she wrote many books, she is best known for her popular Billabong series of novels published between 1910 and 1942. The first, *A Little Bush Maid*, was first published in serial form in the children's pages of the *Leader*. The novels focus on the adventures of the Linton family on Billabong Station in Victoria and in England and Ireland (both countries in which Bruce herself lived for some time). Many of the themes of realistic Australian literature of the 19th and early 20th centuries can be found in these novels: the liberating quality of life in the natural world, the toughness but simultaneous decency of the Australians as inheritors of a challenging land, and the ambiguous relationship between British and Australian cultures. Bruce's patriotic writing was highly influential but is now seen as representing the spirit of a **racist** and class-ridden era, and some recent reprints of the series have been edited to remove material regarded as controversial.

BRUCHAC, JOSEPH (1942–). U.S. author, storyteller, and publisher, and one of the major voices in Native American writing. Although his American Indian heritage is only one part of an ethnic background that includes Slovak and English elements, Bruchac, who holds a PhD in comparative literature, draws in his work mainly on his Abenaki ancestry. He has written more than 70 books for adults and children. These include **historical fiction**, such as *The Arrow over the Door* (1998), which relates an incident concerning an Abenaki and a Quaker boy during the American Revolution, and *Pocahontas* (2003), in which Pocahontas and John Smith narrate alternating chapters, offering the readers a picture of what was happening on both sides. Collections of original **poems** based on traditional songs and prayers, as in *The Circle of Thanks: Native American Poems and Songs of Thanksgiving* (1996), show appreciation for many aspects of nature, and Bruchac has issued collections of stories from various tribes, such as *Flying with the Eagle, Racing the Great Bear: Stories from Native North America* (1993). He combines a conversational style with his vast knowledge of Native American tribes and their traditions to create books that have been both well received and highly praised.

BRUNA, DICK (1927–). Dutch artist, **illustrator**, and author of more than 200 small **picture books** for very young children that are characterized by their clear shapes, heavy graphic lines, and primary colors. His most famous creation is Miffy, created in 1955, a small female rabbit whose name in the original Dutch versions, Mijntje, derives from the young child's pronunciation of the Dutch word for rabbit. *Miffy Loves New York City!* was part of a campaign to promote that city as a family destination in 2003, and Miffy was named New York City's official family-tourism ambassador. Bruna has also created other memorable recurring characters such as Poppy the pig, Snuffy the dog, and Boris the bear. His books have been translated into 40 languages and have sold an estimated 85 million copies worldwide. There is now a TV show named after Miffy and a huge range of Miffy merchandise, and there is a marked similarity between the cat figure **Hello Kitty** by the Japanese Sanrio company and the Dutch rabbit. *See also* ANIMAL FICTION.

BRUNHOFF, JEAN DE (1899–1937) AND LAURENT DE (1925–). French authors and **illustrators**, father and son, best known for their **picture books** about the elephant Babar. Initially made up as a bedtime story for her son Laurent by Cécile de Brunhoff, the story was expanded and illustrated by her husband Jean, and the first picture book, *Histoire de Babar le petit éléphant*, appeared in 1931, with the English **translation**, *The Story of Babar the Little Elephant*, following in 1933. The story tells of Babar's birth and childhood in the great forest, where a hunter kills his mother; he runs away to a city, where he is adopted by a rich old lady who clothes him and gives him a home. Babar becomes a celebrity in the civilized world but later feels drawn back to the forest, to which he returns; finally, he and his cousin Céleste are elected king and queen of the elephants. With their humorous, original, and apparently simple style, de Brunhoff's Babar books headed a revival of high-quality illustrated children's books in 1930s France. The original books were printed on extra-large pages, the lithographed drawings used plenty of color and detail, and the text was handwritten. The story has attracted much criticism: created at the height of the French colonial empire, it raises cultural and political issues as well as issues of race and power. Four Babar sequels appeared before Jean's early death in 1937, after which two unfinished serialized stories were completed by Laurent. Laurent went on to produce countless sequels, including some that teach foreign languages. The Babar stories have been translated into several languages and have inspired musical works, films, and television series. Babar is now one of the global icons of popular culture. *See also* ANIMAL FICTION; ETHNOCENTRISM.

BUNTING, EVE (1928–). Northern Irish–born author of more than 200 books for children, from preschoolers to young adults, in a wide variety of genres and covering a wide range of topics. She began writing after immigrating to the United States in 1958. She has written series aimed at reluctant readers, **nonfiction**, **science fiction**, ghost stories, and romances; but she is perhaps best known for her **picture books**, which often focus on social problems such as homelessness, poverty, and **racism**, but usually offer some sense of hope in the end. **Caldecott Medal** winner *Smoky Night* (1994), illustrated by David Diaz, portrays the 1992 Los Angeles riots through the eyes of a child. *Fly away Home* (1991), illustrated by Ronald Himler, is about how a homeless boy and his father live in an airport, pretending to be travelers.

BUNYAN, JOHN (1628–1688). English preacher, religious writer, and author of *The Pilgrim's Progress from This World to That Which Is to Come* (1678), probably the most famous published Christian allegory. It is a compelling account of the journey of Christian and his friends Faithful and Hopeful, who are beset with all sorts of conflicts, trials, and dangers (such as the Slough of Despond, the Hill of Difficulty, Vanity Fair, and the Valley of the Shadow of Death) that they must pass through before they finally reach the Celestial City. While not specifically written for children, it appealed greatly to them, and numerous retellings and **adaptations** have been made for young readers, one of the first in 1798 in Massachusetts. Bunyan wrote one work specifically for children, *A Book for Boys and Girls, or Country Rhymes for Children* (1686; arguably the first **poetry** book for young readers), in which familiar objects are used to teach spiritual lessons.

BURGESS, MELVIN (1954–). British author of acclaimed and controversial fiction that constantly challenges what is regarded as suitable material for young readers. Heroin addiction and teenage homelessness, for instance, feature in the **Carnegie Medal**–winning *Junk* (1996; published in the United States as *Smack*); *Lady: My Life as a Bitch* (2001) is the story of the metamorphosis of a sexually active teenage girl into a dog; and *Doing It* (2003) focuses on teenage sex and explores relationships, mainly from a male perspective. These books created a stir upon publication due to their uncompromising treatment of teenage sex. Narrative polyphony is a feature of many of Burgess's novels, with diverse points of view and voices generating remarkable moral complexity. *Bloodtide* (1999) is a reworking of the German *Nibelungen* saga, with love, power, blood ties, and violence played out on the streets of a future London.

BURNETT, FRANCES HODGSON (1849–1924). British-born author of fiction and drama for adults and children who immigrated to the United States at the age of 16. A prolific writer, she is remembered today for her three children's classics, *Little Lord Fauntleroy*

(1886), *A Little Princess* (1905), and *The Secret Garden* (1911), in which she succeeds in transforming themes of popular fiction and **fairy tale** into exciting and well-crafted narratives. Common to all three are child figures as outsiders who gradually move toward integration; this often involves scenes in which the identities or true natures of these child protagonists are recognized, and each comes into his or her rightful heritage.

Little Lord Fauntleroy, initially serialized in *St. Nicholas Magazine*, tells the story of Cedric Errol of New York, who, after inheriting an English title, must go to live with his bad-tempered, aristocratic grandfather, who separates him from his middle-class, widowed mother. Mother and son triumph in the end, however, with Cedric's natural gentility moving the old man to recognize the boy as his rightful heir. The book was a commercial success and set a fashion trend in the United States and Great Britain for long curly hair as worn by Cedric and for black-velvet "Fauntleroy suits" with elaborate lace collars, loosely based on children's courtly costume during the 17th century. *A Little Princess* (1905), the expanded version of a story also initially serialized in *St. Nicholas Magazine* under the title *Sara Crewe* (1887–1888), is a Cinderella story about a wealthy girl pupil at Miss Minchin's boarding school for young ladies who, after the death of her father, is forced to work as a servant there. She is sustained by her imagination until her fortune is restored. In *The Secret Garden* (1911), generally regarded as Burnett's masterpiece, rich and spoiled Mary Lennox, **orphaned** in India, is sent to England to live with relatives. There she encounters her cousin Colin, a lonely boy who is lame and bedridden. These two selfish children are gradually transformed through the almost magical agency of a secret garden discovered by Mary, which had been shut up since the death of Colin's mother 10 years earlier. Its cultivation and blossoming serves as a metaphor for the positive changes in Mary and Colin. *The Secret Garden* draws upon Burnett's interest in ideas about the healing powers of the mind, as well as on the Romantic idea of nature as teacher and healer.

These three novels have been **adapted** numerous times for stage and screen (a 1939 film version of *A Little Princess* starred Shirley Temple as Sara). There are Japanese anime versions of all three, and five different new musical versions of *A Little Princess* alone have been produced since 2002. *See also* GENDER.

BURNINGHAM, JOHN (1936–). British writer and **illustrator** of **picture books**. *Borka, the Adventures of a Goose with No Feathers* (1963), his first book, won the **Kate Greenaway Medal**; he received his second for *Mr. Gumpy's Outing* (1970), a mock-serious story about a rowing adventure, in which the pictures do not simply illustrate the words but together with them form a composite text. Burningham's most widely acclaimed picture books were produced in the 1970s and 1980s, when he dropped his painterly style and realistic texts to develop innovative picture books which convey, by visual means, the complex internal world of a child. In *Come Away from the Water, Shirley* (1977), *Time to Get Out of the Bath, Shirley* (1978), and *Where's Julius?* (1986), he uses the left-hand (verso) and right-hand (recto) pages to present distinct and separate narratives and visual styles, thus emphasizing the difference between the adults' dull reality and a child's vivid imagination.

With their creative counterpoint between text and image, Burningham's books realize the full potential of the picture book. *Granpa* (1984), perhaps his most challenging and moving book, is composed of undercoded texts and images with very open links between the two types of pictures and the verbal text. The full-color pictures, in a naive style, show a situation experienced by a granddaughter and grandfather; the facing, faint-sepia ones depict the old man's memories or the child's imaginings; and the fragmentary text consists of snippets of dialogue between the old man and the girl. Burningham has also produced **animal fantasies**, concept books, and stories about young children's everyday problems, and he has illustrated Ian Fleming's *Chitty-Chitty-Bang-Bang* (1964), **Jules Verne**'s *Around the World in Eighty Days* (1972), and **Kenneth Grahame**'s *The Wind in the Willows* (1983). Burningham is married to the illustrator **Helen Oxenbury**.

BUSCH, WILHELM (1832–1908). German painter and poet, best known for his satirical picture stories. *Max und Moritz* (1865; *Max and Maurice: A Juvenile History in Seven Tricks*, 1871), a comic-verse narrative illustrated with grotesque line drawings about two young pranksters who play tricks on the village people, has been translated into more than 100 languages. After the **Grimms**' fairy tales and **Heinrich Hoffmann**'s *Struwwelpeter*, it is the third most popular German children's book of all time. Generally recognized as a precursor of the modern comic strip, it inspired the *Katzenjammer Kids* (1897) by Rudolph Dirks.

BUTTERWORTH, NICK (1946–). English **picture-book** author, writer, and **illustrator** who has collaborated with **Mick Inkpen** on more than 30 highly acclaimed children's books. His most famous individual work comes in the form of the Percy the Park Keeper books, a series that started with *One Snowy Night* (1989). His *B. B. Blacksheep and Company: A Collection of Favourite Nursery Rhymes* (1982) looks at **nursery rhymes** from a fresh, often humorous perspective.

– C –

CALDECOTT MEDAL. Established in 1938 in honor of the **illustrator Randolph Caldecott**, the Caldecott Medal is presented annually by the Association for Library Service to Children (ALSC), a division of the **American Library Association (ALA)**, to the illustrator of the most distinguished **picture book** for children published in the United States in the preceding year. The recipient must be a U.S. citizen or resident. The Caldecott Honor is a citation given to worthy runners-up. (See appendix for list of recipients).

CALDECOTT, RANDOLPH (1846–1886). English artist and **illustrator**. Caldecott, **Walter Crane**, and **Kate Greenaway** comprised a triumvirate as the innovative and significant **picture-book** artists of the late-Victorian era. Caldecott also illustrated novels and accounts of foreign travel, and made humorous drawings depicting hunting and fashionable life, often accompanied by witty captions. Caldecott was discovered by the craftsman-printer Edmund Evans, who commissioned him to produce two picture books a year for Routledge on any subject of his choice. The first two "toy books," to use the trade term, were issued in 1878: *The House That Jack Built* and *The Diverting History of John Gilpin*. Priced at a shilling each, two picture books came out each Christmas for eight years before Caldecott's untimely death at the age of 40. Among the most famous are *Sing a Song for Sixpence* (1880), *Hey Diddle Diddle* (1882), and *A Frog He Would A-wooing Go* (1883).

Caldecott usually chose as text a **nursery rhyme** or a piece of light verse, spread very freely with sometimes only three or four words to a page, and he often alternated full-page color engravings with monochrome drawings in sepia ink. He stretched the story by interpreting the words with his pictures, allowing them to fill in what the words left out, and leaving the words to fill in what the pictures omitted. By using words and pictures to enhance each other in this new way, Caldecott heralded the beginning of the modern picture book. The time settings of his picture books are usually idealized 18th century, and he privileged rural settings, people, and animals, especially dogs and horses. Caldecott had a great ability to capture characters and movement, and his stories are infused with a lightness of spirit and sense of humor, usually especially evident in his original pictorial subplots. The **Caldecott Medal**, awarded annually since 1938 for a distinguished picture book, was named in his honor.

CAMPE, JOACHIM HEINRICH (1746–1818). German educationalist, author, and publisher, and one of the most productive and influential figures in children's literature and education during the German Enlightenment. With his free rendering of **Daniel Defoe**'s *Robinson Crusoe* specifically for a child audience, *Robinson der Jüngere* (1779–1780; *Robinson the Younger*, 1781), Campe created an internationally best-selling and long-selling children's book. His travel writing for young readers also proved widely successful. *Die Entdeckung von Amerika* (1780–1782), an account of the early voyages of discovery of the New World, was published in English in 1799 as *The Discovery of America*.

CANADIAN CRUSOES. *See* TRAILL, CATHERINE PARR.

CARLE, ERIC (1929–). U.S.-born **illustrator** and author raised and educated in Germany, especially known as the creator of *The Very*

Hungry Caterpillar (1969), which has been **translated** into more than 30 languages and has sold more than 20 million copies. Carle has illustrated more than 70 books, many of them best sellers that he has written himself. The recipient of numerous **awards**, he is concerned with the difficult passage from home to school for the young child, and his colorful **picture books** are half book, half toy. His insect trilogy *The Very Hungry Caterpillar*, *The Very Busy Spider* (1984), and *The Very Quiet Cricket* (1990) are great fun while at the same time helping the child to learn about insects, the days of the week, the hours of the day, size concepts, and so on. Using collages of tissue paper, woodcut, and linocut embellished with crayons, tempera, and oil, his books incorporate multisensory elements, such as cutout holes in the pages, that invite preschool readers to manipulate or otherwise investigate the design. In *The Very Busy Spider*, the reader can actually feel how a web is gradually woven, and *The Very Quiet Cricket* comes complete with sound effects.

CARNEGIE MEDAL. Established in 1936 in honor of the Scottish-born industrialist and philanthropist Andrew Carnegie, the Carnegie Medal is presented annually for an outstanding book published in the previous year in Great Britain. Originally restricted to British writers, it has been awarded since 1969 for any book written in English and published first, or concurrently, in Britain. Established by the **Library Association (LA)**, the medal is now awarded by the **Chartered Institute of Library and Information Professionals (CILIP)**. (See appendix for list of recipients).

CARROLL, LEWIS (1832–1898). Pseudonym of Charles Lutwidge Dodgson, English author, photographer, mathematician, and Oxford don most famous as author of *Alice's Adventures in Wonderland* (1865) and its sequel *Through the Looking-Glass, and What Alice Found There* (1871). In his youth Dodgson, the third of 11 children of an Anglican clergyman, invented games for his siblings and edited family magazines for their amusement. Throughout his lifetime, he would feel more comfortable in the company of children than that of adults. After studying mathematics in Oxford, he remained there as a lecturer for the rest of his life, fulfilling the conditions that he not marry and take holy orders. He was very interested in the theater and was a pioneer in the field of photography; his pictures—especially of young girls—are distinguished examples of 19th-century photography. Among the subjects of his pictures were the children of Henry George Liddel, dean of Dodgson's college, with whom he became very friendly, taking a special interest in Alice, the second youngest, to whom the Alice stories were originally told. The genesis of *Alice's Adventures in Wonderland* (or *Alice in Wonderland*, as it is now commonly known) is to be found in stories told to entertain Alice and her sisters on a boating trip on July 4, 1862, which Dodgson subsequently wrote down, furnished with his own illustrations, and presented to Alice Liddel as *Alice's Adventures Under Ground.*

Encouraged by enthusiastic friends, including **George MacDonald**, Dodgson thought to publish the novel; it appeared, illustrated by the political cartoonist John Tenniel, in 1865. In it the seven-year-old protagonist Alice falls down a rabbit hole into a **fantasy** world in which all the rules and norms of behavior, thought, and language are replaced by ones never yet encountered by Alice (or by the reader). She meets numerous peculiar characters taken from the world of **nursery rhymes** (for instance, the Queen of Hearts) or from popular sayings (the Cheshire Cat, the March Hare, and the Mad Hatter) who, although nominally adult, behave like egotistical children. Alice is a curious, open, and spontaneous girl who, despite her frequent and unsettling change of size, rarely forgets her Victorian manners. The novel contains numerous poems and parodies (especially of moral and didactic children's poems) and is full of inventive play with language and logic. Due to the mad unpredictability of its characters, the novel's humor is laced with danger. The narrative takes place within a dream frame: Alice falls asleep, then falls down the rabbit hole; in the end she wakes up after vehemently defending herself against the fantastic figures.

Alice in Wonderland marked the liberation of children's literature from the hands of the moralists and didacts. With its fantastic plot, extravagant characters, parodies of poems and songs, and use of **nonsense**, it revolutionized children's literature and reinstated fantasy to a central position after a long period of rejection by opponents of **fairy tales**. Translated into more than 100 languages, it made literary nonsense a worldwide phenomenon. Close to 150 different artists have **illustrated** *Alice in Wonderland*, including **Arthur Rackham**,

Willy Pogany, Salvador Dalí, **Tove Jansson**, **Anthony Browne**, and **Helen Oxenbury**. The first of many stage versions, a musical, was produced in 1868, and numerous film versions have been made, including the animated feature by **Walt Disney** in 1951 that combines story elements from both *Alice* novels.

The sequel, *Through the Looking-Glass, and What Alice Found There*, features, as did its predecessor, many characters who have become immortal in children's literature and beyond, including the Red and White Queens, Humpty Dumpty, and the White Knight. The two basic conceits are the mirror (encompassing reversals, opposites, time running backward, etc.) and the game of chess. The nonsense is more ruthless here than in the first novel, with the topic of death even more pervasive; and it contains the poem "Jabberwocky," often taken to be the quintessential piece of nonsense verse. Its reception was not as widespread as that of *Alice in Wonderland*, and few artists, other than Tenniel, have illustrated it. But elements from it are often included in film versions, dramatizations, and retellings of the Alice story. Further publications by Lewis Carroll include *The Hunting of the Snark* (1876), a nonsense epic poem, and sentimental novels about two fairy children, *Sylvie and Bruno* (1889) and *Sylvie and Bruno Concluded* (1893). *See also* CROSSOVER BOOKS; FAIRY TALES; HELLO KITTY; LINDSAY, NORMAN; MOSER, BARRY; POETRY; TAYLOR, ANN; WATTS, ISAAC; WIESNER, DAVID; ZWERGER, LISBETH.

CAUTIONARY TALES AND VERSE. Stories or poems giving warning about the dangers of foolish or naughty behavior, which were widespread in the children's literature of many countries from the mid-18th century on. They often fall into three parts: first a prohibition is named—an act, place, or thing supposedly dangerous; then follows the story of someone who disregards the warning; finally the great misfortune that befalls the violator as a direct consequence of the forbidden deed is related. The misfortune or punishment is often widely out of proportion to the original transgression and is usually described in detail. **Heinrich Hoffmann** introduced a new note into the genre with *Struwwelpeter* (1845), which, hovering halfway between real warnings and comedy, converts potential fright into laughter. A complete parody of the genre is **Hilaire Belloc**'s *Cau-*

tionary Tales for Children (1907). The best-known contemporary writer of comical cautionary tales is **Roald Dahl** with *Charlie and the Chocolate Factory* (1964). *See also* COLLODI, CARLO; GOREY, EDWARD ST. JOHN; POETRY.

CAXTON, WILLIAM (ca. 1422–ca. 1491). English **translator** and printer. After learning printing in Cologne, Caxton opened shop in Westminster in 1476; here the first books in England were printed. He translated and printed about 100 books, including the first English collection of Aesop's fables, *Subtyl Historyes and Fables of Esop* (1484). *See also* ILLUSTRATIONS.

CELEBRITY CHILDREN'S BOOKS. Books by famous actors, singers, TV personalities, politicians, and so on. Shirley Temple wrote a series of storybooks in the 1930s, and Prince Charles a picture book, *Old Man of Lochnagar*, in 1980, but celebrity children's books were made a mass phenomenon by the pop star Madonna. *English Roses* appeared in 2003; three years later, her five children's books had sold more than a million copies. In the final months of 2006, the top five slots in the *New York Times* Best Seller List for children's books featured no fewer than three by people famous in other fields: *Is There Really a Human Race?* by the film star Jamie Lee Curtis, *Noelle's Treasure Tale* by the singer-songwriter Gloria Estefan, and the *Big Book of Manners* by the actress Whoopi Goldberg. Celebrity books are of varying quality and accompanied by much hype. Studies have shown that the identity of the author is of little interest to young readers, who care less about this than the appeal of a story.

CHAMBERS, AIDAN (1934–). British novelist, dramatist, critic, editor, and publisher. Chambers's major creative achievement is a sextet of boundary-breaking postmodern novels about adolescence. *Breaktime* (1978), *Dance on My Grave* (1982), *Now I Know* (1987), *The Toll Bridge* (1992), and *Postcards from No Man's Land* (1999) all have young male narrators who explore their new awareness of sexuality and spiritual experience in terms of relationships, language, and cultural symbols. The sixth and final book, *This Is All: The Pillow Book of Cordelia Kenn* (2005), has a young woman at the center of concern. Chambers's postmodern metafictive techniques present a challenge to readers to find their way through the numerous perspectives on offer. Chambers won the **Carnegie Medal** in 1999 for *Postcards from No Man's Land* and the **Hans Christian Andersen Award** in 2002. His interest in teaching literature is mirrored in the much-admired *Tell Me: Children, Reading and Talk* (1993), and his criticism and commentary on children's literature can be found in *Booktalk* (1985) and *Reading Talk* (2001). He was cofounder in the early 1990s of the short-lived publishing company Turton and Chambers, which specialized in English **translations** of European fiction for young people.

CHAPBOOKS. Cheap, popular literature in circulation from the 17th to the 19th centuries, usually sold by peddlers or "chapmen." Short in length, between 16 and 24 pages, and usually **illustrated** with woodcuts, they covered a wide range of subjects, from recipes to jest books and from narratives of recent remarkable events to fortune-telling. Popular chapbooks were those based on romances and popular tales such as *Jack the Giant Killer*, *The Seven Champions of Christendom*, *Guy of Warwick*, and *Doctor Faustus*; and **Aesop**'s **fables**, *Don Quijote, The Pilgrim's Progress*, and *Robinson Crusoe* all appeared in this abridged form. While chapbooks, from the outset, also appealed to young readers in Great Britain and the United States, from the end of the 18th century on they were almost exclusively for this readership. They can thus be regarded as the popular counterpart to improving and instructive material produced for children. Their successors were the **penny dreadful** in Britain and the **dime novel** in the United States. *See also* ADAPTATION; ADVENTURE STORIES; BIBLE IN CHILDREN'S LITERATURE; BUNYAN, JOHN; DEFOE, DANIEL; FAIRY TALES AND FOLKTALES; ILLUSTRATIONS; MORE, HANNAH; PERRAULT, CHARLES; PICTURE BOOKS; POETRY; SWIFT, JONATHAN.

CHARTERED INSTITUTE OF LIBRARY AND INFORMATION PROFESSIONALS (CILIP). Professional organization of librarians and information specialists in the United Kingdom. It was inaugurated on April 1, 2002, following the unification of two predecessor bodies, the **Library Association (LA)** and the Institute of Information Scientists (IIS). CILIP awards the **Kate Greenaway Medal** and the **Carnegie Medal**.

CHILD, LAUREN (1967–). English author, **illustrator**, and creator of **picture books** in an inventive and humorous style with mixed media illustrations that incorporate photography, collage, material, and traditional watercolors. Child's books provide a witty take on everyday situations. *I Will Not Ever Never Eat a Tomato* (2000), which won the **Kate Greenaway Medal**, shows how Charlie uses his ingenuity to get his fussy little sister Lola to eat her dinner. A successful TV series based on Child's Charlie and Lola books was made for **Walt Disney**/BBC. A further popular picture-book series is devoted to the exploits of schoolgirl Clarice Bean, starting with *Clarice Bean, That's Me* (1999). The same protagonist went on to feature in a series of children's novels, from *Utterly Me, Clarice Bean* (2002) on. Child has also produced picture books for preschool children, including the novelty book *My Dream Bed* (2001), which features pop-ups and flaps, and concept board books featuring Charlie and Lola. She won the 2002 Nestlé Smarties Book Prize for *That Pesky Rat*, and her artwork promoted 2002 World Book Day.

THE CHILDREN'S BOOK COUNCIL (CBC). A nonprofit trade association of U.S. publishers and packagers of books for children and young adults. The CBC's aim is to underscore the importance of reading and enjoying children's books and to enhance public perception of that importance. It is responsible for Children's Book Week, celebrated each November in schools, libraries, and bookstores across the United States. It also sponsors educational programs for children's literature professionals.

CHILDREN'S LAUREATE. The role of children's laureate in Great Britain is awarded once every two years to an eminent writer or **illustrator** of children's books to celebrate outstanding achievement in the field. The idea originated from a conversation between (the then) Poet Laureate **Ted Hughes** and children's writer **Michael Morpurgo**. The illustrator **Quentin Blake** was the first children's laureate (1999–2001), followed by the writers **Anne Fine** (2001–2003), **Michael Morpurgo** (2003–2005), **Jacqueline Wilson** (2005–2007), and **Michael Rosen** (2007–2009).

THE CHILDREN'S LITERATURE ASSOCIATION (ChLA). A professional organization founded in 1973 to encourage academic research and scholarship in children's literature. An international, though predominantly North American, group of academics, teachers, librarians, and institutions, the ChLA publishes an annual (*Children's Literature*) and a quarterly journal (*Children's Literature Association Quarterly*). At its annual conference, **awards** for a critical article, a book, an undergraduate and a graduate paper are presented, as well as the Phoenix Award in recognition of the high literary merit of a children's book originally published 20 years previously that did not receive a major award at that time.

CHILDRESS, ALICE (1920–1994). U.S. novelist, playwright, and actress who explored the social problems faced by African Americans in contemporary society. Her first and best-known work for children, *A Hero Ain't Nothin' but a Sandwich* (1973), about a 13-year-old who turns to drugs, caused great controversy and was banned from some libraries; the Supreme Court overturned the censorship. Childress later developed the story into a play and wrote the script for the television movie. In *Hero*, as in her subsequent young adult novels such as *Rainbow Jordan* (1981) and *Those Other People* (1989), Childress narrates from diverse points of view and with different voices to reveal the views of several characters.

CINDERELLA. *See* PERRAULT, CHARLES; GRIMM, JACOB AND WILHELM; PANTOMIME.

CLARE, HELEN. *See* CLARKE, PAULINE.

CLARKE, PAULINE (1921–). British writer who also writes for younger children under the pseudonym Helen Clare. Her best-known book is the **Carnegie Medal**–winning *The Twelve and the Genii* (1962), published in the United States as *The Return of the Twelves*, a **toy story** about a young boy who discovers the toy wooden soldiers of Branwell Brontë in a house near Haworth, and how these come to life.

CLEARY, BEVERLY (1916–). U.S. author of more than 30 works for all ages, which have been translated into 14 different languages.

Cleary is best known as the award-winning author of domestic fiction for middle readers. Her first book, *Henry Huggins* (1950), tells the story of a boy who wants a dog and introduces a pair of sisters, Beezus and Ramona Quimby. Beezus and Ramona later became the main characters in the exceptionally popular Ramona series, which documents the difficulties of school and family life in small-town America. The Ramona books were made into a television series. Cleary has also written romance novels about young adults. *Fifteen* (1956), about a teenage girl who falls in love for the first time, made a major impact in a number of English-speaking countries. The **Newbery Medal**–winning *Dear Mr. Henshaw* (1983) tells the story of a young outsider through his letters to his favorite author. Other popular stories for younger readers include *The Mouse and the Motorcycle* (1965) and *Runaway Ralph* (1970), both of which were made into films.

CLEAVER, BILL (1920–1981) AND VERA (1919–1993). U.S. husband-and-wife team who coauthored some 279 stories and 16 novels for adults and children, many of which are set in the rural South of the United States. Their first novel, *Ellen Grae* (1967), involving issues of divorce and moral choice, is about a child who tells so many tall tales that the ultimate truth she is trying to tell is not believed. Their most widely read novel, *Where the Lilies Bloom* (1969), is about the choices the adolescent Mary Call Luther has to make to keep the family together after her father's death. Many of the Cleavers' stories are a reassessment of classic U.S. stories for children. In *Grover* (1970), a seemingly **Twain**-like story of boyish adventures develops into a tale about a boy trying to cope with his mother's suicide and his father's grief. In *Delpha Green and Company* (1972), the perennially cheerful protagonist in the tradition of ***Rebecca of Sunnybrook Farm*** and ***Pollyanna*** learns that she must change her ways. The Cleavers are known for their lively dialogue and nonpredictable storylines, which often center on the theme of survival.

CLEMENS, SAMUEL LANGHORNE. *See* TWAIN, MARK.

COLE, BABETTE (1950–). British **illustrator** and maker of provocative and original **picture books** for children that depict serious and unusual themes in a naive drawing style and a comic manner. *The Trouble with Mum* (1983) and its sequels about a bizarre family with an alien grandmother question the normality of family relations. Cole operates close to the boundaries of taste in the popular *The Hairy Book* (1984), *The Slimy Book* (1985), and *The Smelly Book* (1987); in *Supermoo* (1993) she addresses ecological issues. *Mummy Laid an Egg!* (1993) is a comic take on sex education featuring two earnest young siblings who instruct their foolish parents in the facts of life. Cole has also written and illustrated **fairy tales** that question their conventions from a **feminist** perspective; in *Princess Smartypants* (1986), the dungarees-wearing title figure doesn't want to be married and cleverly and humorously outwits her parents and numerous suitors. Sometimes anarchic and often satirical, Cole's work frequently has, nonetheless, a discernable didactic purpose. She has authored and illustrated more than 70 children's books that have been translated into many languages.

COLFER, EOIN (1965–). Irish author whose first two realistic and humorous novels, *Benny and Omar* (1998) and *Benny and Babe* (1999), have a strong local flavor while reflecting contemporary Irish preoccupation with changing cultural and sexual identities. In 2001 he achieved international success with *Artemis Fowl*, the first volume in a series of the same name that follows the global adventures of a 12-year-old criminal mastermind. A blend of **science fiction**, action-**adventure**, and **fairy tale** characterized by a dry sense of humor, it combines magic and techno-gadgets, quirky characters, and a fast-moving plot with unexpected and outrageous turns. Colfer himself describes it as "*Die Hard* with fairies." The series, which now incorporates six titles, has been on the *New York Times* Best Seller List and has been translated into numerous languages. Colfer, who appeals especially but not exclusively to boy readers, has also written several books for younger readers, such as *The Legend of the Worst Boy in the World* (2007).

COLLODI, CARLO (1826–1890). Pseudonym of Carlo Lorenzini, Italian author, journalist, and translator best known as the author of the children's classic *Le avventure di Pinocchio* (1881–1882; *The Adventures of Pinocchio*, 1891). Collodi was the name of his mother's hometown, which he adopted after founding the satirical magazine *Il lampione*. Politically progressive, Lorenzini was deeply committed to the creation of a unified Italy, and he fought in the Second War of Independence (1859). He contributed to the revival of Italian theater by editing a new theatrical paper, and he translated a collection of French literary **fairy tales** by **Charles Perrault**, **Marie-Catherine d'Aulnoy**, and others. His *Giannettino* (1876) was a highly successful new type of educational book, which placed less emphasis on instruction than on entertaining tales.

The Adventures of Pinocchio began to appear in serialized form in the magazine *Giornale per i bambini* in July 1881; it was published as a book in 1883. The original publication explains the episodic nature of the various dramatic adventures of the lively, disobedient, curious, cheeky wooden puppet, who is carved by the carpenter Geppetto from a piece of pine (*Pinocchio* means "pine nut" in Tuscany), runs away from home, and dreams of becoming a real boy. The serial was originally to have ended with chapter 15, when Pinocchio is hung from the Great Oak by the murdering Fox and Cat, but for economic and literary reasons it was not expedient for the puppet to die. What follows alters the character of the hero, and the theme of his metamorphosis into a human after learning an important moral lesson about responsibility becomes central. What started out as a **cautionary tale** becomes a novel of childhood itself.

The Adventures of Pinocchio was an immediate success; by the time of Collodi's death in 1890, its fifth Italian edition was being prepared for publication, and it went on to become one of the great international classics of children's literature. The 1940 **Walt Disney** animated film is largely responsible for the legendary status the tale enjoys today, but compared to the novel it is a saccharine version about a cute puppet. The novel has been translated into some 90 different languages, and there are countless abridged editions, as well as **picture-book**, pop-up, and comic-strip versions; numerous Pinocchio films with animatronic puppets or live actors; and animated films and TV series. In addition, the character is featured widely as merchandise. The original novel and its figure are held in high cultural esteem in Italy.

COLUM, PADRAIC (1881–1972). Irish poet, playwright, and storyteller, and leading figure of the Irish Literary Revival. In 1914

Colum immigrated to the United States, where he started writing for children. *The King of Ireland's Son* (1916), his first and most widely known publication, is a collection of Irish **folktales** woven into one narrative and delivered in oral idiom. Among his other renowned retellings are *The Adventures of Odysseus and the Tale of Troy* (1918), ***The Arabian Nights*** (1923), and *Tales and Legends of Hawaii* (1924–1925).

COMENIUS, JOHN AMOS (JAN ÁMOS KOMENSKY) (1592–1670). Czech scientist, educator, and writer. His *Orbis Sensualium Pictus* (1658), an encyclopedic assemblage of captioned illustrations of the natural world in Latin and German, was arguably the very first **picture book** and the first **information book** for children. It remained popular in Europe for two centuries and was translated into numerous languages. An English edition appeared in 1659 under the title *The Visible World in Pictures*. *See also* ILLUSTRATION.

CONLON-MCKENNA, MARITA (1956–). Irish author of fiction for children and adults that explores historical or contemporary events, usually from the perspective of girls or women. She came to national and international prominence with her Children of the Famine trilogy. Set during the Potato Famine in Ireland from 1845 to 1849, *Under the Hawthorn Tree* (1990) recreates the period through the story of three young survivors, Eily, Michael, and Peggy, who set out after their parents' death on a long and testing journey in the hope of finding great-aunts whom they have never met. It was made into a film and translated into several languages. The children's story is continued in *Wild Flower Girl* (1991), in which Peggy, now 13, immigrates to Boston. *The Fields of Home* (1996) concludes the story of the three siblings as adults. The first treatment of the famine theme in Irish children's literature, the trilogy, especially *Under the Hawthorn Tree*, contains graphic descriptions of the famine-devastated countryside juxtaposed with the courage and resourcefulness of the children.

CONLY, ROBERT LESLEY. *See* O'BRIEN, ROBERT C.

COOLIDGE, SUSAN (1835–1905). Pseudonym of Sarah Chauncey Woolsey, American author of family stories for young people. She is best known for her successful series about the motherless Carr siblings: *What Katy Did* (1872), in which the energetic, headstrong title character has to learn to outgrow her tomboy ways; *What Katy Did at School* (1873), an early example of the girls' **school story**; *What Katy Did Next* (1886), in which Katy travels around Europe and, in the end, plans to marry; and the two final volumes, *Clover* (1888) and *In The High Valley* (1890), which were not quite as popular as the first three. The Katy books influenced subsequent writers of girls' books such as **L. M. Montgomery** and **Kate Douglas Wiggin**, and many British girls' school stories were inspired by *What Katy Did at School*. *See also* GENDER.

COONEY, BARBARA (1917–2000). U.S. **illustrator** and author of more than 100 books for children. As an illustrator she perfected the scratchboard technique, but preferred illustrating in full color. She was twice awarded the **Caldecott Medal**, first in 1959 for her **adaptation** of Chaucer's "The Nun Priest's Tale," *Chanticleer and the Fox*, and in 1980 for *Ox-Cart Man*, written by Donald Paul. Cooney carefully researched the art style of the historical period of any text on which she was working, and traveled extensively to support this research. She was especially interested in the themes of self-reliance and the search for beauty, as in her popular *Miss Rumphius* (1982) about an old woman who plants lupines throughout the New England countryside. It was based on a true story, as was its sequel, *The Island Boy* (1988), which recounts the life of John Gilley, a man who lived alone on a New England island.

COOPER, JAMES FENIMORE (1789–1851). Prolific and popular U.S. writer particularly remembered for his *Leatherstocking Tales*, five novels set on the American frontier between 1740 and 1804. These books accompany their hero, Natty Bumppo, scout, hunter, and archetype of the 18th-century frontiersman, from youth to old age. Natty, whose leather stockings give the series its name, lives free, preferring the solitary forest to the wilderness-destroying "civilization" of the settlers. The most celebrated book in the series is *The Last of the Mohicans* (1826), set during the French and Indian War in 1757. The Mohicans of the title are Natty's Indian-chief friend Chingachgook and his son Uncas, who is killed in the course of the novel. The other titles are *The Pioneers* (1823), *The Prairie* (1827), *The Pathfinder* (1840), and *The Deerslayer* (1841). Cooper's books appealed to a broad audience during the 19th century and to older children during the 20th. They have often appeared in abridged versions for children, and many of the **translations**, such as the German ones, were addressed predominantly to a younger audience. Cooper wrote more than 30 novels and has been called the American **Walter Scott**.

COOPER, SUSAN (1935–). British author of fiction for children and adults, television and film screenplays, and works for the stage who moved to the United States in 1963. Her best-known work is the five-volume **fantasy** sequence *The Dark Is Rising*, published between 1965 and 1977. Set in and around England and Wales, it makes use of **mythical** material, most notably the Arthurian cycle, but also other stories, figures, and elements from Celtic and Norse mythology, connecting them with modern England. Cooper wrote one realistic children's novel, *Dawn of Fear* (1970), set in London during World War II. Her recent novels, *The Boggart* (1993) and *The Boggart and the Monster* (1997), provide a humorous take on the device of a fantastic character appearing in everyday surroundings. The boggart of the title is a joke-playing creature inherited by a Canadian family together with a castle in Scotland; it wreaks havoc when the family returns to North America.

CORMIER, ROBERT (1925–2000). U.S. journalist and author whose controversial novels for young adults redefined the genre by defying the convention that a story should always conclude with an element of hope. *The Chocolate War* (1974), adapted into a film in 1988, shows the triumph of evil over good when the protagonist Jerry Renault is violently abused and ultimately defeated by the leader of a school mob, with the support of the shockingly corrupt Catholic-school administration. The polarities of good and evil are also tested in *I Am the Cheese* (1977), a psychological thriller about a troubled protagonist who finds out that his manipulative father has betrayed him. *After the First Death* (1979), the third major novel upon which Cormier's fame rests, presents a dark hijack scenario involving terrorists and a busload of children. Some of Cormier's novels from the

1990s replace anonymous, dark political forces with more personal ones such as guilt, shame, or revenge, as in the love story *We All Fall Down* (1991) or the thriller *In the Middle of the Night* (1995). Cormier is strong on suspense, ambiguity of plot, and characterization, although he is not regarded a great writer. While the relentless pessimism of his vision has earned him much criticism, his bleak takes on such themes as corruption, betrayal, and victimization and the respect he shows toward his readers by refusing to condescend to them are appreciated by many young adult readers.

COUNCIL ON INTERRACIAL BOOKS FOR CHILDREN (CIBC). An organization set up in 1965 as an outgrowth of the U.S. civil-rights movement of the 1960s. Its aims were to "promote a literature for children that better reflects the realities of a multi-cultural society," and to address the issues of **racism** and **sexism** in children's literature, the lack of minority-group writers, and the concerns of all groups that faced discrimination, such as the disabled and homosexual populations. Although it ceased most of its operations in 1990, its checklist "Ten Quick Ways to Analyze Children's Books for Racism and Sexism" is still in use and available through various organizations. *See also* ETHNOCENTRISM; GENDER.

CRANE, WALTER (1845–1915). English lithographer, artist, **illustrator**, and theorist on art and society, and a central figure in the arts and crafts movement. Together with **Randolph Caldecott** and **Kate Greenaway**, Crane set new standards for the **picture book** in the late 19th century. In collaboration with the craftsman-printer Edmund Evans, who aimed to produce artistic and ambitious colored printed books for the mass market, Crane designed some 50 books in the Toy Books series for Warne and Routledge, many of them **nursery rhymes**. His first books included *The House That Jack Built* (1865), *Sing a Song of Sixpence* (1866), and *1, 2, Buckle My Shoe* (1869), which were priced at sixpence; from 1874 his books were published in the larger-format Routledge Shilling Series.

Crane was influenced by Japanese prints, and their black outlines and flat, brilliant colors can be found in his books. He devoted much thought to the significance of pictures for children and to the kind of designs he believed would appeal to them. He was the first artist who regarded each picture book as a designed work in which every element was subordinate to the whole concept, comparing it to a house with a porch and a welcome hallway whence the reader would be taken on a pleasant journey from room to room. His concern that text should be integrated with illustration meant that he frequently calligraphed the text, or part of it. Crane also illustrated books by other authors, such as **Mary Louisa Molesworth**, and he illustrated a new edition of **Nathaniel Hawthorne**'s *Wonder-Book for Boys and Girls* (1892).

CREECH, SHARON (1945–). U.S.-born author of books for children and young adults who moved to England in 1979. *Absolutely Normal Chaos* (1990) is a fictitious diary by a 13-year-old girl, which traces her development during one summer. *Walk Two Moons* (1994), awarded the **Newbery Medal**, is a complex, at times humorous narrative about a girl who, on a long journey across the United States with her grandparents to the place of her mother's fatal accident, passes the time by telling them a story about her bizarre friend Phoebe. In the course of the story, her own confused state of mind and painful acceptance of her mother's death are revealed. *Ruby Holler* (2002), a novel about family and belonging in which an elderly couple adopt two children from the local **orphanage** to accompany them on an adventure, won the **Carnegie Medal** in 2002. Creech was the first author to win both the British Carnegie Medal and the American Newbery Medal. She has also written the texts for several humorous **picture books**.

CREW, GARY (1947–). Australian author of some 40 novels and texts for **picture books** that encompass **fantasy**, **historical novels**, **horror**, and **science fiction**. Many of his novels for older readers are based on historical events and explore postcolonial issues of identity. In *Strange Objects* (1990), which integrates fact and fiction and the colonial past and the present, the imagined fate of two murderous sailors set adrift after the factual wreck of the *Batavia* off the Western Australian coast in 1629 is intertwined with the story of a fictional boy who finds their remains 350 years later. *Mama's Babies* (2000), a fictionalized account of a "baby farmer" who, for profit, takes in unwanted children who later mysteriously disappear, is based on facts revealed at the trials of three women during the 1890s. Crew was the first to write picture books for older readers in Australia in which such themes are explored as the guilt experienced at the death of a sibling (*Lucy's Bay*, 1992; illustrated by Gregory Rogers). *Gulliver in the South Seas* (1994), illustrated by John Burge, is a retelling of **Jonathan Swift**'s classic, situating Lilliput in the Indonesian archipelago and reflecting Crew's rejection of Eurocentric representation. Humorous picture books by Crew include *Troy Thompson's Excellent Peotry Book* (1998), illustrated by Craig Smith, a putative documentation of a sixth-grade boy's yearlong poetry assignment. His recent *Pig on the Titanic: A True Story* (2005), illustrated by Bruce Whatley, tells the story of Maxise, the musical pig, who soothed the fears of a lifeboat full of children. Crew's work has received most of the major Australian children's-book **awards**. *See also* TAN, SHAUN.

CROMPTON, RICHMAL (1890–1969). English writer for both children and adults, most famous for her humorous William stories, which were initially published in a woman's journal but were soon appropriated by children. The first collection, *Just William* (1922), introduces the 11-year-old unruly, rebellious, and opinionated English boy who, joining up with his band of friends known as the Outlaws, escapes from the constraints of family life and his father, long-suffering mother, and older siblings Robert and Ethel. Overall, there were 38 *William* books, which sold more than 12 million copies in Great Britain alone; they were also **adapted** for film, stage, radio, and television.

CROSS, GILLIAN (1945–). English author of **historical fiction**, psychological thrillers, **horror stories**, and **school stories** for children and young adults. *The Demon Headmaster* (1982), the first in a series of six novels about a headmaster with strange powers of control and ultimate ambitions to become a world dictator, was also a successful television series. The intertextual novel *Wolf* (1990), a dark story about a teenage girl whose terrorist father is prepared to murder her, won the **Carnegie Medal**. The picaresque historical novel *The Great Elephant Chase* (1992), set in the 19th century, describes the adventures of a boy, a girl, and a circus elephant on their 1,000-mile journey across the United States. The Dark Ground (2004–2006) is a Kafkaesque trilogy about a teenager reduced to insect size in his now menacing home environment.

CROSSLEY-HOLLAND, KEVIN (1941–). English author of books for adults and children, poet, broadcaster, and translator of Anglo-Saxon texts. His dramatic prose **translation** of *Beowulf* (1982), **illustrated** by **Charles Keeping**, has been much praised; retellings of **myths** and **legends**, such as *British Folk Tales* (1987), demonstrate his ability to speak in a contemporary voice while retaining the rhythms and images of the past. His interest in the magical and the mystical is also apparent in his ghost story, *Storm* (1985), which won the **Carnegie Medal.** The internationally acclaimed Arthurian trilogy *The Seeing Stone* (2000), *At the Crossing-Places* (2002), and *King of the Middle March* (2003) fuses retold legend with a story of rural medieval life at the time of the Crusades.

CROSSOVER BOOKS. A term used to denote books that transcend the boundaries between children's and adult literature. These boundaries have always been permeable, and many works, especially older classics of children's literature such as **Carlo Collodi**'s *The Adventures of Pinocchio*, **Lewis Carroll**'s *Alice in Wonderland*, and **Hans Christian Andersen**'s **fairy tales**, simultaneously addressed or were read by a dual or multiple audience from the outset. **Rosemary Sutcliff**, whose **historical fiction** for children and young adults also appeals to adult readers, said that she wrote for "children of all ages from nine to ninety."

There are different forms of crossover books. Authors may be attracted by the apparent simplicity of children's literature to choose it as the vehicle for a story of childhood written for adults, as in the case of **Antoine de Saint-Exupéry**'s *The Little Prince*. Some books start out for adults, but their media **adaptations** are specifically for children, such as **Felix Salten**'s *Bambi*, made famous in **Walt Disney**'s acclaimed 1942 animation. A change of address can also be brought about in the **translation** process from one language to another; the novels of **Jules Verne** were, until fairly recently, translated almost exclusively for a juvenile market in English, whereas **Anne Fine**'s books for young adults, for instance *Madame Doubtfire* (1987), are issued in an adult imprint in German translation. Crosswriters are those such as **Michel Tournier** who address works to both children and adults, usually in separate works. A recent phenomenon is that of books being marketed in simultaneous editions for adults and for children, with identical texts but different jackets (and prices). The most prominent example of this recent but increasingly widespread "all-ages literature" category is the Harry Potter series by **J. K. Rowling**. *See also* DEFOE, DANIEL; DICKENS, CHARLES; ENDE, MICHAEL; FEELINGS, TOM; GAARDER, JOSTEIN; GRAHAME, KENNETH; HARTNETT, SONYA; HUGHES, SHIRLEY; MAGUIRE, GREGORY; MILNE, A. A.; PULLMAN, PHILIP; RAWLINGS, MARJORIE KINNAN; RUBINSTEIN, GILLIAN; SEWELL, ANNA; SWIFT, JONATHAN; TAN, SHAUN; TOLKIEN, J. R. R.; TWAIN, MARK.

CROSSWRITERS. *See* CROSSOVER BOOKS.

CRUIKSHANK, GEORGE (1792–1878). English artist and caricaturist who produced a vast number of **illustrations** for a variety of texts for adults and children, including **Daniel Defoe**'s *Robinson Crusoe* (1831) and **Charles Dickens**'s *Sketches by Boz* (1836) and *Oliver Twist* (1838). In 1823, he illustrated the first English **translation** of the **Grimms' fairy tales**. The Grimms were so pleased with the pictures, which appealed to both adults and children, that they wanted to use them in later German editions. In the 1850s Cruikshank illustrated and rewrote four well-known fairy tales in which he condemns alcohol. He was one of the foremost English book illustrators of his period.

CRUTCHER, CHRIS (1946–). U.S. novelist and child and family therapist. With his seven young adult novels and his collection of short stories published in the 1980s and 1990s, all coming-of-age stories with male athletes as protagonists, Crutcher produced a body of work that deals with issues of identity and belonging, often in the context of physical and psychological abuse, which boys identify with and read. Each of his books, from *Running Loose* (1983) through *Athletic Shorts: Six Short Stories* (1991) to *Ironman* (1995), was listed among the annual **American Library Association**'s

(ALA) Best Books For Young Adults. He received the ALA Margaret A. Edwards Award for his lifetime contribution in writing for teens in 2000.

CUNNINGHAM, JULIA (1916–2008). U.S. author who lived for a time in France and whose children's books are praised for their originality, idiosyncrasy, and poetic prose. Her first, most famous, and most controversial book, *Dorp Dead* (1965), is about a child with a learning disability, an **orphan** trapped in the home of his murderous adoptive father. This allegory of psychological isolation and personal freedom, combined with an exciting escape story, was one of the first novels to challenge young adult readers with existential themes. Cunningham's books cover a wide variety of genres and are not easy to classify. *The Treasure Is the Rose* (1973) is a **historical novel** with gothic touches; *Flight of the Sparrow* (1980) is a Dickensian novel set in Paris, with a street urchin as its protagonist. She has also written books that feature talking animals who enjoy the fine things in life, such as the hedonistic French title character in *The Vision of François the Fox* (1960), who becomes a reformed character after an uplifting experience in a beautiful cathedral. *See also* ANIMAL FICTION.

CURIOUS GEORGE. *See* REY, H. A. AND MARGRET.

– D –

DAHL, ROALD (1916–1990). British novelist, short-story writer, and screenwriter who ranks among the world's best-selling fiction authors, as well as being one of the most successful writers for children in the second half of the 20th century. Among the best known of his humorous, **fantastic**, and macabre novels for children are *James and the Giant Peach* (1961), *Charlie and the Chocolate Factory* (1964), *The BFG* (1982; the initials stand for "Big Friendly Giant"), *The Witches* (1983), and *Matilda* (1988). They are usually told from the perspective of an innocent child protagonist and involve cruel adults who mistreat children (such as the headmistress Trunchbull in *Matilda*). The villain or villainess is often counteracted by one positive adult figure (Miss Honey in *Matilda* or the good giant in *The BFG*). Grotesque scenarios, gruesome violence, farce, and the ultimate punishment of evildoers feature in most of his fast-paced stories. Dahl was a master of wordplay and made it a central device in the unusual and very funny language of the good giant in *The BFG.*

Dahl is a contentious figure. Hugely popular among children, his stories are seen by many adults as manipulative and opinionated, and his detractors have accused him of **racism**, misogyny, sadism, and anti-Semitism. But his many supporters point out that his forms of excess are in tune with children's carnivalism; that they confront children's worst fears head-on in the form of black humor; and that his plots often tap into familiar **fairy-tale** motifs, such as **orphaned** children, cruel guardians, or miraculous happenings. Dahl also wrote an autobiography, *Boy: Tales of Childhood* (1984), and a volume of alternative fairy tales in verse form, *Roald Dahl's Revolting Rhymes* (1982). Many of his books were **illustrated** by **Quentin Blake** (who used Dahl as a model for his figure of the Big Friendly Giant), and several have been made into popular films. In 2002, the interactive Roald Dahl Museum and Story Centre opened in Great Missenden in Buckinghamshire, the author's former home, to celebrate his work and to encourage children's creativity. *See also* CAUTIONARY TALES.

DANZIGER, PAULA (1944–2004). U.S. author of some 30 books for children and young adults. Her first novel, *The Cat Ate My Gymsuit* (1974), reveals a great understanding of the changing moods of childhood, as well as the anxieties about friends, being overweight, and being an outsider. A compassionate treatment of real-life issues tempered by a great sense of fun, it established the style for which she became known. Popular young adult books include *Can You Sue Your Parents for Malpractice?* (1979) and *There's a Bat in Bunk Five* (1980), which also features Marcy Lewis, the protagonist from her first novel. Popular characters reappear in series of sequels and prequels, such as the fourth-grade girl Amber Brown who first appeared in *Amber Brown Is Not a Crayon* (1994) and has reappeared in 15 different titles since then, including the entertainingly titled *You Can't Eat Your Chicken Pox, Amber Brown* (1995).

D'AULAIRE, EDGAR PARIN (1898–1986) AND INGRI (1904–1980). Swiss-born (Edgar) and Norwegian-born (Ingri) artists, **illustrators**, and writers of children's books who immigrated to the United States in 1929. Their early collaborations focus on the scenery and **folktales** of Norway, but they also wrote children's **biographies** of famous Americans such as *Abraham Lincoln* (1939), which won the **Caldecott Medal**, and *Buffalo Bill* (1952).

D'AULNOY, MARIE-CATHERINE (ca. 1650–1705). French writer of 25 **fairy tales** and one of the central figures in the French fashion for fairy stories in the 17th century. D'Aulnoy was known as an entertaining raconteur whose fairy tales circulated in fashionable circles and female salons. The first three volumes of her *Les contes des fées* (*Tales of Fairys*, 1699) were in print by 1697; *Contes nouveaux, ou Les fées à la mode* [New Tales, or Fairies in Fashion] followed in 1698. Her stories, which include "The Blue Bird," "The White Cat," and "The Yellow Dwarf," were intended for an adult audience and later adapted for children. Married to a baron, she was generally referred to as Comtesse d'Aulnoy.

DAY, THOMAS (1748–1789). English writer, disciple of **Jean-Jacques Rousseau**, and author of the popular *History of Sandford and Merton* (1783), a moral tale about the education of upper-class boys in which the spoiled son of a rich merchant is reformed according to the educational principles espoused in Rousseau's *Émile* (1762). Through his experience, the boy learns to value hard work and to give less weight to class when judging merit, and he gradually becomes more unselfish and resourceful.

DE AMICIS, EDMONDO (1846–1908). Italian novelist, journalist, and short-story writer, best known for his children's novel *Cuore* (1886; *Heart: A School-Boy's Journal*, 1929). This fictional diary of a boy in his first year at secondary school was written to foster children's appreciation of Italy's newfound national unity and is one of the two internationally celebrated 19th-century Italian children's books, the other being **Carlo Collodi**'s *The Adventures of Pinocchio*.

DE JONG, MEINDERT (1906–1991). Netherlands-born author who immigrated to the United States at the age of 8. Many of his 27 children's books are set in the country of his birth; he vividly depicts the Dutch countryside and people and the tension between the dikes and the North Sea storms. In *The Wheel on the School* (1954), illustrated by **Maurice Sendak** and winner of the **Newbery Medal**, Dutch children try to tempt storks to nest on the sharp roof of their village school by placing a wagon wheel on it. *Far Out the Long Canal* (1964) tells the story of a boy who, because of illness, has not yet learned to skate. In his novels set in the United States, life is not always as secure as in the Dutch novels. Set in midwestern farm country, *The Singing Hill* (1962) features a lonely child who has to adjust to changes in the family after his older siblings leave home. *The House of Sixty Fathers* (1956), the tale of a child refugee, takes place in China during World War II. De Jong's special talent lies in the portrayal of the intensity of children's attachments, observations, and opinions. He was the first American to win the **Hans Christian Andersen Award** in 1962, and his books have been translated into several languages.

DE LA MARE, WALTER (1873–1956). English poet and novelist who wrote for both adults and children. His first collection of poems, *Songs of Childhood* (1902; published under the pseudonym Walter Ramal), marked out his special interest in childhood and the imagination; it was followed by the popular collection *Peacock Pie* (1913). *The Three Mulla-Mulgars* (1910), later reissued as *The Three Royal Monkeys*, is a **fantasy** quest tale now known to have influenced **J. R. R. Tolkien**'s *The Hobbit* (1937). The title poem of *The Listeners, and Other Poems* (1912) is still de la Mare's best known. Set in a mysterious landscape and hinting at supernatural events, it begins: "'Is there anybody there?' said the Traveller, / Knocking on the moonlit door." His anthology of **poetry** for children, *Come Hither* (1923), is regarded as the most imaginative one of its period. De la Mare wrote two volumes of short stories for children, *Broomsticks, and Other Tales* (1925) and *The Lord Fish, and Other Tales* (1930). He also retold traditional **fairy stories** and stories from the **Bible**.

DEFOE, DANIEL (1660–1731). English novelist, pamphleteer, and journalist who gained lasting fame for his novel *Robinson Crusoe* (1719), whose full title reads as follows: *The Life and Strange Surprizing Adventures of Robinson Crusoe of York: Mariner: Who lived Eight and Twenty Years, all alone in an un-inhabited Island on the Coast of America, near the Mouth of the Great River of Oroonoque; Having been cast on Shore by Shipwreck, wherein all the Men perished but himself. With: An Account how he was at last as strangely deliver'd by Pyrates. Written by Himself.* One of the first novels in English, this fictional autobiography of the title character recounts the adventures preceding and during the 28 years he spends on a remote island, on which he encounters savages, captives, and mutineers and acquires a personal manservant, Friday, before being rescued. The positive reception of the book was immediate and universal. Within a few years, it had reached an audience as wide as any book ever written in English, and it spawned more **translations**, **adaptations**, and sequels than any other book in the history of Western literature. The term **robinsonade** was coined to describe the different versions and imitations. In *Émile* (1762), **Jean-Jacques Rousseau** declared *Robinson Crusoe* essential reading for adolescent boys and, although not meant for children, it became—usually in abridged form—a classic of children's literature. *See also* ADVENTURE STORIES; CAMPE, JOACHIM HEINRICH; CHAPBOOKS; CRUIKSHANK, GEORGE.

DEPAOLA, TOMIE (1934–). U.S. **illustrator** of more than 200 realistic **picture books**, religious stories, **information books**, and **folktales** and anthologies, roughly half of which he also wrote himself. Particularly popular are the ones inspired by his childhood experiences in an extended Italian-Irish family, many of which feature the popular character Strega Nona ("Grandmother **Witch**"), a kindly, magical old woman who helps those in need. These comical stories often incorporate folk and **fairy-tale** motifs.

DESAI, ANITA (1937–). Indian novelist and short-story writer, daughter of a Bengali father and a German mother. While the vast majority of her work is for adults, she has produced work for children that frequently describes efforts by youngsters to overcome hardship.

The Peacock Garden (1974) tells the story of a Muslim girl caught up in the social turmoil of partition in 1947. Desai received the Guardian Award for children's fiction for the novel *The Village by the Sea* (1982), the story of a family threatened by severe poverty due to the mother's illness and the father's alcoholism but also due to changes in the environment as a result of industrialization. The themes of survival, female experience, and the dynamics of family life are common to Desai's work for adults and for children.

DETECTIVE FICTION. Popular subgenre of fiction that usually involves child characters—alone or in a group—playing a major role in exposing criminals or solving mysteries, with or without assistance from adults. Its origin lies in popular reading matter from narratives of criminal deeds in **chapbooks**, through crime stories in **penny dreadfuls** and **dime novels**. One of the earliest stories featuring a young detective figure was *Young Sleuth, the Detective, in Chicago,* published in the weekly *Boys of New York* in 1882. From the end of the 19th century, detective stories became a popular feature in magazines for both sexes. *Emil and the Detectives* (German original 1929 by **Erich Kästner**) was the first book with a gang of children as protagonists, and this feature was popularized by **Enid Blyton** with her Famous Five and Secret Seven series. Highly popular mystery series by the Stratemeyer Syndicate were the **Hardy Boys** series, featuring the sons of a world-famous detective, from 1927 on, and the **Nancy Drew** series, featuring a female sleuth, from 1930 on. While many series incorporate elements of the **adventure story**, with secret passages, disguises, hidden treasures, and so on, those focusing more on the art of ratiocination include Donald Sobol's Encyclopedia Brown, Boy Detective series from 1963 on, and Robert Arthur's Alfred Hitchcock and the Three Investigators, from 1964 on. Detective stories that do not appear as part of a series tend to rise above formulaic structures and simplified morality. Examples include **E. L. Konigsburg**'s *From the Mixed-Up Files of Mrs. Basil E. Frankweiler* (1967), Joan Lowery Nixon's *The Other Side of the Dark* (1986), and Ruth Thomas's *Guilty* (1993). *See also* AVI; COLFER, EOIN; FITZHUGH, LOUISE; GAARDER, JOSTEIN; JOHNS, CAPTAIN W. E.; LINDGREN, ASTRID; O'BRIEN, ROBERT C.; ROWLING, J. K.; VOIGT, CYNTHIA; WELLS, ROSEMARY.

DICAMILLO, KATE (1964–). U.S. author of children's stories that often feature touching relationships between humans and **animals**. *Because of Winn-Dixie* (2000), about a lonely girl who befriends a dog named after the supermarket in which she finds him, relates the adventures that come about as a result of the dog winning his way into the hearts of original characters in their small town in Florida. The best seller was made into a film in 2005. *The Tale of Despereaux* (2003) is an animal **fantasy** with elements of the classical **fairy tale**, about a small mouse with large ears who falls in love with a princess. Written in short chapters in a deceptively simple style and with a narrator who directly addresses the readers, this tale was a **Newbery Medal** winner. *The Miraculous Journey of Edward Tulane* (2006) tells the story of the china rabbit of the title and his journey through various stations, from arrogance to redemption through love.

DICKENS, CHARLES (1812–1870). English author and most popular Victorian writer whose most famous novels were written for adults but read by readers of all ages. *A Christmas Carol* (1843), *Oliver Twist* (1837–1839), and *David Copperfield* (1849–1850) have frequently been **adapted** for children both in English and in **translation**. Works that Dickens wrote specifically for children enjoyed neither critical nor commercial success. *A Child's History of England* (1851–1853) is a strange and imbalanced account; *Holiday Romance* (1868) consists of four stories narrated by four different children (two **adventure stories**, a **fairy tale**, and a topsy-turvy story in which grown-ups have to obey the children); and, published after his death, *The Life of Our Lord* (1934) was written for his own children. Dickens was a great champion of the fairy tale and strongly condemned attempts to change them for didactic purposes. He protested fiercely when his old illustrator **George Cruikshank** bowdlerized some well-known fairy tales.

DICKINSON, PETER (1927–). British writer born in Northern Rhodesia (now Zambia). His Changes trilogy (published in reverse order of reading), *The Weathermonger* (1968), *Heartsease* (1969), and *The Devil's Children* (1970), is set in a futuristic Great Britain that has reverted to a medieval state in which the majority rejects anything technological. Dickinson's books combine an interest in ecology and politics with **science-fiction** elements and **fantasy**. In *The Gift Boat* (2004; U.S. title *Inside Grandad*), a Scottish boy tries to communicate with his grandfather, who is paralyzed and dumb after a stroke. He achieves this with magical help from selkies, seal people purportedly able to pass for humans. *Tulku* (1979), set in China during the Boxer Rebellion, won the **Carnegie Medal**, and Dickinson was awarded it once more in 1980 for *City of Gold, and Other Stories from the Old Testament*, **biblical** stories told by contemporary observers. His realistic novel *AK* (1990) is the story of a boy soldier in a guerrilla band in the Nagala bush. It won the Whitbread Children's Book **Award**.

DILLON, DIANE (1933–) AND LEO (1933–). U.S. husband-and-wife artist team who collaborate on **illustrations**, the production of book jackets, and children's books. They describe the products of their unusual way of working as emanating from "a third artist," as syntheses that neither of them could have produced alone. With *Why Mosquitoes Buzz in People's Ears: A West African Tale* (1975), written by **Verna Aardema** and illustrated in a style reminiscent of African batiks, and *Ashanti to Zulu* (1976), by Margaret Musgrove, an **alphabet book** about 26 African cultures, they produced two **Caldecott Medal**–winning books. They were the first illustrators to win the medal twice, and Leo was the first African American winner. Working in a wide range of media and with various techniques of painting, their warm and often humorous images celebrate African American and African cultures in such works as *The People Could Fly* (1985) and *Her Stories: African American Folk Tales, Fairy Tales and True Tales* (1995), both by **Virginia Hamilton**. They provided playful and imaginative pictures for **Nancy Willard**'s *Pish, Posh, Said Hieronymus Bosch* (1991) and paid homage to a famous African American performer in the only book for which they also wrote the text, *Rap a Tap Tap: Here's Bojangles—Think of That!* (2002).

DILLON, EILÍS (1920–1994). Irish writer and author of almost 40 books for children, from **picture books** to **adventures** for older readers, a number of them in the Irish language. Although some of her **historical fiction** is set in Italy, and her final novel, *The Children of Bach* (1992), follows the trials of three Hungarian Jewish children during the Holocaust, Dillon is best known for her adventure stories set on fictional islands off the western coast of Ireland. In *The Lost Island* (1952), *The Island of Horses* (1956), and *The Singing Cave* (1959), her (usually male) teenage protagonists are anxious to prove their bravery, and the difficult lives of the traditionally Irish-speaking communities who live on the very edge of the western seaboard are depicted with sympathetic detail. *The Island of Ghosts* (1990) won the Irish Bisto Book of the Year **Award**. The annual Eilís Dillon Award for the author of an outstanding first children's book was established in her honor in 1995.

DIME NOVELS. Popular series fiction mass-produced in the United States during the late 19th and early 20th centuries, printed on cheap paper in weekly installments costing 10 cents, and primarily aimed at a youthful, working-class audience. In the early phase, western and frontier series dominated; these were later joined by **detective** series. Popular series characters included Buffalo Bill, Deadwood Dick, and the first dime-novel detective, Frank Reade. In Great Britain the novels were known as **penny dreadfuls**.

DISNEY, WALT (1901–1966). U.S. animator, filmmaker, and founder of a global entertainment empire. Disney began his career as an animator. Mickey Mouse, his most famous creation, first featured in the 1928 cartoon *Steamboat Willie*. His first animated feature film was based on one of the **Grimms' fairy tales**, *Snow White and the Seven Dwarfs*, and was a spectacular hit in 1937. *The Adventures of Pinocchio* (1940), based on **Carlo Collodi**'s tale and considered by many to be his greatest work, was acclaimed for the quality of its animation; the song "When You Wish upon a Star" won an Oscar. *Fantasia* (1940) brought together classical music and animation. *Bambi* (1942) romanticized **Felix Salten**'s tale of forest life but also ensured the lasting fame of the figure and story. After World War II, Disney continued his **adaptation** of folklore and children's literature, adding live-action films to his repertoire with *Treasure Island* (1950), ***Pollyanna*** (1960), and *Mary Poppins* (1964), based on stories by **Robert Louis Stevenson**, Eleanor H. Porter, and **P. L. Travers**, respectively. *Mary Poppins* was the only one of his live-action films nominated for an Academy Award for best picture. In the 1950s, Disney branched out into the world of television and amusement parks.

After Disney's death the company declined somewhat; since the mid-1980s new management structures and the use of new technologies, such as computer animation, have succeeded in recapturing success. *The Little Mermaid* (1989), *Beauty and the Beast* (1991), *Aladdin* (1992), and *The Lion King* (1994) did spectacularly well, with *Beauty and the Beast* and *The Lion King* later turned into live Broadway musicals. Hits at the beginning of the 21st century included *Peter Pan: Return to Neverland* (2002), *Finding Nemo* (2003), and *Pirates of the Caribbean* (2003).

The name "Walt Disney" stands for a particular approach to family entertainment and, above all, for the commodification of children's literature, children's culture, and folklore. The commercialism; Disney's role in the globalization of American culture; and the ideology underlying many of Disney's products, especially when it relates to the sanitization of traditional stories such as **Hans Christian Andersen**'s "The Little Mermaid" and the need for a happy-ever-after ending, have all attracted hefty criticism. On the other hand, Disney's innovation in the area of animation, the quality of some of the songs from the soundtracks, the magic he brought to family entertainment, and the influence of his original cartoon characters Mickey Mouse, Donald Duck, and Goofy on children's **illustrators** such as **Maurice Sendak**, have been justifiably praised. *See also THE ARABIAN NIGHTS*; BARRIE, SIR J. M.; CARROLL, LEWIS; HARRIS, JOEL CHANDLER; KIPLING, RUDYARD; LEWIS, C. S.; MILNE, A. A.; NORTON, MARY.

DIXON, FRANKLIN W. Pseudonym of the authors of the **Hardy Boys** mystery series created by the Stratemeyer Syndicate from 1927 on; these authors included Edward Stratemeyer and Leslie McFarlane.

DODGE, MARY ELIZABETH MAPES (1831–1905). U.S. editor and author of *Hans Brinker; or, The Silver Skates* (1865). Set in Holland, a country never visited by Dodge, the novel tells of Hans and his sister Gretel, who want to win silver skates in a skating match so that they can use the money for their poor father, who lost his job after a fall from scaffolding. It contains the famous tale "The Hero of Haarlem," about a Dutch boy who saves the land by keeping his finger in a hole in the wall of a dike all night long. The hero is actually anonymous, but the adventure is usually (falsely) attributed to Hans Brinker. The novel was an immediate success, and more than 100 editions were issued in at least six languages before the end of the century. Hans Brinker became a Dutch icon in the United States; and, although he was hitherto unknown in the Netherlands, the Dutch Bureau for Tourism erected a statue of Hans at Spaarndam in 1950 to commemorate this fictitious hero and event, in order to satisfy American tourists. From 1873 to 1888 Dodge was the first editor of *St. Nicholas: A Magazine for Boys and Girls*, an ambitious literary magazine that published work by such authors as **Louisa May Alcott**, **Mark Twain**, **Joel Chandler Harris**, **Frances Hodgson Burnett**, and **Rudyard Kipling**; poets such as **Henry Wadsworth Longfellow**; and artists like **Howard Pyle**.

DOHERTY, BERLIE (1943–). English novelist, poet, and playwright for both children and adults who has written some 30 novels and **picture books** for children, many of which draw on her experience as a social worker. Her acclaimed account of a teenage pregnancy, written in the form of letters from the mother to her unborn child, *Dear Nobody* (1991), won the **Carnegie Medal**; and child trafficking and African AIDS **orphans** are central themes in her novel *Abela: The Girl Who Saw Lions* (2007). Doherty's own family background has also inspired some of her work. In *Granny Was a Buffer Girl* (1986), for which Doherty won her first Carnegie Medal, the past and present are intertwined to reveal the layers of a Sheffield family's history. Most of her novels have a strong sense of time and place, and she usually focuses on family life and relationships, love, and other difficult emotions honestly, while managing to avoid sentimentality.

DOLL AND TOY STORIES. Stories that feature **anthropomorphic** dolls and toys have a special place in children's **fantasy**. Early examples include the dark fantasy *Nussknacker und Mausekönig* (1816; *Nutcracker and Mouse King,* 1853), by **E. T. A. Hoffmann**, and *The Adventures of Two Dutch Dolls and a "Golliwogg"* (1895), by **Bertha and Florence Upton**. The first major classic of the genre was **Carlo Collodi**'s *The Adventures of Pinocchio* (Italian original 1881–1882), which explores the conditions of becoming human and growing up. Doll and toy stories generally enable an exploration of the boundaries between the human and the nonhuman, and, when a story depicts the relationship between a child owner and his or her toy, it can explore questions of mutual affection, loyalty, and responsibility, with the toy or doll traditionally even more vulnerable than the child protagonist.

Different conventions govern the interaction between toys and humans. In some stories toys only become alive when human beings are not present, such as in **Hans Christian Andersen**'s "The Steadfast Tin Soldier," and Anne Parrish's *Floating Island* (1930), a **robinsonade** featuring a shipwrecked doll family. In others, live toys interact with their child owners, for instance in **Margery Williams**'s *Velveteen Rabbit, or How Toys Become Real* (1922), where the love of a child enables his pet rabbit to become real; in **A. A. Milne**'s *Winnie-the-Pooh* (1926); and in *The Indian in the Cupboard* (1980), by **Lynne Reid Banks**. **Russell Hoban**'s *The Mouse and His Child* (1967) and The Mennyms series (1993–1996) by **Sylvia Waugh** address philosophical questions of existence. The theme of toys coming to life is given an extensive and action-packed treatment in the highly successful films *Toy Story* (1995) and *Toy Story 2* (1999). *See also* CHILDRESS, ALICE; COLFER, EOIN; GODDEN, MARGARET RUMER; GRUELLE, JOHNNY.

DOYLE, BRIAN (1935–). Canadian author of more than a dozen books for young people that are both widely popular and critically acclaimed, particularly for the strength and clarity of voice and the rooted sense of place. He spent his youth in the Gatineau Hills north of Ottawa, the setting of many of his books. A number of his stories take place in the late 1940s to about 1950, when Doyle was around the same age as his readers, and often his narrators. He has won several **awards** and his books have been translated into French, Italian, German, Dutch, and Spanish, bringing the tales of the Ottowa Valley to a worldwide audience. Although they contain tall-tale episodes and eccentric characters, Doyle's novels address serious themes such as death (*Up to Low*, 1982), love and abuse (*Boy O'Boy*, 2003), and changing attitudes toward one's parents (*Hey Dad!* 1978). Doyle won the 2005 NSK Neustadt Prize for Children's Literature.

DOYLE, RODDY (1958–). Irish novelist, playwright, and screenwriter whose Dublin novels *The Commitments* (1987), *The Snapper* (1990), and *The Van* (1991) were made into successful films. Doyle has written six children's novels—some that center on the theme of family, such as *Wilderness* (2007) and *Her Mother's Face* (2008), and three zany, scatological "Rover Adventures" involving a Dublin dog, his family, and their friends, which are full of playful postmodern elements: *The Giggler Treatment* (2000), *Rover Saves Christmas* (2001), and *The Meanwhile Adventures* (2004).

DU BOIS, WILLIAM PÈNE (1916–1993). U.S. author and **illustrator** who spent six years of his childhood in France. Admired for his originality and humor, Du Bois was fascinated by islands, utopias, and inventions (he illustrated books by **Jules Verne**), as can be seen in his best-known and **Newbery Medal**–winning book *The Twenty-One Balloons* (1947), a tall tale of a 19th-century mathematics professor who is stranded when his balloon crashes on the fabulous island of Krakatoa.

– E –

EASY READERS. Also known as *beginner books*. Relatively short fiction and **nonfiction** books written for beginning readers, typically five to seven years old, to read independently. Usually between 32 and 64 pages long with a word count between 200 and 2,000 words, they build a bridge between **picture books** read aloud by adults and longer books for older children. They are characterized by age-appropriate language, concepts, and topics, with **illustrations** playing an important supportive role. The earliest easy readers came from Ladybird Books in Great Britain in the 1940s; the first ones in the United States came out in the mid-1950s. **Dr. Seuss**'s *The Cat in the Hat* (1957) changed the face of beginner books, showing how entertaining reduced-vocabulary books could be. In his honor, the **American Library Association (ALA)** awards the annual Theodor

Seuss Geisel **Award** to the most distinguished beginning reader book published in the United States during the preceding year. The award is to "recognize the author(s) and illustrator(s) of a beginning reader book who demonstrate great creativity and imagination in his/her/their literary and artistic achievements to engage children in reading." Easy readers in the form of modern and classical texts simplified to appropriate levels of linguistic proficiency also have an important place in foreign-language learning. *See also* ABBOTT, JACOB; EDGEWORTH, MARIA; LOBEL, ARNOLD; NAPOLI, DONNA JO.

ECKERT, HORST. *See* JANOSCH.

EDGEWORTH, MARIA (1767–1849). Irish novelist and daughter of Richard Lovell Edgeworth, with whom she shared a keen interest in education. *The Parent's Assistant; or, Stories for Children* (1796) is a collection of moral tales in which children learn for themselves to see the error of their ways. Blending the real with the moral and using a lively style, Edgeworth intended these stories to entertain her readers. Her Early Lessons (1801), whose large print and small size appealed to children just learning to read, was a series of story books that combined simple reading matter with practical information. Edgeworth was also a successful adult novelist.

ENDE, MICHAEL (1929–1995). German author of internationally successful **fantasy** fiction. His first children's book, *Jim Knopf und Lukas der Lokomotivführer* (1960; *Jim Button and Luke the Engine Driver*, 1963), is a gentle fantasy for young readers set on a minute island with five inhabitants. His two most successful fantasy novels, the allegorical *Momo* (1973) and *Die unendliche Geschichte* (1979; *The Neverending Story*, 1983), invite older children and adults alike into worlds full of visionary symbolic power; they advocate imagination as an antidote for such ills of modern times as materialism and rationalism. *The Neverending Story* was made into a film in 1984. Ende did much for fantasy writing in Germany at a time when realism prevailed. His works have received several **awards** and have been translated into more than 40 languages.

ETHNOCENTRISM. *Ethnocentrism* (the tendency of an ethnic group or a nation to award itself greater significance than and to place itself above all other ethnic groups, cultures, and nations) and *racism* (the belief that racial differences produce inherent superiority or inferiority) have been features of European and American children's literature since the 19th century. In the era of colonialism, such writers as **R. M. Ballantyne**, **G. A. Henty**, **Rudyard Kipling**, and **Henry Rider Haggard** upheld the ideology of empire, and their white, British protagonists purportedly represented the pinnacle of civilization. Exotic settings in the mid-19th-century **adventure novels** of the German author Karl May also served to celebrate the supremacy of European culture. In the United States, a white-supremacist tradition that relegated black characters to the roles of fools or villains, and the Native American to that of a "savage," was thoughtlessly perpetuated until the rise of the civil-rights movement in the late 1950s brought about a gradual change in perception.

An awareness of all forms of bias—**gender** bias, racial bias, and class bias—in children's literature increased during the 1960s and 1970s with the founding of such organizations as the **Council on Interracial Books for Children (CIBC)**, established in 1965 to address racism, sexism, and related issues in children's literature, and the British National Committee on Racism in Children's Books, founded in 1976. During the 1970s, studies such as *Catching Them Young: Sex, Race and Class in Children's Fiction*, by Bob Dixon, drew critical attention toward children's classics such as **Helen Bannerman**'s *Little Black Sambo* (1899), **Hugh Lofting**'s *The Story of Dr. Dolittle* (1920; the book contains a subplot involving the black Prince Bumpo's desire to become white), and the books of **Enid Blyton**, and these gradually became the focus of campaigns by teachers and librarians against racial bias in children's books. One of the most controversial examples of classic American novels challenged on the basis of racial bias is **Mark Twain**'s *Adventures of Huckleberry Finn* (1884), which has been the target of censorship over use of the term "nigger."

Many contemporary authors explore the injustice of racism in their novels; these include **Beverley Naidoo**, who has also published critical works on racism in children's literature, and **Mildred D. Taylor**, who, in her Logan-family saga, presents a history of institutionalized racism in the United States. With their studies on how (if at all) the various ethnic groups in the United States were represented in children's literature, the CIBC revealed stereotypes associated with Asian Americans, Chicanos, Latinos, Mexicans, and other groups. These surveys highlighted the necessity of information about and portrayal of cultural and racial diversity, which in turn led the way to the development of multicultural literature in the United States. **Prizes** have been created in many countries for multicultural children's literature, and exploring diversity through children's and young adult books has become a key area in teaching and researching children's literature today, with numerous institutions (such as the National Council of Teachers of English) issuing multicultural book lists for schools and for recreational reading. There are also several websites devoted to this important topic. *See also* BRUCE, MARY GRANT; BRUNHOFF, JEAN DE AND LAURENT DE; DAHL, ROALD; FOX, PAULA; GUY, ROSA; HAMILTON, VIRGINIA; HARRIS, JOEL CHANDLER; SCHOOL STORIES.

– F –

FABLES. Short narratives in prose or verse that usually feature **anthropomorphic** animals and illustrate a moral lesson. Fables are a form of didactic literature that comments, often satirically, on human conduct. One of the most enduring forms of folk literature, they can be found in almost every country, and they played a large part in children's reading before books intended specifically for them were published. The author of the most important body of fables in Western literature is **Aesop**, who lived during the 6th century BC. In the Eastern tradition, Indian fables told by a Brahmin called Bidpai (or Pilpay) were influential; they were first published in Europe during the 13th century, and versions for children appeared from the mid-18th century on. **Jean de la Fontaine** composed literary fables in verse form in 17th-century France, which became as famous as Aesop's and provided a model for subsequent fabulists. In the late 19th century, Joel Chandler Harris popularized African American tales of Brer Rabbit, which can be traced back to the trickster figures in Africa. Stories from this tradition are also included in **Virginia Hamilton**'s

The People Could Fly: American Black Folktales (1985). In his *Just So Stories* (1902), **Rudyard Kipling** developed fables based on myths of origins, especially of the animal species. *See also* AYMÉ, MARCEL; HUGHES, TED; LEAF, MUNRO; LIONNI, LEO; LOBEL, ARNOLD; PINKNEY, JERRY.

FAIRY TALES AND FOLKTALES. *Folktales* are narratives from the oral-storytelling tradition, with every region throughout the world having its own distinctive tradition. *Fairy tales*, *fairy stories*, or *wonder tales*, a subdivision of folktales that usually involve magic, tell of transformations and wondrous changes in fortune of a disadvantaged protagonist, usually culminating in a happy end. Folktales and fairy tales were not originally told—or later written—specifically for children, although they are now one of the dominant forms of children's literature. Among the most popular and widespread fairy tales for children today are "Cinderella," "Little Red Riding Hood," "Beauty and the Beast," "Sleeping Beauty," "Hansel and Gretel," and "Rapunzel." Oral folktales and fairy tales, originally told by adults to an audience that was primarily made up of adults but could also include children, were traditionally a form of shared literature with a ritualistic nature. This can still be seen in formulaic expressions such as "once upon a time"; familiar plot patterns and character types; stock situations; and overt symbolism. These tales addressed the deep-seated fears, hopes, and dreams of a given community and helped to reinforce cultural and moral values.

The earliest written collections are the Indian *Panchatantra* (ca. 6th century) and the Oriental ***Arabian Nights*** (ca. 10th century). The first recorded variation of "Cinderella" can be found in a Chinese book of folktales from the mid-9th century. In Europe the genre of the literary fairy tale developed after the introduction of printing in the 15th century. The first printed collections of wonder tales from the oral tradition set down to amuse educated readers were in Italian: Giovanni Francesco Straparola's *Piacevoli notti* (1550–1553; *The Facetious Nights*) and Giambattista Basile's *Lo cunto de li cunti* (1634–1636), also known as the *Pentamerone*. However, it was in the salons of late-17th-century France that fairy tales first gained literary respectability and widespread popularity among the educated classes. **Marie-Catherine d'Aulnoy** was one of the first to coin the term *conte de fées*, or fairy tale; her three volumes of tales were already in print by 1697, the date of publication of her compatriot **Charles Perrault**'s famous collection *Histoires, ou Contes du temps passé* (1697; *Histories, or Tales of Past Times*, 1729). After publication and **translation**, these literary fairy tales for adults were published in **adapted** form, shortened and simplified, and as **chapbooks** that were then widely disseminated and read to children. Educators in the Puritan tradition rejected fairy tales for their lack of moral instruction and because they purportedly encouraged superstition.

The German Romantic movement at the beginning of the 19th century heralded a major shift in the development of the literary fairy tale, with works by authors such as **E. T. A. Hoffmann** and Ludwig Tieck. Folktales and fairy tales from the oral tradition were collected throughout Europe; this was inspired by the celebrated collection by the brothers **Grimm**, *Kinder- und Hausmärchen* [Children's and Household Tales], first published in 1812 and 1815. From 1819 on, the Grimms revised their collections to make them suitable for children. The English translation of these tales by Edgar Taylor, *German Popular Stories* (1823), brought about a change in attitude toward this genre for children in the English-speaking world, leading to the recognition that imaginative literature was an important element for children's recreation. This favorable climate enabled the immediate and widespread reception in translation of the 19th-century master of the literary fairy tale, **Hans Christian Andersen**. The development of **fantasy** for children owes much to this trend: the first major works in the genre by authors such as **George MacDonald** and **Lewis Carroll** were produced in the wake of the early-19th-century popularity of fairy tales.

Fairy tales have always been popular among **illustrators**, and the 20th century saw republications of illustrated collections of fairy tales by Charles Perrault, the Grimms, and Hans Christian Andersen by artists such as **Arthur Rackham**, Harry Clarke, and **Johnny Gruelle**; individual tales have been notably illustrated by such artists as **Trina Schart Hyman**, **Anthony Browne**, **Lisbeth Zwerger**, and **P. J. Lynch**. Some illustrators, such as **Wanda Gág** and **Paul O. Zelinsky**, have both retold and illustrated their own versions. Today the fairy tale has advanced to canonized reading matter in schools and libraries, a positive development theoretically underpinned by

Bruno Bettelheim's study *The Uses of Enchantment* (1976) and its claims about the psychologically beneficial aspects of fairy tales. It is now a staple element in all media produced to entertain children, especially in the realm of animated film in the wake of the great impact produced by the major **Walt Disney** films *Snow White and the Seven Dwarfs* (1937), *Cinderella* (1950), and others. A recent trend in fairy tales since the 1960s has been their politicization to comment on ecological, class, race, and **gender** issues. Alison Lurie, Angela Carter, **Tanith Lee, Jane Yolen, Babette Cole**, and others have written revisionist **feminist** fairy tales for adults and children. Black folktales and fairy tales have been issued by authors such as **Julius Lester** and **Virginia Hamilton**, and Asian ones by **Laurence Yep**. Parodies have been produced by many, including **Janosch**; fresh revisitings by authors like **Donna Jo Napoli**; and postmodern versions with fractured and new perspectives by **Jon Scieszka** and **Lane Smith**, by **David Wiesner**, and in films such as *Shrek* (2001). *See also* AARDEMA, VERNA; ACHEBE, CHINUA; AHLBERG, ALLAN AND JANET; ASBJØRNSEN, PETER CHRISTEN; BAUM, L. FRANK; BERRY, JAMES; BIERHORST, JOHN; BLOCK, FRANCESCA LIA; BRUCHAC, JOSEPH; COLUM, PADRAIC; D'AULAIRE, EDGAR PARIN AND INGRI; GERAS, ADÈLE; GUY, ROSA; HARRIS, JOEL CHANDLER; HAUFF, WILHELM; HUGHES, SHIRLEY; JACOBS, JOSEPH; JANOSCH; KIMMEL, ERIC A.; LAGERLÖF, SELMA; LANG, ANDREW; LEE, TANITH; SÉGUR, SOPHIE, COMTESSE DE; STORR, CATHERINE; TRIVIZAS, EUGENE; WILDE, OSCAR.

FANTASY. The origins of fantasy lie in **myths, legends**, and folklore, and these continue to provide plots, motifs, and characters for works of fantasy today. Although it may appear in many forms, from **picture books** to **poems**, the predominant fantasy genre is the novel. Fantasy may take place entirely in an alternative universe with its own history, geography, and so on, which **J. R. R. Tolkien** called a "secondary world"; in such fantasy, the secondary world is closed or self-contained. Another form sees characters transported from a realistic setting, or a primary world, into a magical secondary world via a passage between them, such as the wardrobe through which Narnia is visited in **C. S. Lewis**'s *The Lion, the Witch and the Ward-*

robe (1950), or the book in **Michael Ende**'s *The Neverending Story* (German original 1979). Fantasy can also involve the intervention of supernatural beings (Mary Poppins, Pippi Longstocking), objects (magic rings, the pencil in **Catherine Storr**'s *Marianne Dreams*, 1958), or events (such as metamorphosis) from an implied secondary world into a realistic setting in a quotidian world. Fantasy can feature **anthropomorphic** animals (**E. B. White**'s *Charlotte's Web*, 1952) or **toys** (**A. A. Milne**'s *Winnie-the-Pooh*, 1926; **Sylvia Waugh**'s Mennyms series, 1993–1996), time travel (**E. Nesbit**'s *The Story of the Amulet*, 1906; **Philippa Pearce**'s *Tom's Midnight Garden*, 1958), or imaginary locations (Neverland in **Sir J. M. Barrie**'s *Peter Pan*, 1904). It may incorporate elements from other traditions and genres to create a hybrid form such as the **school story**–fantasy in **J. K. Rowling**'s Harry Potter series (1997–2007).

Prior to the 19th century, imaginative narratives were rejected by the gatekeepers of children's literature, and it was not until after the Romantic movement that they advanced to a dominant form; indeed, a large number of the texts commonly regarded as international classics of children's literature today belong to the fantasy genre. The beginnings of modern fantasy can be found in the pioneering German literary **fairy tale** *Nussknacker und Mausekönig* (1816; *Nutcracker and Mouse King*, 1853), by **E. T. A. Hoffmann**, which depicted for the first time a realistic modern setting in which the protagonist experiences another, fantastic world. Following in the tradition of German Romanticism, **Hans Christian Andersen** created his famous and original literary fairy tales, in turn influencing the development of English fantasy in the second half of the 19th century, often called the "golden age of children's literature." **Lewis Carroll**'s *Alice's Adventures in Wonderland* (1865) was without precedent in original imaginative literature, and it served as a touchstone for later works. Blending parody, satire, and **nonsense**, it showed how limitless the possibilities of fantasy were and how liberating it could be for children. Further highlights in the English tradition have included **George MacDonald**'s *At the Back of the North Wind* (1871), **Oscar Wilde**'s *The Happy Prince, and Other Tales* (1888), E. Nesbit's *Five Children and It* (1902), Sir J. M. Barrie's *Peter Pan* (1904), A. A. Milne's *Winnie-the-Pooh* (1926), and **P. L. Travers**'s *Mary Poppins* (1934).

While the British tradition is particularly strong, other countries have, of course, produced notable works of fantasy, such as **Carlo Collodi**'s *The Adventures of Pinocchio* (Italian original 1881–1882), **Selma Lagerlöf**'s *The Wonderful Adventures of Nils* (Swedish original 1906–1907), **Antoine de Saint-Exupéry**'s *The Little Prince* (French original 1943), **Astrid Lindgren**'s *Pippi Longstocking* (Swedish original 1945), **Tove Jansson**'s *Moomin* books (Finnish/Swedish originals from 1945 on), **Alf Prøysen**'s *Mrs. Pepperpot* tales (Norwegian originals from 1956 on), **Otfried Preussler**'s *The Little Water-Sprite* (German original 1956), and Michael Ende's *The Neverending Story* (German original 1979), to name but a few. **L. Frank Baum** is seen as one of the founders of a specific American tradition of fantasy; his *Wizard of Oz* (1900) is a masterpiece that sets out in Kansas and addresses the American Dream.

High fantasy, usually epic in form and serious in tone, creates a secondary world of mythic proportion, with the story often spread over a number of volumes. It draws on mythic structures and the quest motif, and frequently involves a young hero discovering his or her own identity. Tolkien is seen as the initiator of this tradition with *The Hobbit* (1937) and The Lord of the Rings trilogy (1954–1955). The struggle between good and evil is one of the basic structures of high fantasy, which often also maps the progression from youth to maturity of the central characters. The best fantasy explores this struggle with great seriousness, as well as a mindfulness of ethical and philosophical dimensions, in series set in alternative realms. Examples are **Ursula Le Guin**'s Earthsea novels (1968–2001), *The Chronicles of Prydain* by **Lloyd Alexander** (1964–1968), **Susan Cooper**'s The Dark Is Rising (1965–1977), and **Philip Pullman**'s His Dark Materials trilogy (1995–2000). The latter combines an exciting adventure plot with a reconsideration of creation, the soul, death, and religion in a retelling and inversion of John Milton's *Paradise Lost* (1667). From his first novel, *The Weirdstone of Brisingamen* (1960), **Alan Garner** created a new type of fantasy that blended myths with contemporary settings and insights, and this new tradition is continued in the works of Susan Cooper, **Peter Dickinson**, **Penelope Lively**, and **Patricia Wrightson** (who draws on Australian Aboriginal legends). So-called sword-and-sorcery novels, a popular form of high fantasy, have enjoyed widespread popularity since the 1980s.

Far from the seriousness of epic high fantasy is the tradition of comic fantasy, which can be traced back to Lewis Carroll and sometimes involves nonsense or absurd elements. The Australian classic *The Magic Pudding* (1918), by **Norman Lindsay**, and the comic-grotesque novels of **Roald Dahl** occupy the carnivalesque end of this tradition, with **Hugh Lofting**'s Dr. Dolittle stories (from 1920 on) and E. B. White's *Stuart Little* (1945), to name but two, representing the more gentle, humorous end.

In the aftermath of the unprecedented popularity and huge commercial success of the Harry Potter novels and films, fantasy has been enjoying a strong wave of interest; Harry Potter has had a knock-on effect that has catapulted the genre to the top of the popularity stakes in reading matter and spawned endless new series. The film versions of Harry Potter (starting in 2001) and the three Lord of the Rings films (2001–2003) brought in their wake numerous successful motion-picture **adaptations** of fantasy classics such as C. S. Lewis's The Chronicles of Narnia and Susan Cooper's The Dark Is Rising series. *See also* AIKEN, JOAN; ALMOND, DAVID; AYMÉ, MARCEL; BABBITT, NATALIE; BANKS, LYNNE REID; BOSTON, LUCY M.; COLFER, EOIN; DE LA MARE, WALTER; FUNKE, CORNELIA; GRIPE, MARIA; JONES, DIANA WYNNE; KINGSLEY, CHARLES; LEE, TANITH; L'ENGLE, MADELEINE; LINKLATER, ERIK; LOWRY, LOIS; MAAR, PAUL; MAGUIRE, GREGORY; MAHY, MARGARET; MONTEIRO LOBATO, JOSÉ; NORTON, ANDRE; NORTON, MARY; NÖSTLINGER, CHRISTINE; O'BRIEN, ROBERT C.; PRATCHETT, TERRY; RUBINSTEIN, GILLIAN; SACHAR, LOUIS; SCHMIDT, ANNIE M. G.; THOMPSON, KATE; UTTLEY, ALISON.

FARJEON, ELEANOR (1881–1965). English children's writer, **poet**, playwright, and broadcaster. Farjeon, who enjoyed an unorthodox childhood in a creative household, produced some 30 books of verse for children, many of them sequences of linked poems, often with strong rhythms and onomatopoeic elements. Her best-known poem today is the hymn "Morning Has Broken," which was popularized by Cat Stevens in the 1970s. Her numerous plays for children were popular for school performances throughout the 1950s and the 1960s, and *The Little Bookroom* (1955), a selection of short stories, won the

Carnegie Medal. Farjeon received the **Hans Christian Andersen Award** in 1956. The annual Eleanor Farjeon Award, presented by The Children's Book Circle in recognition of an outstanding contribution to the world of children's books by an individual or organization, was established in her memory.

FEELINGS, TOM (1933–2003). U.S. **illustrator** of some 20 books, including 7 for children, usually with African or African American themes. *Moja Means One: A Swahili Counting Book* (1974) and *Jambo Means Hello: A Swahili Alphabet Book* (1971), both written by his then wife Muriel Feelings, were chosen as **Caldecott** Honor Books, making him the first African American to win this distinction. *Jambo* also won the prestigious **Biennial of Illustrations Bratislava (BIB) Award**. His best-known work is *The Middle Passage: White Ships/Black Cargo* (1995), a wordless **picture book** of 60 black-and-white illustrations that powerfully depict the slave trade, starting in an African village before its invasion by slave traders, through the dreadful ship passage to the United States where Africans were sold as slaves. The book, more for young adults and adults than for children, took Feelings over two decades to complete.

FEMINISM. *See* GENDER.

FÉNELON, FRANÇOIS (1651–1715). French archbishop and author of what is often regarded as the first novel for young readers, *Les aventures de Télémaque* (1699; *The Adventures of Telemachus, Son of Ulysses*, 1699). A keen pedagogue, Fénelon wrote *Télémaque* and other fictional texts to increase the impact of his lessons after he became tutor to the grandchildren of Louis XIV. Intended as a sequel to the fourth book of *The Odyssey* and written in ancient epic style, it portrays an adolescent hero in search of his father. Louis XIV recognized in it a fierce attack on the divine right of monarchy and withdrew Fénelon's title of tutor to the heir to the throne. *Télémaque* was translated and read widely throughout 18th-century Europe.

FIELDING, SARAH (1710–1768). English author of *The Governess, or Little Female Academy* (1749), regarded as the first full-length novel written expressly for girls. It follows the lives of nine girls and their governess, Mrs. Teachum, through 9 days of their time together at boarding school. The girls narrate their life histories and tell stories to each other including, unusual in publications at that time, two **fairy tales**. *See also* GENDER.

FINE, ANNE (1947–). British author for both adults and children who has written some 50 books for younger readers, middle readers, and adolescents. Her books can be classified as social realism; she is especially interested in family relationships and their impact on her child characters, as well as the influence of peers. The wide range of humor, from witty and sparkling to dark comedy, with which she balances serious issues has won her critical acclaim as well as huge popularity. Books for younger readers include *The Diary of a Killer Cat* (1994) and the gently funny and perceptive *Jamie and Angus Stories* (2002), which won the Boston Globe–Horn Book **Award**. In *Crummy Mummy and Me* (1988), for middle readers, the parent and child roles are reversed; in *Bill's New Frock* (1989), an award-winning, lighthearted look at **gender** stereotyping, Bill wakes up one morning to find that he is a girl. Family warfare is the theme of some of Fine's novels for older children; *Madame Doubtfire* (1987; U.S. title *Alias Madame Doubtfire*, 1988), which was made into the film *Mrs. Doubtfire* (1993) starring Robin Williams, is the story of a divorced father who disguises himself as a nanny to be able to have access to his children.

Through all the fun, Fine never trivializes the pain of family problems for any of her characters. *Goggle-Eyes* (1989; U.S. title *My War with Goggle-Eyes*), for which she won the **Carnegie Medal**, deals in a humorous way with the difficult relationship between the narrator Kitty and her mother's boyfriend; it was adapted for BBC television. Fine won the Carnegie Medal again for *Flour Babies* (1992), a poignant story about the growing self-awareness of a semidelinquent boy during a science project on parenting that has schoolboys care for sacks of flour as if they were babies. One of her darkest novels, *The Tulip Touch* (1996), explores a relationship in which evil Tulip, a victim turned victimizer, plays wild and sinister games with her outsider friend Natalie. Fine was the second **children's laureate** from 2001 to 2003, during which time she encouraged children to own, read, and enjoy books. During these years, she also put together the *Shame to*

Miss collections of her favorite poems, in three volumes for different age groups. In 2003, Fine was appointed OBE in recognition of her contribution to literature for children.

FITZHUGH, LOUISE (1928–1974). U.S. author and **illustrator** best known for *Harriet the Spy* (1964). This groundbreaking satirical novel has as its realistically flawed, unconventional heroine an 11-year-old spoiled, independent, outspoken aspiring writer and spy. She is ostracized after her notebook containing brutally honest observations of the people in her environment is found by her classmates. It was made into a film in 1996.

FLEISCHMAN, PAUL (1952–). U.S. author of fiction and **poetry** known for the musical texture and lyrical quality of his language and for his experimentation with form and perspective. His *Joyful Noise: Poems for Two Voices* (1988), a celebration of the insect world in verses to be read aloud by alternating voices, was only the second book of poetry ever to have won the **Newbery Medal**, and this award made him part of the only father-son pair who have both won Newbery awards. (His father is the author **Sid Fleischman**.) His young adult novel *Bull Run* (1993), a fictional recreation of a battle in the American Civil War, is also notable for its use of multiple voices; it is composed of 60 monologues delivered by 16 characters who represent North, South, male, female, black, and white.

FLEISCHMAN, SID (1920–2010). U.S. writer known for his tall tales, slapstick humor, and fast-paced plots. His first children's book, *Mr. Mysterious and Company* (1962), was written for his own children but was so successful that he turned to writing children's books almost exclusively. He received the **Newbery Medal** for *The Whipping Boy* (1986), a melodramatic story reminiscent of **Mark Twain**'s *The Prince and the Pauper* (1881), in which a spoiled prince of an imaginary kingdom in an unspecified past learns about real life from his liberated whipping boy. He is part of the only father-son pair who have both won Newbery awards. (His son is the author **Paul Fleischman**.) Artists such as **Peter Sís** and **Quentin Blake** have **illustrated** his books.

FOLKTALES. *See* FAIRY TALES AND FOLKTALES.

FOREMAN, MICHAEL (1938–). English **illustrator** and **picture-book** maker. Foreman has illustrated more than 150 books for all ages, covering a wide range of genres. These include classics such as **Sir J. M. Barrie**'s *Peter Pan and Wendy* (1988) and **Antoine de Saint Exupéry**'s *The Little Prince* (1995), contemporary fiction like **Alan Garner**'s *The Stone Book Quartet* (1976–1978), **poetry** such as *A Child's Garden of Verses* by **Robert Louis Stevenson** (1985), **information books**, and **fairy tales**. His unsentimental illustrations for Angela Carter's *Sleeping Beauty, and Other Favourite Fairy Tales* (1982) won the **Kate Greenaway Medal**, and he illustrated his own collection *World of Fairy Tales* (1990) in styles and colors appropriate for the cultures from which the stories originated. Foreman has a distinctive style that creates its effects through luminous color washes (with blue featuring largely in his illustrations), combined with line drawing, pastel, and crayon. He has created more than 20 picture books of his own, which address the themes of aggression and war as well as the environment. These include *War and Peas* (1974); *War Boy* (1989), a personal account of his childhood during World War II that won Foreman his second Kate Greenaway Medal; and *War Game* (1993), which combines black-and-white drawings, factual information, and atmospheric painting to recreate the experiences of young British and German soldiers during World War I.

FOX, MEM (1946–). Australian **picture-book** author, storyteller, and university lecturer specializing in literacy education. Fox's first book, *Possum Magic* (1983), **illustrated** by **Julie Vivas**, is a humorous story of Hush the possum and her Grandma, who search throughout Australia for a cure for Hush's invisibility. It holds the record for best-selling Australian children's book, with more than half a million copies sold worldwide and an industry of associated merchandise. Intergenerational relationships are a dominant theme in many of Fox's picture books: *Wilfrid Gordon McDonald Partridge* (1984) tells of a young boy who helps an elderly neighbor recover her lost memory through simple gifts; and the cycle of life is celebrated in *Sophie* (1989), in which the birth of her first child helps Sophie to cope with her grandfather's death. Fox was awarded the Dromkeen Medal for Services to Children's Literature in 1990.

FOX, PAULA (1923–). U.S. author of novels for adults and children. Fox's controversial and award-winning children's books are in the realist tradition and tend to focus on isolated children. She addresses such difficult subjects as disease, death, homelessness, and disability in novels like *Blowfish Live in the Sea* (1970), *One-Eyed Cat* (1984), and *Monkey Island* (1991); but as she focuses on the young protagonists' emotional landscapes and processes of learning about themselves and the world, these rise above simple "problem novels." Fox won the **Newbery Medal** for *The Slave Dancer* (1974), a historical novel about a boy press-ganged onto a slave ship in 1840. It remains controversial in some quarters because of its liberal use of derogatory terms for black people, and the author has been accused of **racism** in her portrayal of the black characters and their history. Fox received the **Hans Christian Andersen Award** in 1978.

FREEDMAN, RUSSELL (1929–). U.S. author of a wide range of **nonfiction** books. His **biography** of Abraham Lincoln embellished with period photographs, *Lincoln: A Photobiography* (1987), won the **Newbery Medal**, and was followed by several volumes composed in the same manner, such as *Eleanor Roosevelt: A Life of Discovery* (1993) and *The Life and Death of Crazy Horse* (1996). He has written full-length biographies of Louis Braille (1997) and Confucius (2002) and more than 20 books about animal behavior, including *Animal Fathers* (1976) and *How Birds Fly* (1977). The quality of his work has been influential in the revitalization of nonfiction over the past 25 years; Freedman himself prefers to be called a "factual author," because he believes people think "nonfiction is less important than fiction."

FRITZ, JEAN (1915–). U.S. author born to American missionaries in China, where she spent the first 12 years of her life. She is best known for her historical work for children. Working against the perception that history is dull, Fritz helps her readers to experience the human qualities of historical figures in engaging **biographies** for both young and older readers. Her **picture-book** biographies began with *And Then What Happened, Paul Revere?* (1973), which was followed by further factually accurate, stylistically inviting, and often humorous biographies such as *What's the Big Idea, Ben Franklin?* (1976). Engaging biographies for older readers include *The Double Life of Pocahontas* (1983) and *You Want Women to Vote, Lizzie Stanton?* (1995). Fritz has also authored two semiautobiographical accounts of her childhood in China, *Homesick: My Own Story* (1982) and *China Homecoming* (1985).

FUNKE, CORNELIA (1958–). German author of some 40 novels who had her international breakthrough when her **fantasy adventure** novel about two orphaned brothers set in Venice, *Herr der Diebe* (2000), was translated into English as *The Thief Lord* (2002). It won the **Mildred L. Batchelder Award** and was released as a major film in 2006. It, as well as subsequent novels by Funke, stormed the *New York Times* Best Seller List for children's books, earning Funke the epithet "Germany's **J. K. Rowling**." Among these books was *Tintenherz* (2003; *Inkheart*, 2003), the first in the Inkworld trilogy of fantasy novels about fiction and reading, in which the protagonist's father can release fictional characters from their books when he reads aloud. *Inkheart* was released as a major movie in 2008.

– G –

GAARDER, JOSTEIN (1952–). Norwegian philosophy teacher and writer, and author of the international best seller *Sofies verden* (1991; *Sophie's World*, 1994), which combines a **mystery** plot with a popular history of world philosophy. Sold as a children's book in Scandinavia and Germany, although possibly read there by more adults than young readers, the book was marketed in Great Britain for adults. It was translated into 50 languages, and a film version appeared in 1999. Gaarder has written subsequent **fantasy** titles for children and adults, such as in *Julemysteriet* (1994; *The Christmas Mystery*, 1996) and *Kabalmysteriet* (1990; *The Solitaire Mystery*, 1996), which often address existential questions and employ complex narrative devices, including intertextuality and metafiction.

GÁG, WANDA (1893–1946). U.S. graphic artist, **picture-book** creator, and translator most famous for *Millions of Cats* (1928), an original, humorous **fairy tale** in which an old man goes in search of a cat. Its black-and-white, double-spread **illustrations** and hand-lettered text are presented in a dynamic layout, and the text has a memorable refrain. A classic today, it achieved both critical and popular success, has never been out of print, and is regarded as one of the first true modern American picture books. Gág's training as a graphic artist and her exposure to European **folktales** during her childhood were the two most important influences on her work. Her translations of many of the **Grimm** brothers' fairy tales were published from 1936 on. Other notable picture books include *The ABC Bunny* (1933), *Snow White and the Seven Dwarfs* (1938), and *Nothing At All* (1941).

GALDONE, PAUL (1914–1986). Hungarian-born **illustrator** who immigrated to the United States in his early teens. He is especially remembered for the numerous **folktales** he illustrated, many of which he retold himself, including *The Three Wishes* (1961), *Little Red Riding Hood* (1974), and *Hansel and Gretel* (1982). His style of illustration was influenced by **Arthur Rackham** and **Walter Crane**, and his mainly humorous drawings are done in pen, ink, and wash, with free-flowing strokes. Galdone provided illustrations for the works of many major authors, including Edgar Allan Poe and **Henry Wadsworth Longfellow**.

GARFIELD, LEON (1921–1996). British author of **picture books**, **historical fiction**, and retellings of **myths** and **legends**. Garfield saw his novels for young readers as being in the tradition of the old-fashioned family novel; because of his interest in exploring life in the lower classes of British society and his flamboyant writing style he has often been compared to **Charles Dickens**. **Robert Louis Stevenson** was a further influence, as can be seen in the sea **adventure** *Jack Holborn* (1964), his first published novel, and *Devil-in-the-Fog* (1966), about a working-class boy who learns that he is actually of noble birth. In it, we find a frequent theme of Garfield's: the quest for identity, which is also central in his Dickensian tale of a pickpocket, *Smith* (1967), which won the **Children's Literature Association**'s Phoenix Award in 1987. *Garfield's Apprentices* (1976–1978), a series of 12 linked long short stories about the lives of London apprentices during the late 18th century, focuses on the characters rather than the era and again explores the processes of identity formation, as well as the ambiguous nature of good and evil. *The God Beneath the Sea* (1970), a contemporary retelling of Greek myths cowritten with Edward Blishen, won the **Carnegie Medal**; a sequel, *The Golden Shadow*, followed in 1971. Garfield was elected a Fellow of the Royal Society of Literature in 1985.

GARNER, ALAN (1934–). English novelist, playwright, and reteller of **fairy tales** for children who, since the 1990s, has also written for adults. His work, usually set in rural communities, displays a keen interest in how history, **myths**, and landscape interact. From his earliest novels *The Weirdstone of Brisingamen* (1960), *The Moon of Gomrath* (1963), and *Elidor* (1965), Garner blended the mythical with the modern world. The Carnegie Medal–winning *The Owl Service* (1967) made Garner's name. It is a complex and demanding novel with three levels of narrative: Blodeuwedd's story of violence, passion, and betrayal from the *Mabinogion*; the story of three contemporary teenagers on holiday in a Welsh valley whose tense relationship resembles a reenactment of the Celtic myth; and the story of a similar tragedy that happened a generation earlier, involving the youngsters' parents. This threefold structure of enmeshed narratives also features in *Red Shift* (1973), which similarly ends with no clear resolution. While *The Owl Service* was criticized for making few concessions to young readers, *Red Shift* was widely attacked for incomprehensibility.

Garner's native Cheshire, its landscape, its history, and its dialect are celebrated in his books, and the acclaimed *Stone Book* quartet, consisting of the four novellas *The Stone Book* (1976), *Granny Reardun* (1977), *Tom Fobble's Day* (1977), and *The Aimer Gate* (1978), pay tribute to the working-class artisan tradition of his family and to craftsmanship itself. It won the **Children's Literature Association**'s Phoenix Award in 1996. Garner has published a number of collections of retold traditional **folktales** and fairy tales, as well as a locally set nativity play, *Holly from the Bongs* (1966), in which the shepherds perform a mummers' play, a traditional English folk drama, in Cheshire dialect. Garner is one of the leading figures in

British children's **fantasy** who blend mythological material with contemporary settings, and his work has influenced numerous other writers in this tradition, such as **Susan Cooper** and **Penelope Lively**. He was appointed OBE in 2001 for services to literature.

GARNETT, EVE (1900–1991). British author and **illustrator** who is credited with writing the first acclaimed children's book about working-class life, *The Family from One End Street* (1937), which won the **Carnegie Medal**. These episodic tales of the large and cheerful Ruggles family—the father is a dustman, the mother a washerwoman—were later criticized for being condescending; but they represented a breakthrough in British children's books of the 1930s, which had hitherto featured only middle-class and upper-class families, and the adventures are described with warmth and humor. Garnett also illustrated **Robert Louis Stevenson**'s *A Child's Garden of Verses* in 1948.

GEISEL, THEODOR SEUSS. *See* SEUSS, DR.

GENDER. From the beginning, children's literature distinguished between the genders. **John Newbery**'s *A Little Pretty Pocket-Book* (ca. 1744), widely considered the first modern children's book and the first marketing tie-in, was sold with gender-specific toys: a ball for boys, a pincushion for girls. These differences soon found their way into the texts themselves, and from the mid- to late 18th century on, children's literature became a medium of socializing children in the gender roles foreseen for them as adults. Until the 1960s, a broad tendency was to characterize boys as resourceful and active, in contrast to passive, emotional, and dependent girls whose primary role would be that of wife and mother.

Following the publication of the first English novel for girls, **Sarah Fielding**'s *The Governess* (1749), books for girls and books for boys developed as separate forms, even if many children read across gender boundaries. Girls especially have always read boys' stories, and many boys read their sisters' books. Traditionally gendered genres include the **adventure story**, the war story, the sports story, the **robinsonade**, and many types of "how to" **information books** for boys; typical genres for girls include family stories in a realistic mode and female coming-of-age novels in a domestic setting, such as **Louisa May Alcott**'s *Little Women* (1868), **Susan Coolidge**'s *What Katy Did* (1872), **Frances Hodgson Burnett**'s *A Little Princess* (1905), and **L. M. Montgomery**'s *Anne of Green Gables* (1908). Also traditionally categorized as "girls'" reading were **horse and pony stories**. Gender-specific **school stories** were widespread for both readerships.

An awareness of gender bias in children's literature, together with other forms such as **racial** bias and class bias, increased during the 1960s with the founding of such organizations as the **Council on Interracial Books for Children (CIBC)**, established in 1965 to address racism, sexism, and related issues in children's literature. Since then, traditional roles have been increasingly questioned, and in particular children's literature has seen a gradual increase in intelligent, active, and resourceful female main characters, in novels by authors such as **Madeleine L'Engle**, **Virginia Hamilton**, **Margaret Mahy**, **Robin Klein**, **Norma Klein**, **Cynthia Voigt**, and **Jacqueline Wilson** (a leading popular author of contemporary girlhood). Traditional roles in **fairy tales** have been subverted by a number of authors whose revisionist versions often focus on the role of the princess. These include **Babette Cole**'s humorous **picture book** *Princess Smartypants* (1986), as well as longer narratives by **Tanith Lee**, **Jane Yolen**, and **Donna Jo Napoli**. *See also* BALLANTYNE, R. M.; BLOCK, FRANCESCA LIA; BLYTON, ENID; FINE, ANNE; FOX, PAULA; HENTY, G. A.; HUGHES, SHIRLEY; HUGHES, THOMAS; JANOSCH; KONIGSBURG, E. L.; LE GUIN, URSULA; NANCY DREW; PANTOMIME; TREASE, ROBERT; TURNER, ETHEL SIBYL MARY BURNWELL; URE, JEAN; YONGE, CHARLOTTE M.

GEORGE, JEAN CRAIGHEAD (1919–). U.S. author of more than 100 children's novels, **picture books**, and **nonfiction** titles on nature and survival. After coauthoring six books with her ornithologist husband, George took to writing individually. Her first novel, *My Side of the Mountain* (1959), is a survival story about a New York teenager, Sam, who runs away from home and lives alone in the Catskill Mountains for a year. In it George blended her extensive knowledge of science, nature, and survival into a fictional framework. It is now a classic of its genre, and it was made into a movie in 1969. Its success prompted George to write two sequels, *On the Far Side of the Mountain* (1990) and *Frightful's Mountain* (1999). Her **Newbery Medal**–winning *Julie of the Wolves* (1972) reflects her interest both in Inuit culture and in wolves, which prompted her travels to Alaska in the 1960s. This outdoor survival story is about the girl Miyax, whose American name is Julie, who is torn between Inuit and American cultures when, after the death of her parents, the traditional "child marriage" custom is forced upon her. Julie escapes from this arranged marriage, loses her way on the tundra, but manages to save her life by learning how to communicate with wolves. Miyax's story is continued in the sequels *Julie* (1994) and *Julie's Wolf Pack* (1997).

GERAS, ADÈLE (1944–). British author for adults and children who was born in Jerusalem and spent her early childhood in many different countries due to her father's employment by the Colonial Service. Geras has published 4 novels for adults and more than 90 books for children and young adults, which are noted for their versatility and emotional range. They include novels influenced by Jewish culture and history, such as *The Girls in the Velvet Frame* (1978), about five Jerusalem sisters who send their photograph to a New York newspaper on the eve of World War I in the hope of contacting their brother; and *Voyage* (1983), a moving narrative about emigration from eastern Europe to the United States in 1904. Her interest in the supernatural is evident in the collection of stories *Letters of Fire* (1984) and *A Lane to the Land of the Dead* (1994); the supernatural in a humorous guise turns up in the stories about the eccentric Fantora family, *The Fabulous Fantora Files* (1988) and *The Fabulous Fantora Photographs* (1993). She has used **fairy tales** in an innovative way in her Egerton Hall series of three novels about girls at the end of their boarding-school careers; these echo "Rapunzel" (*The Tower Room*, 1990), "Sleeping Beauty" (*Watching the Roses*, 1991), and "Red Riding Hood" (*Pictures of the Night*, 1992). *Troy* (2000), which met with much critical approval, is a monumental version of the last weeks of the Trojan War from the point of view of two young sisters.

GODDEN, MARGARET RUMER (1907–1998). British author of some 70 books for adults and children who spent her childhood and long periods of her adult life in India. Some of her novels for adults, such as *The Greengage Summer* (1958), are based on autobiographical experience and have been read and enjoyed by adolescents. A number of Godden's children's books feature miniature characters and settings: examples are **dolls** and their houses in *The Doll's House* (1947) and *Miss Happiness and Miss Flower* (1961), and a mouse in *The Mousewife* (1951). *The Diddakoi* and *The Doll's House* were made into BBC films as *Kizzy* and *Totty*. Godden was appointed OBE in 1993.

GOFF, HELEN LYNDON. *See* TRAVERS, P. L.

GOLLIWOG(G). *See* UPTON, BERTHA AND FLORENCE K.

GOODRICH, SAMUEL GRISWOLD (1793–1860). U.S. bookseller, publisher, and author of more than 100 **information books** for children. Most of these were written under the pseudonym Peter Parley, derived from the French word *parler* ("to talk"), because he wanted to write for children as he would have spoken to them. *Tales of Peter Parley about America* (1827) was the first, followed by *Tales of Peter Parley about Europe* (1828), with books on Asia and Africa following in 1830. Goodrich abhorred **fairy tales** and **nursery rhymes**, and his "Parley tales," in opposition to **fantasy**, were offered as reasonable and truthful children's books with subjects such as history, natural science, geography, biography, and occasional fiction. Their success led to many imitations and to other authors using his pseudonym. In 1833 he established *Parley's Magazine*, a twice-monthly periodical published in Boston; it had no connection with the British *Peter Parley's Magazine*, published monthly from 1839, which imitated his tone as well as his formula of stringing information on a thread of narrative. Goodrich was the first best-selling American children's author, and the first to achieve fame beyond the United States.

GOREY, EDWARD ST. JOHN (1925–2000). U.S. author, artist, and **illustrator** known for macabre drawings in small, illustrated volumes, some for children, which frequently satirize the conventions of didactic children's books. Often set in a surreal, pastiche version of late-Victorian or Edwardian England, they tell tales of children killed or maimed or carried off by giant insects, such as in his **alphabet book** *The Gashlycrumb Tinies* (1963). More than 50 of these small volumes are collected in the anthologies *Amphigorey* (1972), *Amphigorey Too* (1975), and *Amphigorey Also* (1983). His work is difficult to classify; he himself saw it as literary **nonsense**. Gorey also worked as a theater designer, and illustrated works by Samuel Beckett, T. S. Eliot, and **Edward Lear**. *See also* CAUTIONARY TALES.

GRAHAME, KENNETH (1859–1932). Scottish author and bank official whose only children's book, the **animal fantasy** *Wind in the Willows* (1908), is a major classic. It began as a series of bedtime stories told to his son Alastair; the protagonists are animals with whom Grahame and his son were familiar from their boating trips, Mole, Rat, Toad, and Badger. There are two narrative strands. A reflective strand tells the story of Mole, who is enticed by the spring to leave his safe burrow and seek adventure and an exciting life by the river, where he meets his new friend, the Water Rat. They share a love of home, one of the most important themes of the story, and their friendship celebrates the virtues of loyalty, respect, and affection. This story is a vision of perfect fellowship where bachelors—females don't feature much in the novel—fill their days with picnics and pleasant conversation. The second, opposing, narrative strand contains the action-packed, anarchic, and at times farcical adventures of Toad. Vain, egocentric, and impulsive, Toad is a very funny character who is determined to speed in stolen cars and ends up in prison; at the end of the book his friends, under the leadership of the patriarchal Badger, may have cured him of his passion.

Grahame wished to discourage readers from believing that the book had hidden meaning. He wrote to Theodore Roosevelt: "Its qualities, if any, are mostly negative—i.e. no problems, no sex, no second meaning—it is only an expression of the very simplest joys of life as lived by the simplest beings of a class that you are specifically familiar with and will understand." This quote actually betrays the fact that the book is not really about animals at all. Although they do have some animal qualities, the characters change size according to the demands of the moment: Toad can both drive a car and be picked up easily and hurled through the air by a bargewoman. The behavior of the animals, who represent different types of human behavior, conforms to the rules of etiquette of upper-middle-class Edwardian England. Contemporary fears of the lower classes and the threat they offered to a social stability based on the landowning classes retaining their privileges are reflected in the episode where Toad Hall is occupied by the masses of stoats and weasels from the Wild Wood.

All age groups have enjoyed the novel, with different elements appealing to the different readers. The unobtrusive case in the novel for a conservative social order and the nostalgic creation of a preindustrial life in nature belong to the aspects likely to appeal to adult readers, while children delight in Toad's adventures. In 1991, Jan Needle wrote a sequel from the perspective of the masses called *Wild Wood*, and William Horwood wrote four sequels in the 1990s, *The Willows in Winter*, *Toad Triumphant*, *The Willows and Beyond,* and *The Willows at Christmas*. **A. A. Milne** wrote the first dramatization in 1924, based on Toad's adventures; Alan Bennett's stage adaptation, *The Wind in the Willows* (1991), was a major critical and commercial success. There are also a number of film and television versions.

GREEN, ADAM. *See* WADDELL, MARTIN.

GREENAWAY, KATE (1846–1901). English artist, **illustrator**, and writer of verses. She is famous for her vision of flowers and gardens in perennial blossom, and charming scenes of playing children dressed in imaginary late-18th-century costumes with high-waisted garments and big bonnets—which inspired a fashion in children's dress. After having worked as a freelance illustrator, her breakthrough success occurred with the publication, in 1878, of *Under the Window*, 43 rhymes composed by the artist and furnished with illustrations. Some 100,000 copies were sold, including editions for the French and German markets. Further successful titles followed, including *The Birthday Book for Children* (1880), an edition of ***Mother Goose*** (1881), and *A Apple Pie* (1886). Greenaway's books were hugely popular in Great Britain and the United States during the 1880s, as were Greenaway items such as wallpaper, plates, scarves, and dolls. Her delicate line drawings and watercolors created an idealistic and nostalgic vision of childhood that caught the public imagination and inspired countless imitators. Her artwork has endured, with several of her books still in print, and it is widely merchandised today. In 1955 the **Library Association (LA)** of the United Kingdom established the **Kate Greenaway Medal**, awarded annually for distinguished illustration; it is considered the highest honor that can be conferred on a British illustrator. Greenaway, **Walter Crane**, and **Randolph Caldecott** constituted a triumvirate of major Victorian illustrators who greatly influenced the development of the **picture-book** genre.

GRIMM, JACOB (1785–1863) AND WILHELM (1786–1859). German philologists and collectors of **fairy tales**. Stimulated by their friends Clemens Brentano and Achim von Arnim, Romantic poets and collectors of folk songs, the Grimm brothers started collecting fairy tales in 1806. They believed that the traditional tales of the common people were the basis from which high culture emanated, and they wanted to save this rich tradition from oblivion, insisting on the importance of the tales as part of the nation's literary history. In all, the Grimms collected more than 200 folktales and fairy tales, published as *Kinder- und Hausmärchen* [Children's and Household Tales] in 1812 (volume 1) and in 1815 (volume 2). One of the most popular collections of fairy tales in the world, it inspired collectors and folklorists in many countries. Among the best-known stories are "Hansel and Gretel," "Cinderella," "Rumpelstiltskin," "Snow White," "Briar Rose," "Little Red Cap," and "The Golden Goose." Seventeen different editions of the *Märchen* were published during the Grimms' lifetimes, and some stories underwent major changes, making them more suitable for children (for whom the first edition was not exclusively intended). Edgar Taylor undertook the first English **translation** of selected tales in *German Popular Stories* (1823), and it revolutionized the traditional English attitude toward fairy tales. **Illustrated** by **George Cruikshank**, it inspired the Grimms themselves to issue an illustrated edition of the tales in German in 1825. The tales have been translated into more than 100 languages and in numerous forms are part of today's global children's culture. They have inspired filmmakers such as **Walt Disney**, and many authors have written their own versions of Grimms' fairy tales for children and adults.

GRIPE, MARIA (1923–2007). Swedish author of children's books who, along with **Astrid Lindgren**, is regarded as one of the most important Scandinavian authors for children. She studied philosophy and history of religion, and these interests are visible behind the treatment of social and psychological issues in her books. Finding one's place in the world is a major theme in her fiction, both realistic and fantastic; in fact, Gripe often transcends the conventional boundaries between these two realms. She strives to convey the innermost thoughts, fears, and joys of her child protagonists, both in her predominantly realistic novels and in those with a stronger **fantasy** dimension. The first group includes *Josefin* (1961; *Josephine*, 1973), *Hugo och Josefin* (1962; *Hugo and Josephine*, 1969), and *Hugo* (1966; *Hugo*, 1970), about a lonely and unhappy girl who is forced to live in her imagination before becoming friends with Hugo; *Glasblåsarns barn* (1964; *The Glassblower's Children*, 1973) and *Landet utanför* (1967; *The Land Beyond*, 1974) belong to the second. She has written **historical novels** for older readers that display strong traits of the gothic. Unlike many socially committed Swedish authors writing in the 1960s and the 1970s, Gripe continues to be widely read because of the literary quality of her work. She received the **Hans Christian Andersen Award** in 1974.

GRUELLE, JOHNNY (1880–1938). U.S. cartoonist, writer, **illustrator**, and toy designer most famous for the creation of the rag **dolls** Raggedy Ann and Raggedy Andy. The greater part of Gruelle's career was spent as a newspaper artist, producing cartoons on political, sports, and current-events topics, as well as comic strips. From 1908 on, he also produced features for children, including the popular "Mr. Twee Deedle," and he provided color illustrations for a 1914 edition of ***Grimms' Fairy Tales***. In 1915, he designed and patented the Raggedy Ann doll, created for his daughter Marcella, which had red yarn for hair, black shoe-button eyes, a triangular nose, and a wide smile. Gruelle wrote stories based on the figure, in which she comes to life when humans are not looking, and his publishers arranged to sell the dolls as well as the first collection of stories in 1918. The tie-in proved a great marketing success, and Gruelle authored a new book of Raggedy Ann and Raggedy Andy stories every year for 20 years. A Johnny Gruelle Raggedy Ann and Andy Museum opened in Illinois in 1999, and Raggedy Ann was inducted into the National Toy Hall of Fame in 2002.

GULLIVER'S TRAVELS. *See* SWIFT, JONATHAN.

GUY, ROSA (1928–). West Indian–born author for adults and children who immigrated to the United States in the early 1930s. Guy grew up in Harlem, where she was orphaned at an early age. She was active in the civil-rights movement and helped to found the Harlem Writers Guild in the late 1940s. Many of her novels are about children from the West Indies, often **orphaned**, growing up in Harlem. These include the trilogy *The Friends* (1973), *Ruby* (1976), and *Edith Jackson* (1978), which traces the story of the immigrant sisters Phyllisia and Ruby Cathy, and their outspoken friend Edith Jackson. Guy has worked in a number of genres. Two teen romances, *Mirror of Her Own* (1981) and *The Music of Summer* (1992), explore intraracial class differences, and she has written humorous **picture books** for younger readers such as *Billy the Great* (1992), which explores interracial friendships across ages. She has retold Caribbean **folktales** in *Mother Crocodile* (1981), and, in 1970, she issued a collection of oral histories of young African Americans, *Children of Longing*.

– H –

HAGGARD, HENRY RIDER (1856–1925). English author of some 60 **adventure novels** with exotic locations. As a young man, Haggard was appointed to a government post in South Africa, and his reputation is based on three novels set in that continent: *King Solomon's Mines* (1885), about tracing a man gone missing while searching for the treasures of the legendary diamond mines of the title; its sequel, *Alan Quatermain* (1887); and *She* (1887), a **fantasy** about the 2,000-year-old queen Ayesha. Haggard was awarded a KBE for his public services in 1912. *See also* ETHNOCENTRISM.

HAMILTON, VIRGINIA (1936–2002). African American author of fiction and **nonfiction** for children and young adults, regarded as one of the most important U.S. children's authors of the late 20th century. Hamilton has written prizewinning books in a wide variety of genres, predominantly addressing African American history and culture. The descendent of a fugitive slave, she grew up in a rich oral-storytelling community that influenced her development as a writer; the joy of telling is evident in her varied narrative voices in both fiction and nonfiction. Storytelling, along with embedded stories and other metafictional techniques, features in a number of novels, such as *A White Romance* (1987) and *Plain City* (1993). Hamilton's fiction is characterized by a depth generated by stories operating on different levels—sometimes literal, sometimes metaphorical—and by the way she challenges the distinction between **fantasy** and realism. An example is *Jaguarundi* (1995). On one level it can be read as a fantasy in the tradition of African folklore, on another as an **information book** about endangered species, and on a third as a narrative about interracial tolerance.

Family and history are strong themes in Hamilton's work. In *The House of Dies Drear* (1968), which won the Edgar Allan Poe Award, an African American family is confronted with black history after moving home; in *M. C. Higgins, the Great* (1974), which won the **Newbery Medal**, making Hamilton the first African American to win this **award**, the male teenage protagonist seeks a solution to save his family's land. Psychic powers and the power of the imagination as a means of escape play a central role in female coming-of-age stories such as *Zeely* (1967) and *Sweet Whispers, Brother Rush* (1982), in which the protagonist is endowed with the magic ability to see into her family's past. The use of psychic powers also features in the Justice **science-fiction** trilogy, *Justice and Her Brothers* (1978), *Dustland* (1980), and *The Gathering* (1981). Hamilton's nonfiction includes historical reconstruction such as *Anthony Burns: The Defeat and Triumph of a Fugitive Slave* (1988) and **biographies** of W. E. B. Du Bois (1972) and Paul Robeson (1974). Her acclaimed collections of traditional tales include *The People Could Fly: American Black Folk Tales* (1985); *In the Beginning: Creation Stories from around the World* (1988); *When Birds Could Talk and Bats Could Sing: The Adventures of Bruh Sparrow, Sis Wren, and Their Friends* (1996); and *Bruh Rabbit and the Tar Baby Girl* (2003). Hamilton received the **Hans Christian Andersen Award** in 1992 in honor of her lifetime achievement.

HANDLER, DANIEL. *See* SNICKET, LEMONY.

HANS BRINKER; OR, THE SILVER SKATES. *See* DODGE, MARY ELIZABETH MAPES.

HANS CHRISTIAN ANDERSEN AWARD. Established in 1956 in honor of the author **Hans Christian Andersen**, the Hans Christian Andersen Award is presented by the **International Board on Books for Young People (IBBY)** every 2nd year to an author and, since 1966, an **illustrator** in recognition of their entire body of work. The nominations are made by the national sections of IBBY and the recipients selected by an international jury of children's literature specialists. (See appendix for list of recipients).

THE HARDY BOYS. Popular **mystery** series created by the Stratemeyer Syndicate and produced by different authors including Edward Stratemeyer, Leslie McFarlane, and others under the pseudonym Franklin W. Dixon. It features the exciting, mystery-solving adventures of Frank and Joe Hardy, sons of a famous detective, and their friends, all of whom enjoy seemingly unlimited freedom. The original Hardy Boys mystery stories series ran from 1927 to 1975, and it was succeeded by a number of updated series, including The Hardy Boys Casefiles for older readers and The Clues Brothers aimed at younger readers. They were teamed up with **Nancy Drew** in the Nancy Drew and Hardy Boys SuperMystery series authored by "**Carolyn Keene**." The Hardy Boys have also featured in television shows and animated series.

HARRIS, JOEL CHANDLER (1845–1908). U.S. journalist and writer best known for his Uncle Remus stories, eight titles starting with *Uncle Remus: His Songs and His Sayings* (1880). These trickster tales about the crafty Brer Rabbit and his adversary Brer Wolf, based on the African American oral-storytelling tradition, are narrated by the fictional character Uncle Remus, a kind old slave who passes on the **folktales** to the children sitting at his feet. The stories are told in plantation Negro dialect that was praised for its authenticity when the stories were first published, and Harris's attitude toward black culture was enlightened for his day. However, contemporary African American writers view his work, especially the frame story of Uncle Remus, less favorably. **Walt Disney** produced an **adaptation** of Harris's stories, *The Song of the South*, in 1946.

HARRY POTTER. *See* ROWLING, J. K.

HÄRTLING, PETER (1933–). German poet, author, and essayist, equally acclaimed for his work for children and for adults. Härtling is one of the leading representatives of a generation of writers for children in Germany who championed realistic stories, often told from a child's perspective and using age-appropriate syntax and vocabulary, that address such themes as death, war, and sexuality. His own biographical experience as a child during and after World War II is evident in his work for adults and for children. Among his most popular novels for children are *Oma* (1975; *Oma*, 1977), an intergenerational story about an **orphan** who is brought up by his grandmother; and *Ben liebt Anna* (1979; *Ben Loves Anna*, 1990), the story of a friendship between the German Ben and Anna, a Polish immigrant, both age 10, which develops into love. *Krücke* (1986; *Crutches*, 1988) is set in the aftermath of World War II and recounts the wanderings of 12-year-old refugee Thomas and a one-legged former German officer in their search for food and family. Härtling is the recipient of numerous German literary **awards**.

HARTNETT, SONYA (1968–). Australian author of more than a dozen novels who made her publishing debut at the age of 15. Hartnett prefers not to specify which age group she writes for and has expressed her dissatisfaction at being pigeonholed as an author for young adults. Her thematically challenging books, which lean toward the darker elements of life, depict with great psychological depth and narrative skill the circumstances of young people, and cross the divide between young adult and adult fiction. *Sleeping Dogs* (1995), set in a trailer park, is about the dysfunctional Willow family; *Black Foxes* (1996), written in three sections with gaps in time between them, traces the life of Lord Tyrone Sully during the late 19th century. *Of a Boy* (2000; published in Great Britain as *What Birds See*, 2003) follows nine-year-old Adrian's effort to understand the disappearance of three local children. *Thursday's Child* (2002) is about a family's struggle to survive during the Great Depression. Hartnett received the **Astrid Lindgren Memorial Award** in 2008 as "one of the major forces for renewal in modern young adult fiction."

HAUFF, WILHELM (1802–1827). German poet and novelist who published three collections of **fairy tales**, a number of which were **translated** into English from the 1840s onward; many are still popular in Germany today. Combining realism with satire and **fantasy**, most of Hauff's tales are placed within a narrative frame and are set either in the Orient, like "Der kleine Muck" ("Little Mook") and "Kalif Storch" ("Caliph Stork"), or in Germany, like "Der Zwerg Nase" ("Dwarf Long-Nose") and "Das kalte Herz" ("The Cold Heart"). All were published in his *Märchenalmanache* [Fairytale Almanacs] of 1826, 1827, and 1828. *Dwarf Long-Nose* was **illustrated** in 1960 by **Maurice Sendak**.

HAUGEN, TORMOD (1945–2008). Norwegian author acclaimed for his creative use of narrative techniques and his blending of genres to chart the darker side of childhood. Loneliness, oppression, and even despair feature in novels such as *Nattfuglene* (1975; *The Night Birds*, 1982), about imaginary and real fears; *Zeppelin* (1976; *Keeping Secrets*, 1994), an atmospheric story with a mysterious fantasy element, narrated in poetic form; and the dystopian *Øglene kommer* [The Lizards are Coming] (1991). Haugen, who won the **Hans Christian Andersen Award** in 1990, has also **translated** literature from many languages into Norwegian, including **C. S. Lewis**'s *Chronicles of Narnia*.

HAWTHORNE, NATHANIEL (1804–1864). U.S. novelist and short-story writer, and the first major American writer to write specifically for children. He edited *The American Magazine of Useful and Entertaining Knowledge* in 1837, compiled *Peter Parley's Universal History* (1838) for **Samuel Goodrich**, and published *Grandfather's Chair*, *Famous Old People*, and *Liberty Tree* (all 1841), historical and biographical accounts for children, before his highly successful (adult) novel *The Scarlet Letter* (1850). *A Wonder-Book for Girls and Boys* (1852), which included the popular story "The Golden Touch" based on the tale of King Midas, was one of the first retellings of

Greek **myths** for children. A second volume, *Tanglewood Tales*, followed in 1853.

HAZARD, PAUL (1878–1944). French comparative-literature scholar, whose *Les livres, les enfants et les hommes* (1932; *Books, Children and Men*, 1944) was a highly influential early study of children's literature from a literary viewpoint. Setting out from an image of childhood that owes much to the Romantic tradition, Hazard emphasizes the imagination as the child's strongest urge, as well as the distance between childhood and adult realms. The broad international reception of Hazard's book after World War II focused especially on the idea of the humanizing function of books in a universal republic of childhood.

HEARN, LIAN. *See* RUBINSTEIN, GILLIAN.

HEIDI. *See* SPYRI, JOHANNA.

HEINLEIN, ROBERT A. (1907–1988). U.S. writer of **science-fiction** stories and novels seen by many as one of the most influential authors of that genre. Having studied mathematics and physics and with a background in engineering, Heinlein based his science fiction on real scientific discoveries and well-founded speculation about future technology. His 13 novels for young readers, such as *Rocket Ship Galileo* (1947) and *Farmer in the Sky* (1950), are in the tradition of the *bildungsroman*; the (usually teenage boy) protagonist is educated, for instance, through encounters with aliens in space to understand the universe more completely, as well as his role, and future role, in it. Self-reliance, discipline, and respect for others, are key elements in these narratives.

HELLO KITTY. A white cat character with a red bow and no visible mouth; one of the most successful marketing brands in the world. Created in 1974 by the designer *Ikuko Shimizu* for the Japanese Sanrio company and apparently inspired by the (black) kitten in **Lewis Carroll**'s *Through the Looking-Glass, and What Alice Found There* (1871), Hello Kitty is devoid of any specific identifying characteristics other than cuteness, ensuring that she is a character upon which anything can be projected and whose expressionless face can be read in any way international buyers want. The first Hello Kitty product came out in 1974 in Japan and 1976 in the United States, and since then the figure has developed into a multi-billion-dollar global commodity that appeals not only to children around the world, but also to adults (mainly women in their twenties and thirties). In 2004 the distinct face of Hello Kitty appeared on some 50,000 different products, which were sold in about 60 countries and generated close to $1 billion in revenue. Products included dolls, key chains, stationery, school supplies, clothes, credit cards, laptops, mobile phones, toasters, and even cars. Hello Kitty **picture books** for children in a variety of languages include board books, cutout books, **ABC books**, and books about countries (such as *Hello Kitty Hello World!* and *Hello Kitty Hello USA*). The Japanese anime series *Hello Kitty and Friends* aired on TV Tokyo in Japan and CBS in the United States in 1991. Hello Kitty has also featured as the protagonist in animated film versions of children's classics such as ***Alice in Wonderland***, ***Heidi***, and *Snow White*. *See also* BRUNA, DICK.

HENTY, G. A. (GEORGE ALFRED) (1832–1902). British journalist, writer, and editor of the *Union Jack* and the *Boy's Own Magazine*, and a dominant figure in boys' fiction during the last two decades of the 19th century. Author of more than 90 books for boys, which sold an estimated 30 million copies across the English-speaking world, Henty is best remembered for his series of **historical adventure stories**, starting with *Out on the Pampas; or, The Young Settlers* (1871). Many of his novels follow a formula. The hero is a boy of 15 or 16, well endowed with "manly skills," physically fit, brave, and with a good heart, whose bravery is tested when he becomes embroiled in a great historical event such the Punic War or the American Civil War. These heroes frequently acquire faithful followers, usually of the private-soldier class, and the plot often ends with maturity brought on by the responsibilities of leadership, with social and financial gains providing the appropriate reward.

Henty was a distinguished war journalist, and he succeeded in transferring the experience of being present at historic and critical moments to his fiction. He knew how to teach accurate history while mingling it with personal adventures, placing his young protagonists in the thick of the action, and his contemporaries praised him for understanding boys' tastes better than any other living author. His moral purpose was to teach his readers to be brave and honorable, and his work is characterized by his belief in the British Empire and its values. *See also* ETHNOCENTRISM.

HERALD, KATHLEEN. *See* PEYTON, K. M.

HESSE, KAREN (1952–). U.S. writer and **poet** whose work covers a wide range of genres, from **picture books** like *Come On, Rain* (1999), which celebrates the natural phenomenon of a summer storm, to well-researched **historical fiction** like *Letters From Rifka* (1992), about a young Jewish woman who escapes persecution in the Ukraine by migrating to the United States. *Stowaway* (2000) is based on the true story of a boy who stowed away on Captain James Cook's ship *Endeavour* in 1768, and *Witness* (2001) is the story of the Klu Klux Klan's attempt to recruit members in a small town in Vermont in 1924, told in the voices of 11 different residents. *Out of the Dust* (1997), a **Newbery Medal** winner, is the story of a family's struggle in the Dust Bowl during the Depression, told from the perspective of a 14-year-old girl. This striking novel is organized as a diary and written in free verse, with the form and tone of the **poems** reflecting the subject matter. In *Aleutian Sparrow* (2003) Hesse uses free-verse poems to narrate a story of Japanese occupation during World War II.

HINTON, S. E. (SUSAN ELOISE) (1948–). U.S. author whose first novel, *The Outsiders* (1967), published when she was only 17, was a resounding success among readers and critics and is regarded as one of the first genuine young adult novels. A first-person narration, this coming-of-age novel explores the troubling circumstances of a male teenager caught up in the groundless violence between two rival gangs, the lower-class Greasers and the upper-class Socs. Three further young adult novels followed, all of them fast paced and realistic, with sympathetic portrayals of tough but vulnerable young males: *That Was Then, This Is Now* (1971), *Rumble Fish* (1975), and *Tex* (1979). All four novels have been made into films; Francis Ford Coppola directed both *The Outsiders* (1983) and *Rumble Fish* (1983).

Hinton has also authored two books for young children, *Big David, Little David* (1995) and *The Puppy Sister* (1995).

HISTORICAL FICTION. Historical fiction generally refers to realistic narratives set in a time that predates that of their writing, usually but not necessarily by at least 50 years. In them, authors generally try to present events and people from the past in a story that makes them interesting and intelligible for contemporary readers; this also ensures historical fiction's popularity and usefulness as a teaching resource. The level of engagement with the past can range from authors using a historical setting merely as an exotic backdrop, to their painstakingly recreating the atmosphere, events, and culture of a bygone time. Historical fiction invariably selects and embellishes facts and presents invented as well as historical figures. While works that include elements of **fantasy** rarely qualify as historical fiction, there are some notable exceptions, such as **Joan Aiken**'s "alternative history" series of novels set in a plausible 19th-century England ruled by King James III, who never actually existed.

Sir Walter Scott, the father of the historical novel, was widely read by young readers although he did not write specifically for them. *Waverley* (1814), *Rob Roy* (1817), and *Ivanhoe* (1819) were especially popular and influenced many later authors for children. One of the first historical novels specifically for young readers was **Captain Frederick Marryat**'s *The Children of the New Forest* (1847), set in the English Civil War. With some exceptions, such as **Charlotte Yonge**'s *The Little Duke* (1854) and **Robert Louis Stevenson**'s *Kidnapped* (1886), most British historical fiction of the 19th century consisted of **adventures** incorporating heroism, chivalry, and military glory, such as the tales by **R. M. Ballantyne** and **G. A. Henty**. In the United States, **Howard Pyle** wrote and **illustrated** remarkable versions of **legends** such as *The Merry Adventures of Robin Hood* (1883) and a four-volume cycle of Arthurian stories, as well as the medieval historical novels *Otto of the Silver Hand* (1888) and *Men of Iron* (1892). The American Civil War, one of the most popular settings in U.S. historical fiction for children, received an early treatment in an eight-volume epic about cousins on opposite sides by Joseph A. Altsheler (1914–1916).

The 20th century saw a shift of emphasis in subject matter and treatment, with novels focused more and more on the lives of ordinary people in historical contexts, such as **Laura Ingalls Wilder**'s Little House series (1932–1946), an autobiographically informed account of the domestic life of a prairie settler family. From the 1930s, **Geoffrey Trease** started to produce a new type of historical fiction that was written from a radical standpoint and generally more interested in character than in historical events. This focus on the lower classes and their struggles, as well as the moral challenges faced by individuals during times of conflict, came to replace the heroic adventures of the 19th century. A leading author in this genre is **Rosemary Sutcliff**, who covered a wide range of historical themes and times. Since the 1970s, there have been numerous novels about World War II based on the childhood experiences of authors. These include **Robert Westall**'s *The Machine-Gunners* (1975), **Nina Bawden**'s *Carrie's War* (1973), and **Judith Kerr**'s novels about the European odyssey of a Jewish family fleeing from Nazi Germany. The Holocaust has been the theme of several recent historical novels; striking examples are **Gudrun Pausewang**'s *Reise im August* (1992; *The Final Journey*, 1996), about a girl's journey to a death camp; **Lois Lowry**'s *Number the Stars* (1989); and **Roberto Innocenti**'s **picture book** *Rose Blanche* (1985).

The second half of the 20th century saw a great expansion in themes and approaches in historical fiction. In the United States it now addresses aspects including history from a Native American perspective in the works of **Joseph Bruchac** and others, and slavery and its aftermath in books by **Julius Lester**, **Paula Fox**, **Gary Paulsen**, and **Mildred D. Taylor**. **Laurence Yep** has produced remarkable historical novels about Asian Americans. Further notable contemporary U.S. authors include **Avi**, **Julia Cunningham**, and **Karen Hesse**. Contemporary British authors include **Gillian Avery**, **Gillian Cross**, **Jill Paton Walsh**, and **Berlie Doherty**. Among the key Australian contributors are **Gary Crew**, **Robin Klein**, **Colin Thiele**, and **Nadia Wheatley**. And in Ireland, historical fiction is written by **Mark O'Sullivan**, Aubrey Flegg, **Siobhan Parkinson**, and **Marita Conlon-McKenna**, author of the acclaimed Children of the Famine trilogy (1990–1996) about the Potato Famine in Ireland from 1845 to 1849.

The last two decades of the 20th century saw the appearance of a number of new, highly marketed series of historical fiction. Scholastic issued their Dear America series of 36 books between 1996 and 2002, each written in the form of a diary of a fictional young woman who lived during an important period in American history. It inspired a nine-episode TV series on HBO, as well as other series by Scholastic, including fictional journals of young American men from the past in My Name Is America, and of famous royal women throughout world history in their teenage years in The Royal Diaries. Similar series published by Scholastic's international divisions include Dear Canada, Dear India, My Australian Story, and My Story (published by Scholastic New Zealand). The American Girls, a major brand name initiated in 1986 that produces dolls, clothing, and furniture, also issues a line of short books featuring characters from American history, marketed with matching dolls, accessories, and activities. *See also* DILLON, EILÍS; GARFIELD, LEON; GRIPE, MARIA; KONIGSBURG, E. L.; MORPURGO, MICHAEL; NAPOLI, DONNA JO; O'DELL, SCOTT; PATERSON, KATHERINE; PRESSLER, MIRJAM; TREECE, HENRY.

HOBAN, RUSSELL (1925–). U.S. author of Jewish Ukrainian descent, who settled in England in 1969. A prolific writer in numerous genres whose experimental work has a cult following, Hoban has authored more than 14 novels, 60 children's books including **picture books** and volumes of verse, a number of plays, and films. He is best known for his adult novel *Riddley Walker* (1980), a post-Holocaust novel narrated in corrupted English, and his children's novel *The Mouse and His Child* (1967), illustrated by his first wife, Lillian Hoban. This Beckett-like, satirical **fable** about joined clockwork toy mice and their quest to become self-winding is regarded a children's classic, although the author sees it as his first novel rather than a book specifically for children. An animated film version in 1977 featured the voices of Peter Ustinov and Chloris Leachman. Hoban has collaborated with a number of different **illustrators**, notably with **Quentin Blake**, on titles such as *How Tom Beat Captain Najork and His Hired Sportsmen* (1974) and *The Twenty Elephant Restaurant* (1978).

HOFFMANN, E. T. A. (ERNST THEODOR AMADEUS) (1776–1822). German author, composer, jurist, and one of the key writers of the Romantic movement. Hoffmann's major contribution to children's literature lies in his creation of **fantasy** in which the wondrous world coexists easily with the modern one, and is peopled by psychologically realistic child figures that inhabit both of these worlds. His children's story *Nussknacker und Mäusekönig* (1816; *Nutcracker and Mouse King,* 1853) is regarded as one of the founding texts of the genre of fantastic children's literature, preparing the way for such 19th-century English texts as **Lewis Caroll**'s *Alice's Adventures in Wonderland* (1865). It inspired Tchaikovsky's ballet *The Nutcracker* (1892). Other stories were the basis for Jacques Offenbach's opera *The Tales of Hoffmann*, first performed in 1882.

HOFFMANN, HEINRICH (1809–1894). German physician and psychiatrist and writer best known for *Der Struwwelpeter* (1845; *The English Struwwelpeter,* 1848), usually called *Slovenly Peter* or *Shock-headed Peter* in English, eight rhyming **cautionary tales** about children who get severely punished for minor transgressions. Hoffmann created the **picture book** for his three-year-old son after finding the children's books on offer too perfectly illustrated, excessively moralizing, and full of abstract admonitions such as "Be clean!" and "Be obedient!" He believed that a single tale would impress a child more than a hundred general warnings. The stories include "The Story of Augustus Who Would Not Have Any Soup" and who starves to death within the space of five days; "The Story of Little Suck-a-Thumb" who disobeys his mother's warning and has his thumbs chopped off by a mysterious tailor with a giant pair of scissors; and "The Dreadful Story about Harriet and the Matches," in which the girl plays with the forbidden toy and ends up igniting her own funeral pyre. One of Hoffmann's great innovations was to bring **illustration** and text together as equal components to tell a story. Much of the comic potential of the book lies in the interaction between moralizing texts, which parents would read to their children, and the grotesque, exaggerating, caricature-like pictures, the center of focus for the listening child. The first edition was published under the title *Lustige Geschichten und drollige Bilder mit 15 schönen* *kolorierten Tafeln für Kinder von 3 bis 6 Jahren* [Funny Stories and Merry Pictures with 15 Prettily Colored Pictures for Children from 3 to 6]; the initial 1,500 copies were sold out in a matter of weeks. To date more than 15 million copies in more than 30 languages have been sold worldwide. There are at least 8 different British and 10 different American translations of the text, the most famous one, more inventive than faithful, by **Mark Twain**. *Struwwelpeter* found many imitators and parodists; indeed there is a genre known as "Struwwelpetriaden." *Struwwelpeter* is the German children's book that, next to the **Grimms' fairy tales**, has enjoyed the greatest international success.

HORROR STORIES. Young readers have consumed horror stories in the form of comics, films, or novels not necessarily intended for them since around the middle of the 20th century, and Stephen King has enjoyed huge popularity among young readers since the 1980s. Horror as a genre for children entered, and indeed partly dominated, the children's book publishing market in the 1990s with series and collections bearing titles such as *Are You Afraid of the Dark? Point Horror*, *Tremors*, and *Scary Stories for Seven-Year-Olds*. One of the best-selling children's authors of all time, **R. L. Stine**, creator of the Goosebumps series, is active in this segment. Surveys have shown that, contrary to assumptions, girls read more horror fiction than boys do. In contrast to horror for adults, which often leaves readers feeling fearful and uncertain as to whether the events actually happened or whether they could recur, horror for children usually offers closure instead of ambiguity and explains the apparently inexplicable, making safe what seemed threatening and dangerous. *See also* AIKEN, JOAN; CREW, GARY; CROSS, GILLIAN; LEE, TANITH; MEYER, STEPHENIE; PECK, RICHARD; PENNY DREADFULS; STEVENSON, ROBERT LOUIS; SWINDELLS, ROBERT.

HORSE AND PONY STORIES. The beginnings of narratives about horses and ponies as a distinctive type of **animal story** can be found in the classic text *Black Beauty* (1877), by **Anna Sewell**, with its sympathetic treatment of horses. However, it was not until about 50 years later that a wave of books about horses and ponies began to appear. Enid Bagnold's *National Velvet* (1935), like *Black Beauty* originally intended for adults, was particularly popular among children, especially after the successful film version in 1944. Many features which later became formula for the genre make their first appearance in *National Velvet*: an adolescent girl who longs for a horse or pony beyond the financial means of her family but who achieves her wish through hard work or luck (in this case by winning a raffle), and the ultimate and unexpected victory of horse and rider (here winning the Grand National). Equally influential was the novel *A Pony for Jean* (1936), about a girl learning to ride on a neglected pony. Written by Joanna Cannan, it was dedicated to her daughters Josephine, Diana, and Christine Pullein-Thompson, who later became famous for their own contributions to the genre.

Successful combinations of the horse/pony story with other genres include Primrose Cumming's *Silver Snaffles* (1937), which contains elements of **fantasy**, and **Mary Treadgold**'s *We Couldn't Leave Dinah* (1941), which in a World War II setting blends the threat of Nazi occupation with the pony story. Under the pseudonym Kathleen Herald, **K. M. Peyton** produced *Fly-by-Night* (1968) and its sequels, in which the protagonist develops from pony lover to teenage mother, thus incorporating elements of the problem novel. While pony stories featuring female protagonists were popular in Great Britain, the horse story was more predominant in U.S. fiction. Pioneering titles included Will James's *Smoky, the Cowhorse* (1926), a **Newbery Medal** winner, Stephen Meader's *Red Horse Hill* (1930), and Colonel S. P. Meek's *Frog, the Horse That Knew No Master* (1933). Western life, dogs, and working life on ranches feature in many of these horse novels, one of the most popular being *My Friend Flicka* (1941), by Mary O'Hara, and its two sequels. All three novels came out as films within three years of publication, and they were made into a popular television series in the 1950s.

The popularity of horse and pony stories reached its peak in the mid-20th century. Later series of pony stories include the Jill books (1949–1962) by Ruby Ferguson, the Jacky books (1958–1984) by Judith M. Berrisford, and the recent, formulaic series The Saddle Club (1986–2001) by Bonnie Bryant and ghostwriters, made into a TV series in 2001. Today's pony series are predominantly for younger girls. Although the popularity of this genre has waned in the last decades, and it has often been criticized for being formulaic and socially exclusive, books such as these obviously satisfy an important need, offering wish fulfillment and satisfaction in a context not easily available to many readers in real life. In the past they also offered girl readers instances of women succeeding in sports, often against men, at a time when there were few prominent female athletes. *See also* GENDER.

HOWKER, JANNI (1957–). British author for children and young adults based in the north of England whose work has a strong regional flavor. Howker has, to date, produced half a dozen titles, most of which have won **awards** and commendations. Her first book, *Badger on the Barge, and Other Stories* (1984), a collection of five subtle and powerful long short stories, each about the relationship between a young and an old person, was named best book of the year by the **American Library Association (ALA)**. It was followed by *The Nature of the Beast* (1985), a fable about an economically depressed, working-class community threatened by a mysterious beast that, savaging the farmers' existence, stands for the collective misery of the community. It won the Whitbread Children's Book Award, and Howker adapted it for the screen. Her next two novels, *Isaac Campion* (1986) and the **historical** novel *Martin Farrell* (1994), also address adolescent struggles rife with social and economic issues. *Walk with a Wolf* (1997) is an **illustrated** story for younger readers about an old wolf living in Canada.

HUGHES, LANGSTON (1902–1967). African American poet, novelist, and playwright, and one of the leading figures of the Harlem Renaissance of the 1920s. Although primarily known for his work for adults, Hughes also wrote many books for children; the best known is his collection *The Dream Keeper, and Other Poems* (1932). He collaborated with another major figure of the Harlem Renaissance, Arna Bontemps, to produce *Popo and Fifina: Children of Haiti* (1932), an **adventure story** now regarded as an early African American children's classic. Hughes also produced a number of **nonfictional** titles about African American history and the history of black people in other countries. These include *The First Book of the Negroes* (1952) about black leaders, *The First Book of the West Indies* (1956), and *The First Book of Africa* (1964). He introduced children to the rhythms surrounding them in *The First Book of Rhythms* (1954).

HUGHES, SHIRLEY (1927–). English **illustrator** and creator of **picture books** who started her career illustrating texts by other authors such as **Frances Hodgson Burnett**, **William Mayne**, and **Margaret Mahy.** Her picture books, of which there are more than 30, have met with great critical and commercial success and have been translated into several languages. Hughes's knowledge of what it is to be a child is evident in the dramas of everyday life in her books for younger readers, and she has produced a number of memorable, endearing characters. *Dogger* (1977), winner of the **Kate Greenaway Medal**, is about a few days in a small boy's life during which his favorite toy dog has gone missing. Her most popular figures around whom series are based are Lucy and Tom, and Alfie. Hughes won her second Kate Greenaway Medal for her retelling of the Cinderella story with a subversive end for her self-empowered 1920s protagonist, *Ella's Big Chance: A Jazz-Age Cinderella* (2003). Sepia or black line and watercolor are central media in her graphic style, and she integrates elements of strip comics and graphic novels, especially in her work for **all ages** or older readers. These include *Up and Up* (1979), a wordless picture book, and the metafictive *Chips and Jessie* (1985). In 1999, she was appointed OBE for services to children's literature, and she was made a fellow of the Royal Society of Literature in 2000.

HUGHES, TED (EDWARD JAMES) (1930–1998). British poet, playwright, author, and translator who was poet laureate from 1984 until his death. Regarded as one of the major poets of the second half of the 20th century, Hughes was also a significant author for children. A sequence of comic family poems, *Meet My Folks!* (1961), was followed by two books dedicated to the children of his first marriage (to the poet Sylvia Plath), the prose **fables** *How the Whale Became* (1963) and the modern **myth** *The Iron Man* (1968; U.S. title *The Iron Giant*), about a mysterious, destructive giant who, in the face of threats to world order, finds a way to save the planet. *The Iron Woman* (1993), for older readers, addresses the topic of environmental pollution. The natural world and the innocent savagery of animals were a source of great inspiration for Hughes, and he produced several volumes of children's **poetry** on these themes, including *Season Songs* (1975), *Moon Whales, and Other Poems* (1976), and *What Is the Truth?* (1984), written for the Farms for City Children Scheme and winner of both the Signal Prize for children's poetry and the Guardian Award. Together with **Michael Morpurgo**, Hughes proposed the creation of a **children's laureate** position. The volumes *Collected Plays for Children* (2001) and *Collected Poems for Children* (2005), **illustrated** by **Raymond Briggs**, include, respectively, all of Hughes's dramatic output and most of his poems.

HUGHES, THOMAS (1822–1896). British writer best known for *Tom Brown's School Days* (1857), based on his own experiences at Rugby from 1834 to 1842. The book charts the development of Tom, who is portrayed as a typical middle-class English schoolboy from rural Berkshire who goes up to the English "public school" (i.e., private school) Rugby. There he is introduced to its world of lessons, sports, and bullying. After getting into trouble, Tom has to share his room with a timid new pupil, Arthur, whose Christianity greatly affects his roommate. The book was immediately successful, has never been out of print, and has been **adapted** for film, television, and radio. Written partly to praise the leadership and reforms of Dr. Thomas Arnold, the legendary headmaster of the school during Hughes's attendance, it was hugely influential on the genre of the British **school story**, not least in its rating sports over academic achievement.

HYMAN, TRINA SCHART (1939–2004). U.S. artist and **illustrator** of more than 150 books by such diverse authors as Geoffrey Chaucer, **Mark Twain**, **Howard Pyle**, **Astrid Lindgren**, and **Lloyd Alexander**. Hyman, who trained as an artist in the United States and Sweden, is particularly acclaimed for her illustrations of **fairy tales** and **folktales**, especially for her versions of *Snow White* (1974), *Sleeping Beauty* (1977), and *Little Red Riding Hood* (1983). Indeed, her **picture-book** autobiography for children, *Self-Portrait* (1981), presents itself in the style of a fairy tale. *Saint George and the Dragon* (1984), **adapted** by Margaret Hodges from Edmund Spenser's *The Faerie Queene* and illustrated by Hyman, won the **Caldecott Medal** in 1985. Hyman was one of the first white American illustrators to include realistic-looking black characters in her pictures. She was art director of *Cricket* magazine from 1972 to 1979 and contributed regularly to the magazine until her death.

– I –

ILLUSTRATIONS. Illustrations are a central element in children's literature, providing in books and magazines pictorial representations and interpretations of fiction and **nonfiction**. The degree of illustration can range from a single picture to central graphic prints, from decorated initial letters to vignettes. Illustrations, which use most available art media—from woodcut, engraving, and lithography, through watercolor and collage, to computer graphics—are an applied form of art, not generally intended to stand alone but traditionally playing a subservient role based on a preexisting verbal text. In **picture books**, on the other hand, a more recent invention, the pictures are as important as the words, and the total effect depends on the interplay between the visual and the verbal.

The first printed books with illustrations were not intended for children, but there can be no doubt that children who had access to **William Caxton**'s *Subtyl Historyes and Fables of Esop* (1484) enjoyed looking at the woodcut illustrations. Biographical accounts of first reading experiences frequently indicate how child readers first accessed texts originally for adults, such as **John Bunyan**'s *Pilgrim's Progress* (1678), **Daniel Defoe**'s *Robinson Crusoe* (1719), or **Jonathan Swift**'s *Gulliver's Travels* (1726), through the accompanying illustrations. Martin Luther was one of the first to emphasize the importance of illustrations for an illiterate audience, although he meant primarily adults. This idea was later adopted by educationalists, who realized that children could better grasp and remember things that were seen rather than merely read about. A pioneering publication was **John Amos Comenius**'s *Orbis Sensualium Pictus* (1658), a pictorial encyclopedia for children that assembled 150 small woodcut illustrations of the natural world with Latin and German captions. In *Some Thoughts concerning Education* (1693), **John Locke** emphasized the educational importance of pictures for children as a means "to encourage enquiry and knowledge." In seeking to combine instruction with entertainment, Locke exercised great influence on the development of children's literature and the growth of illustrated children's books in the 18th century. A famous early example is **John Newbery**'s *A Little Pretty Pocket-Book* (1744), considered one of the first entertaining books for children, which was furnished with woodcut illustrations. The cheap and popular **chapbooks** that boomed in the 18th century were also illustrated with frequently recycled woodcuts. **Thomas Bewick**, who made the work of the illustrator as important as the text in books for children in such works as *Aesop's Fables* (1818), influenced artists like **George Cruikshank**, illustrator of the first English translation of the **Grimms**' fairy tales in 1823.

Advancements in printing technology during the 19th century led to an improvement in children's book illustrations. Woodcuts and wood engravings were gradually replaced by engravings on copper and steel plates that, when used by increasingly professional engravers, ensured distinct printing of the original image. The new technology of chromolithography, invented in 1799, became widespread on the continent of Europe; one of the early examples of colored chromolithography is **Heinrich Hoffmann**'s *Der Struwwelpeter* (1845), in which the lithographer, on Hoffmann's insistence, reproduced his deliberately amateurish style without any correction or improvement. By the second half of the 19th century, colored illustrations could be produced relatively cheaply; this led to significant developments in picture books and illustrated books for children. Three key British artists of the late 19th century, **Randolph Caldecott**, **Kate Greenaway**, and **Walter Crane**, worked together with the printer and engraver Edmund Evans to produce striking quality illustrations, as made possible by Evans's three-color-printing process.

In the United States, the prime medium and vehicle for illustrated works was the periodical, specifically the magazines for children from the middle of the 19th century on, such as *Our Young Folks* and *St. Nicholas*. The artist known as the father of American children's book illustration, **Howard Pyle**, started his creative career illustrating for magazines, including *St. Nicholas*. Although influenced by European artists and known for his medieval style and his attention to book design, Pyle promoted a distinctively American form of art in his teaching, and his painterly style influenced pupils including Maxfield Parrish and **Jessie Wilcox Smith**.

At the turn of the century, children's book illustration reflected contemporary developments in the world of art, with the arts and crafts movement in Great Britain producing richly decorated books for children by Aubrey Beardsley and others; in Europe, the French **Louis Maurice Boutet de Monvel**, the Swiss **Ernst Kreidolf**, the Swedes Elsa Beskow and Carl Larsson, and the Russian Ivan Bilibin all produced children's books that linked illustration to the fine arts. The most common form of illustration in children's books of the 20th century was the line drawing, and several British and U.S. artists in the 20th century worked exclusively as line illustrators of the works of others. Notable examples are **E. H. Shepard**, **Walter Trier**, Ilon Wikland (illustrator of **Astrid Lindgren**'s work), and **Garth Williams**. A number of artists who have created their own picture books have also illustrated fiction by other authors, sometimes in the early days of their career, but not necessarily exclusively so. Such artists include **Edward Ardizzone**, **Charles Keeping**, **Quentin Blake**, **Shirley Hughes**, **Michael Foreman**, **Anthony Browne**, and **Jan Ormerod**.

The 1930s saw the rise of the American comic book, a popular form that induced anxieties among educationalists about declining literary standards. In the 1940s, Simon and Schuster's Little Golden Books (LGB) series of inexpensive, well-illustrated, high-quality children's books costing 25 cents became a publishing phenomenon. From the perspective of book-buying parents, these were a good and economical alternative to the comic book, and many of the early contributors went on to become noted authors and illustrators, including the author **Margaret Wise Brown** and the illustrators Gustaf Tenggren, **Richard Scarry**, and Garth Williams. The LGBs were astonishingly successful: the eighth book in the series, *The Poky Little Puppy* (1942) by Janette Sebring Lowrey, was, prior to **Harry Potter**, one of the top-selling children's hardcover books of all time. Indeed, 5 of the top 10 best-selling hardcover children's books are LGBs.

Apart from picture books, which have become by far the most commonly illustrated printed medium, illustrations in children's books today occur most frequently in books for preschool children and **easy readers**, where they primarily aid comprehension; in **information books**; in **poetry** editions for children; in collections of **fairy tales** or folktales; and in selected classics. Many of these have been reillustrated by several artists—**Robert Louis Stevenson**'s *A Child's Garden of Verses* (1885), for instance, has been illustrated by Millicent Sowerby, Charles Robinson, Jessie Wilcox Smith, **Eve Garnett**, **Brian Wildsmith**, and Michael Foreman. Other repeatedly reillustrated titles include **Lewis Carroll**'s *Alice's Adventures in Wonderland* (1865), **Charles Dickens**'s *A Christmas Carol* (1843), and **Carlo Collodi**'s *The Adventures of Pinocchio* (1881–1882), a recent, acclaimed version of which was by **Roberto Innocenti**. Notable illustrations of folktales from other countries have been created by **Marcia Brown**, **Leo** and **Diane Dillon**, **Trina Schart Hyman**, and **Jerry Pinkney**. The most frequently illustrated and reillustrated works are undoubtedly the fairy tales of **Charles Perrault**, the Brothers Grimm, and **Hans Christian Andersen**; illustrators include **Arthur Rackham**, **Johnny Gruelle**, **Maurice Sendak**, Trina Schart Hyman, **Lisbeth Zwerger**, **Janosch**, and **P. J. Lynch**; some illustrators, such as **Wanda Gág**, Marcia Brown, and **Paul O. Zelinsky**, have also retold or translated the versions they have illustrated. Major **prizes** awarded to illustrators are the **Astrid Lindgren Memorial Award**, the **Caldecott Medal**, the **Hans Christian Andersen Award**, and the **Kate Greenaway Medal**. *See also* BLAKE, WILLIAM; BROOKS, RON; BROWN, MARC; BUTTERWORTH, NICK; FEELINGS, TOM; GALDONE, PAUL; INGPEN, ROBERT; JANSSON, TOVE; KEATS, EZRA JACK; LAWSON, ROBERT; LENSKI, LOIS; LOBEL, ANITA; LOBEL, ARNOLD; MACAULAY, DAVID; MOSER, BARRY; OXENBURY, HELEN; PINKNEY, JERRY; ROSS, TONY; SÍS, PETER; WILLARD, NANCY; YOUNG, ED.

INFORMATION BOOKS. A major umbrella category also called *nonfiction*, although many authors dislike the negative classification. **Russell Freedman** argues that it leads people to believe that "nonfiction is less important than fiction"; he elects to call himself a "factual author." Information books inform readers about the real world: people, places, history, art, science, the environment, and ideas. The first information book for children was **John Amos Comenius**'s

Orbis Sensualium Pictus (1658); development in the United States started with books by **Samuel Goodrich** and **Jacob Abbott**. The scope of information books ranges from encyclopedias, such as Comenius's work, to in-depth examinations of a single topic, such as the acclaimed *Cathedral* (1973) by **David Macaulay**. Categories include concept books for the young; through how-to-books that invite children to participate actively and guide them step by step through activities such as cooking or science experiments; to extended narratives that inform children about their country's geography, such as **Selma Lagerlöf**'s *Wonderful Adventures of Nils* (Swedish original 1906–1907).

Information can be presented in a variety of ways: A narrative approach may dominate in some biographies, for instance in *You Want Women to Vote, Lizzie Stanton?* (1995), by **Jean Fritz**; or they can be embellished with period photographs, as in the **Newbery Medal**–winning *Lincoln: A Photobiography* (1987), by Russell Freedman. Information books can be presented in **picture-book** form—as in Holling C. Holling's *Paddle-to-the-Sea*, about an expedition from the Great Lakes to the Atlantic Ocean—or in a pop-up-book format.

Contemporary developments in the media—up-to-date, attractive, user-friendly, and interactive digital media as well as sophisticated printing techniques and paper engineering—have led to dramatic changes in style of presentation. The design has become more eye-catching, the books work with a variety of media and graphics in new forms and formats, and we find nonsequential organization, with some designs aiming to replicate Internet screens. Series, which have become prolific, usually opt for distinctive formats, notably those produced by Dorling Kindersley such as the Eyewitness books. A recent trend is the introduction of humor: an example is the Magic School Bus series, by Joanna Cole and Bruce Degen, which combines fact and fiction in comic-style format.

Information books have not enjoyed as much critical attention as other forms of children's literature, although there have been some significant contributions since the 1970s. One of the earliest **awards** for nonfiction was the West German government's (now German government's) Deutscher Jugendliteraturpreis; a nonfiction prize was included among the prize categories as early as the 1960s. In 1976, the Boston Globe–Horn Book Award for Nonfiction was established, and the 1980s and 1990s saw awards for information books established in Canada and Australia. These have insured greater visibility for children's nonfiction, as well as encouraging high standards in authorship and production. *See also* ASIMOV, ISAAC; BUNTING, EVE; DEPAOLA, TOMIE; EASY READERS; FOREMAN, MICHAEL; GENDER; GEORGE, JEAN CRAIGHEAD; HAMILTON, VIRGINIA; HUGHES, LANGSTON; ILLUSTRATIONS; INGPEN, ROBERT; KIMMEL, ERIC A.; LENSKI, LOIS; LESTER, JULIUS; LOBEL, ARNOLD; MYERS, WALTER DEAN; PAULSEN, GARY; PINKNEY, JERRY; SCARRY, RICHARD; SCIENCE FICTION; STREATFEILD, NOEL; WIESE, KURT; YONGE, CHARLOTTE M.

INGPEN, ROBERT (1936–). Australian writer and **illustrator** of more than 100 works of fiction and **nonfiction** for children and adults. His first illustrations were for the 1974 edition of **Colin Thiele**'s *Storm Boy*. Environment, heritage, and the Australian landscape are central to many of Ingpen's illustrations, and he is a talented creator of **fantasy** creatures and mythological worlds. His acclaimed work includes illustrations for Michael Page's *Encyclopedia of Things That Never Were* (1985) and Philip Wilkinson's *Encyclopedia of Events That Changed the World* (1991). He has also illustrated a number of international classics, including **Rudyard Kipling**'s *Jungle Book* and **Hans Christian Andersen**'s *The Ugly Duckling*. Great Ormond Street Hospital for Children invited him to illustrate the centenary edition of **Sir J. M. Barrie**'s *Peter Pan and Wendy* in 2004. The widely popular Australian Gnome series (1979–1981), authored and illustrated by Ingpen, about hairy gnomes from Peru who travel to Australia in a "poppykettle," gave rise to an annual Poppykettle Festival in Geelong. Ingpen won the **Hans Christian Andersen Award** in 1986.

INKPEN, MICK (1952–). British **picture-book** artist and writer. He worked in collaboration with **Nick Butterworth** for many years, creating the successful comic strip *The Mice of Upney Junction*; the popular Jasper books starting with *Just like Jasper!* (1989); *The Nativity Play* (1985), a funny and moving story of children preparing for the Christmas pageant; and *Animal Tales* (1999), a collection of

Bible stories told from the perspective of animals. With *The Blue Balloon* (1989), Inkpen launched his solo career, and one of its characters, the lovable but unfortunate dog Kipper, has since become the popular subject of a number of books. Another animal protagonist, Wibbly Pig, features in a successful series for preschool children.

INNOCENTI, ROBERTO (1940–). Self-taught Italian **illustrator** of classic works such as **Carlo Collodi**'s *The Adventures of Pinocchio*, **Charles Perrault**'s *Cinderella*, **Charles Dickens**'s *A Christmas Carol*, and **E. T. A. Hoffmann**'s *Nutcracker*. His most famous book, *Rose Blanche* (1985), was conceived and illustrated by Innocenti himself with an original French text by the Swiss author Christophe Gallaz. It tells of the final phase of World War II in a small town in Germany, from the perspective of a nine-year-old girl who is confronted with the awful truth of the Holocaust after she discovers a concentration camp in the woods outside the town. She displays instinctive compassion and civil disobedience by sneaking food to the Jewish child prisoners. In the end, Rose is killed by a soldier's stray bullet. The book has been **translated** into 10 different languages, and it won several **awards**, including the Golden Apple at the **Biennial of Illustrations Bratislava (BIB)**. Innocenti's style is hyperrealistic and highly detailed; his pictures are carefully crafted, with layer upon layer of historically authentic material. He was the recipient of the **Hans Christian Andersen Award** in 2008.

THE INTERNATIONAL BOARD ON BOOKS FOR YOUNG PEOPLE (IBBY). A nonprofit organization founded in October 1953 in Zurich, Switzerland, which represents a network of people from all over the world committed to bringing books and children together. Composed of 70 national sections, its mission is to promote international understanding through children's books, to give children everywhere the opportunity to have access to books with high literary and artistic standards, and to encourage the publication and distribution of quality children's books, especially in developing countries. Every two years it presents the **Hans Christian Andersen Award** to an author and an **illustrator**, and issues an IBBY Honor List consisting of two books from each country, nominated by its national section, as representative of the best in children's literature. It also publishes the quarterly journal *Bookbird*. As a nongovernmental organization with an official status in the United Nations Educational, Scientific and Cultural Organization (UNESCO) and the United Nations International Children's Emergency Fund (UNICEF), IBBY has a policy-making role as an advocate of children's books.

THE INTERNATIONAL RESEARCH SOCIETY FOR CHILDREN'S LITERATURE (IRSCL). A professional organization founded in 1970 to promote academic research and scholarship in children's literature, reading, and related fields, and to facilitate cooperation between researchers in different countries. The IRSCL organizes a congress every two years and publishes a journal (*International Research in Children's Literature*). In 2008, the IRSCL had more than 250 members from more than 40 countries.

THE INTERNATIONAL YOUTH LIBRARY (IYL). Founded by **Jella Lepman** in 1946 to foster international understanding through children's books, the IYL is the world's largest library for international children's literature. It houses a collection of 500,000 volumes of children's books in more than 130 languages; some 1,000 publishers send sample copies of their latest titles to the library each year. Its reference collection, used by scholars from all over the world, comprises around 30,000 volumes of secondary literature and almost 300 professional periodicals. The IYL also maintains a public lending library and offers foreign-language and art courses. It is housed in the 15th-century Blutenburg Castle in Munich.

– J –

JACOBS, JOSEPH (1854–1916). Australian folklorist and Jewish historian who immigrated to England in 1872 and to the United States in 1900. In the spirit of the **Grimm** brothers, he wanted to bring together native **folktales** in a standard edition before they were lost. The first of his collections, *English Fairy Tales* (1890), contained such tales as "Jack and the Beanstalk," "Jack the Giant Killer," "Whittington and His Cat," and "The Story of the Three Little Pigs," as well as British variants of well-known European stories. Several volumes followed, including *More English Fairy Tales* (1894), *Celtic Fairy Tales* (1892 and 1894), and *Indian Fairy Tales* (1912). Jacobs intended his folktale collections specifically for young readers, but they also include extensive notes on the origins of the stories and his own modifications. Jacobs also produced major works on Jewish history and was editor of the *Jewish Encyclopedia.*

JANEWAY, JAMES (1636–1674). English Puritan minister and author of *A Token for Children: Being an Exact Account of the Conversion, Holy and Exemplary Lives, and Joyful Deaths of Several Young Children* (1671). Next to the **Bible** and *The Pilgrim's Progress* by **John Bunyan**, it was for some time the most widely read book in nurseries in England.

JANOSCH (1931–). Pseudonym of Horst Eckert, German author, painter, and **illustrator** who has been living on the Canary Islands since 1980. Janosch has produced a number of novels for adults, as well as a collection of graphic art predominantly of a satirical and erotic nature—but it is for his children's books, which are more than 100 in number and which have been **translated** into more than 30 languages, that Janosch is most famed. He has a marked interest in eccentric characters and trickster figures, and many traditional forms of literature—**fairy tales**, **nursery rhymes**, and tall tales—can be found in different variations in his work. These include his collection of mildly subversive rhymes *Heute um neune hinter der Scheune* (1965; *Tonight at Nine*, 1967) and his parodies of the **Grimms**' fairy tales, *Janosch erzählt Grimm's Märchen* (1972; *Not Quite as Grimm*, 1974), in which the heroes swap roles and **genders**.

The style of illustration with which Janosch is now most associated—pastel-colored drawings and round, curved forms—was established in the late 1970s in his famous Little Tiger and Little Bear stories. These feature **anthropomorphic** animal figures in idyllic miniature worlds and focus on issues relevant for young children like friendship, loneliness, and misunderstandings. *Oh, wie schön ist Panama* (1978; *The Trip to Panama*, 1981), the first of these, is his best-known book. His stories reached a wide audience through the TV series *Janoschs Traumstunde* [Janosch's Dream Hour], and images of his creations currently feature on more than 1,700 articles, making him one of the premier objects of merchandising in Germany today. Four out of five Germans are familiar with his figures the Little Tiger, the Little Bear, and his hybrid invention "Tigerente" [Tiger Duck].

JANSSON, TOVE (1914–2001). Finnish artist and writer who belonged to the small Swedish-speaking minority in Finland. She achieved international fame for her novels, **picture books**, and comic strips about the Moomins, which have been **translated** into some 35 languages. In the first stories, starting with *Småtrollen och den stora översvämningen* [The Moomins and the Great Flood] (1945) and *Kometjakten* (1946; *Comet in Moominland,* 1968), Jansson creates a childhood utopia in a Moominvalley inhabited by imaginary, troll-like, round characters who vaguely resemble hippopotamuses with human features. The most important are the family that consists of Moominmamma, Moominpappa, and their son Moomintroll. The later books, such as *Sent i November* (1970; *Moominvalley in November,* 1971), are darker in tone and often regarded as more suitable for an adult audience. After completing the series of nine Moomin books, Jansson no longer wrote specifically for children but continued her writing for adults. She **illustrated** the Moomin novels herself as well as Swedish translations of **J. R. R. Tolkien**'s *The Hobbit* and **Lewis Carroll**'s *Alice in Wonderland.* As with other figures of classic children's literature, the Moomins are licensed today and can be found on toys, candy, and other merchandise, as well as in film and animated cartoon versions. There is a theme park devoted to the Moomins in Finland. Tove Jansson received the **Hans Christian Andersen Award** in 1966.

JOHNS, CAPTAIN W. E. (WILLIAM EARL) (1893–1968). British writer who, after having served as a pilot in the Royal Flying Corps during World War I, became one of the most popular British authors in the mid-20th century. Ninety-six of his approximately 170 books are about the hero Biggles. This pilot, adventurer, and detective, whose full name and title is Major James Bigglesworth, D.S.O., M.C., first appeared in the magazine *Popular Flying* founded by Johns; the first Biggles book, *The Camels Are Coming*, was published in 1932. At the instigation of the Air Ministry during

World War II, he created the highly skilled heroine "Worrals of the WAAF." (WAAF stands for "Women's Auxiliary Air Force.") Johns later came into criticism for **racism** and violence; but his popularity as an author was surpassed only by **Enid Blyton**'s, and his books have been **translated** into many languages.

JONES, DIANA WYNNE (1934–). British author for children and adults and prolific writer of **fantasy**. Jones's inventive novels and short stories avoid or subvert the widespread conventions of the fantasy genre. Written with a light, often comic, touch and with original plots, they present complex narratives that often explore interpersonal and family relationships and social and ethical issues. Among her best-known works are *Howl's Moving Castle* (1986) and the Chrestomanci series (1977–2006). The former book, a Boston Globe–Horn Book **Award** winner, is set in the magical kingdom of Ingary, in which **fairy-tale** tropes determine the lives of the characters. (Hayao Miyazaki made it into an acclaimed anime in 2004.) The Chrestomanci series involves powerful, nine-lived enchanters named Chrestomanci and is based on the idea that there are multiple universes, each the result of a different possibility or choice made in history. Following the widespread interest in fantasy generated by the success of the Harry Potter novels, many of Jones's earlier children's books that were out of print were reissued. In *The Tough Guide to Fantasyland* (1996), Jones wittily parodies the clichés of sword-and-sorcery fantasy. *The Dark Lord of Derkholm* (1998), which can be regarded as a sequel, is set in a fantasy world that maintains all these clichés for the benefit of tourists. It won the Mythopoeic Fantasy Award for Children's Literature.

– K –

KÄSTNER, ERICH (1899–1974). German journalist, poet, satirist, and writer of screenplays and novels for both adults and children. Kästner is arguably the best-known German children's author of the 20th century; his most famous novel, *Emil und die Detektive* (1929; *Emil and the Detectives,* 1930) was **translated** into 57 different languages. His children's novels enjoyed widespread international success during the 1930s and 1940s, at a time when the Nazis had burned his satirical works for adults and forbidden his publication in Germany. *Emil und die Detektive*, Kästner's first novel for children, is the first **detective** novel for children to feature a gang of children as protagonists, a feature later copied and popularized by **Enid Blyton**. Set in contemporary Berlin, it tells the story of a poor provincial boy whose money has been stolen on his way to the city, and how he joins forces with a gang of young Berliners to catch the thief without any adult assistance. It transpires that the crook was a bank robber, and the happy ending includes a large financial reward for Emil. A striking feature of the novel is the modernity of the setting: a huge city with its bright lights, cinemas, and public transport. The plot even features a telephone used to coordinate operations, a relatively rare commodity in Berlin in 1929. **Walter Trier** illustrated the novel with stylized figures and reduced forms, introducing *Neue Sachlichkeit* (new objectivity) into children's **illustration**. Most translated editions appear with Trier's illustrations, which have the same classic status as the text.

In this and other novels, Kästner takes children seriously and trusts their inherent and uncorrupted moral sense. He saw himself as a writer in the Enlightenment tradition, but he was also a consummate entertainer who created a humorous, ironic, and sometimes theatrical narrative voice in numerous paratexts such as prefaces, introductions, and metafictional commentaries. Following *Emil* in terms of international popularity is *Das doppelte Lottchen* (1949; *Lottie and Lisa*, 1950; U.S. title *Lisa and Lottie*, 1969) and *Pünktchen und Anton* (1931; *Annaluise and Anton*, 1932). Kästner also published an autobiographical account of his childhood for children, *Als ich ein kleiner Junge war* (1957; *When I Was a Little Boy*, 1959), and retold such classic texts as ***Gulliver's Travels*** (1961). Many of his novels were made into films, *Emil and the Detectives* and *The Parent Trap* (based on *Das doppelte Lottchen*) in a number of different versions. His books have been used in special editions for teaching German as a foreign language throughout the world. Kästner was one of the founding members of the **International Board on Books for Young People (IBBY)**, was awarded the German Order of Merit (Bundesverdienstkreuz) in 1959, and won the **Hans Christian Andersen Award** in 1960. *See also* KRÜSS, JAMES.

KATE GREENAWAY MEDAL. Established in 1955 in honor of the **illustrator Kate Greenaway**, the Kate Greenaway Medal is presented annually for distinguished illustration in a book for children published in Great Britain in the previous year. Established by the **Library Association (LA)**, the medal is now awarded by the **Chartered Institute of Library and Information Professionals (CILIP)**. (See appendix for list of recipients).

KEATS, EZRA JACK (1916–1983). U.S. author and creator of **picture books**, especially known for his bright stories set in inner-city neighborhoods. Keats **illustrated** more than 80 books for children and wrote the stories for 24 of them. *The Snowy Day* (1962), about the joy a young child has in the first snow of the season, received the **Caldecott Medal**. Its protagonist, Peter, who features in six more books (getting a little older through the years), was the first black child to appear in full color in an American picture book. Keats's vibrant books, which often blend watercolor with paper or fabric collage and marbled paper, illustrate family life, daily routines, and seasonal highlights such as puppet shows, Halloween nights, and birthday parties, as well as difficulties that face young children, such as bullying or a new baby in the family. Other popular protagonists include the shy, Hispanic protagonist in *Louie* (1975) and *The Trip* (1978), and the bespectacled Archie in *Goggles!* (1969) and *The Pet Show* (1972).

KEENE, CAROLYN. Pseudonym of the authors of the Nancy Drew **mystery** series—Mildred Wirt Benson, Walter Karig, and others—hired by its publisher Stratemeyer Syndicate from 1930 on. Other ghostwriters using this name have included Priscilla Doll, Charles Strong, and Susan Wittig Albert.

KEEPING, CHARLES (1924–1988). English artist, **illustrator**, and creator of **picture books**. Regarded as one of the most original British artists who produced for children in the 20th century, Keeping illustrated close to 200 books for children and adults, first coming to prominence with his illustrations for **Rosemary Sutcliff**'s **historical novels** in the 1950s. His illustration of the complete works of **Charles Dickens** (1978–1988) reveals his intimate knowledge of the vanishing world of industrial London. His first picture books, *Black Dolly* and *Shaun and the Carthorse*, both published in 1966, were about working horses. *Charley, Charlotte and the Golden Canary* (1967), a story with **fairy-tale** qualities about two children who are separated when one is moved from their inner-city dwelling to a new tower block, won Keeping his first **Kate Greenaway Medal**. He won his second for his illustration of Alfred Noyes's poem *The Highwayman* (1981), notable for its gruesome details. His illustrations for *Beowulf* (1982), **adapted** from the Anglo-Saxon epic by **Kevin Crossley-Holland**, present a sympathetic view of the monster, subverting the view of the text. Keeping was attracted to subjects such as death, violence, and loneliness, and applied contemporary styles and techniques not often found in the children's literature of his time.

KERR, JUDITH (1923–). German-born British writer who had to flee with her family from Berlin when Adolf Hitler came to power in 1933; her father was the famous theater critic of Jewish origin, Alfred Kerr. After studying art and working for the BBC, Judith Kerr produced her first **picture books** for young readers, *The Tiger Who Came to Tea* (1968) and *Mog the Forgetful Cat* (1970), humorous stories featuring **anthropomorphic** animals in a domestic context. Mog the cat went on to become the main character in a series of 17 books, ending with his death in *Goodbye, Mog* (2002). Kerr has also authored three autobiographical novels—*When Hitler Stole Pink Rabbit* (1971), *The Other Way Round* (1975), and *A Small Person Far Away* (1978)—about her childhood in Berlin, her family's exile, and how she, although not her parents, ultimately adapted to the English way of life.

KEY, ELLEN (1849–1926). Swedish **feminist**, author, and educator. Her most influential book was *Barnets århundrade* (1900; *The Century of the Child*, 1909), which presented changes she believed were necessary in child care for the 20th century, advocated children's rights, and called for parents and carers to listen more closely to children. Key's ideas played a decisive role in the pedagogical debate of the 20th century, and were highly influential on the development of Swedish children's literature, especially after World War II, in the way it focuses on children's rights and child psychology.

KIMMEL, ERIC A. (1946–). U.S. storyteller and author of more than 50 children's books, especially acclaimed for bringing folklore to contemporary children. Kimmel has retold **folktales** from many cultures. These include titles such as *Three Sacks of Truth: A Story from France* (1993), *The Three Princes: A Tale from the Middle East* (1994), *Sword of the Samurai: Adventure Stories from Japan* (1998), and *The Rooster's Antlers: A Story of the Chinese Zodiac* (1999), as well as Eastern European Jewish tales such as the **picture book** *Hershel and the Hanukkah Goblins* (1989), **illustrated** by **Trina Schart Hyman**, and *The Jar of Fools: Eight Hanukkah Stories from Chelm* (2000). Kimmel has also modernized **fairy tales** by the **Grimms**, retold **Bible** stories, and authored abridged classics such as *Don Quixote and the Windmills* (2004) as well as **information books** on Judaism, like *Bar Mitzvah: A Jewish Boy's Coming of Age* (1995). Before becoming a professional storyteller and author, Kimmel was professor of education at Portland State University.

KINGSLEY, CHARLES (1819–1875). English author and clergyman, who was involved in forming the Christian Socialist movement in 1848. His **historical novel** *Westward Ho!* (1855) was widely read by adults and children; *The Heroes* (1856) is a retelling of the Greek **myths** for his own children; but it is above all for *The Water-Babies* (1863) that Kingsley is remembered. Regarded today as one of the first classic English **fantasies**, it follows the adventures of a small **orphan**, Tom, who has to work for the depraved chimney sweep, Grimes. Tom's moral education starts after he falls into a river and is transformed into a water-baby. In this state he experiences sometimes painful adventures in order to become a moral creature. He is finally redeemed because he does a thing he does not like; he helps Grimes to see the light. At the end of the novel he becomes, in true Victorian tradition, a great man of science. While the story is largely concerned with Christian redemption, Kingsley's interest in social reform and criticism of enforced child labor is evident. Many of his polemical comments on the scientific and educational disputes of the day were addressed to adult readers rather than children.

KING-SMITH, DICK (1922–). British farmer, teacher, and popular and prolific author of more than 100 children's books, mainly inventive and humorous **animal stories** for young readers. His most famous book, *Sheep-Pig* (1983; U.S. title *Babe: The Gallant Pig*), winner of the Boston Globe–Horn Book **Award** and the Guardian Children's Fiction Award, is about a pig who can herd cattle better than a dog. It was made into an Oscar-nominated movie, *Babe*, in 1995. His animals are **anthropomorphic** to the extent that they can speak, but the reality of farm life is portrayed unsentimentally. King-Smith is adept at representing different forms of speech such as dialect, especially idiosyncratic language spoken by his animal characters, and at wordplay. He has also retold traditional tales in rhymes in *The Topsy-Turvy Storybook* (1992) and produced an entertaining collection of **nonsense poems**, *Alpha Beasts* (1992), **illustrated** by **Quentin Blake**.

KIPLING, RUDYARD (1865–1936). British poet, novelist, and short-story writer for both children and adults. Kipling was one of the most popular writers in English in the late 19th and early 20th centuries. He declined most of the many honors offered to him, including a knighthood and the poet laureateship, but he accepted the Nobel Prize for Literature in 1907. Kipling was born in India and spent his first five happy years there, speaking Hindustani as his second language, before being sent to school in England, which he described as a traumatic experience. He returned to India at the age of 16 and worked there as a journalist for seven years before returning to England. India provided the background for his most famous children's books, *The Jungle Book* (1894) and *The Second Jungle Book* (1895), and for *Kim* (1901), more a novel about childhood than for children, about the relationship between an **orphaned** British boy and a lama from Tibet.

The Jungle Books are collections of stories (interspersed with poems), mostly about **anthropomorphic** animals—such as "Rikki-Tikki-Tavi," about a mongoose who defends a human family against a pair of cobras. Most famous today are the eight stories about the boy Mowgli, a child raised among the wolves and trained in the law of the jungle. **Walt Disney**'s film *The Jungle Book* (1967) popularized these, but few of Kipling's central themes, such as initiation, loyalty, personal responsibility, and skill, are to be found in the animated musical. *Just So Stories* (1902) is another outstanding children's book, with fantasized origin stories told by Kipling to his own children. Striking both for their vivid imagery and for the oral quality of the tales, they give an account of how various phenomena came about, for instance "How the Camel Got His Hump," or "How the Alphabet Was Made." *Puck of Pook's Hill* (1906) and *Rewards and Fairies* (1910) are collections of tales based on English history, interspersed with poems and linked by a frame narrative of two children. Kipling made a major contribution to the genre of the **school story**, as well as giving an insight into the brutalities of school life, with *Stalky and Co.* (1899).

Kipling was a poet of Empire, and some of his work represents extremes of imperialism and **ethnocentrism**, although these do not feature in the works written specifically for children. The best-loved British poem in a survey carried out by the BBC in 1995 was Kipling's poem "If."

KLEIN, NORMA (1938–1989). U.S. author for adults and children. Klein's novels represent an important contribution to the development of the *problem* or *issue* novel. She openly addressed formerly taboo subjects, such as nontraditional families in *Mom, the Wolfman, and Me* (1972), abortion in *It's Not What You Expect* (1973), and masturbation, homosexuality, and female sexuality in *It's Okay If You Don't Love Me* (1977). While the issues take center stage in these novels, they also frequently feature interesting, articulate, and confident young female protagonists, predominantly from an urban Jewish background. *See also* GENDER.

KLEIN, ROBIN (1936–). Australian author of more than 50 novels, **picture books**, and collections of stories and verses for children and young adults, who enjoys both popular and critical success. Klein combines a strong sense of humor with a focus on the themes of friendship, family, adolescence (usually female), struggling under pressure, and outsiders. Her best-known novel, *Hating Alison Ashley* (1984), also made into a film, is a comedy that addresses the pressures of growing up, the power of friendship, and the pursuit of happiness. *Halfway across the Galaxy and Turn Left* (1985) is about an alien family who seek refuge in a small Australian town. It focuses on the daughter, X, who is forced to take responsibility for her family while trying to adapt to the strange Earth customs. It was made into a television series in 1991–1992. Klein's wordplay and quirky humor characterize her work for younger readers, such as the picture book *The Giraffe in Pepperell Street* (1978), **illustrated** by Jill Tumblin, and *Birk the Berserker* (1987), illustrated by Allison Lester, which features a timid Viking and humorously challenges stereotypes. Klein has won most of the major Australian literary **awards**, as well as the Australian Human Rights Award for Literature in 1989 for *Came Back to Show You I Could Fly* (1989), about two young outsider friends, 11 and 20 years old respectively, and the issue of drug dependency.

KONIGSBURG, E. L. (ELAINE LOBL) (1930–). U.S. author and **illustrator**. Konigsburg is the only writer to have won the **Newbery Medal** and the Newbery Honor Book citation in the same year with her first and second novels. The Newbery winner *From the Mixed-Up Files of Mrs. Basil E. Frankweiler* (1967) is about siblings who run away from home, stay at the Metropolitan Museum of Art in New York, and become fascinated with the question of the origin of a statue previously owned by the Mrs. Frankweiler of the title. *Jennifer, Hecate, Macbeth, William McKinley, and Me, Elizabeth* (1967), the Honor book, is the story of an empowering friendship between two outsiders, the lonely narrator and the unconventional Jennifer, who claims that she is a **witch**. Characteristics common to many of Konigsburg's novels are evident here: they are thought-provoking stories primarily interested in characters—especially articulate and highly intelligent suburban children in search of their identity—and their development. "Frankweiler" has remained her most famous book, but other notable titles include *(George)* (1970), a challenging account of a talented young schizophrenic, and the two **historical novels** *A Proud Taste for Scarlet and Miniver* (1973), about Eleanor of Aquitaine, and *The Second Mrs. Giaconda* (1975), about Leonardo da Vinci. Twenty-nine years after winning her first Newbery Medal, Konigsburg was awarded it once again for *The View from Saturday* (1996), the story of four 6th-grade children who are chosen to compete in an academic bowl, told in alternating chapters of third-person omniscient narrative and first-person narratives by each of the characters.

KORCZAK, JANUSZ (1878–1942). Pseudonym of Henryk Goldszmit, Polish-Jewish writer and educator. He was closely associated with two orphanages in Warsaw from 1912 on, one for Jewish and one for Christian children, in which he developed and applied his progressive educational ideas. When the Nazis took the Jewish children to the Treblinka death camp in 1942, Korczak refused offers of sanctuary and went with them. His most famous book for children, *Król Maciuś Pierwszy* (1923; *King Matt the First*, 1986; in adapted form as *Matthew, the Young King*, 1945) has been **translated** into many languages. It is a childhood utopia but without a happy ending. Upon the death of his father, six-year-old Matt becomes king of a fictional kingdom. Good and naive, he wants to bring about the happiness of his people and introduce reforms, and he sets up a children's parliament. In one episode adults and children trade places, but while the adults have fun at school the children bring total chaos to the country with breakdowns in law and order, communications and transport, and industry. A forged letter ostensibly leads the neighboring country to declare war, and he is sentenced to exile on a desert island. In the end Matt, who has traveled throughout the world gathering experience and making numerous friends in the process, is deposed because, as the novel suggests, a child's idealism alone is not sufficient qualification to rule a country or to be able to cope with adult corruption and betrayal.

KREIDOLF, ERNST (1863–1956). Swiss artist, poet, and **illustrator** famous for his original **picture books** with stories about **anthropomorphic** plants and animals. Influenced by Art Nouveau, his most successful books, which have remained popular, are *Die Blumenmärchen* (1898; *Flower Fairy Tales*, 1979) and *Der Traumgarten* (1912; *Dream Garden*, 1979). His books communicate a sense of wonder about nature, with lots of flowers, elves, and other creatures of the woodlands portrayed in a spare and fantastic style. Kreidolf's approach to illustration and his careful attention to book production showed how the quality of pictures could be improved, and had a significant effect on the development of 20th-century picture books.

KRÜSS, JAMES (1926–1997). German storyteller, poet, author, anthologizer, and **translator**. Encouraged by **Erich Kästner** in the late 1940s to write for children, Krüss went on to become one of the most important postwar German authors. Like Kästner, he believed that children's books could change the world. In all he authored more than 80 **picture books**, several of them **illustrated** versions of his poems; some 40 predominantly prose works; and 2 major collections of poems. He also produced 4 important anthologies of **poetry**, including the first German anthology of **nonsense** poems for children, *Seifenblasen zu verkaufen* [Bubbles for Sale] (1972), many of which he translated himself. In 1959, he published *Mein Urgroß-vater und ich* (*My Great-Grandfather and I*, 1962), which looks back to his childhood spent on the island of Helgoland and presents, with great affection and in a form that suited his imagination and love of wordplay, a series of connected short stories, tall tales, and poems. It won the German state **prize** for children's literature, the Deutsche Jugendbuchpreis. *Tim Thaler oder das verkaufte Lachen* [Tim Thaler, or The Traded Laughter] (1962), which was later filmed, tells of a boy who sells his laughter to a sinister baron, who is in fact the devil, in exchange for winning all bets. As an author who had experienced World War II, Krüss wrote books that stressed the need for peace, freedom, and humanity, as in the utopian *Die glücklichen Inseln hinter dem Winde* (1958; *The Happy Islands behind the Winds*, 1966). He himself translated from 12 different languages, and his books have been translated into more than 30. Krüss received the **Hans Christian Andersen Award** in 1968.

– L –

LA FONTAINE, JEAN DE (1621–1695). *See* FABLES.

LAGERLÖF, SELMA (1858–1940). Swedish author and first woman to win the Nobel Prize in Literature. Her most famous book, and the only one she wrote for children, is *Nils Holgerssons underbara resa genom Sverige* (1906–1907; *The Wonderful Adventures of Nils*, 1907). Commissioned from the Swedish national teachers' association as a geography reader for schools, it is a work of fiction whose frame story involves a naughty boy reduced to the size of a dwarf. He undertakes journeys with wild geese, during which he must change for the better in order to return to his normal size. The episodes that make up his adventures are based on well-known **fairy tales** and incorporate the history, geography, and folklore of Sweden as well as thoughts on contemporary social issues such as industrialization, women's rights, and ecology.

LANG, ANDREW (1844–1912). Scottish poet, folklorist, translator, and editor of collections of fairy stories for children. Lang is best known for the series of 12 "colored" fairy books that began with *The Blue Fairy Book* (1889)—an anthology of French **fairy tales**, tales from ***The Arabian Nights***, Greek **myths**, and English **chapbook** tales—and ended with *The Lilac Fairy Book* (1910). Lang neither wrote the stories himself nor collected them from the oral tradition, but selected them from a wide range of sources, arranged for their **adaptation** and **translation**, and wrote the prefaces. His wife, Leonora Blanche Alleyne, was a major collaborator who did most of the retellings from the third book on. Lang also issued *The Arabian Nights Entertainments* (1898) in an edition especially for children.

LAWRENCE, JACOB (1917–2000). U.S. painter famous for his narrative paintings of African American historical figures. Influenced by the socialist-realist movement of the 1930s and by African art, Lawrence's work is known for its bold use of color, striking patterns, flat shapes, and sophisticated composition. Using material from his 30-paneled *Harriet Tubman Series* (1939–1940), he wrote a book for children, *Harriet and the Promised Land* (1968), with **illustrations** and rhymes documenting Tubman's Underground Railroad network of activists who helped slaves escape from the South. Excerpts from other series were used in children's books such as *John Brown: One Man against Slavery* (1993), with a text by Gwen Averett. *See also* BIOGRAPHY.

LAWSON, ROBERT (1892–1957). U.S. author and **illustrator**. His friend **Munro Leaf** wrote *The Story of Ferdinand* (1936) for Lawson to illustrate in black and white, a pacifist **fable** about a bull that has been bred to fight in the bullring but prefers to smell flowers. It went on to become an international classic. *Ben and Me: An Astonishing Life of Benjamin Franklin by His Good Mouse Amos* (1939) was the first of a series of humorous **biographies** written from the perspective of a companion animal. Lawson is one of the few people to have won both the **Newbery Medal** and the **Caldecott Medal.** He won the Newbery for *Rabbit Hill* (1944), a utopian **animal fantasy**, and the Caldecott for *They Were Strong and Good* (1940), a **picture-book** account of his family history.

LE GUIN, URSULA (1929–). U.S. author of **fantasy** and **science-fiction** novels for adults and children who has also written poetry and essays. Approximately one-third of her 40 books of fiction have been for young adults and children. In her most famous work of fantasy, the prizewinning Earthsea sextet (1968–2001), Le Guin responded to the secondary world in **J. R. R. Tolkien**'s Lord of the Rings trilogy (1954–1955) by creating one of her own. In a vast archipelago complete with history, languages, **myths**, and **legends** informed by her background in anthropology and Jungian psychology, she explores ideas about the creation of the universe. The sextet developed as two trilogies; the first, published between 1968 and 1972, features young adults as the main protagonists and is considered children's or young-adult fantasy. The second, published between 1990 and 2001, is a type of revision of her earlier fantasy resulting from her growing awareness of feminism and the relationship between **gender** and power. Le Guin has also written a highly regarded realistic novel for young adults, *Very Far Away from Anywhere Else* (1976). In Le Guin's books for children, we find creative use of **anthropomorphism**; among the most popular are her Catwings books (1988–1999) about six kittens, five of whom are winged.

LEAF, MUNRO (1905–1976). U.S. writer and **illustrator** best known for *The Story of Ferdinand* (1936) with illustrations by **Robert Lawson**, a pacifist **fable** about a bull that has been bred to fight in the bullring but prefers to smell flowers. Released at the outbreak of the Spanish Civil War, it became a right-wing target and was banned in many countries, including Nazi Germany, because of its pacifist message. It was made into an animated feature film by **Walt Disney** and was subsequently the object of corresponding merchandising materials. Today, it is a classic of modern children's literature.

LEAR, EDWARD (1812–1888). British artist, traveler, and **nonsense** poet. The second youngest of 21 children, Lear was educated at home but was obliged to start earning his living as an artist at the age of 15. He was commissioned to make drawings of the parrots in the London Zoo, and was engaged as an artist by the future Earl of Derby, who kept a menagerie at Knowsley Hall. There Lear came across one of the first collections of limericks published in English, *Anecdotes and Adventures of Fifteen Gentlemen* (1821), which inspired him to compose some with accompanying drawings, to entertain the grandchildren of his patron. Their publication in 1846, under the title *A Book of Nonsense* and the pseudonym Derry Down Derry, ultimately established Lear as one of the founding fathers of literary nonsense. His name first appeared on the enlarged third edition published in 1861.

Lear was not the inventor of this short, humorous verse form, but he succeeded in popularizing it. His limericks are carefully crafted in their use of rhyme and meter; they brim with eccentric behavior, celebrate the inconsequential, and often present arbitrary and violent behavior. They are, for the most part, nonsensical and devoid of any punch line. In the accompanying drawings, Lear deliberately distorts the human figure, for instance by putting huge birdlike heads on tiny bodies. *A Book of Nonsense* saw 19 editions during Lear's lifetime, and he published three further collections of nonsense: *Nonsense Songs* (1871); *More Nonsense* (1872); and *Laughable Lyrics* (1877), which contains 12 nonsense songs (**poems**), two stories, a number of nonsense **ABCs**, a nonsense botany, and nonsense recipes. One of his most famous poems is *The Owl and the Pussycat.* In his later, longer poems we find a change in tone to a more a melancholy and nostalgic key. Lear's poems and stories are characterized throughout by verbal creativity; he delights in the sound of his invented words. Among the whimsical neologisms are the names of characters and places, such as the "Great Gromboolian Plain," and adjectives like "scroobius."

LEE, TANITH (1947–). British author of more than 55 novels and almost 200 short stories for adults and for children in the **science-fiction**, **horror**, and **fantasy** genres. Her first books for younger readers were the novel *Dragon Hoard* (1971), about a shape-changing prince; a collection of **feminist** fairy tales, *Princess Hynchatti, and Some Other Surprises* (1972); and a **picture book**, *Animal Castle* (1972). Her unicorn series, comprising *Black Unicorn* (1991), *Gold Unicorn* (1994), and *Red Unicorn* (1997), mixes science fiction with gothic **folktale** elements. The *Claidi Journals* series, *Wolf Tower* (2000), *Wolf Star* (2000), *Wolf Queen* (2001), and *Wolf Wing* (2002), maps the journey of the protagonist Claidi Wolf from slavery to freedom in the form of journal entries, starting when she is 16.

LEESON, ROBERT (1928–). British critic and author of more than 70 books in a wide range of genres, from **historical fiction** and **school stories** to **science fiction**. Many of them reflect his thoughts about poverty, class, sexism, and **racism**, as well as his firm belief, stated in his critical writing, in books as a means of liberation and empowerment of readers. His best-known titles are the Grange Hill school stories, set in a comprehensive school and based on the BBC television series. Leeson responds to literary classics in innovative ways; *Silver's Revenge* (1978) is a humorous and subversive sequel to **Robert Louis Stevenson**'s *Treasure Island*, and *Candy for the King* (1983), echoing Voltaire's *Candide*, is about an innocent giant whose nobility is not recognized by the world. Leeson's novels featuring young people from disadvantaged backgrounds are seen as a central achievement, especially the It's My Life trilogy (1980–1990), about a 16-year-old girl suddenly deserted by her mother, and *Red White and Blue* (1995), about an adolescent boy trying to come to terms with a new school and his father's missing-in-action status in the Falklands War. Leeson has also written acclaimed critical studies, including *Reading and Righting*, published in 1985; in the same year he received the Eleanor Farjeon **Award** for his services to children's literature.

LEGENDS. *See* MYTHS AND LEGENDS.

L'ENGLE, MADELEINE (1918–2007). U.S. author of more than 60 novels, plays, **poems**, and religious works for adults and children. Her writing for young adults includes espionage thrillers and what can be roughly classified as domestic fiction, such as the series about the fabulously gifted Austin family. Her most famous work for this age group is *A Wrinkle in Time* (1962), an intellectually challenging

fantasy and winner of the **Newbery Medal**, in which Meg Murry, the adolescent female protagonist, seeks her missing physicist father, discovering her own individuality in the process. It combines fantasy, science (the theories of Albert Einstein and Max Planck), and theology as the protagonists travel through the fourth dimension to confront the evil entity who rules the planet. The two families in this novel, the Murrys and the O'Keefes, feature in eight different novels by L'Engle. The first five were *A Wrinkle in Time*; *A Wind in the Door* (1973), which uses cellular biology to explore the universe; *A Swiftly Tilting Planet* (1978), featuring the threat of nuclear war; *Many Waters* (1986); and *An Acceptable Time* (1989). These books involve Meg, her young brother, and their friend Calvin O'Keefe trying to save the world from evil forces. Each involves time travel, and together they constitute what is known as The Time Quintet. L'Engle received the **American Library Association**'s **(ALA)** Margaret A. Edwards Lifetime Achievement **Award** in 1998, and a National Humanities Medal in 2004.

LENSKI, LOIS (1893–1974). U.S. author and **illustrator** of children's books in a variety of genres, including **picture books**, **information books**, and **historical fiction**. She illustrated some 150 books and wrote the text for around 100. She is known for her series of realistic accounts of geographically and culturally diverse lives of children across the United States, incorporating some 17 titles. These include her most famous novel, *Strawberry Girl* (1945), the **Newbery Medal**–winning story of migrant laborers in Florida; *Blue Ridge Billy* (1946); and *Prairie School* (1951). For younger readers, Lenski wrote the Roundabout America series that includes titles such as *We Live by the River* (1956) and *We Live in the Country* (1960).

LEPMAN, JELLA (1891–1970). Daughter of a German-Jewish factory owner, who worked as a journalist and published children's books before fleeing the Nazi regime. She immigrated to England in 1936 and returned to Germany in 1945 as advisor for women's and youth affairs in the American "Re-Education" program. In 1946, Lepman turned to 20 nations, most of which had been at war with Germany only a year before, asking for donations to set up an international exhibition of children's literature in Munich. In her autobiography, *Die Kinderbuchbrücke* (1964; *A Bridge of Children's Books*, 1969), she recounts how her appeal ran: "Bit by bit . . . let us set this upside down world right again by starting with the children. They will show the grown-ups the way to go." The exhibition formed the basis of the **International Youth Library (IYL)**, which Lepman founded in 1946. In her work at the IYL, Lepman put the ideal of international understanding through children's literature into practice through a range of activities, and she went on to cofound the **International Board on Books for Young People (IBBY)** in 1953.

LESTER, JULIUS (1939–). U.S. poet, author of fiction and **nonfiction**, professor of Judaic studies, civil-rights activist, and folk musician. Lester's reputation as a teller of African American history was established by his collection of slave narratives *To Be a Slave* (1968). He has compiled several collections of **folktales** that include retellings of the Uncle Remus stories, and he also retold ***Little Black Sambo*** as *Sam and the Tigers* (1996), **illustrated** by **Jerry Pinkney**. It retains and heightens the humor of the original, gives it a new Southern black setting, and reduces many of the perceived **racist** and stereotypical elements of the original.

LEWIS, C. S. (CLIVE STAPLES) (1898–1963). Irish academic, medievalist, essayist, Christian apologist, and author of the **fantasy** classic Chronicles of Narnia. Born and raised in Belfast, Lewis, known to his friends as Jack, studied and spent almost 30 years as a fellow at Oxford University, moving later to Cambridge University, where he was the first professor of medieval and Renaissance English. Along with his close friend **J. R. R. Tolkien** and others, he was a member of the famous all-male Oxford literary discussion group the Inklings, which encouraged the writing of fantasy. The Chronicles of Narnia is a series of seven fantasy novels: *The Lion, the Witch and the Wardrobe* (1950), *Prince Kaspian: The Return to Narnia* (1951), *The Voyage of the Dawn Treader* (1952), *The Silver Chair* (1953), *The Horse and His Boy* (1954), *The Magician's Nephew* (1955), and *The Last Battle* (1956). In it, children are transported from their everyday world to the magic kingdom of Narnia with its talking **animals**, where they help the lion Aslan and play a key role in the battle between good and evil. The series is rooted in Greek and Roman mythology, Irish **fairy tales**, and, especially, Christian ideas. It has sold some 120 million copies in more than 40 languages, and has been adapted several times for radio, television, stage, and film. The most recent film versions of the first two volumes were released by **Walt Disney** Pictures in 2005 and 2008.

LIBRARY ASSOCIATION (LA). Professional body founded in 1877 that represented those working in the library and information services in Great Britain. The LA established both the **Caldecott Medal** and the **Kate Greenaway Medal**. It was merged with the Institute of Information Scientists in 2002 to create the **Chartered Institute of Library and Information Professionals (CILIP)**.

LINDGREN, ASTRID (1907–2002). Swedish author and editor and one of the most acclaimed European authors of the 20th century. Lindgren grew up in a small rural village in Småland, southern Sweden, and many of her books are based on her family and childhood memories, most famously those set in the idyllic universe of Bullerbyn (in English translation, Noisy Village). She worked as a journalist and secretary before her first book, a girl's novel *Britt-Mari Lättar Sitt Hjärta* [Britt-Mari Opens Her Heart] (1944), won second prize in a competition run by the newly founded publishing house Rabén & Sjögren (for whom she later worked as an editor from 1947 to 1970). She won first prize in the same competition the following year, with a story first told to her daughter that went on to become one of the most widely read and popular children's **fantasies**, *Pippi Långstrump* (1945; *Pippi Longstocking*, 1950). Pippi Longstocking, a self-assured, red-headed, nine-year-old **orphan** of supernatural strength, has a house and wealth of her own, is not subject to any adult supervision or rules, and lives and behaves exactly as she chooses. She refuses to be socialized and does not want to grow up.

This anarchic protagonist, who fulfills every child's dream of freedom, was condemned by some contemporary commentators as a bad example for children; the novel is now acknowledged as one of the first to truly celebrate childhood autonomy. An irreverent attitude toward adult authority is a general characteristic of Lindgren's work. The further adventures of Pippi and her two friends are told in *Pippi Långstrump Går Ombord* (1946; *Pippi Goes on Board*, 1957) and *Pippi Långstrump I Söderhavet* (1948; *Pippi in the South Seas,* 1957), and they feature in a number of original **picture books**.

Lindgren published more than 100 books in a range of genres—photo-documentary books about children's lives in different countries; bad-boy stories in the Emil series; bad-girl stories about *Madicken* (English Meg or Mardie); and **detective stories**, starting with *Mästardetektiven Kalle Blomqvist* (1946; *Bill Bergson, Master Detective*, 1952)—but she is particularly acclaimed for her fantasy novels. Apart from the Pippi Longstocking novels, these include the female coming-of-age story *Ronja Rövardotter* (1981; *Ronia, the Robber's Daughter*, 1983) and the psychodramas *Mio, min Mio* (1954; *Mio, My Son,* 1956) and *Bröderna Lejonhjärta* (1973; *The Brothers Lionheart,* 1975), each written in first-person narrative perspective with an open ending, both unusual features in children's fantasy. *The Brothers Lionheart*, a serious tale about death and reincarnation, raised considerable controversy because it contradicts traditional religious teachings and purportedly celebrates suicide.

Lindgren was an active and public supporter of children's rights and animal rights, and she received the Alternative Nobel Prize in 1993 for "her commitment to justice, non-violence, and understanding of minorities as well as her love and caring for nature." She is the most prominent Swedish children's author of the 20th century and is credited with changing the face of Swedish children's literature and its status in society. Her books bore a significant influence on children's literature in other countries. They have been **translated** into more than 80 languages, have sold some 150 million copies worldwide, and have been made into film, television, and radio versions both in Sweden and in other countries. Lindgren won numerous awards, including the **Hans Christian Andersen Award** in 1958, and, in her honor, the Swedish government established the **Astrid Lindgren Memorial Award** in 2002.

LINDSAY, NORMAN (1879–1969). Australian author and **illustrator** who, inspired by a passage in **Lewis Carroll**'s *Through the Looking-Glass, and What Alice Found There* (1871), wrote his famous children's book *The Magic Pudding: Being the Adventures of Bunyip Bluegum and His Friends Bill Barnacle and Sam Sawnoff* (1918). The story features the adventures of the sailor Bill Barnacle, the koala Bunyip Bluegum, and the penguin Sam Sawnoff, who own a walking, talking pudding that never runs out, and their struggles against two thieves, a wombat and a possum. The episodes during which the parties move about Australia are interspersed with many short songs. *The Magic Pudding* established a new **nonsense** tradition in Australia and is considered one of the classics of Australian children's literature. Lindsay, who started his career as a cartoonist, illustrated the book himself with numerous black-and-white drawings.

LINGARD, JOAN (1932–). British novelist who was born in Edinburgh and who lived in Belfast from age 2 to age 18. Those formative years are responsible for her Kevin and Sadie quintet of novels about Northern Ireland—*The Twelfth Day of July* (1970), *Across the Barricades* (1972), *Into Exile* (1973), *A Proper Place* (1975), and *Hostages to Fortune* (1976)—which explore Catholic-Protestant strife by means of the relationship between children across the religious divide. The young couple Kevin and Sadie are forced, by the time of the third novel in the series, to leave Belfast and live in exile. Another remarkable Northern Irish novel is *The File on Fraulein Berg* (1980), about three Belfast schoolgirls who, in 1944, persecute their new German teacher, failing to realize that, rather than representing the enemy whom Great Britain is currently fighting in World War II, the woman is a Jewish refugee whose family has been murdered in the German concentration camps. Lingard is committed to writing about political and social issues for children, and many of her books touch on the theme of displacement. These include many set on mainland Europe, such as *Tug of War* (1989) and *Night Fires* (1993), inspired by the forced relocation of her husband's family from Latvia to Canada during World War II. Lingard's oeuvre also includes **historical novels** set in Scotland, as well as more lighthearted contemporary teenage novels. She was appointed MBE for services to literature in 1998.

LINKLATER, ERIK (1899–1974). Scottish author of literature for adults who wrote two **fantasies** for children. *The Wind on the Moon* (1944), which won the **Carnegie Medal**, is about two sisters who magically transform themselves into kangaroos to help a number of animals and people escape captivity. It culminates in the rescue of their father, imprisoned in a dungeon in Bombardy by Hitlerian dictator Count Hulagy Boot. The book is characterized by wild inventiveness, humor, wordplay, and arbitrary turns of plot, which reflect its origin in stories told to Linklater's daughters. His second children's fantasy, *The Pirates in the Deep Green Sea* (1949), features two brothers involved in a struggle between good sailors and bad pirates. In both fantasies children save the world from evil; and, written during World War II and the Cold War respectively, they feature elements of topical political satire in the guise of adventure.

LIONNI, LEO (1910–1999). Dutch-born cosmopolitan artist and **illustrator** who lived in Italy during the 1930s as a respected painter; in the United States from 1939–1960, where he worked in advertising; and from 1960 on in Italy again, where he began his career as a children's book author and illustrator. Lionni produced some 40 books for children that work with different styles and techniques such as collage, textile and paper patterns, marbling, and vibrant colors, and these reveal his sense of design, honed in his years of experience as a professional graphic artist. His first book for children, *Little Blue and Little Yellow* (1959), tells a story by using abstract shapes and colors only; it is one of very few children's books to do so, and an exception in Lionni's oeuvre. His **fables** usually feature **animal** characters, very often mice; and some of these are artists, like *Frederick* (1967), his best known. His books are didactic to varying degrees, and recurring themes are outsiders and their ultimately beneficial differences; finding one's place in the world; living in harmony with nature; and strength in unity. This last theme is central to *Swimmy* (1963), the story of a small, black outsider fish who convinces his red fish siblings to join forces to simulate a much larger animal, to save themselves from a predator. *Swimmy* won the Golden Apple at the first **Biennial of Illustrations Bratislava (BIB)**, and it was the first of four **Caldecott** Honor books by Lionni; the other three were *Inch by Inch* (1960), *Frederick* (1967), and *Alexander and the Wind-Up Mouse* (1969). Lionni was the recipient of the 1984 American Institute of Graphic Arts Gold Medal.

LITTLE BLACK SAMBO. *See* BANNERMAN, HELEN.

A LITTLE PRINCESS. *See* BURNETT, FRANCES HODGSON.

LITTLE WOMEN. *See* ALCOTT, LOUISA MAY.

LIVELY, PENELOPE (1933–). British author of fiction who was born in Cairo and spent her childhood there, before being sent to boarding school in England at the age of 12. Lively is a prolific and popular author of fiction for both adults and children who enjoys great critical acclaim in both fields. She first achieved success with her children's fiction, winning the **Carnegie Medal** for *The Ghost of Thomas Kempe* (1973), in which a 300-year-old sorcerer's ghost haunts the 11-year-old protagonist, and the Whitbread Children's Book **Award** for *A Stitch in Time* (1976). Both of these, as indeed most of her novels for both audiences, are characterized by an interest in the history of a particular location—building or landscape—the passage of time, the power of memory, and the impact of the past upon the present. She was awarded the Booker Prize for her adult novel *Moon Tiger* (1987) and has been shortlisted a further three times. A Fellow of the Royal Society of Literature, Lively was appointed CBE in 2001.

LOBEL, ANITA (1934–). Polish-born U.S. **illustrator** and maker of **picture books** whose style of illustration, with its use of bright colors and floral patterns, is influenced by the art of her native country. After studying art at the Pratt Institute, where she met and married fellow student **Arnold Lobel**, she initially worked in the area of fabric design. Her first picture book, *Sven's Bridge*, was published in 1965; since then she has illustrated nearly 40 books, many of them also written by her. She collaborated with her husband on four books—he provided the text and she the illustrations—including the acclaimed **alphabet book** *On Market Street* (1981). She has produced a series of alphabet books on such different themes as flower paintings, animal antics, and (in *Away from Home*, 1994) architecture and travel.

LOBEL, ARNOLD (1933–1987). U.S. author and **illustrator** of **poetry**, fiction, and **nonfiction**. He is known for his books in the I Can Read series for beginner readers, both written and illustrated by him, which include the humorous and touching *Frog and Toad* stories. He studied art at the Pratt Institute, where he met his wife **Anita Lobel**.

Lobel was happy to acknowledge the influence of **Edward Lear** on his work, and it is nowhere more evident than in *The Book of Pigericks: Pig Limericks* (1983), **nonsense** verses and illustrations about pigs that even include an illustrated pig version of Lobel himself. He wrote or illustrated more than 100 children's books during his career and received the **Caldecott Medal** for *Fables* (1980), an original collection of modern **fables** on the virtues and foibles of society, with colorful and exuberant drawings. Lobel was praised for his illustrations for *The Random House Book of Poetry for Children* (1983) and *The Random House Book of Mother Goose* (1986). He collaborated with his wife on four books, including the acclaimed **alphabet book** *On Market Street* (1981).

LOCKE, JOHN (1632–1704). English philosopher, one of the most influential thinkers of the Enlightenment, and author of *Some Thoughts concerning Education* (1693), a founding text of modern education. Locke formulated the notion that the mind of a young child was similar to a blank slate (tabula rasa) just waiting to be written upon. He argued against set curricula and corporal punishment, and for treating children (mainly boys) in a humane and liberal manner. Believing in the effectiveness of learning through play, he sought to combine instruction with amusement. *See also* ILLUSTRATIONS.

LOFTING, HUGH (1886–1947). British author and civil engineer who spent much of his adult life in the United States. He is famous as the creator of the fictional veterinarian Doctor Dolittle, who first appeared in letters he wrote to his children while in Flanders during World War I. The series, starting with *The Story of Dr. Dolittle* (1920), encompasses 13 books, 3 of them published posthumously, and tells the adventures of the gentle animal doctor who can talk to **animals** and who sees each one as equal to human beings. **Illustrated** by Lofting with pen-and-ink drawings, the books blend the **fantastic** with the everyday, showing the doctor sharing his household in Puddleby-on-the-Marsh with the parrot Polynesia, who teaches Dolittle animal languages; the duck housekeeper, Dab-Dab; a pig named Gub-Gub; Chee-Chee the chimp; and Jip the dog. Tommy Stubbins, a boy from the village who becomes the doctor's assistant, narrates several of the stories. A constant worry is finding enough money to run the motley household, and this motivates the search for all sorts of strange and wonderful solutions. The second book in the series, *The Voyages of Doctor Dolittle* (1922), won the **Newbery Medal**.

In recent times, the books have been accused of **racism**, specifically for a scene in which a black prince longs for a white face, and Lofting's treatment of native peoples is seen as **ethnocentric**. (Later editions of some of the books have removed illustrations and passages regarded as offensive.) Despite such concerns, many critics emphasize the positive values underlining the series, such as kindness to humans and animals, and antimaterialism. A *Doctor Dolittle* film musical in 1967 starred Rex Harrison in the title role, and Eddie Murphy played Doctor Dolittle in two films in 1998 and 2001.

LONGFELLOW, HENRY WADSWORTH (1807–1882). U.S. **poet** whose narrative poems, especially on American historical themes, have been popular with children and are frequently anthologized for use in schools. These include "Paul Revere's Ride" (1863) and "The Wreck of the Hesperus" (1841). His epic poem *The Song of Hiawatha* (1855), based on traditional Ojibwa stories and described by Longfellow himself as his Indian edda, has been published in numerous illustrated editions and retellings.

LORENZINI, CARLO. *See* COLLODI, CARLO.

LOVELACE, MAUD HART (1892–1980). U.S. author best known for her popular Betsy-Tacy series set in the fictional town of Deep Valley, Minnesota, and initially told to her daughter about her own childhood. The first book in the series was published in 1940, and the 10th and last, *Betsy's Wedding*, in 1955, after Lovelace had followed Betsy's girlhood, school, and high-school adventures from the age of 5 to marriage.

LOWRY, LOIS (1937–). U.S. author of children's fiction in a variety of genres. Her first novel, the semiautobiographical *A Summer to Die* (1977) about the relationship between two sisters after one is diagnosed with cancer, launched her career as a writer for children and young adults. A series of nine popular humorous novels followed, based on a precocious and headstrong 10-year-old Bostonian, starting with *Anastasia Krupnik* (1979) and concluding with *Anastasia Absolutely* (1995). Anastasia's younger brother Sam also features as a protagonist in four comic novels for younger readers, beginning with *All About Sam* (1988). Her most critically acclaimed novels are *Rabble Starkey* (1987), a Boston Globe–Horn Book **Award** winner about the daughter of a single mother in rural Virginia and their relationship with the wealthy family for whom the mother works; the **Newbery Medal**–winning *Number the Stars* (1989), set in Nazi-occupied Denmark when ordinary citizens tried to smuggle Jews out of the country; and *The Giver* (1993), the first of a trilogy of futuristic dystopian novels, for which Lowry won her second Newbery Medal. In it, 12-year-old Jonas is selected to bear all the memories of pain and pleasure of his seemingly utopian community that has renounced these in order to achieve a society without hunger, prejudice, or insecurity. However, their world is also free of choice, love, joy, and sorrow. In order to restore humanity and individuality, Jonas decides to flee, unleashing all of the memories back into the community. The controversial themes of *The Giver* and its dystopian view of a future society also feature in the two subsequent novels in the trilogy, *Gathering Blue* (2000) and *Messenger* (2004). These three books are among the most thought-provoking speculative novels for young adults.

LULLABY. A song or chant usually sung to children or babies to lull them to sleep. Common to all cultures, they form an ancient body of the earliest folk **poetry** and song. While many lullabies are comforting for caregiver and infant, others, such as the well-known "Hush-a-Bye, Baby, on the Tree Top," may, despite their soothing melodies and rhythms, nonetheless convey through the words meanings that are anything but reassuring, possibly arising from parental fears. Most lullabies known to modern children feature in collections of **nursery rhymes**. The composed lullaby offers a particular challenge for poets; famous examples can be found in collections from **Ann and Jane Taylor**'s *Original Poems for Infant Minds* (1804) to **James Berry**'s *When I Dance* (1988).

LYNCH, P. J. (PATRICK JAMES) (1962–). Irish **illustrator** and **picture-book** artist who, as a student, collaborated with **Alan Garner** on *A Bag of Moonshine* (1986), which won him the first of many **awards**. Working mainly in watercolor and gouache, Lynch has a painterly style that is distinguished by its factual detail, the perspectives from which he chooses to illustrate a theme, and his attention to effects of light. He meticulously researches each of his books; for *East o' the Sun and West o' the Moon* (1991), a Norwegian **folktale**, he visited Norway to study the architecture, fishing boats, and carvings. Lynch has illustrated **fantasy** and **fairy tales**, including different tales by **Hans Christian Andersen**; *Catkin* (1994), Antonia Barber's tale of a child taken by the Little People; and Irish **myths** and **legends** in Marie Heaney's *The Names upon the Harp* (2000). He has also illustrated texts in the realistic mode, usually set in the historical past, which suits Lynch's traditional style. These include *The Christmas Miracle of Jonathan Toomey* (1995), by Susan Wojciechowski, which shows how the heart of an embittered carpenter is softened by a young widow and her son. It won the **Kate Greenaway Medal**, an accolade again received by Lynch for *When Jessie Came across the Sea* (1997). Written by Amy Hest, it traces the fate of a young Jewish girl who migrates from Eastern Europe to the United States in the early years of the 20th century.

LYNCH, PATRICIA (1894–1972). Irish novelist and author of some 50 books for children, including collections of short stories and retellings of Irish **legends**. From the 1930s to the 1960s, Lynch was arguably Ireland's best-known and most popular children's writer, and she enjoyed a considerable international reception. Her best-known books are *The Turf-Cutter's Donkey* (1934) and *Brogeen Follows the Magic Tune* (1952), both of which are characterized by an emphasis on transformational magic. Reality in much of Lynch's writing is juxtaposed with supernatural events resonant of Irish **myths** and **folktales**. Lynch also wrote **historical fiction** such as *Fiddler's Quest* (1941), which combines the quest motif with a theme related to Irish nationalism, and predominantly realistic **adventure stories**, such as *The Bookshop on the Quay* (1956).

– M –

MAAR, PAUL (1937–). German author, **illustrator**, and playwright who has written more than 40 books in a broad spectrum of genres including **easy readers**, **picture books**, **fantasy**, and young adult novels (often illustrated by himself), as well as plays and screenplays. He is currently the most frequently performed children's playwright in theaters in German-speaking countries. Among his plays translated into English is *Kikerikiste* (1972; *Noodle Doodle Box*, 1979), an absurdist piece centered on the relationship between two clownish characters. His most famous creation in Germany is the anarchic, carnivalistic figure Sams from the novel *Eine Woche voller Samstage* [A Week of Satur-Days] (1973), who owes his existence to (virtually untranslatable) wordplay on the German names of the days of the week. Playful use of language dominates in Maar's work, and he enjoys both critical acclaim and widespread popularity. He has received several national and international **prizes**, and his books have been **translated** into more than 20 languages, although very few have been published in English. In 1998, Maar was awarded the German Order of Merit (Bundesverdienstkreuz) for his life's work.

MACAULAY, DAVID (1946–). English-born U.S. author and **illustrator** whose family immigrated to the United States when he was 11. Macaulay studied architecture, and many of his successful books have been on architectural themes, starting with *Cathedral: The Story of Its Construction* (1973), an **information book** whose black pen-and-ink illustrations on large white pages show the process of building, as well as the cultural and historical contexts in which the cathedral came to be. Macaulay used the same successful approach in *City: A Story of Roman Planning and Construction* (1974), *Pyramid* (1975), *Mill* (1983), *Mosque* (2003), and other titles. In a different, at times humorous, vein is the monumental *The Way Things Work: From Levers to Laser, Cars to Computers; A Visual Guide to the World of Machines* (1988), which, in color, and with a woolly mammoth leading readers through the technology, translates concepts and information to the printed page. Ten years later Macaulay revised and expanded the book to include explanations of digital technology in *The New Way Things Work* (1998). His fictional **picture books** incorporate satire and humor and frequently refuse to follow a linear narrative. *Black and White* (1990), a **Caldecott Medal** winner, defies picture-book conventions by simultaneously telling four tales that do not necessarily take place at the same moment in time, and may not even be one story.

MacDONALD, GEORGE (1824–1905). Scottish author and Congregationalist minister, and one of the most important Victorian authors of original fairy stories and **fantasies**. His three major novels for children, *At the Back of the North Wind* (1871), *The Princess and the Goblin* (1872), and *The Princess and Curdie* (1883), were published when he was in his late forties. MacDonald had a clear moral agenda, and his enigmatic tales contain intertextual references to authors from Dante to the German Romantic author Novalis. In his essay "The Fantastic Imagination" (1893), he compares the **fairy tale** to music: with form but no definite meaning, its task is to awaken readers' imaginations rather than telling them what to think. MacDonald's writings are characterized by a symbolic richness and have often been described as mystical and allegorical, although it is not always clear how they are to be read. His use of fantasy as a medium for exploring the human condition influenced such writers as **J. R. R. Tolkien**, **C. S. Lewis**, and **Madeleine L'Engle**. The MacDonald family was responsible for encouraging **Lewis Carroll** to publish *Alice's Adventures in Wonderland.*

MacDONALD, GOLDEN. *See* BROWN, MARGARET WISE.

MACHADO, ANA MARIA (1941–). Brazilian painter, scholar, and author of more than 100 books for children and adults. She has received numerous literary honors, including the **Hans Christian Andersen Award** in 2000. Though they are hugely popular in Brazil and throughout Latin America, few of Machado's books have been **translated** into English. Among her books available in English are *How the Leopard Got His Spots: A Brazilian Folktale* (1984); *Exploration into Latin America* (2001), a history for young people; and *Me in the Middle* (2002; Brazilian original *Bisa Bea Bisa Bel*, 1982), about a 10-year-old girl who becomes possessed by competing voices after finding a photo of her great-grandmother. Machado works with the rich oral tradition of Brazilian literature and combines this with her own creative style. Published in 17 different countries, her books have sold more than 8 million copies worldwide.

MacLACHLAN, PATRICIA (1938–). U.S. author of fiction and **picture books**. *Sarah, Plain and Tall* (1985), which won the **Newbery**

Medal, is a frontier story set in the late 19th century, about a widowed father of two who advertises in the newspaper for a new wife. The Sarah of the title responds, and the novel focuses particularly on the warm relationship between the children and Sarah, whom they hope will become their stepmother. Recurrent themes in MacLachlan's fiction are family, home, parent-child relationships, and new siblings, usually in a contemporary setting. Her style is lyrical and sparse, and she is capable of portraying strong emotions in few words. In *Journey* (1991), the protagonist struggles to come to terms with the disappearance of his mother. In *Baby* (1993), a family fosters an abandoned baby, although they know that her mother will return for her; only after this renewed loss can they finally talk about the death of a baby in their own family. Many of MacLachlan's novels have been **translated** into other languages, and a number have been **adapted** into films.

MAGORIAN, MICHELLE (1947–). British actress and author of a number of novels that examine the impact of war on family relationships and social organization, the most successful of which is *Goodnight Mister Tom* (1985). Winner of the Guardian **Award** and now regarded a modern classic, it tells the tender and moving story of nine-year-old inner-city evacuee William Beech, who, during the World War II bombing raids on London, is sent to a country village to stay with Tom, an elderly widower. There the abused child of a sin-obsessed mother finds kindness and love and gradually blossoms under the care of the old man. There is a musical version of the novel, and it was adapted for television in 1999. The year 2008 saw the publication of another major success by Magorian, *Just Henry*, a 750-page novel about a 15-year-old cinema fanatic, set in 1949. Much of the novel is devoted to Henry's film projects, part of the plot concerns the revelation of the truth about his father, an assumed war hero, and this in turn leads to dramatic events including blackmail and kidnapping. It won the 2008 Costa Children's Book of the Year award.

MAGUIRE, GREGORY (1954–). U.S. author of novels for adults and children, commentator on children's books, and cofounder of the Children's Literature New England group. Maguire's early work was mostly in the **fantasy** genre, and he has rewritten stories of figures from folklore and classic literature. His **crossover** title *Wicked: The Life and Times of the Wicked Witch of the West* (1995) tells the story of ***The Wizard of Oz*** from the perspective of the green-faced wicked **witch**. He has also written humorous books for younger children, such as *Seven Spiders Spinning* (1994); realistic fiction that raises social questions, as in *Missing Sisters* (1995), in which a handicapped **orphan** discovers she has an identical twin; and **historical fiction** such as *The Good Liar* (1999), about the lives and loyalties of a young boy's family in German-occupied France during World War II. Maguire has also written and coedited critical essays on children's literature.

MAHY, MARGARET (1936–). Acclaimed and prolific New Zealand author of **picture books**, novels for children and young adults, **nonfiction**, **poetry**, and plays. Mahy's first publications were five picture books featuring individualistic lions (e.g., *A Lion in the Meadow*, 1969, illustrated by Jenny Williams) and dragons (e.g., *The Dragon of an Ordinary Family*, 1969, illustrated by **Helen Oxenbury**, winner of the **Kate Greenaway Medal**). During an era dominated by realistic fiction in New Zealand, Mahy's stories about **witches**, **wizards**, and dragons were rejected by local publishers as being "too English"; but they were snapped up by publishers in the United States and Great Britain, who thereby launched the career of a writer who was to become the most famous New Zealand author for children. Numerous picture books and story collections followed during the 1970s. The predominant modes are **fantasy** and **adventure**, but Mahy's fabulous characters engage fully with the ordinary world. She specializes in a humoristic, sometimes parodistic or even satirical tone in her picture books and stories for young readers. Her first two novels, *The Haunting* (1982) and *The Changeover* (1984), both won the **Carnegie Medal**.

Mahy's language is rich in poetic imagery and wordplay, and she specializes in strong (usually female) characters. In her adolescent novels, she blends the themes of growing up and human relationships with plots that contain supernatural elements—for instance in *The Haunting*, *The Changeover*, *Dangerous Spaces* (1991), and *The Tricksters* (1986)—creating a metaphorical arena for the expression of adolescence and the theme of establishing autonomy. The relationship between the truth of the imagination and factual truth is a central preoccupation in Mahy's work. She has also written for television—*Maddigan's Quest* is a **fantasy**-based TV series set in a postapocalyptic future—and she adapted *The Haunting* as a feature film. Mahy's books have been translated into more than 15 languages and have won many national and international **awards**; in addition to the Carnegie Medals, she won the Phoenix Award in 2005 for *The Catalogue of the Universe* (1986), and in 2007 for *Memory* (1987). She received the **Hans Christian Andersen Award** in 2006. The Margaret Mahy Medal Award was established by the New Zealand Children's Book Foundation in 1991 to provide recognition of excellence in children's literature, publishing, and literacy in New Zealand. Mahy was made a Member of the Order of New Zealand in 1983 for her contributions to children's literature. She became an official New Zealand Arts Icon, as part of a program that celebrates living artists, in 2005.

MARRYAT, CAPTAIN FREDERICK (1792–1848). British naval officer and author of some of the most successful 19th-century **adventure stories**. Marryat initially wrote novels such as *Mr. Midshipman Easy* (1836) for adults; he later began to write specifically for children, producing *Masterman Ready* (1841) after his children said that they would like to read a continuation of ***The Swiss Family Robinson***. Further titles included *The Settlers in Canada* (1844), an account of life on the frontier, and *The Children of the New Forest* (1847), a story of the English Civil War and the first enduringly popular British **historical novel** for children.

MARY POPPINS. *See* TRAVERS, P. L.

MAYNE, WILLIAM (1928–2010). English author whose work has received great critical acclaim although not widespread popularity. His novels are regarded as stylistically challenging for young readers as they reject many of the conventions of children's literature, which typically aid its accessibility. They reveal a fascination with place and its historical or mythological past, and how this is revealed to its inhabitants—for instance in his Earthfasts trilogy (1966, 1995, and 2000). There is frequently a gulf between the worlds of adults and children in Mayne's novels, and children's belief in magic and its power is vindicated in novels such as *A Grass Rope* (1957), which won the **Carnegie Medal**, and *Low Tide* (1992), a survival story set in New Zealand in the aftermath of a tidal wave (in which a Maori **legend** plays a key role). Mayne is probably best known for his Choir School series (1955–1963), a sequence of four novels based on his own experience as a chorister at the Canterbury Cathedral Choir School.

McCAUGHREAN, GERALDINE (1951–). English author of more than 150 books and plays for adults and children. Her writing for children includes **picture books**, retellings of classics such as *The Canterbury Tales* (1984), **myths** and **legends** from around the world, and novels, such as the metafictional *A Pack of Lies* (1988), which won the **Carnegie Medal**. Her *Peter Pan in Scarlet* (2006), an official sequel to **Sir J. M. Barrie**'s *Peter Pan*, addresses the conflict between the delights of eternal childhood and the price to be paid for them, and delivers fresh insights into the energizing potential of children's imagination. It was published simultaneously in 31 languages.

MEYER, STEPHENIE (1973–). U.S. author of the hugely popular Twilight series of young-adult vampire novels that focus on 17-year-old Isabella "Bella" Swan, who falls in love with a vampire, Edward Cullen. *Twilight* (2005), *New Moon* (2006), *Eclipse* (2007), and the final volume of the series, *Breaking Dawn* (2008), all dominated the *New York Times* Best Seller List, and tell a romantic tale of forbidden love and lustful abstinence. They are a conservative example of the young-adult vampire subcultures established by *Buffy the Vampire Slayer*. The first film of the Twilight saga was released in 2008.

McKEE, DAVID (1935–). British author and **illustrator** of more than 30 **picture books**. McKee's commercially most successful creation is the colorful elephant from *Elmer, the Patchwork Elephant* (1968), who is the subject of different types of books (board books, coloring books, etc.), has spawned a range of merchandise, including stuffed animals, and has been **translated** into 20 languages. Other popular series characters include King Rollo and Mr. Benn. McKee exploits the ironic potential of picture books to contrast what is said in the text with what is shown in the pictures, both to comic and to critical effect, in books such as *Not Now, Bernard* (1980)—which shows parents ignoring their son, who is trying to alert them to his imminent danger of being eaten by a monster, underscoring the complete miscommunication between the child and his parents. Similarly, *I Hate My Teddy Bear* (1982) pits a mundane conversation beween two children against mysterious and exciting activities in the pictures. McKee is cofounder of the company King Rollo Films, which specializes in animated film version of picture books such as his own Elmer series, **Tony Ross**'s Towser books, Eric Hill's *Spot the Dog*, and others.

MILDRED L. BATCHELDER AWARD. Established in 1966 to honor a former executive director of the Association for Library Service to Children (ALSC) and believer in the importance of good books for children in **translation** from all parts of the world. The award is granted to a U.S. publisher for a children's book considered to be the most outstanding of those originally published in a foreign language and subsequently translated into English. It is presented annually by the ALSC, a division of the **American Library Association (ALA)**. (See appendix for list of recipients).

MILNE, A. A. (ALAN ALEXANDER) (1882–1956). English playwright, **poet**, and author, best known for four children's classics written for his young son Christopher Robin: the verse collections *When We Were Very Young* (1924) and *Now We Are Six* (1927), and two collections of stories, *Winnie-the-Pooh* (1926) and *The House at Pooh Corner* (1928). All four books, **illustrated** by **E. H. Shepard**, were hugely successful among child and adult readers, and they have never been out of print. The Pooh stories are framed by a father-son storytelling situation and narrate the adventures of **anthropomorphic** toy animals. The lovable, if not too bright, teddy-bear poet Pooh, the pedant Owl, the pessimist donkey Eeyore, bouncy Tigger, and others live in the Hundred Acre Wood, an enchanted place regularly visited by the young boy Christopher Robin. It is a safe world in which the main occupations are eating, exploration, and visiting friends, a lost paradise of childhood that invites adults to engage with the story on a nostalgic level. The most familiar image of Winnie the Pooh today is the (de-hyphenated) **Walt Disney** one seen in numerous cartoon films that have starred the bear and other characters since 1966. Pooh videos, teddy bears, and other merchandise items, from clothes to furniture, generate substantial revenues for the company today, and the figure of Pooh also appears at Disney parks and resorts.

MOE, JØRGEN ENGEBRETSEN (1813–1882). *See* ASBJØRNSEN, PETER CHRISTEN.

MOLESWORTH, MARY LOUISA (1839–1921). Prolific and popular late-19th-century author of some 100 books for children. Best remembered today is *The Cuckoo Clock* (1877), about a lonely girl befriended by a fairy who occupies the cuckoo clock in her great-aunts' house. In the realistic mode was *Carrots* (1876), illustrated by **Walter Crane**, about a six-year-old redhead and his difficult relationship with his father. One of Molesworth's great strengths was her ability to make observations about children and empathize with them; but her use of **fantasy** as a vehicle for moral instruction and her habit of making small children talk in baby language diminish the attractiveness of her work for modern readers.

MONTEIRO LOBATO, JOSÉ (1882–1948). Brazilian writer, translator, editor, and entrepreneur regarded as the father of Brazilian children's literature. The publication in 1920 of *A menina do narizinho arrebitado* [The Little Girl with the Snub Nose] was a watershed in Brazilian children's literature, which up to this point had been dominated by Portuguese imports and **translations**. It was the first of 16 books set on Sitio do Picapau Amerelo (Yellow Woodpecker Ranch), which is occupied by the elderly widow ranch owner Dona Benta and her two grandchildren, Lúcia (whose nickname is Narizinho) and Pedrinho. In these books, written in a contemporary, colloquial, and innovative Brazilian Portuguese, three realms are intertwined: everyday farm life, the children's fantasy worlds, and stories steeped in Brazilian tradition, told by Dona Benta and Tia Nastácia, the black cook. While playfulness and fantasy predominate in these books, Monteiro Lobato also wanted to impart knowledge; he deals with serious questions such as politics and science in a way that is accessible for children, and some of the stories told by Dona Benta address subjects that children may not like at school, such as mathematics or national history. His books have been translated into Spanish but not into English, and they have been **adapted** no fewer than five times into hugely popular TV series (the first made in the 1950s, the most recent in the 2000s). Monteiro Lobato also translated and retold a number of children's classics, including ***Alice in Wonderland*** and ***Peter Pan***.

MONTGOMERY, L. M. (LUCY MAUD) (1874–1942). Canadian author of domestic fiction, famous for the hugely popular series of novels beginning with *Anne of Green Gables* (1908). In it, an elderly brother and sister who live in the fictional community Avonlea on Prince Edward Island are mistakenly sent a lively, redheaded 11-year-old **orphan** girl, Anne Shirley, instead of the boy they had wanted to work on their farm. After many adventures in their home, Green Gables, and in the village, the outspoken, independent, and talented girl succeeds in softening the hearts of the Cuthbert siblings, turning Green Gables into a loving home and, later, winning a scholarship to college. This she gives up in order to look after Marilla Cuthbert after the death of her brother. The novel was followed by the sequels *Anne of Avonlea* (1909), *Anne of the Island* (1915), *Anne of Windy Poplars* (1936), *Anne's House of Dreams* (1917), and *Anne of Ingleside* (1939).

Anne of Green Gables is one of the most popular "girls' stories" of all time, and it inspired many later authors in Canada and elsewhere. Its influence is evident in novels such as Eleanor H. Porter's ***Pollyanna*** (1913) and, later, **Astrid Lindgren**'s *Pippi Longstocking* (Swedish original 1945). Lindgren proclaimed Anne one of her favorite heroines, and Pippi's red hair, freckles, and unconventionality pay homage to Montgomery's creation. *Anne of Green Gables* is Canada's most famous literary figure and ambassador. The novels have been **translated** into numerous languages and **adapted** for the stage and the screen in several animated and live-action TV series and movies. *See also* GENDER.

MORE, HANNAH (1745–1833). British writer and evangelical especially known for her *Cheap Repository Tracts* (1795–1798). This was a series of pamphlets written for working-class children learning to read in Sunday schools, in which More successfully copied the format and style of the popular **chapbooks**. The best known was *The Shepherd of Salisbury Plain* (1795), about a poor but pious shepherd who, despite great hardship, is content with his lot. It enjoyed great popularity in the United States.

MORPURGO, MICHAEL (1943–). British author of more than 100 books, most of them for children, and cofounder of the charity Farms for City Children, which provides children from inner-city areas with experience of the countryside. Children's welfare, animal welfare, and pacifism are central preoccupations in Morpurgo's work. One of his own favorite novels, *War Horse* (1982), describes the terrible destruction at the front during World War I from the perspective of the horse Joey, and a further **historical novel** of World War I bears the title *Private Peaceful* (2003). **Orphaned** and dispossessed children feature in many novels, from his first, *Long Way Home* (1975), about a boy living in care; through *Waiting for Anya* (1990), which relates how the villagers in a small village in France smuggled Jewish children over the border to Spain; to *Alone on a Wide, Wide Sea* (2006), about English orphans transported to Australia after World War II. A number of Morpurgo's books have been made into films, and some have been **adapted** for television. The idea for the **children's laureate** was first mooted in a conversation between Morpurgo and **Ted Hughes**, and Morpurgo himself held the title from 2003 to 2005. In 1999, he and his wife Claire were appointed MBE for services to literature in recognition of their services to youth, and in 2006 Morpurgo was appointed OBE.

MOSER, BARRY (1940–). U.S. **illustrator** of more than 100 books for adults and children. Moser's favorite media are wood engraving and watercolor, and he has illustrated many classics, including Herman Melville's *Moby Dick* (1978), **Lewis Carroll**'s Alice novels (1982), and **Mark Twain**'s *Adventures of Huckleberry Finn* (1985). Illustrations of works by contemporary authors include **Virginia Hamilton**'s *In the Beginning: Creation Stories from around the World* (1988) and Van Dyke Parks's retellings of Brer Rabbit stories, starting with *Jump! The Adventures of Brer Rabbit* (1986). He has also retold and **adapted folktales** such as *Tucker Pfeffercorn* (1992) and *The Three Little Pigs* (2001).

MOTHER GOOSE RHYMES. *See* NURSERY RHYMES.

MULTICULTURALISM. *See* CREW, GARY; ETHNOCENTRISM; HAMILTON, VIRGINIA; PICTURE BOOKS; SAY, ALLEN; TAN, SHAUN; WHEATLEY, NADIA; YEP, LAURENCE.

MYERS, WALTER DEAN (1937–). African American poet and author of **picture books**, **fantasy**, **historical fiction**, and **nonfiction**. Author of more than 50 books for children and young adults, Myers is regarded as one of the most important voices in contemporary young adult literature, especially for his novels depicting urban African American youth. Many of his novels are based in Harlem, where he grew up, and address such topics as gang life, drug use, and violence. His books are infused with a belief in education, in family bonds—especially those between father and son—and in the positive influence of friends. Among his notable young adult novels are *Fast Sam, Cool Clyde, and Stuff* (1975), and *Fallen Angels* (1988), about a young soldier's tour of duty in Vietnam. He has written picture books with texts in verse form, such as *Glorious Angels* (1997); a poem, *Harlem* (1997), which was illustrated by his son Christopher; and the biography *Malcolm X: By Any Means Necessary* (1994). He is a five-time winner of the Coretta Scott King Award and was the recipient, in 1994, of the **American Library Association**'s **(ALA)** Margaret A. Edwards Award for his lifetime contribution to young adult literature.

MYSTERY FICTION. *See* DETECTIVE FICTION.

MYTHS AND LEGENDS. Narratives that are passed down traditionally from generation to generation. Traditional narratives are commonly arranged into three groups: myths, legends, and **fairy tales and folktales**. Myths are narratives about divine or heroic beings, linked to the spiritual life of a community or culture and arranged in a coherent system. They usually provide an explanation for the beginning of the universe, the early history of a society ("creation myths" and "founding myths"), natural phenomena, and anything else for which no simple explanation exists. Among the most widely known bodies of myths from particular cultures or regions are Greek mythology, Egyptian mythology, and Norse mythology. Retellings of myths have been a staple of children's literature from its inception. These popularly include stories about the Greek gods, Theseus and the Minotaur, King Midas, the Trojan Horse, and Jason and the Golden Fleece; stories from Norse mythology, such as "How Thor Got His Hammer," "The Golden Apples," and "The Death of Balder"; and tales about the Egyptian gods Ra, Osiris, Isis, Thoth, and others.

Legends, on the other hand, generally focus on human heroes or events. While tellers regard the events upon which legends are based as having occurred in a definite historical time, mythic events are seen as having occurred before historical time, when the nature of the world differed from the one we know today. Legends are usually believable, although they are not necessarily believed. Famous legends often center on heroic figures, either secular or religious, such as Saint George, King Arthur and the Knights of the Round Table, **Robin Hood**, William Tell, Joan of Arc, Geronimo, Pocahontas, Annie Christmas, or Sister Fox and Brother Coyote; legendary animals include the Yeti and the Loch Ness monster. Legends are a part of every known culture; their role in national and cultural socialization and in the creation of national identification is strong. The canon of national heroes in the United States and Great Britain has been relativized in recent years, with the addition of different legends and interpretations of the national histories and with a more prominent position given to female figures. *See also* ADAPTATION; BRUCHAC, JOSEPH; BURGESS, MELVIN; COOPER, SUSAN; CROSSLEY-HOLLAND, KEVIN; GARFIELD, LEON; GARNER, ALAN; HAWTHORNE, NATHANIEL; HISTORICAL FICTION; KINGSLEY, CHARLES; LEWIS, C. S.; LYNCH, PATRICIA; MCCAUGHREAN, GERALDINE; MAYNE, WILLIAM; PIUMINI, ROBERTO; PREUSSLER, OTFRIED; PYLE, HOWARD; SUTCLIFF, ROSEMARY; THOMPSON, KATE; TOURNIER, MICHEL; YOLEN, JANE.

– N –

NAIDOO, BEVERLEY (1943–). South African children's author who grew up under apartheid and joined the resistance movement as a teenager. She moved to Great Britain in 1965. Naidoo's first novel, *Journey to Jo'burg* (1985), banned in South Africa for many years, tells of two South African children who journey to find their mother in Johannesburg without possessing the papers that allow them, as blacks, to leave their designated area. A sequel, *Chain of Fire*, followed in 1989. *No Turning Back* (1995) features children living on the streets of Johannesburg; the **Carnegie Medal**–winning *The Other Side of Truth* (2000) is about two Nigerian **orphans** uprooted to Great Britain; and *Burn My Heart* (2007) is a tale of friendship and betrayal in colonial Kenya. Naidoo explicitly wrote these novels to encourage children to explore the injustice of **racism**, ask fundamental questions, and engage imaginatively in the lives of others. Naidoo has also published critical works on racism and children's literature: *Censoring Reality: An Examination of Books on South Africa* (1985) and her doctoral thesis, *Through Whose Eyes? Exploring Racism: Reader, Text and Context* (1992). *See also* ETHNOCENTRISM.

NANCY DREW. Amateur detective and fictional heroine of a popular **mystery** series of the same name published by the Stratemeyer Syndicate under the pseudonym **Carolyn Keene**. The at times impossibly perfect Nancy, one of the first female action heroines, uses her intelligence to solve mysteries and crimes, usually committed in her hometown. Sixteen years old at the beginning of the series and gradually aging to 18, she is an independent-minded, courageous, and accomplished young woman who escapes villains by driving her blue roadster, later a blue convertible, at high speed. The original series of 56 titles was published between 1930 and 1979; more than 100 further titles came out in the modern Nancy Drew Mystery Stories between 1979 and 2003; and a new, revamped series with a very modern Nancy Drew hit the bookstores in 2004. A spin-off, The Nancy Drew Files, targeted an older teenage audience, while The Nancy Drew Notebooks addresses younger readers. Crossover series with **The Hardy Boys** were published in the 1980s, and in 2007, and a number of interactive computer games were based on Nancy Drew titles. The most recent of many movie adaptations was released in 2007.

NAPOLI, DONNA JO (1948–). U.S. author for children and young adults and professor of linguistics. Napoli's writing ranges from **pic-**

ture books and **easy readers** to contemporary realism, **fantasy**, and **historical novels** for young adults, many of which, such as *Daughter of Venice* (2002), are set in Italy. She is perhaps best known for revisiting **fairy tales** to provide fresh and absorbing new versions. These can be in a lighthearted mode for younger readers, as in the hilarious *Prince of the Pond: Otherwise Known as De Fawg Pin* (1992), which features a frog-prince with a communication problem: he cannot roll up his tongue. In a darker mode for older readers is *The Magic Circle* (1993), which revisits "Hansel and Gretel" from the perspective of the **witch**, who has sought refuge in the wood to prevent herself from eating children. Other notable revisited fairy tales include "Rapunzel" in *Zel* (1996), "Beauty and the Beast" in *Beast* (2000), and "The Pied Piper of Hamlin" in *Breath* (2003). The Angelwings series of 16 easy readers (1999–2001) features apprentice angels who help children in need. Napoli has also written a number of books geared toward helping deaf people learn to read. Her books have been **translated** into many languages.

NAYLOR, PHYLLIS REYNOLDS (1933–). U.S. author of a number of popular children's series. In the Alice series, starting with *The Agony of Alice* (1985), an average female adolescent narrates her experiences in school, with friends, at summer camp, with boyfriends, at the time of her first menstruation, and so on. *Witch's Sister* (1975) was the first in a series about two girls who try to fight a local **witch**. Naylor's novel *Shiloh* (1991) is about an 11-year-old country boy, Marty, who empathizes with animals and protects an abused dog, Shiloh. A **Newbery Medal** winner, it was made into a movie and was followed by several sequels.

NESBIT, E. (EDITH) (1858–1924). English writer for adults and children, political activist, and cofounder of the Fabian Society. The children's books for which Nesbit is celebrated were published from 1899 on, after she had spent two decades supporting her unconventional family with hack writing in almost every genre. Her children's books were published under the name E. Nesbit, with the bare initial often leading readers to assume that she was a man, to her apparent delight. Most of them began as serials in different magazines and were later issued as books. Her first major success was *The Story* *of the Treasure Seekers* (1899), the initial volume of the Bastable trilogy about an impoverished middle-class family of six inventive, motherless children. Each episode in the book describes a different ploy by the children for making money, all of which end in disaster and comedy. *The Wouldbegoods* (1901) and *The New Treasure Seekers* (1904) complete the trilogy and made Nesbit's name as a children's writer. They have been called the first truly contemporary realistic stories for children, and they blend comedy with realistic accounts of children's play, as well as their quarrels and faults. In this series and her other books, Nesbit was one of the first writers to use a child first-person narrator who possesses a genuine childlike view of the world. The narrator of *The Treasure Seekers* plays with the reader, admitting he is one of the Bastable children "but I shall not tell you which"; but the number of complimentary references to Oswald in the narrative makes it very clear that it is, in fact, he. *The Railway Children* (1906), Nesbit's most popular work and one that has been repeatedly **adapted** for stage and screen, is about three children whose father has been imprisoned as a suspected spy.

In her **fantasy** novels, Nesbit departs from the principle of heroic fantasy to locate the fantastical in everyday life; and, in this, she is considered the founder of modern fantasy for children. In *Five Children and It* (1902), five ordinary children undergo a series of magical adventures after encountering an odd, bad-tempered sand fairy, a so-called Psammead, who has the power to grant them one wish per day. Regardless of what the children wish—to be able to fly or to possess great beauty, for instance—each wish has unforeseen, humorous consequences. When they wish for money, they get a sandpit full of ancient coins that can buy nothing. More magical adventures showing how tricky magic can be follow in the sequel, *The Phoenix and the Carpet* (1904). In *The Story of the Amulet* (1906), the first children's book to introduce the idea of time displacement, the five children travel to Atlantis, ancient Egypt, Roman Britain, and a utopian future society based on Fabian socialist ideals. Time travel also features in *The House of Arden* (1908) and *Harding's Luck* (1909). The fantasy that Nesbit created is sometimes called "domestic fantasy" because of its use of everyday settings and objects, or "humorous fantasy" because it flouts the conventions of traditional folktales and **fairy tales** to comic effect. She is regarded as one of the most innovative writers for children of the early 20th century and has had a major influence upon other writers for the young, including **C. S. Lewis**, **P. L. Travers**, and **J. K. Rowling**.

NEWBERY, JOHN (1713–1767). English publisher and bookseller who was the first to realize the commercial potential of publishing for children. His *A Little Pretty Pocket-Book, Intended for the Instruction and Amusement of Little Master Tommy and Pretty Miss Polly, with Two Letters from Jack the Giant Killer . . . to Which Is Added a Little Songbook, etc.* (ca. 1744), which contains a play **alphabet**, songs, and moral tales, is widely considered the first modern children's book. It was the first storybook marketed as pleasure reading in English; and, as it was sold with a ball (for boys) and a pincushion (for girls), it was also the first marketing tie-in. Another Newbery publication was *The History of Little Goody Two Shoes* (1765), the most popular novel for children of the period, which has been variously attributed to Oliver Goldsmith; to Giles Jones, an author employed by Newbery; and to Newbery himself. The **Newbery Medal**, established in 1922, was named in his honor.

NEWBERY MEDAL. Established in 1922 in honor of the publisher **John Newbery**, the Newbery Medal is presented annually by the Association for Library Service for Children (ALSC), a division of the **American Library Association (ALA)**, to the author of the most distinguished contribution to American literature for children published in the United States in the preceding year. The award is limited to residents or citizens of the United States. The Newbery Honor is a citation given to worthy runners-up. (See appendix for list of recipients).

NICHOLS, GRACE (1950–). Guyanese author of **poetry** and prose for adults and children who moved to Great Britain in 1977. In her poems for children, Nichols's inspiration comes from the sights, sounds, storytelling, and language of her Guyanese childhood. She fuses Standard English and Caribbean Creole in her collection *Come On into My Tropical Garden* (1988). She has edited a number of anthologies of Caribbean poetry, many of them, including *A Caribbean Dozen: Poems from Caribbean Poets* (1994), with her partner **John**

Agard. She and Agard coauthored the collection of **nursery rhymes** *No Hickory, No Dickory, No Dock* (1991).

NONFICTION. *See* INFORMATION BOOKS.

NONSENSE. Poetry and prose texts that play with the conventions of language and logic while maintaining a coherent structure; the balance of sense and non-sense elements characterizes nonsense texts and distinguishes their playful subversion of temporal, spatial, and semantic norms from pure gibberish. There are two major forms of nonsense, *folk nonsense* and *literary nonsense*. Examples of folk nonsense can be found in most cultures in poems from the oral tradition that celebrate contradictions and play with the sound of language. "One bright day in the middle of the night" is one example, the **nursery rhyme** "Hey diddle diddle, the cat and the fiddle" another. The writers who popularized literary nonsense are **Edward Lear** and **Lewis Carroll**, although literary nonsense, which combines intellectual nonsense with folk elements, predates them. Lear's limericks and Carroll's Alice novels are regarded by many as prototypical nonsense. While nonsense is an important element in many works for adults by authors such as James Joyce, Flann O'Brien, Spike Milligan, and Eugene Ionesco, its absurd logic, playfulness, delight in sound, and subversiveness make it particularly popular among children and writers for children. These include the Australian **Norman Lindsay**, the Germans Christian Morgenstern and Joachim Ringelnatz, the Americans **Dr. Seuss** and **Shel Silverstein**, the English **Michael Rosen**, and the Dutch **Annie M. G. Schmidt**. *See also* ABC BOOKS OR ALPHABET BOOKS; FANTASY; GOREY, EDWARD ST. JOHN; KING-SMITH, DICK; LOBEL, ARNOLD; POETRY; PRATCHETT, TERRY; SANDBURG, CARL.

NORTON, ANDRE (1912–2005). U.S. author of **science fiction** and **fantasy**. Regarded, like **Robert A. Heinlein**, as a major science-fiction writer for young adults, Norton rose to fame with the publication of *Star Man's Son: 2250 A.D.* (1952), and is especially known for her Witch World series starting with *Galactic Derelict* (1959). Exploring a wide range of issues in her books, she authors so-called hard science fiction based on the "hard" sciences of physics and chemistry and emphasizing technology, in contrast to its counterpart "soft" science fiction, which is more interested in the human sciences of psychology and sociology. In 2005, The Science Fiction and Fantasy Writers of America (SFWA) created in her honor the annual Andre Norton Award for an outstanding young adult science-fiction or fantasy book.

NORTON, MARY (1903–1992). British author of **fantasy** for children. Her first two books, *The Magic Bedknob* (1943) and *Bonfires and Broomsticks* (1947), humorous time-shift fantasies, were brought together in *Bedknob and Broomsticks* (1957) and made into a musical film by **Walt Disney** in 1971. Norton is most famous for her Borrowers series of fantasy novels about the adventures and travels of miniature people who "borrow" things from human beings and keep their existence a secret. It started with *The Borrowers* (1952), which won the **Carnegie Medal**, and was followed by *The Borrowers Afield* (1955), *The Borrowers Afloat* (1959), *The Borrowers Aloft* (1961), and *The Borrowers Avenged* (1982). The central characters are the Clock family of father, mother, and teenage daughter, whose names—Pod, Homily, and Arrietty—reflect their penchant for mispronouncing names and words (they call human beings "human beans"). *The Borrowers* was **adapted** for United States (1977) and British (1992–1993) television, and a film version was released in 1997.

NÖSTLINGER, CHRISTINE (1936–). Austrian author, journalist, and graphic artist, one of the leading authors for young readers in Germany during the second half of the 20th century and the one most widely translated into English. Nöstlinger's international accolades have included the **Hans Christian Andersen Award** in 1984 and the first **Astrid Lindgren Memorial Award**, which she won together with **Maurice Sendak** in 2002. Her work for children and young adults covers many genres and creatively blends **fantasy** with social realism to create texts that are both socially critical and entertaining. Patriarchal authority is one recurring topic, most famously in *Wir pfeifen auf den Gurkenkönig* (1972; *The Cucumber King,* 1975). In it, a despotic and grotesque fantasy figure, the Cucumber King Kumi-Ori II, ousted from his cellar kingdom by his oppressed subjects, tries to impose his will on a Viennese family and, to the dismay of the children, wins the allegiance of their father. Other popular titles include her first novel, *Die feuerrote Friederike* (1970; *Fiery Frederica,* 1975), and *Konrad oder Das Kind aus der Konservenbüchse* (1975; *Conrad: The Factory-Made Boy*, 1976), both of which address issues of conformism and emancipation. In the 1980s she wrote a series of novels for older readers about Gretchen Sackmeier and her family, but she turned her attention increasingly to younger readers, creating a popular series of stories about the children Franz and Mini. Her autobiographical novel *Maikäfer flieg!* (1973; *Fly Away Home,* 1975) is an account of the final days of the war in Austria and the Russian occupation. Nöstlinger's work is full of humor and wordplay, which her **translator** Anthea Bell successfully recreates in English.

NURSERY RHYMES. Verses that are recited or sung to small children. The chief characteristics of nursery rhymes are their brevity and strongly marked rhythm, both of which ensure memorability; some are narratives that pack a whole drama into a limited number of lines. **Iona and Peter Opie** collected around 550 traditional, orally transmitted rhymes in their definitive study *The Oxford Dictionary of Nursery Rhymes* (1951). Most rhymes date from the beginning of the 17th century on, and at least half of those in circulation today are believed to have been current by the mid-18th century. The majority of nursery rhymes were not initially composed for children: they were preserved by the nursery rather than coming from the nursery. Some are fragments of ballads or folk songs or remnants of ancient custom and ritual; others are based on proverbs, rude gests, or romantic lyrics. Of the older nursery rhymes, the only ones composed especially for children are the rhyming alphabets, the infant amusements accompanying a game, the jog-along knee songs, and the **lullabies**. When publications specifically for children started to appear around the mid-18th century, publishers began to document the songs found in the nursery and put them into print. After the publication of the influential booklet *Mother Goose's Melody, or Sonnets for the Cradle* in 1765, the rhymes were known as Mother Goose rhymes, a term still used in the United States today. *See also* AGARD, JOHN; AHLBERG, ALLAN AND JANET; BAUM, L. FRANK; BRIGGS, RAYMOND; BUTTERWORTH, NICK; CALDECOTT, RANDOLPH;

CARROLL, LEWIS; CRANE, WALTER; GREENAWAY, KATE; NICHOLS, GRACE; POETRY; POMBO, RAFAEL; RACKHAM, ARTHUR; SENDAK, MAURICE; WILDSMITH, BRIAN.

– O –

O'BRIEN, ROBERT C. (1918–1973). Pseudonym of Robert Leslie Conly, a U.S. journalist, under which he published four children's books. The first two were for younger readers, *The Silver Crown* (1968) and *Mrs. Frisby and the Rats of NIMH* (1971), a **fantasy** about phenomenally intelligent laboratory rats who become self-sufficient. It won the **Newbery Medal** and was made into an animated film, *The Secret of NIMH*, in 1982. His later novels *A Report from Group 17* (1972) and *Z for Zachariah* (1975), the latter published posthumously and written from the perspective of a 16-year-old survivor of a nuclear war, are darker, dystopian novels for young adult readers. His last title received the Mystery Writers of America Award in 1976 for the best juvenile **mystery**.

O'DELL, SCOTT (1898–1989). U.S. author who published his first children's novel, *Island of the Blue Dolphins* (1960), at the age of 62 and completed a further 25 before his death almost 30 years later. O'Dell specialized in **historical novels** with non-European American first-person narrators, strong characters with an intense sense of personal morality, and exciting survival plots that incorporate criticism of destructive periods in the history of the Americas. *Island of the Blue Dolphins* is a female **robinsonade** based on the true story of Juana Maria, a Nicoleño Indian marooned for 18 years on San Nicolas Island off the California coast in the mid-19th century. It won the **Newbery Medal**, and a film version was released four years after the novel's publication. **Translated** into numerous languages, it earned O'Dell his international reputation. He received the **Hans Christian Andersen Award** in 1972.

OPIE, IONA (1923–) AND PETER (1918–1982). Husband-and-wife team of British folklorists who applied modern research methods to document the continuity of children's folklore and traditional games.

Among their most important publications are *The Oxford Dictionary of Nursery Rhymes* (1951), *The Lore and Language of School Children* (1959), and *Children's Games in Street and Playground* (1969). The Opies amassed one of the richest collections of children's books and ephemera from the 16th to the 20th century; their collection of children's books, containing approximately 1,200 titles, is now in the Bodleian Library, Oxford University. The collection of historic toys and games is still in the position of Iona Opie.

ORBIS SENSUALIUM PICTUS. *See* COMENIUS, JOHN AMOS (KOMENSKY, JAN ÁMOS).

ORLEV, URI (1931–). Polish-born Israeli writer for adults and children, and translator. Orlev has published some 30 books for children and young adults, most of them realistic novels about the Holocaust from a child's perspective, which draw on his own wartime childhood in the Warsaw Ghetto and the Bergen-Belsen concentration camp. *The Lead Soldiers* (Hebrew in 1956, English in 1979) is an account of how two young protagonists respond to the horrific events of the Holocaust by escaping into games and stories. *The Island on Bird Street* (Hebrew in 1981, English in 1984), also adapted into a play and a film, is the story of a boy's survival in the Warsaw Ghetto. *The Man from the Other Side* (Hebrew in 1988, English in 1991) is based on the experiences of a Polish journalist; blending elements of moral conflict and action, it describes how a 14-year-old Polish Catholic boy helps to hide a Jewish man from the Warsaw Ghetto. The English **translations** of the last two titles—as well as those of *Run, Boy, Run* (Hebrew in 2001, English in 2003) and *The Lady with the Hat* (Hebrew in 1991, English in 1995), set in postwar Palestine—all won the **Mildred L. Batchelder Award**. Orlev received the **Hans Christian Andersen Award** in 1996 in recognition of his entire body of work.

ORMEROD, JAN (1946–). Australian **illustrator** and author of more than 60 books published in more than 21 countries. Her first **picture book**, *Sunshine* (1981; winner of the Australian Picture Book of the Year Award), and its sequel *Moonlight* (1982) are wordless picture books that depict in detail unremarkable events of everyday life in the family of a young girl and her parents. The subject of much of Ormerod's work is the closeness between parents and children, often depicted through body language and facial expressions, and her picture books for young children capture with great detail, humor, and gentleness her keen observations of small children and their world. She has written numerous board books—some of which, such as *Hat Off, Baby!* (2002), incorporate flaps for toddlers to lift—and pop-up books such as *Rock-a-Baby* (1997). Her popular *Lizzie Nonsense* (2004) is a picture book depicting the life of a pioneer woman and her young daughter in Western Australia. She has illustrated picture books written by others, including works by classic authors such as **Sir J. M. Barrie**'s *Peter Pan* (1987).

ORPHANS. Orphaned characters are strikingly common as protagonists in children's literature and have their origin in folklore, where the prerequisite for a successful rite of passage is often the symbolic removal of parents. Orphans nearly always succeed in the end and receive a reward in the form of wealth, status, and marriage. Passing from the oral to the written tradition, the orphan tale occupied a firm place in European and American children's literature by the 19th century. Prominent female orphans feature in **Johanna Spyri**'s *Heidi* (1880), Eleanor H. Porter's ***Pollyanna*** (1913), **Frances Hodgson Burnett**'s *A Little Princess* (1905) and *The Secret Garden* (1911), and **L. M. Montgomery**'s *Anne of Green Gables* (1908). Orphans, especially female orphans, often end up with relatives or other adults who do not want to have them, but their sweet nature often transforms their environment and turns rejection into love. Male orphans feature in **Charles Dickens**'s *Oliver Twist* (1837–1839) and *David Copperfield* (1849–1850) as well as in **Mark Twain**'s *The Adventures of Tom Sawyer* (1876) and *Adventures of Huckleberry Finn* (1884). The most famous orphan in recent children's fiction is **J. K. Rowling**'s *Harry Potter* (1997–2007), while **Lemony Snicket**'s *A Series of Unfortunate Events* (1999–2006) parodies the orphan genre. Orphans are attractive characters for authors because, released from parental control and familial obligation, they are free to pursue adventures at their own risk. They frequently have a heightened sense of their own identity through trying to discover their roots. *See also* AVERY, GILLIAN; BOSTON, LUCY M.; CUNNINGHAM,

JULIA; DAHL, ROALD; DOHERTY, BERLIE; GENDER; KIPLING, RUDYARD; LINDGREN, ASTRID; MORPURGO, MICHAEL; NAIDOO, BEVERLEY; SHERWOOD, MARY MARTHA; STREATFEILD, NOEL.

O'SULLIVAN, MARK (1954–). Irish author of predominantly realistic novels for young adults. *Melody for Nora* (1994), O'Sullivan's first novel, merges the personal and political in a story set against the backdrop of the Irish Civil War. It explores complex political allegiances, the horror of war, and difficult family circumstances through the eyes of its central character, Nora. Its sequel, *Wash-Basin Street Blues* (1995), follows Nora from Ireland to New York. *More Than a Match* (1996), a novel about a German-Irish family, addresses themes of national and cultural identity and competitive sport. In *Angels without Wings* (1997), a cleverly plotted story in a German setting that plays sophisticated games with the notion of fiction, the characters of a book come alive in order to try to prevent the manipulation of their story according to the dictates of Nazi ideology. The burning of **Erich Kästner**'s books in 1933 inspired the plot. *White Lies* (1999) is about an adopted black Irish teenager who begins to doubt the details of her adoption in Africa. *Silent Stones* (1997) returns to the theme of how war destroys families, by portraying two adolescents caught up in a mode of living that is historically imposed on them; the father of one was an Irish Republican Army man killed in an ambush before his son was born.

OXENBURY, HELEN (1938–). British **picture-book** author and **illustrator**. Oxenbury is acclaimed for her innovative contribution to the development of board books for prereaders in the series Heads, Bodies, and Legs; First Picture Books; and Tom and Pippo (the latter featuring a small boy and his toy monkey). Her illustrations of *The Quangle-Wangle's Hat* (1969) by **Edward Lear** and *The Dragon of an Ordinary Family* (1969) by **Margaret Mahy** won the **Kate Greenaway Medal**, an accolade she received a second time for her modern interpretation of **Lewis Carroll**'s *Alice's Adventures in Wonderland* (2000). She furnished **Michael Rosen**'s hugely popular *We're Going on a Bear Hunt* (1989) with alternating black-and-white and color illustrations; it went on to win the Smarties Book

Prize. Subsequent winners were the hilarious *Farmer Duck* (1991), a collaboration with **Martin Waddell,** and *So Much* (1994), by Trish Cooke with vibrant pictures by Oxenbury. A recent joint undertaking with **Mem Fox** produced a celebration of babies from all over the world in the form of *Ten Little Fingers and Ten Little Toes* (2008). Oxenbury is married to the illustrator **John Burningham**.

– P –

PACOVSKÁ, KVĚTA (1928–). Czech artist and **illustrator** who has produced an oeuvre of original, often whimsical, and ultramodern **picture books** for children. Pacovská treats the picture book as an object, which she tries to make tactile and three-dimensional. Her illustrations use bold, saturated colors, geometric and abstract shapes, collages, mirrors, and superimpositions of different kinds of paper. *Midnight Play* (1993) creates a miniature theater with cutouts; in *Alphabet* (1996), made into an award-winning interactive CD-ROM by Jean-Jacques Birgé, Frédéric Durieu, and Murielle Lefèvre in 1999, letters and numbers merge with her quirky-faced creatures. A recent work, *Unfold-Enfold* (2005), is an expandable object almost 20 feet in length, folded into a book of 100 pages, incorporating cutouts and pop-up elements. Other popular books by Pacovská include *One, Five, Many* (1990) and *Little Flowerking* (1991). Pacovská won the Golden Apple at the **Biennial of Illustrations Bratislava (BIB)** in 1983 and the **Hans Christian Andersen Award** in 1992. Her art has featured in several major international exhibitions.

PADDINGTON BEAR. An **anthropomorphic** small bear found at Paddington railway station in London by Mr. and Mrs. Brown, whose adventures feature in more than 10 books by Michael Bond, starting with *A Bear Called Paddington* (1958) and *More about Paddington* (1959). Paddington is extremely polite and obliging, likes marmalade sandwiches and cocoa, and frequently creates mayhem. Unlike the adventures of other fictional bears, his take place in the real world of suburban London. Paddington is one of the icons of English children's literature; the books have been **translated** into 30 languages, and the figure widely merchandised. Especially popular is the toy

Paddington bear dressed in a dark blue duffle coat, shapeless bush hat, and Wellington boots.

PANTOMIME. A form of traditional theatrical entertainment for children and parents performed during the Christmas and New Year holiday season. With a plot very loosely based on a **fairy tale** such as "Cinderella," "Puss in Boots," or "**Aladdin**," it incorporates song, dance, slapstick, audience participation, mild sexual innuendo, and **gender** crossing. The leading male character (the "principal boy") is often played by a young woman, the "pantomime dame," an older woman, usually by a man in drag. In its modern form, pantomime is a British invention, also successfully adopted by former colonies such as Australia and Ireland.

PARKINSON, SIOBHAN (1954–). Irish author for children and adults, and editor. A prolific writer of fiction, Parkinson writes books that are intelligent, experiment with narrative forms, and are full of dry humor. Her earliest works of fiction, *Amelia* (1993) and its sequel *No Peace for Amelia* (1994), are **historical novels** about a young Quaker girl in Dublin in 1914 and 1916; the comical story *The Leprechaun Who Wished He Wasn't* (1993) concerns two opposites who are dissatisfied with themselves. *Sisters . . . No Way!* (1996) presents diverging accounts of the same events by two stepsisters. These are arranged back-to-back, so that the reader can choose which one to start with. Boundaries between **fantasy** and reality, between fact and fiction, and between madness and sanity are called into question in *Four Kids, Three Cats, Two Cows, One Witch (Maybe)* (1997), which parodies the **adventure** form used by **Enid Blyton** and others. Considered by many to be her best novel, it explores personal identity and shows how the protagonists rewrite themselves by telling their own stories. The changing face of Irish ethnic diversity is addressed in *The Love Bean* (2002), an investigation of similarity and difference featuring two sets of twins at two distinct periods in Irish history, each of which encounter an attractive young man completely alien to their culture. Parkinson has won a number of **awards**, and her books have been **translated** into several European languages.

PARLEY, PETER. *See* GOODRICH, SAMUEL GRISWOLD.

PATERSON, KATHERINE (1932–). U.S. novelist for children. Born in China to Christian missionaries, Paterson spent much of her childhood there and later, after studying Christian education, worked as a missionary in Japan. She studied both Japanese and Chinese culture and these, as well as her religious belief, greatly influence her writing. Her first novel, *The Sign of the Chrysanthemum* (1973), was the first of four **historical novels** set in Japan. U.S. history features in some of her later novels, such as *Jip: His Story* (1996), which, in attempting to produce a more accurate account of slavery, is a modern reply to *Uncle Tom's Cabin.* She has also authored **picture books** and **nonfiction**, but it is above all for her contemporary psychological novels for children that Paterson has been widely acclaimed. In these, she presents in contemporary social settings and with great seriousness difficult topics such as loneliness, the death of a child, insufficient parental love, betrayal, and bereavement, often integrating a mythical level as an underlying textual structure.

Some novels are innovative in their use of unreliable first-person narrators. Topics such as feeling betrayed by a parent feature in *Park's Quest* (1988) and *Come Sing, Jimmy Jo* (1985), which, like *The Great Gilly Hopkins* (1978), have as their central theme a child seeking a parent. In the **Newbery Medal**–winning *Bridge to Terabithia* (1977), her most famous novel, two lonely children create a magical world inspired by **C. S. Lewis**'s *Narnia* books, in which they name themselves king and queen. After Leslie's tragic death, Jess is left to cope with his grief. It was one of the first U.S. children's books to feature a child's response to a close friend's death. Paterson won the Newbery Medal for a second time with *Jacob Have I Loved* (1980), again a first-person narrative that presents sibling rivalry between Louise and her more talented and prettier twin sister Caroline, and Louise's attempt to free herself from her sister's shadow up into adulthood.

Regarded by some critics as too religious, many of Paterson's novels have also come in for criticism by conservative Christians. Highly serious in her moral vision, Paterson sets high aesthetic standards for children's literature, about which she has also written a number of critical essays. Her work has been honored by the two most important international **prizes** for children's literature, the **Hans Christian Andersen Award** in 1998 and the **Astrid Lindgren Memorial Award** in 2006.

PAULSEN, GARY (1939–). U.S. author of more than 175 books and 200 shorter pieces of fiction and **nonfiction** for adults and children. Paulsen's favored genre is the plot-driven **adventure novel**, often featuring characters that must rely on themselves to survive extreme challenges, both physical and emotional. *Hatchet* (1987) is the story of a 13-year-old boy who crash-lands a plane in the Canadian wilderness and has to survive for months with a hatchet as his only tool. Paulsen's love of dogs and his experience of having twice run the 1,180-mile Alaskan dogsled race, the Iditarod, feature in *Woodsong* (1990), his autobiographical account for young adults, and in *Winterdance: The Fine Madness of Running the Iditarod* (1994) for adults. *Dogsong* (1985) is a coming-of-age story about an Inuit boy who learns to run sled dogs. In his **historical novel** *Nightjohn* (1993), Paulsen addresses the grim realities faced by African American slaves. His juvenile nonfiction includes a series of humorous sports books such as *Dribbling, Shooting, and Scoring—Sometimes* (1976). *The Amazing Life of Birds: The Twenty-Day Puberty Journal of Duane Homer Leech* (2006) is a comic take on adolescence in journal form. Together with his wife, the artist Ruth Wright Paulsen, Paulsen has created a number of **picture books**, including *The Tortilla Factory* (1998) and *Dogteam* (1999).

PAUSEWANG, GUDRUN (1928–). German author of numerous books for children and young adults, which critically examine social and political issues. Among her best known are the two speculative, dystopian novels about nuclear disasters, *Die Wolke* (1987; *Fall-Out*, 1995), which was made into a film in 2006, and *Die letzten Kinder von Schewenborn* (1983; *The Last Children of Schevenborn*, 1988). *Reise im August* (1992; *The Final Journey*, 1996) is a remarkable fictional account of the train journey of a Jewish girl to the Auschwitz extermination camp. Pausewang, who lived in South America for 16 years, also wrote several novels set in that continent, as well as a trilogy of autobiographical novels, *Rosinkawiese* (1980–1990), about her childhood in the German-speaking area of Czechoslovakia, the Sudetenland, during the Nazi era and World War II. She has received numerous national and international **awards**.

PEARCE, PHILIPPA (1920–2006). English scriptwriter, radio producer, children's editor, and author of novels and short stories.

Pearce's first novel, *Minnow on the Say* (1955; published in the United States as *The Minnow Leads to Treasure*), was inspired by a canoe trip she had made several years previously and is, as all of her fiction, informed by a clear sense of place in and around Cambridge, where she spent most of her life. Her most famous book and an acclaimed masterpiece of English children's literature is the **Carnegie Medal**–winning *Tom's Midnight Garden* (1958), a time-shift **fantasy** that draws on the notion that different times can coexist and blend. Young Tom, who visits his old aunt and uncle in a house in the country, discovers a beautiful walled garden that appears every night, in which he meets Hatty, an **orphan** from Victorian times, who is bored and lonely like he is. They become friends and enjoy a few weeks of happiness together, but Hatty becomes older in each successive meeting and finally, almost an adult, disappears from the midnight garden. After having wanted to arrest time and stay in the garden, a symbol of childhood paradise, Tom comes to realize that living in a fantasy world is no long-term alternative to everyday life; he is finally ready to face the psychological challenge of growing up. At the end of the novel, the old proprietor of the house, resident in an upstairs apartment, is revealed to be Hatty, and there is a moving moment of recognition between her and Tom. Further acclaimed novels by Pearce include *A Dog So Small* (1962), *The Children of the House* (1968; later reissued as *The Children of Charlecote*), *The Battle of Bubble and Squeak* (1978), and *The Little Gentleman* (2004). Pearce was appointed OBE in 1997 for her services to children's literature.

PECK, RICHARD (1934–). U.S. novelist, poet, and short-story writer considered one of the pioneers of young adult literature. His realistic novels for this age group deal with a wide variety of difficult social and personal issues, such as dysfunctional families in *Father Figure* (1978), rape in *Are You in the House Alone?* (1976), and suicide and divorce in *Remembering the Good Times* (1985). Peck extended the generic boundaries of the serious coming-of-age novel to include **horror stories** (e.g., *Ghosts I Have Been*, 1977), comedy (e.g., *The Teacher's Funeral: A Comedy in Three Parts*, 2004), and **fantasy** (e.g., *Lost in Cyberspace*, 1995). His humorous, **Newbery Medal**–winning novel, *A Year Down Yonder* (2000), follows city kids from Chicago who go to stay with their eccentric grandmother in a country town during the Depression years. Peck has also edited and published a number of anthologies of **poems** and short stories.

PECK, ROBERT NEWTON (1928–). U.S. writer for adults and children whose poignant and partly autobiographical novel, *A Day No Pigs Would Die* (1972), depicts a 16-year-old protagonist who experiences the clash of cultures between the life led by his Shaker family and the modern world to which he is increasingly exposed. Suddenly becoming the breadwinner of the family after his father falls ill, he has to butcher his pet pig. A sequel, *A Part of the Sky* (1994), followed it. His *Soup* stories, humorous bad-boy tales with echoes of *Tom Sawyer*, are particularly popular among young readers. They include *Soup and Me* (1975), *Soup on Wheels* (1981), and *Soup for President* (1978). A number of these have been **adapted** for television.

PENNY DREADFULS. Cheap printed entertainment—serial-story papers, magazines, and novelettes—which emerged in mid-19th-century Great Britain. Mass-produced by anonymous authors, the stories were sensationalist and designed to arouse horror and delight. They featured such heroes and villains as Varney the Vampire, Rob Roy, Sweeney Todd, and Dick Turpin. Printed on cheap paper and sold in weekly installments for a penny, this popular literature was aimed primarily at youthful, working-class audiences. Many U.S. **dime novels**, the counterpart of the penny dreadfuls, were rewritten for a British audience who enjoyed reading the escapades of Frank Reade, Buffalo Bill, and Deadwood Dick.

PERKINS, LUCY FITCH (1865–1937). U.S. author and **illustrator** of the popular Twins series of books, which includes such titles as *The Dutch Twins* (1911), *The Irish Twins* (1913), and *The Eskimo Twins* (1914) and describes life in other countries. They were widely read in schools and homes all over the United States and were **translated** into several languages.

PERRAULT, CHARLES (1628–1703). French writer, poet, and member of the Académie Française, and one of the founders of the literary **fairy tale** in Europe. Perrault became acquainted with fairy tales in the literary salons of **Marie-Catherine d'Aulnoy** and others, and it was under their influence that he published his collection of eight tales, *Histoires, ou Contes du temps passé* (1697; *Histories, or Tales of Past Times*, 1729). It included versions of "Sleeping Beauty," "Bluebeard," "Cinderella," "Tom Thumb," and "Puss in Boots." Written for adults, Perrault's tales made their way into children's literature through **chapbooks** in the 18th century. Today his tales are published in **illustrated** collections and **picture-book** versions of individual tales. They have been made into operas and ballets, as well as films, both live-action and animated. *See also* ADAPTATION.

PETER PAN. *See* BARRIE, SIR J. M.

PETER RABBIT. *See* POTTER, BEATRIX.

PEYTON, K. M. (1929–). British author of more than 50 novels, many of them **pony stories** published under the pseudonym Kathleen Herald. She is best known for her Flambards series of novels set before, during, and after World War I, centered on the **orphan** Christina Parsons. Christina stays with her uncle and her cousins Mark and William, members of the landed gentry, on their run-down estate in *Flambards* (1968). Historical change in ways of life in the process of modernization features in this romantic but realistic series that traces the demise of the old patriarchal order, which is forced to make way for a new social and economic one. The second, **Carnegie Medal**–winning, novel, *The Edge of the Cloud* (1969), covers Christina and her cousin William's elopement against the backdrop of the upcoming war and William's passion for flying. In the third volume, *Flambards in Summer* (1969), Christina, now a war widow, returns to the big house, and falls in love with and marries the former stable boy, Dick. What was originally planned as a trilogy was followed by a fourth volume, *Flambards Divided* (1981), which sees a partial restoration of the old social order with Christina leaving Dick and planning to marry her cousin Mark; it dissatisfied many fans. The Flambards trilogy was made into a popular television series in 1979. A further series for young adults by Peyton is Pennington, published in the 1970s, which features a troubled and aggressive working-class protagonist who is a gifted musician.

PICTURE BOOKS. Composite texts that usually rely for their effects on the interdependence of pictures and words. From the very beginning, printed children's books were **illustrated**, initially with crude woodcuts or with more sophisticated engravings. The pictures in illustrated books traditionally play a subservient role, based as they are on a preexisting verbal text. In picture books, on the other hand, the pictures are as important as the words, and their synergetic relationship means that the total effect depends not only on the union of the visual and the verbal elements but also on the interaction between them. This can take numerous different forms, ranging from parallel storytelling, in which words and pictures tell the same story, to contradictory or ironic interaction, in which words and pictures tell two different stories. In the past few decades, postmodern picture books have experimented with nonlinear narrative forms, metafiction, and deconstruction.

The origins of the picture book lie in educational publications and encyclopedias such as **John Amos Comenius**'s *Orbis Sensualium Pictus* (1658) and in the popular **chapbooks**. The picture book itself is a relatively recent invention, the development of which hinged on advancements in printing technology during the late 19th and early 20th centuries. The development of lithography provided the technical means of printing quality pictures in multiple colors in close proximity with the text, a prerequisite for the picture book. By the second half of the 19th century, technological advances in color printing meant that high-quality picture books could be produced relatively cheaply for a mass market. A milestone in the development of the picture book was **Heinrich Hoffmann**'s *Stuwwelpeter,* published in Germany in 1845. A trio of British artists during the late 19th century, **Randolph Caldecott**, **Kate Greenaway**, and **Walter Crane** provided a further significant influence on its development. They, together with the printer and engraver Edmund Evans, who recruited all three and who was a pioneer in the area of reproduction of quality illustrations, transformed earlier forms into what can be regarded as the modern picture book. Of the three, Caldecott has been the most influential; his humorous interpretation of rhymes and the witty and often surprising interaction between text and picture have been greatly admired by such picture-book artists as **Beatrix Potter**, whose *Tale of Peter Rabbit* was published in 1902, and **Maurice Sendak**.

In the 1920s, color photo-offset lithography that could reproduce art media with a high degree of accuracy was used for William Nicholson's *Clever Bill* (1926), with its hand-lettered text. The possibilities of this technology were further exploited by **Edward Ardizzone** in 1930s Great Britain in his Little Tim books, and by **Jean de Brunhoff** in France in his hugely popular Babar series, starting in 1931. Of central importance for the development of the American picture book was **Wanda Gág**'s *Millions of Cats* (1928), a story in **folktale** mode about a castaway, with black-and-white illustrations and attractive hand lettering. It was the first picture book to receive the Newbery Honor citation, which Gág received again five years later for *The ABC Bunny* (1933).

Acknowledging the development of the picture book as a form that merited its own award, the **American Library Association (ALA)** established in 1938, as a sister **award** to the **Newbery Medal**, the **Caldecott Medal**, to be given annually to the most distinguished children's book illustration. Significant collaborative picture books in the 1930s include *The Story about Ping* (1933), with text by Marjorie Flack and pictures by **Kurt Wiese**, and the antiwar picture book *The Story of Ferdinand* (1936), written by **Robert Lawson** and illustrated in black and white by **Munro Leaf**. The year 1937 saw the publication of *And to Think That I Saw It on Mulberry Street* by **Dr. Seuss**, a graphic artist and humorist who broke the traditional picture-book mold with his imaginative cartoon pictures and anarchic language games. Other Dr. Seuss favorites followed, such as *Horton Hatches the Egg* (1940) and, in 1957, the wildly imaginative *Cat in the Hat*, a story using only 223 distinct words that changed the face of **easy readers**. A further milestone in picture-book innovation was Maurice Sendak's *Where the Wild Things Are* (1963), with its use of visual symbolism to explore the child's interior world. This and subsequent picture books by Sendak marked an increase in sophistication in this art form.

The comic strip has had an important influence on the development of the picture book, and contemporary picture-book artists such as **Shirley Hughes**, **Raymond Briggs**, **Tony Ross**, and **Babette Cole** have explored its possibilities. The influence of the cinema is evident in many works, from Lawson and Leaf's *The Story of Ferdinand* to the cold images in **Chris van Allsburg**'s *Polar Express*

(1985). The 1970s saw the introduction of new forms; *Look Again!* (1971), by Tana Hoban, was one of the first picture books to feature photographs as the medium. In the same decade, the wordless picture book evolved; examples include fully formed nonverbal narratives such as Raymond Briggs's *The Snowman* (1978); and books by the Japanese artist **Mitsumasa Anno**, such as *Anno's Journey* (1977) and *Anno's Britain* (1982), which invite the reader to scrutinize detailed scenes and discover clever instances of pictorial quotations or interpicturality on the way. A further development was the trend toward **nonfiction** picture books; one of the leading artists in this subgenre is **David Macaulay**, with his books on architecture. Cultural diversity has gradually gained recognition in the picture books of the leading **multicultural** nations. An early example is **Ezra Jack Keats**'s *The Snowy Day* (1962), one of the first picture books to feature an African American boy. Leading African American artists and writers committed to cultural diversity include **Leo and Diane Dillon** and **Tom Feelings**. In Australia, *The Giant Devil-Dingo* (1973), by Aboriginal artist Dick Roughsey and Percy Trezise, was the first picture book from an Aboriginal perspective. An example of a striking expansion of visual and verbal cultural references in Great Britain is James Berry's *Celebration Song* (1994), the story of Jesus' birth in a Caribbean setting, with pictures by Louise Brierly.

The most recent trend consists of postmodern picture books that defy the usual linear organization of storybooks, often incorporating self-referential elements, intertextuality, and metafiction. These are playful texts that demand a high degree of readers' involvement in constructing meaning. Precursors included **John Burningham**, who playfully subverted rules and conventions by exploiting the gap between pictures and words in books such as *Come Away from the Water, Shirley* (1977); and **Allan and Janet Ahlberg**, with their playful exploration of the book's physical structure in *The Jolly Postman* (1986) and their wide-reaching but always accessible and funny, intertextuality in the Jolly Postman books and *Each Peach, Pear, Plum* (1978). **David Wiesner**'s use of postmodern elements in *The Three Pigs* (2001) is more radical; here the very act of world making is foregrounded. The pigs fall out of the frame and hence out of the story, only to return to wander through other stories, thereby taking control of their own tale. Metafictionality and interrupted narratives can also be found in books by **Jon Scieszka** and **Lane Smith**, most famously in *The Stinky Cheese Man* (1992). *See also* ABBOTT, JACOB; ANIMAL FICTION; BANNERMAN, HELEN; BERRY, JAMES; BLAKE, QUENTIN; BROOKS, RON; BROWNE, ANTHONY; BRUNA, DICK; BUTTERWORTH, NICK; CARLE, ERIC; CHILD, LAUREN; CREW, GARY; FOREMAN, MICHAEL; FOX, MEM; FRITZ, JEAN; GUY, ROSA; ILLUSTRATIONS; INKPEN, MICK; KEEPING, CHARLES; KERR, JUDITH; KREIDOLF, ERNST; LOBEL, ANITA; LOBEL, ARNOLD; LYNCH, P. J.; MAHY, MARGARET; MCKEE, DAVID; ORMEROD, JAN; OXENBURY, HELEN; PACOVSKÁ, KVĚTA; REY, H. A. AND MARGRET; ROSEN, MICHAEL; RUBINSTEIN, GILLIAN; SAY, ALLEN; SCHAMI, RAFIK; SÍS, PETER; STEIG, WILLIAM; TAN, SHAUN; VAN ALLSBURG, CHRIS; WADDELL, MARTIN; WILD, MARGARET; WILDSMITH, BRIAN; WILLARD, NANCY; WYNNE-JONES, TIM: YOUNG, ED; ZOLOTOW, CHARLOTTE; ZWERGER, LISBETH.

PINKNEY, JERRY (1939–). U.S. **illustrator** who has worked with many celebrated writers for children such as **Mildred Taylor**, **Virginia Hamilton**, **Verna Aardema**, and **Julius Lester**. With his distinctive watercolors and underlying pencil sketches he has illustrated traditional stories, **poetry**, **information books**, and novels from a variety of cultures, such as **Hans Christian Andersen**'s *The Ugly Duckling* (1999), **Aesop**'s ***Fables*** (2000), and his own *Noah's Ark* (2002), with African and African American subjects receiving a special focus throughout his career. Especially notable are his collaborations with Julius Lester, which include four volumes of *Uncle Remus* stories (from 1987) and *Sam and the Tigers* (1996), a retelling of **Little Black Sambo**. Pinkney has been a role model for other African American artists, and his sons Brian and Myles Pinkney also write and illustrate children's books.

PINKWATER, DANIEL (1941–). U.S. author, **illustrator**, and broadcaster. Pinkwater is especially known for humorous books that combine slapstick with absurd situations and present sympathetic, nonconformist protagonists in plots combining elements of **science fiction** and **fantasy**. Titles for children include *The Hoboken Chicken*

Emergency (1977) and *Fat Men from Space* (1977); for teenagers he has written such books as *Alan Mendelsohn, the Boy from Mars* (1979) and *Young Adult Novel* (1982), a satirical take on the "problem novel." His **picture books** include *The Big Orange Splot* (1977) and *Guys From Space* (1989). Pinkwater has illustrated many of the 50 books he has authored, but a number are also the result of collaboration with his wife, the illustrator Jill Pinkwater.

PINOCCHIO, THE ADVENTURES OF. *See* COLLODI, CARLO.

PIPPI LONGSTOCKING. *See* LINDGREN, ASTRID.

PIUMINI, ROBERTO (1947–). Italian author of novels for children and adults, plays, **poems**, **fairy tales**, screenplays, and songs. One of Italy's leading contemporary authors for children, Piumini has produced work covering a range of genres and themes, from retellings of **myths** and classical works such as *La nuova Commedia di Dante* [The New Divine Comedy] (2004); through a touching psychological novel about the acceptance of death, *Mattia e il nonno* (1993; *Matti and Grandpa,* 1993); to **picture-book** collaborations: his collaboration with artist Piet Grobler, for example, produced the amusing *Il medico Me-Di-Cin* (2001; *Doctor Me Di Cin*, 2001), in which a wise doctor tricks a sick young Chinese prince into curing himself without drugs or medication. Piumini's highly acclaimed, multilayered, and lyrical books have been **translated** into some dozen languages.

POETRY. The earliest poems for children derived from oral traditions, and included proverbs, rhyming alphabets, jog-along knee songs, riddles, and **lullabies**. Many now belong to the body of what we call **nursery rhymes** or Mother Goose rhymes. While children also enjoyed the broadside ballads printed in **chapbooks**, collections specifically made for them were issued by the Puritans of the 17th century, who saw poetry as a means of religious instruction. **John Bunyan**'s *A Book for Boys and Girls* (1686) was arguably the first poetry book for young readers. A little milder in tone was **Isaac Watts**'s *Divine Songs, Attempted in Easy Language for the Use of Children* (1715), which was in circulation for more than two centuries and widely read. **William Blake**'s *Songs of Innocence* (1789), which anticipated the Romantic movement, were written in the hymn tradition but addressed children in ways that were radically new, and they criticized contemporary social and moral behavior. *Original Poems for Infant Minds* (1804) by **Ann and Jane Taylor**, the first English poets exclusively for children, had an important influence on the development of child-centered children's poetry.

During the 19th century, poetry for children broke away from its religious roots to become more lighthearted. In the United States, Clement Clarke Moore's "A Visit from St. Nicholas" (1823), more widely known as "The Night Before Christmas," celebrated the modern American Santa Claus. A few decades later, major works of **nonsense** were published in Great Britain: **Edward Lear**'s humorous and linguistically inventive *A Book of Nonsense* (1846), and **Lewis Carroll**'s *Alice's Adventures in Wonderland* (1865), which contained numerous parodies and nonsense verses that poked liberating fun at the earlier tradition of moral verse. **Heinrich Hoffmann**'s *Struwwelpeter* (1845) comically subverted the genre of **cautionary tales and verses**, and remained popular throughout the 19th and 20th centuries. **Robert Louis Stevenson**'s *A Child's Garden of Verses* (1885) marked the emergence of poetry that tried to speak with an authentic child's voice and to portray the world from a child's point of view; Stevenson greatly influenced later poets such as **Walter de la Mare**, especially his collections *Songs of Childhood* (1902) and *Peacock Pie* (1913). Following in this tradition and adding his own brand of humor was **A. A. Milne**, with *When We Were Very Young* (1924) and *Now We Are Six* (1927).

In her study of 300 years of poetry for children, *From the Garden to the Street* (1998), Morag Styles identifies a shift in poetry for children from pastoral innocence to urban knowingness. One of the few major English-language nature poets for children in the second half of the 20th century was the poet laureate **Ted Hughes**; otherwise comic poetry dominates, with notable authors such as **Shel Silverstein**, **Allan Ahlberg**, Roger McGough, **Roald Dahl**, and **Dr. Seuss**. Authors of challenging works that encourage children to engage with traditions and new forms of poetry include **Nancy Willard**, whose *A Visit to William Blake's Inn: Poems for the Innocent and Experienced Travellers* (1981) was the first book of poetry to win the **Newbery Medal**; and **Paul Fleischman**, who received the same accolade for his *Joyful Noise: Poems for Two Voices* (1988).

One of the most striking developments in children's poetry in the late 20th century was the increasing significance of poetry written in an idiom not predominantly white, middle class, and Standard English. African American poets feature in the anthologies *Shimmy Shimmy Shimmy Like My Sister Kate: Looking At the Harlem Renaissance through Poems* (1996), edited by Nikki Giovanni, and Nikki Grimes's *A Pocketful of Poems* (2001). Native American poems based on traditional songs and prayers are collected in **Joseph Bruchac**'s *The Circle of Thanks: Native American Poems and Songs of Thanksgiving* (1996) and in Brian Swann's *Touching the Distance: Native American Riddle Poems* (1996). The vibrant voices of Caribbean poets in England, such as **John Agard**, **James Berry**, **Grace Nichols**, and Benjamin Zephaniah, have greatly enriched contemporary British poetry for children and adults. *See also* AWARDS; BARBAULD, ANNA LAETITIA; BELLOC, JOSEPH HILAIRE PIERRE RENÉ; BROWN, MARGARET WISE; FARJEON, ELEANOR; KIPLING, RUDYARD; LONGFELLOW, HENRY WADSWORTH; ROSEN, MICHAEL; SCHMIDT, ANNIE M. G.; WEISSE, CHRISTIAN FELIX; YOLEN, JANE.

***POLLYANNA*.** Best-selling novel by the author Eleanor H. Porter, published in 1913, about an eternally cheerful and optimistic **orphan**, 11-year-old Pollyanna Whittier, who goes to live with her aunt Polly. Her philosophy of life centers on "the glad game," which she plays to find something positive to be glad about in every situation, even when she loses the use of her legs in an accident. The book was an international best seller, and the adjective "Pollyannaish" has since then been used to describe someone who is naively optimistic.

POMBO, RAFAEL (1833–1912). Colombian poet, journalist, and translator. Pombo lived and worked in the United States from 1855 to 1872, during which time he translated **nursery rhymes** from the Anglo-Saxon oral tradition into Spanish. The result was two volumes of narratives in verse and prose known throughout the Spanish-speaking world, *Cuentos pintados para niños* [Illustrated Tales for Children] (1867) and *Cuentos morales para niños* [Moral Tales for Children] (1869). He also published many popular children's **fables**.

Pombo became the first *poeta nacional* (national poet) in Colombia in 1905 and is regarded as one of the great poets of that country.

PONY STORIES. *See* HORSE AND PONY STORIES.

PORTER, ELEANOR H. *See POLLYANNA.*

POTTER, BEATRIX (1866–1943). English author and **illustrator** best known for her 23 small-format **picture books**, most of them published between 1902 and 1916, which feature **anthropomorphic** animal characters. Potter spent a sheltered and isolated Victorian childhood and young adulthood in London and on extended family holidays in Scotland and the Lake District, where she observed and drew plants and animals. Being a woman in that era, with parents who discouraged both her intellectual development and her independence, meant that a career in biology, her main interest next to drawing, was out of the question. She was 36 when she published her first book, the highly successful *Tale of Peter Rabbit* (1902), and the royalties from this and other books eventually enabled her to become financially independent of her parents and buy her own property in 1909.

The Tale of Peter Rabbit, first told in a picture-letter to the son of Potter's former governess, tells the story of a young rabbit who ignores his mother's warning and enters Mr. McGregor's garden, where he feasts on vegetables. Discovered by Mr. McGregor, Peter is chased and almost caught but just manages to escape, losing his blue jacket and shoes in the process. Rather than punishing his disobedience, his mother tucks him into bed with chamomile tea for his indigestion, while his sisters enjoy their supper of bread and milk and blackberries. Peter is one of many naughty children in Potter's works; and, although they are not permitted to get away with it, their disobedience, especially toward their parents, is the prerequisite for the adventure and excitement of the story. Two further books feature Peter Rabbit: *The Tale of Benjamin Bunny* (1904), which tells how Peter and Benjamin try to retrieve Peter's clothes from Mr. McGregor's garden, and *The Tale of the Flopsy Bunnies* (1909). Other well-known titles include *The Tale of Squirrel Nutkin* (1903), *The Tale of Jemima Puddle-Duck* (1908), and *The Tale of Pigling Bland* (1913).

Potter never underestimated her young audience, and she neither sentimentalized her **animal** protagonists nor played down the cruelty of nature. She integrated words and images in an innovative way and drew animals from life with great skill; despite the anthropomorphic elements of clothing and speech, she attributed to them perfectly appropriate animal behavior. Potter's language is sophisticated and witty, and her dry understatement and caricature of social behavior have led to her being called the Jane Austen of the nursery. She married in 1913, against the wishes of her parents, and from then on her main interest was in farming and sheep breeding. One of the leading conservationists of her day, she bought property in the Lake District to protect the area from developers, which she bequeathed to the National Trust.

Potter was one of the first authors to exploit the merchandise possibilities of her fiction, making a Peter Rabbit doll and issuing painting books, jigsaw puzzles, and wallpaper. With 450 licensees worldwide, her characters are among the most widely merchandised today. Film versions of the stories include a ballet version, *The Tales of Beatrix Potter* (1971), and an animated series, *The World of Peter Rabbit and Friends* (1992), produced by the BBC. The BBC also produced *The Tale of Beatrix Potter* (1982), a dramatization of her life; and a biopic starring Renée Zellweger, *Miss Potter*, was released in 2006. Potter's books have been **translated** into numerous languages and continue to sell well today.

PRATCHETT, TERRY (1948–). English author of **fantasy** and **science fiction** for adults and children. Pratchett is best known for his Discworld series of comic fantasy novels, starting with *The Colour of Magic* (1983) and encompassing, by 2009, 37 novels. They are set in a flat world that balances on the backs of four enormous elephants. These, in turn, are standing on the back of a giant turtle, Great A'Tuin, which swims through space. The series offers an irreverent take on high fantasy, contains forms of humor from **nonsense** to parody and satire, and incorporates details of popular culture, current technology, and science. It appeals to a wide range of readers who appreciate Pratchett's humor and the intellectual challenges he offers, including the reflections on death in many of his novels. While the Discworld series is enjoyed by younger readers, only four of the novels are specifically addressed to this age group: *The Amazing Maurice and His Educated Rodents* (2001), a parody of the Pied Piper story that won the **Carnegie Medal**, and three that feature trainee **witch** Tiffany Aching and her battles against the forces of evil—*The Wee Free Men* (2003), *A Hat Full of Sky* (2004), and *Wintersmith* (2006). Other children's books by Pratchett include a trilogy about Johnny Maxwell and his friends, who, in *Johnny and the Dead* (1992), save the local cemetery from property developers; *Only You Can Save Mankind* (1993) is about computer games; and *Johnny and the Bomb* (1996) is a time-slip fantasy in which Johnny finds himself in his hometown during World War II. Pratchett's acclaimed *Bromeliad* trilogy for children—*Truckers* (1989), *Diggers* (1990), and *Wings* (1990)—is about a miniature world of gnomes, their forced flight from home, and a search for safety that leads them to discover their amazing origins. His novels have been **translated** into more than 30 languages and have sold more than 55 million copies worldwide. Pratchett was appointed OBE for services to literature in 1998 and was knighted in 2009.

PRESSLER, MIRJAM (1940–). German author of more than 30 novels for children and young adults and **prize**winning **translator** from Hebrew, Dutch, and English. While her early novels often address social difficulties experienced by contemporary children, later novels address broader political issues in a historical setting. *Malka Mai* (2001; *Malka,* 2003) is the moving odyssey of a seven-year-old Jewish girl abandoned by her mother during the flight from Poland and the Nazis; the **historical novel** *Shylocks Tochter* (1999; *Shylock's Daughter*, 2000) addresses the anti-Semitism of 16th-century Venice and its effects on Shylock—the figure from Shakespeare's *Merchant of Venice*—and his daughter Jessica. Pressler, who wrote a **biography** of Anne Frank in 1992, coedited the definitive version of the girl's diary published in Dutch in 1991 and in English as *Anne Frank: The Diary of a Young Girl* in 1995. Pressler won a special German Youth Literature **Award** (Deutscher Jugendliteraturpreis) for her lifetime achievements as a translator in 1994 and, in 2004, was awarded the German Order of Merit (Bundesverdienstkreuz) for her entire literary production.

PREUSSLER, OTFRIED (1923–). German author in the **fantasy** tradition, many of whose figures and topics originate in Slavic and German **myths**, **legends**, and folk tradition. His best-known titles include *Der kleine Wassermann* (1956; *The Little Water-Sprite,* 1961); *Die kleine Hexe* (1957; *The Little Witch,* 1961), about a trainee **witch** only 127 years young who uses her magic powers to bring about good instead of evil; the comic tales in three volumes about the *Räuber Hotzenplotz* (1962–1973; *The Robber Hotzenplotz*, 1965 and 1971); and *Krabat* (1971; *The Satanic Mill*, 1972), a dark story for older readers that focuses on the lure of evil. It was reissued in English under the title *The Curse of the Darkling Mill* in 2000, and a movie **adaptation** was released in 2008. Hugely popular in Germany, Preussler's books have been **translated** into more than 50 languages and have sold some 40 million copies worldwide.

PRIMER. Originally the name for a small prayer book used to teach children how to read; a famous example is the *New England Primer* (ca. 1690). By the early 19th century, the term had come to denote a small introductory book on any subject used to teach children their letters.

PRIZES. *See* AWARDS.

PRØYSEN, ALF (1914–1970). Norwegian author best known for his lively, magical tales about the adventures of Mrs. Pepperpot (1956–1966), an old woman who can shrink in size. (Teskjekjerringa, her Norwegian name, literally means "teaspoon lady.") In diminished form, she can understand and speak to animals and act as a magical helper. Prøysen's stories, originally written for the radio, were discovered by **Astrid Lindgren** when she was working as an editor. The first of many collections was published in Swedish in 1956, with the Norwegian edition, *Kjerringa som ble så lita som ei teskje*, following in 1957. The English **translation**, *Little Old Mrs. Pepperpot, and Other Stories*, was issued in 1959. The stories have been translated into more than 20 languages.

PULLMAN, PHILIP (1946–). English writer who covers a wide range of genres and styles, from graphic novels (*Clockwork, or All*

Wound Up, 1996) to **fairy tales** (*The Firework-Maker's Daughter*, 1995) to **historical thrillers** set in the 19th century (the Sally Lockhart series). He is best known for his epic **fantasy** trilogy His Dark Materials (1995–2000), comprising *Northern Lights* (published in the United States as *The Golden Compass*), *The Subtle Knife*, and *The Amber Spyglass*, which won the Whitbread Children's Book **Award** and went on to become the first children's book ever to win the overall Whitbread Book of the Year. Pullman describes His Dark Materials as "*Paradise Lost* for teenagers," and the title of the trilogy is drawn from Book One of Milton's epic poem. It tells of the struggle between good and evil and between love and hatred, and it is centered on the young protagonists Lyra and Will from an alternate world. The trilogy has been widely acclaimed for its gripping plot, its absorbing characters, and its exploration of big ideas, from the nature of hell to the existence, or otherwise, of God. One of its most striking and moving inventions is the concept of *daemons*, animal-shaped manifestations of the soul that cannot be separated from their humans. Children's daemons change form at will, but during puberty a daemon settles into the form that reflects his or her human's personality. The trilogy, a best seller for both adult and young readers, is an outstanding contemporary contribution to children's literature. Pullman was appointed CBE in 2004; in 2005 he won the **Astrid Lindgren Memorial Award**.

PUNCH AND JUDY. Main characters in a traditional British hand-puppet show that dates back to the 17th century. Punch, originally derived from the *commedia dell'arte* figure Pulcinella, has an oversized, hooked, red nose, bright red cheeks, and a long club used to bash his victims. These are, in the main, his wife Judy, their baby, the hangman, and the devil, the latter replaced by a crocodile in most modern versions. Punch and Judy shows now feature chiefly at the seaside, at funfairs, or at children's birthday parties, and are the first theatrical experience of many British children, who enjoy the knockabout comedy and the violence.

PYLE, HOWARD (1853–1911). U.S. **illustrator**, author, and teacher. Pyle started his creative career illustrating for magazines, including *St. Nicholas*, and went on to illustrate and write some 13 books for children. The first book for which he provided both text and illustrations was *The Merry Adventures of* ***Robin Hood*** (1883), a retelling in mock-medieval style of the classic stories he read in his childhood. This beautifully designed book is notable for its full-page illustrations framed in imitation of medieval manuscript illumination. His fascination with the medieval period is also evident in *Otto of the Silver Hand* (1888), set in 16th-century Germany, *Men of Iron* (1892), set in England in the early 15th century, and his four-volume version of the Arthurian legends, *The Story of King Arthur and His Knights* (1903). *Pepper and Salt* (1886) and *The Wonder Clock* (1888) are retellings of European **folktales** in the colloquial style of the **Grimm** brothers. Pyle believed that the artist should address the whole text, he was always mindful of the total appearance of a book and a page, and his illustrations are notable for their dynamism and depiction of action. Although his work reveals the influence of European artists such as Albrecht Dürer and his style has been compared to that of the Pre-Raphaelites in England, Pyle promoted a distinctively American form of art and, as a teacher, believed that his art students should seek their training and inspiration in the United States. His illustrations of Civil War subjects are still widely used in American history books.

– R –

RACISM. *See* ETHNOCENTRISM.

RACKHAM, ARTHUR (1867–1939). British artist who **illustrated** more than 50 books, mainly for children, most famously *Fairy Tales of the Brothers Grimm* (1900), *Alice's Adventures in Wonderland* (1907), and *Mother Goose: The Old Nursery Rhymes* (1913). One of the leading illustrators of his time, Rackham was influenced by Japanese prints and the Pre-Raphaelites. His watercolor paintings, with their delicate fairies and barely-hidden details, create an otherworldly quality, and their foreboding atmosphere reflects his understanding of the dark undercurrents beneath **fairy tales**. Rackham's style was highly influential in the area of **fantasy** illustration.

RAGGEDY ANN. *See* GRUELLE, JOHNNY.

RAMAL, WALTER. *See* DE LA MARE, WALTER.

RANSOME, ARTHUR (1884–1967). English novelist best known for his Swallows and Amazons series of 12 novels (1930–1947). The books, which were very popular in both Great Britain and the United States during the author's lifetime and beyond, involve the **adventures** of a group of children during their school holidays between the two world wars. Set mainly in a fictionalized version of the Lake District, a lot of attention is devoted to holiday activities such as sailing, camping, and fishing. The characters grow older and mature as the series progresses, and the narrative structures gain in complexity. The sixth book, *Pigeon Post* (1936), won the first **Carnegie Medal** awarded for children's literature. The seventh, *We Didn't Mean to Go to Sea* (1937), in which four children in a yacht drift out into the North Sea, eventually ending up in the Netherlands, is generally regarded as Ransome's best novel.

RAWLINGS, MARJORIE KINNAN (1896–1953). U.S. author of novels, short stories, and autobiographical essays primarily for adults. She is best known for her Pulitzer Prize–winning *The Yearling* (1938), a story about childhood set in the 1870s on a poor farm in Florida. Now regarded a children's classic but originally published for an adult readership, it follows a year in the life of 11-year-old Jody and his forced transition into adulthood when he has to kill his pet deer to save his family from starvation. The book was made into a film in 1946 and into a television version in 1994.

REBECCA OF SUNNYBROOK FARM. *See* WIGGIN, KATE DOUGLAS.

RELIGIOUS TRACT SOCIETY. Publisher and distributor of many 19th-century children's books. The society was founded in 1799, in the context of the evangelical revival, to publish and promote religious tracts for the poor. It specifically set out to counteract the effects of purportedly antireligious and sensational writing by providing literature designed to improve a semiliterate audience. The society began to publish specifically for children around 1812, providing tracts at reduced prices to Sunday Schools, where poor children received them as rewards. Two types of narratives dominated these early publications: the conversion narrative and the child-deathbed story. So-called "street arab" stories were also very popular. The society founded many magazines, including the *Boy's Own Paper* (1879–1967) and the *Girl's Own Paper* (1880–1956). By the end of the 19th century, the society's publications were free of overtly religious content, and, in the 1930s, the Religious Tract Society became the Lutterworth Press. A similar organization was set up in the United States in 1814 as the New England Tract Society, renamed the American Tract Society in 1825. Both the American and the British organizations had a significant effect on the growth of the juvenile sector of the book trade and in shaping the direction of children's literature in the 19th century.

REY, H. A. (HANS AUGUSTO) (1898–1977) AND MARGRET (1906–1996). German-born husband and wife who immigrated to Brazil, spent a number of years in Paris, fled from the Nazis, and moved to New York in 1940. There they published the first of seven Curious George **picture books** (1941–1966), brightly colored, dynamic, episodic stories about a mischievous monkey who has been taken from his African home by "the Man with the Yellow Hat" to live with him in a big city. In titles such as *Curious George Rides a Bike* (1952) and *Curious George Goes to the Hospital* (1966), the young monkey's curiosity brings about comic mishaps similar to those experienced by any young and curious child. The Curious George books have been **translated** into numerous languages, and there have been countless **adaptations** and spin-offs. An animated film was released in 2006 and a new TV series in the same year; there are board books with scenes from the original picture books, books adapted from the TV series, new adventures **illustrated** in the style of the Reys, a video game, and countless items of licensed Curious George merchandise.

RHODEN, EMMY VON (1829–1885). Pseudonym of the German author Emmy Friedrich, author of one of the most famous German girls' stories, *Der Trotzkopf* (1885; *Taming a Tomboy*, 1898). The novel, a "taming of the shrew" type narrative set mainly in a girls' boarding school, was an immediate success, running to 55 editions by 1909. As von Rhoden had died shortly before her novel was issued, her daughter, Else Wildhagen, carried on the *Trotzkopf* legacy by writing three sequels in 1892, 1895, and 1930. A TV miniseries was made in 1983.

RHUE, MORTON (1950–). Pseudonym of U.S. author Todd Strasser, who has written more than 130 novels for young readers and is especially known for his documentary-style novels for young adults that address themes such as fascism, bullying, homelessness, and school shootings. His most famous novel, *The Wave* (1981), is about a school experiment on Nazism that gets out of control. It was made into a television movie in 1981 and a feature film in 2008. *Give a Boy a Gun* (2000), presented as a series of fictional interviews, is loosely based on the Columbine High School massacre in 1999. Both novels have been translated into a number of languages and are read widely in schools.

ROBIN HOOD. Outlaw hero of numerous tales and **legends** set in medieval England. Few stories have been retold as often as that of Robin Hood, and the legend has been subject to many shifts throughout its history; each age's version develops the hero and his company of merry men according to the needs and ideologies of the time. This is in part possible because no single narrative was passed down through the ages, nor are there historical records, and the origins of the legend are uncertain. The earliest sources, from the 14th century, are ballads, which describe a bandit, or criminal. Only gradually in the course of the development of the legend did Robin evolve into a chivalric figure who famously robs the rich to provide for the poor and fights against injustice and tyranny. Robin Hood and his band of seven "Merry Men" are usually associated with Sherwood Forest; the romantic interest is Maid Marian, and the enemy the Sheriff of Nottingham.

The first scholarly edition of the Robin Hood stories was by Joseph Ritson in 1795. It validated the romantic image of Robin Hood as a noble rebel, but also gave the story a politically radical inflection picked up by many later retellers. **Sir Walter Scott** introduced Robin Hood and Friar Tuck into *Ivanhoe* (1819), and Alexander Dumas wrote two Robin Hood novels in the 1870s. The first retellings for young readers were published in the 19th century, the most distinguished being **Howard Pyle**'s lengthy and lavishly illustrated *The Merry Adventures of Robin Hood* (1883). Notable 20th-century versions include **Geoffrey Trease**'s *Bows against the Barons* (1934), which openly depicts class warfare, and **Rosemary Sutcliff**'s *The Chronicles of Robin Hood* (1950). The material has proved attractive to filmmakers since the early days of Hollywood; *Robin Hood* (1922), starring Douglas Fairbanks, was a major success, and a definitive film version starring Errol Flynn, *Adventures of Robin Hood*, followed in 1938. A number of popular TV series have also told the Robin Hood story.

ROBINSON CRUSOE. *See* DEFOE, DANIEL.

ROBINSONADES. Stories based on the model of *Robinson Crusoe* (1719), by **Daniel Defoe**, which was so popular that it immediately inspired imitations. Although the first robinsonades were for adults, like Defoe's novel they were adopted by children. One of the first **adaptations** for children was *Robinson der Jüngere* (1779–1780; *Robinson the Younger*, 1781), by the educationalist **Joachim Heinrich Campe**, a book that enjoyed wide international reception and became one of Germany's most successful children's books. *Der Schweizerische Robinson* (1812–1813; *The Swiss Family Robinson*, 1814), one of the most famous robinsonades, was written by the Swiss pastor **Johann David Wyss**.

In a traditional robinsonade, the protagonist is suddenly isolated from the comforts of civilization. It often begins with a shipwreck and arrival on a desert island; the protagonist must then improvise the means of survival from the limited resources at hand. The narrative generally ends with a return to civilization. The archetypal motif of the desert island serves as a metaphor of solitude, and the protagonist frequently has to deal with loneliness, fear, and depression. While many 19th-century British robinsonades, such as **Frederick Marryat**'s *Masterman Ready* (1841) or **R. M. Ballantyne**'s *The Coral Island* (1857), praised the values of colonialism and imperialism, many contemporary robinsonades have questioned or subverted the Crusoe **myth**. In the dystopian *Lord of the Flies* (1954), by William Golding, for instance, the isolation produces depravity and violence, and **Michel Tournier**'s *Vendredi, ou La vie sauvage* (1971; *Friday and Robinson*, 1972) provides an ironic treatment of the myth.

Robinsonades set in (former) British colonies, such as *Canadian Crusoes* (1852) by **Catherine Parr Traill** and **Ivan Southall**'s Australian robinsonade, *To the Wild Sky* (1967), transferred the setting from an island to a wilderness in which the young protagonists have to survive. There are **science-fiction** robinsonades, **fantasy** robinsonades, and **picture-book** robinsonades; they can feature male, female, animal, or even **doll** protagonists, and the settings range from outer space, through the American desert, to an urban Holocaust hideaway in **Uri Orlev**'s *Island on Bird Street* (1984). The majority of contemporary robinsonades are realistic novels for adolescents; examples include **Scott O'Dell**'s *Island of the Blue Dolphins* (1960), Theodore Taylor's *The Cay* (1969), Harry Mazer's *The Island Keeper* (1981), and **Gary Paulsen**'s *The Island* (1988). *See also* ADVENTURE STORIES; ETHNOCENTRISM; GENDER.

RODARI, GIANNI (1920–1980). Italian author and journalist, regarded as one of the leading writers for children in 20th-century Italy. Rodari trained as a teacher but spent most of his life writing and working for educational reform. A campaigner for egalitarianism and humanism, he introduced new themes such as pacifism and the exploitation of workers into Italian children's literature in the 1950s. His work incorporates features of folklore, and he worked in collaborative projects with children. Topsy-turvy, parody, and wordplay feature in his books, as do products of modern technology such as televisions and telephones. His very short tales told by a father to his child on the telephone each evening, *Favole al telefono* (1962; *Telephone Tales*, 1965), are now regarded as classics in Italy. Rather than as a form of escape from reality, Rodari regarded **fantasy** as a means to understand it; this and other reflections on storytelling are in his *Grammatica della Fantasia* (1973; *The Grammar of Fantasy*, 1996). He received the **Hans Christian Andersen Award** in 1970.

ROSEN, MICHAEL (1947–). British **poet**, performer, broadcaster, and author of **nonfiction**, **picture books**, and retellings of classics and **folktales** from other cultures. The winner of several **awards**, Rosen is especially known for his collections of humorous verse for children, whose titles echo the language of the playground—such as *Mind Your Own Business* (1974), *Quick Let's Get Out of Here* (1983), or *Tea in the Sugar Bowl, Potato in My Shoe* (1997)—or have playfully nonsensical titles such as *Lunch Boxes Don't Fly* (1999) or *Spollyollydiddlytiddlyitis* (1987). **Quentin Blake**, who catches the quirky and fun elements of the poems, **illustrated** these, as well as many other collections and books by Rosen.

Rosen draws closely on his own childhood experiences in London to create poetry written not only from the perspective of a child but also in the voice of a child, using the ordinary language, speech rhythms, and thought patterns of contemporary children. He uses free verse in his anecdotal poems, with much use of repetition and near rhyme in many, but he also uses more formal rhyme structures in his **nonsense** poetry. Rosen's love of storytelling comes through as strongly in his poems as in his fiction for children. His storybook *We're Going on a Bear Hunt* (1989), with illustrations by **Helen Oxenbury**, has become a modern classic shared by children, adults, teachers, and pupils alike. His poignant *Michael Rosen's Sad Book* (2004), illustrated by Quentin Blake, addresses his bereavement after the death of his teenage son in 1999.

Rosen has broadcast and lectured widely on children's literature and frequently visits schools to share his passion for poetry with children. He has been involved in producing more than 140 children's books, including anthologies. Regarded as one of the most significant figures in contemporary children's poetry, Rosen was **children's laureate** from 2007 to 2009.

ROSS, TONY (1938–). British **illustrator** and creator of **picture books**. With *Goldilocks and the Three Bears* (1976), Ross established a reputation for updated, humorous, and flamboyantly colored **fairy-tale** versions; many more followed. He is the author and illustrator of the popular series about the dog Towser, starting with *I'm Coming to Get You* (1984), as well as the Little Princess series for young children, which includes the prizewinning *I Want My Potty* (1986) and, numerous titles later, *I Don't Want to Go to Bed* (2005). He created the subversively humorous Dr. Xargle series together with Jeanne Willis, starting with *Dr. Xargle's Book of Earthlets* (1988), which purportedly documents a lesson by the teacher of the title for his class of alien children about the strange customs of the planet Earth. Ross has illustrated books by numerous authors, including **Allan Ahlberg**, **Eoin Colfer**, **Roald Dahl**, **Paula Danziger**, and **Margaret Mahy**. He also furnished the illustrations for Francesca Simon's internationally successful Horrid Henry series. Ross's books have been translated into some 40 languages, and he has won several international prizes.

ROUSSEAU, JEAN-JACQUES (1712–1778). Swiss philosopher of the Enlightenment and author of *Émile; ou, De l'éducation* (1762; *Emile*, 1762), one of the most widely read books on the subject of education. Rousseau criticized traditional education and schools and depicted the ideal education of a fictional boy in a natural setting, where he learns from his experiences rather than from books. Above all, he believed that the uncorrupted child was to be protected from the corrupting influence of social institutions. Rousseau's work was banned by the church because of its attack on organized religion. *See also* DAY, THOMAS; DEFOE, DANIEL; SPYRI, JOHANNA.

ROWLING, J. K. (JOANNE KATHLEEN) (1965–). British author whose Harry Potter **fantasy** novels about a young wizard achieved unprecedented worldwide popularity and commercial success, broke all previously held literary sales records, and made her one of the richest women in Great Britain. By June 2008, more than 400 million copies of the novels had been sold, and they had been **translated** into some 70 languages. The series consists of the following novels, a number of which won literary **awards**: *Harry Potter and the Philosopher's Stone* (1997; published in the United States as *Harry Potter and the Sorcerer's Stone*), *Harry Potter and the Chamber of Secrets* (1998), *Harry Potter and the Prisoner of Azkaban* (1999), *Harry Potter and the Goblet of Fire* (2000), *Harry Potter and the Order of the Phoenix* (2003), *Harry Potter and the Half-Blood Prince* (2005), and *Harry Potter and the Deathly Hallows* (2007).

Elements of the **school story**, fantasy, and **mystery** are blended in this bildungsroman, which follows Harry's development from the age of 11 to 17 in seven novels, each covering a single year at Hogwarts School of Witchcraft and Wizardry. The novels get increasingly complex and darker as the series proceeds, with the evil

wizard Lord Voldemort, Harry's nemesis, becoming more powerful in his quest for immortality and ultimate power over both the wizard and the nonwizard (or Muggle) world. Central themes in Harry Potter include finding one's identity, free will and predetermination, power and its abuse, and racial persecution. The core virtues celebrated are courage, loyalty, tolerance, love (especially parental love), and friendship. One of the strengths of the series is a moral complexity that reveals the capacity for both good and evil in some characters. The inventiveness and wit of the author (especially in furnishing the details of her magic world), as well as her linguistic creativity, are key features of the novels and have ensured their popularity among both children and adults.

The huge success of the Harry Potter series spawned many imitations, and the popularity of the film versions by Warner Brothers (starting in 2001) paved the way for **adaptations** of many other fantasy classics. Harry Potter is now a global brand name worth an estimated $15 billion in 2008. Rowling was appointed OBE in 2000 and is the recipient of numerous honorary degrees.

RUBINSTEIN, GILLIAN (1942–). English-born Australian playwright, journalist, and author of books for children and young adults in a large range of genres. Rubinstein, who moved to Australia in 1973, has written eight plays, several short stories, and more than 30 books, many of them **award** winning, which have established her reputation as a challenging writer whose multilayered **fantasy** and **science-fiction** novels explore ethical and environmental issues, power relationships in families and in society, and adolescent anxieties. Her first novel, *Space Demons* (1986), and its sequel, *Sky Maze* (1989), tell of four children drawn into a sinister computer game. In the acclaimed but controversial *Beyond the Labyrinth* (1988), a 14-year-old seeks escape from his fears of nuclear annihilation and his problematic family in choose-your-own-adventure games. Rubinstein leaves the reader to choose between two endings by rolling a die.

Rubinstein studied modern languages and speaks Japanese, and she likes to experiment with language, for instance by inventing a pidgin for a group of kidnapped children in *Galax-Arena* (1992). Wordplay is evident in her humorous stories for younger readers, such as the rhyming *Sharon, Keep Your Hair On* (1996), **illustrated** by David Mackintosh. Among her successful **picture-book** scripts is *Dog In, Cat Out* (1991), illustrated by Ann James, which uses only four words in varying order. Under the pseudonym Lian Hearn, Rubinstein published the internationally best-selling, five-book series Tales of the Otori (2002–2007). The historical fantasy series is set in a fictional nation resembling feudal Japan and integrates elements of Japanese legends and drama. It follows the fate of a young warrior, Takeo, who is torn between conflicting obligations to his adoptive and his biological fathers amid a power struggle involving dozens of clan lords and thousands of warriors, and who is also in pursuit of the woman he loves. The highly acclaimed novels have become best-selling **crossover books** marketed under adult, children's, and young adult imprints.

– S –

SACHAR, LOUIS (1954–). U.S. author of children's books. His publishing debut was *Sideways Stories from Wayside School* (1978), zany, **fantastic** stories set in an elementary school that has supernatural elements and is populated by eccentric children. It was followed by three sequels. His novels for middle-graders, such as *There's a Boy in the Girls' Bathroom* (1987) and *Dogs Don't Tell Jokes* (1991), reveal his capacity to portray both the pain and the humor of young teenage life. He is best known for *Holes* (1998), which won the **Newbery Medal**. Set in a juvenile detention facility in Camp Green Lake, it features an unlucky adolescent, wrongly accused of theft, who has to dig a hole 5 feet wide and 5 feet deep. It is a cleverly constructed, complex novel about justice, punishment, family folklore, friendship, and redemption, told in a deceptively simple style. It surprisingly and satisfyingly brings together all the narrative strands in the end. **Walt Disney** Pictures made it into a successful film in 2003.

SAINT-EXUPÉRY, ANTOINE DE (1900–1944). French aviator and writer, most famous for his *Le Petit Prince*, published simultaneously in French and in English (as *The Little Prince*) in 1943, a year before the author disappeared while flying on a mission during World War II. Ostensibly a children's book, *The Little Prince* is a poetic tale about childhood **illustrated** by the author, in which the aviator narrator, stranded in a desert, meets and hears the story of the Little Prince, a young boy from a tiny asteroid. The book contains several seemingly profound observations about life and love, summed up in the famous line uttered by the Fox to the Little Prince: "It is only with the heart that one can see rightly; what is essential is invisible to the eye." One of the most **translated** French books, it has sold more than 50 million copies worldwide. In it, society and the follies of the adult world are criticized through the joint perspectives of the uncorrupted, innocent child observer from a distant planet and the world-weary narrator. It has always been more popular among adults, to whom it is addressed, than among children.

SALTEN, FELIX (1869–1945). Pseudonym of Siegmund Salzmann, Austrian writer, famous for his novel *Bambi, ein Leben im Walde* (1923; *Bambi*, 1927), an occasionally dark **animal** tale about growing up and surviving in a harsh world. **Walt Disney**'s acclaimed 1942 animation romanticized the tale of forest life and transformed it into a children's story, but it also ensured the lasting fame of the figure and story. Salten had sold the rights to his book in 1933, so the success of the film brought him no financial gain.

SANDBURG, CARL (1878–1967). U.S. poet, writer, folk musician, and winner of two Pulitzer Prizes. His notable contribution to children's literature consists of improvised **nonsense** stories that he told to his own three children, which celebrate the Midwestern landscape: *Rootabaga Stories* (1922), *Rootabaga Pigeons* (1923), *Rootabaga Country* (1929), and *Potato Face* (1930). He also wrote two books of **poems** for children, *Early Moon* (1920) and *Wind Song* (1960).

SANRIO. *See* HELLO KITTY.

SAY, ALLEN (1937–). Japanese-born Asian American author and **illustrator** who immigrated to the United States when he was 16. Say's work, which often contains autobiographical elements, primarily focuses on Japanese and Japanese American characters and explores cross-cultural experiences, immigrant identity, and the effects of cultural dislocation. His **Caldecott Medal**–winning **picture book** *Grandfather's Journey* (1994), illustrated in a range of different styles, traces the migration of his grandfather from Japan to America and its consequences for his children and his children's children, including Say himself. Further acclaimed titles include *The Bicycle Man* (1982), set in Japan during World War II, and *Tea With Milk* (1999), with episodes from his mother's life. In *Home of the Brave* (2002), an enigmatic picture book, Say departs from a realistic sequence of events to portray a nightmare-like scenario in which a man symbolically confronts the trauma of his family's incarceration in the infamous Japanese internment camps in the United States during World War II. Say's picture books enjoy both critical acclaim and popularity.

SCARRY, RICHARD (1919–1994). U.S. author and **illustrator** of more than 300 **picture books** that have sold more than 300 million copies worldwide. Scarry's books combine fact and fiction, presenting themes like weather, food, and jobs in combination with simple stories involving recurring and popular characters (e.g., Huckle Cat, Miss Honey, Rudolf Strudel), in books such as *Richard Scarry's Great Big Air Book* (1971) and *Richard Scarry's Best First Book Ever!* (1980). His breakthrough came in 1963 with the large-format book *Richard Scarry's Best Word Book Ever*, in which he identified more than 400 objects with labels. For this, he developed a new technique of drawing the lines with pencil and painting in the colors separately onto blueboards. Scarry had an instinctive knowledge about what interests children in terms of information and what they like in terms of amusement. His drawings depict everyday activities in minute detail while emphasizing action, and they use animals instead of people for extra appeal. Critics dislike Scarry's cluttered layout and repetitiveness, but his books remain popular with children throughout the world and have been **adapted** into animated series.

SCHAMI, RAFIK (1946–). Pseudonym of Syrian-born German-language children's author Suheil Fadéla; it means "he who comes from Damascus." After immigrating to and studying in Germany, Schami was able to establish himself as a professional storyteller and author from the late 1970s. The affinity of his style to Arabic oral and literary storytelling traditions is one of its overriding characteristics. The structure and title of ***The Arabian Nights*** are echoed in his novel *Erzähler der Nacht* (1989; *Damascus Nights*, 1993; literally "Storyteller of the Night") and in his many collections of stories in which storytelling itself features as a theme and activity. Together with German **illustrators** such as Wolf Erlbruch and Peter Knorr, he has created some memorable **picture books**, most notably *Der Wunderkaste* [The Box of Delights] (1990), a clever and moving visual account of the negative influence of the Western way of life on the culture and indigenous tradition of storytelling in Damascus. The English **translation** of his semiautobiographical *Eine Hand voller Sterne* (1987; *A Handful of Stars*, 1990) received the **Mildred L. Batchelder Award**. Schami's books have won numerous literary prizes in Germany and Austria.

SCHMID, CHRISTOPH VON (1768–1854). German educator, Catholic priest, author of more than 100 stories for children, and one of the most popular children's writers in 19th-century Germany. His books have been **translated** into more than 20 languages, and their value has been acknowledged by both Catholic and Protestant educators. Schmid's stories were not initially meant for publication, but were written for the children whom he taught and to whom he read after school as a reward. His writings reveal a familiarity with children's language and thought, and he used his narratives as a medium to instill religious ideas and Christian moral principles. His stories were often allegorical, illustrating how good is rewarded with wealth and happiness, and the child characters embody key Christian virtues. His best known narrative, translated into many European languages, is *Die Ostereyer* (1816); *Easter Eggs*, 1829). He was appointed canon of the Cathedral of Augsburg in 1826.

SCHMIDT, ANNIE M. G. (1911–1995). Dutch author for adults and children of radio and TV series, plays and musicals, **poetry**, and fiction. Regarded as the Netherlands' most versatile, talented, and beloved children's author of the 20th century, she received the **Hans Christian Andersen Award** in 1988. Schmidt introduced a new dimension into Dutch children's literature after World War II with her ironic tone, her amusing style, and a happy, anarchistic artistic world free of moralism. Almost everyone in the Netherlands is able to recite at least a line or two from one of her songs or poems; these are full of elements of folk poetry such as repetitions, alliteration, quirky characters, and, especially in her many **nonsense** poems, illogical associations. An anthology of her poetry in English translation, *Pink Lemonade*, was published in the United States in 1981. Her fiction for children, much of it **fantasy** stories with realistic, contemporary settings, often addresses the struggle of children and nonconventional adults against a repressive establishment; an example is *Minoes* (1970; *Minnie*, 1992), a story about a woman who was formerly a cat. Schmidt's books have appeared in **translation** all over the world, although very few of them in English. Several of her children's books have been successfully adapted for the screen.

SCHOOL STORIES. Genre that centers on school both as a setting and as the reason for the narrative. British in origin, it is the product of educational reforms in the Victorian era that brought about the development of modern "public schools" (in fact private schools) for boys of the middle and upper classes. **Thomas Hughes**'s *Tom Brown's School Days* (1857) is generally regarded as the first boys' school story, and it celebrates Rugby School under the headmastership of Dr. Arnold, its famous, reforming headmaster. Focusing on the moral, emotional, and social—rather than academic—development of the young male protagonist away from his family's influence, *Tom Brown's School Days* established key generic conventions. The dominant feature of the school story is a closed community with its own values, norms, and traditions, such as the prefect system and the house system with its interhouse rivalries, and its emphasis on games and the schoolboy code of honor. Plot elements can include midnight feasts and breaking rules, punishment of individuals or groups, and visits to the local town. Virtues prized include decency, pride in one's nation, bravery, loyalty, fairness, and, due to the significance of team sports in the boarding-school concept, team spirit. While the dominant mode was affirmative, critical treatments of the school story can be found, for instance, in **Rudyard Kipling**'s *Stalky and Co.* (1899).

The 1880s saw the development of the girls' school story with its first prolific author L. T. Meade, author of some 40 girls' school stories starting with *A World of Girls* (1886). One of the most commercially successful authors was **Angela Brazil**, with titles such as *The Luckiest Girl in the School* (1916); another, later, was Elinor M. Brent-Dyer, who situated her *School at the Chalet* (1925) and its numerous sequels in a Swiss location. From the 1940s, **Enid Blyton** contributed prolifically to this genre with her Naughtiest Girl, Malory Towers, and St. Claire's series. By this time, however, the genre and its reputation were in rapid decline. The boys' school story had degenerated into tales about the comic-grotesque figure Billy Bunter of Greyfriars School, hero of a seemingly endless series by Frank Richards (pseudonym of Charles Hamilton) that ran from 1908 into the 1940s in the boys' magazines *Magnet*, *Gem*, and *Boys' Friend*, and achieved further fame between 1952 and 1962 in BBC television series.

The demise of the school novel has been linked to the introduction in 1944 of free secondary education for all children in England and Wales; no longer viewed as a privilege that enabled greater opportunity, education now became something to be taken for granted. Much of the appeal of the ultimately escapist school story lay in its setting in a privileged environment inaccessible to the majority of its readers, and in its avoidance of real-life issues such as unemployment and class friction. Among the last school stories set in private schools were the four novels about Canterbury Cathedral Choir School by **William Mayne**, starting with *A Swarm in May* (1955). Coeducational state comprehensive schools, often with an inner-city setting, gradually came to replace the traditional public school setting as the more appropriate, modern form in Great Britain. One of the most successful series of this type was Grange Hill, written for TV in the 1970s by Phil Redmond and subsequently as tie-in novels by **Robert Leeson**.

Just as critics had reached the consensus that the school story was dead, **J. K. Rowling** came on the scene with Harry Potter (seven novels from 1997 to 2007), which, with Hogwarts School of Witchcraft and Wizardry, creates a boarding school with all the traditional elements of the school story—but defamiliarized, and hence injected with new life. Rowling cleverly sticks to the known forms—lessons, houses, uniforms, lists of items to be purchased before the beginning of every school year—but the similarity is only a formal one;

in each case she invents a comic and **fantastic** alternative, such as Quidditch, a game played on broomsticks, which substitutes for the traditional rugby or hockey. A feature of some contemporary American school stories, such as **Paula Danziger**'s first novel *The Cat Ate My Gymsuit* (1974) or **Louis Sachar**'s *There's a Boy in the Girls' Bathroom* (1987), is the relationship between pupils and an inspirational teacher, who is often rejected by a hostile school environment. This found popular expression in the film *The Dead Poets' Society* (1989), starring Robin Williams. How school as an institution can breed corruption and abuse of power is strikingly demonstrated in **Robert Cormier**'s *The Chocolate War* (1974), and the corruption of both teachers and students in a large state school is revealed in Tom Perrota's *Election* (1998).

The traditional school story was often criticized because it featured exclusively upper- and middle-class white children, but recent novels have tackled issues of race, ethnicity, **gender**, and disability. The problems a third-grade Hispanic girl has with so-called assimilation in school features in Alma Flor Ada's novella *My Name Is María Isabel* (1993), and the question of gender gets a humorous but serious treatment in **Anne Fine**'s *Bill's New Frock* (1989), in which Bill wakes up one morning to find that he has turned into a girl. Disability, illness, and children's fears when confronted with them feature in **Virginia Hamilton**'s *Bluish* (1999). Many young adult novels and popular television series (such as the American *Beverly Hills 90210*, 1990–2000) with a contemporary school setting focus on conditions of being a teenager in a world in which adults and young people alike are flawed. *See also* BEMELMANS, LUDWIG; BURNETT, FRANCES HODGSON; COOLIDGE, SUSAN; CROSS, GILLIAN; DE AMICIS, EDMONDO; FIELDING, SARAH; SPINELLI, JERRY; TREASE, GEOFFREY; VOIGT, CYNTHIA.

SCHUBIGER, JÜRG (1936–). Swiss psychotherapist and author for adults and children. Schubiger specializes in simple, often cryptic, stories about everyday life and different generations, told with subtle humor and a gently psychological approach to his characters. Known as the philosopher among Swiss children's authors, Schubiger addresses fundamental questions of interest to both children and adults. He came to fame with his collection *Als die Welt noch jung war*

[When the World Was Still New] (1995) and his family story *Vater, Mutter, ich und sie* [Father, Mother, Me and Her] (1997). He has also authored an original retelling of the story of William Tell (2003). Schubiger received the **Hans Christian Andersen Award** in 2008, the first Swiss author to be granted this honor.

SCIENCE FICTION. A broad genre, also sometimes called *speculative fiction*, that usually involves speculations based on discoveries and developments in science and technology and on how these might affect and change the individual, human relations, and society itself. The science-fiction mode can be found in long and short fictional texts, films, television series, comic books, and computer games, and it has always been popular among children and teenagers, especially boys and young men. Although the first classic authors of the genre, **Jules Verne** and H. G. Wells, did not write specifically for a young audience, they were immediately read by them, and they influenced numerous works of fiction at the end of the 19th century, a time now regarded as fostering the first wave of science fiction. These works included **Mark Twain**'s *A Connecticut Yankee in King Arthur's Court* (1889), **E. Nesbit**'s time-travel novels such as *The Story of the Amulet* (1906), and Sir Arthur Conan Doyle's *The Lost World* (1912). During the same period, a number of boys' magazines, like *The Boys of New York* in the United States and *The Boy's Own Paper* in Great Britain, started publishing fiction and **nonfiction** articles on scientific matters. They reacted to the success of **dime novels** and **penny dreadfuls** about the adventures of scientists by commissioning authors to create series about young inventors. With heroes like Frank Reade, who first featured in *Frank Reade and His Steam Man of the Plains* (1876), Tom Edison, Jr., and Tom Swift, hero of 38 volumes from 1910 on, they emphasized the adventures of young male inventors, often in exotic locations in which they defend themselves and their marvelous inventions against the evil intentions of villains.

In 1947, Scribners published *Rocket Ship Galileo* by **Robert A. Heinlein**, one of the founders of modern science fiction for young adults, and with it established the genre as a separate publishing category. This novel, in common with later ones by Heinlein such as *The Rolling Stones* (1952) and *Citizen of the Galaxy* (1957), features interesting characters and thoughtful plots rather than pure adventure. They reflect the general loss of innocence of science fiction in the wake of World War II and the development and use of atomic weapons, which revealed the darker side of technology. Questioning the utopianism of earlier science fiction, the genre became more complex and innovative in form and content. With her novel *Star Man's Son: 2250 A.D.* (1952), **Andre Norton** joined Heinlein as a major science-fiction writer for young adults. Especially known for her Witch World series, Norton is an author of "hard" science fiction, based on the "hard" sciences of physics and chemistry and emphasizing technology. Its counterpart, "soft" science fiction, is more interested in the human sciences of psychology and sociology. Prominent authors of the latter type include **Madeleine L'Engle**, whose novel *A Wrinkle in Time* (1962), on the nature of good and evil, was the first science-fiction novel to win the **Newbery Medal**; and **Virginia Hamilton**, who addresses the use of psychic powers in her *Justice* trilogy, starting with *Justice and Her Brothers* (1978).

Science fiction has come to take an ever more dystopian view of the future, with many young adult novels exploring the possibility of surviving a nuclear holocaust or environmental disaster. Examples include **Robert C. O'Brien**'s *Z for Zachariah* (1975), written from the perspective of a 16-year-old girl who survives a nuclear war in a small American town; and **Gudrun Pausewang**'s socially critical novel *Die Wolke* (1987; *Fall-Out*, 1995), which examines the threat of nuclear accidents, and her post–nuclear holocaust novel *Die letzten Kinder von Schewenborn* (1983; *The Last Children of Schevenborn*, 1988). In the same vein is **Robert Westall**'s *Future Track 5* (1983), set in a totalitarian society in 21st-century Great Britain that is stratified by class and controlled by a single national computer.

The best examples of the genre, such as **Lois Lowry**'s *The Giver* (1993), reveal the potential of science fiction to serve as a metaphor for the choices facing young readers seeking a place for themselves in an ever-changing and adult-dominated society. *The Giver*, like many other dystopian science-fiction novels for young readers, was accompanied by controversy on its appearance, and criticism that its subject matter was inappropriate for young readers; it was nonetheless awarded the 1994 Newbery Medal. Science fiction for young readers explores issues central to the lives of children and teenagers, such as computer games and their dangers in **Gillian Rubinstein**'s

Space Demons (1986), or teen sexuality in **Peter Dickinson**'s *Eva* (1988), but it also addresses issues concerning the whole of mankind, such as overpopulation in Margaret Peterson Haddix's *Among the Hidden* (1998), **racism** in Alison Goodman's *Singing the Dogstar Blues* (2002), and consumer culture and totalitarianism in M. T. Anderson's *Feed* (2002). *See also* ASIMOV, ISAAC; LE GUIN, URSULA; LEE, TANITH; PINKWATER, DANIEL; PRATCHETT, TERRY, SWINDELLS, ROBERT; ROBINSONADES; YOLEN, JANE.

SCIESZKA, JON (1954–). U.S. author of **picture books** and fiction for young readers. His inventive and irreverent picture books, produced in collaboration with the **illustrator Lane Smith**, are credited with having introduced postmodernism, with its elements of pastiche and metafiction, into children's literature, and both older children and adults enjoy them. They include *The True Story of the Three Little Pigs! by A. Wolf* (1989), a slyly humorous revised **fairy tale** in which the wolf gets to tell his version, and *The Stinky Cheese Man, and Other Fairly Stupid Tales* (1992), which takes the deconstruction of fairy tales a step further by playing with the materiality of the book itself: Jack the narrator moves the closing endpaper further forward in the book to trick a character into thinking it is over. Scieszka has also produced revised fairy tales with other illustrators such as Steve Johnson (*The Frog Prince, Continued*, 1991). The Time Warp Trio, a series of **adventure-story** spoofs for middle-graders involving three boys who travel through time and space, was made into an animated television series.

SCOTT, SIR WALTER (1771–1832). Scottish poet and novelist who established the **historical novel**. His tales of heroism and adventures in past times have always appealed to younger readers; *Ivanhoe* (1819), a tale of chivalry set in the age of Richard the Lion-Hearted, and *Rob Roy* (1817), about a highland chief who was one of Scotland's greatest heroes, remain popular today, especially in media adaptations. Scott influenced many novelists, including **James Fenimore Cooper** and **Jules Verne**.

THE SECRET GARDEN. *See* BURNETT, FRANCES HODGSON.

SEFTON, CATHRINE. *See* WADDELL, MARTIN.

SÉGUR, SOPHIE, COMTESSE DE (1799–1874). Russian-born novelist who settled and married in France and initially authored **fairy tales** for children (*Nouveaux contes de fées* (1857; *Fairy Tales for Little Folks*, 1869) at the age of 57 but left this genre to write some 20 novels for young readers that explore developmental and social issues. The most famous of these, *Les malheurs de Sophie* (1859; *The Misfortunes of Sophy*, 1937), is about a willful small girl whose behavior gets her into trouble. It was **translated** into many languages and was an international success. Her novel about two boys, *L'auberge de l'ange gardien* (1863), first translated in 1897, was translated by **Joan Aiken** as *The Angel Inn* in 1976.

SENDAK, MAURICE (1928–). U.S. **illustrator** and creator of **picture books**. The son of Polish-Jewish immigrants, Sendak started illustrating children's books in the 1950s; among his earliest are **Marcel Aymé**'s *The Wonderful Farm* (1951) and Ruth Krauss's *A Hole Is to Dig* (1952). He has illustrated more than 70 children's books by other authors, including **Isaac Bashevis Singer**, **George MacDonald**, and the **Grimm** brothers, usually adopting a distinctive style for each author and story. Sendak has produced more than a dozen self-authored picture books. The most famous, *Where the Wild Things Are* (1963), a milestone in the development of the picture book, established him as one of the most challenging and innovative voices in children's literature. In it, he uses visual symbolism to explore the child's interior world, and he shows how Max, punished for his unseemly behavior, creates a liberating fantasy world populated by wild monsters whom he tames. A **Caldecott Medal** winner, it has sold more than 2 million copies in 15 languages, even though the depiction of the grotesque, fanged, and clawed Wild Things caused initial concern among parents. Sendak, who has also designed operas and ballets, adapted *Where the Wild Things Are* into an opera in 1979.

In the Night Kitchen (1970), a further exploration of a child's fantasy world in the style of comics art, is also widely popular, although it has been subject to censorship in the United States for its drawings of a naked young boy. The darker *Outside Over There* (1981), in the style of the European Romantic artists, is the third book in what Sendak regards a trilogy on the subject of make-believe and the unconscious. Further successful titles include his early work *The Sign on Rosie's Door* (1960), featuring a plucky, imaginative girl, and *Higglety Pigglety Pop! or There Must Be More to Life* (1967), which was later transformed into an opera. In it, as in *We Are All in the Dumps with Jack and Guy* (1993), **nursery rhymes** are evident as a source of inspiration. Sendak collaborated with the playwright Tony Kushner on an English version of the Czech children's opera *Brundibár*, originally performed in the 1940s by the children in Terezín (Theresienstadt) concentration camp. Kushner and Sendak's opera premiered in 2003, the same year in which the picture-book version was issued. In 1970, Sendak became the first American to win the **Hans Christian Andersen Award**; in 2003, he received the **Astrid Lindgren Memorial Award**.

SEUSS, DR. (1904–1991). Pseudonym of Theodor Seuss Geisel, U.S. humorist, cartoonist, and creator of 44 **picture books** noted for their humorous rhymes, quirky characters, bright and distinct cartoon graphics, imaginative and subversive storylines, and celebration of the power of childhood imagination. Seuss started out as a cartoonist and author of humorous articles for magazines; he also drew advertising for firms such as General Electric and, during World War II, joined the army to write films in support of the U.S. war effort, some of which won Academy Awards. No fewer than 27 publishers rejected his first children's book, *And to Think That I Saw It on Mulberry Street* (1937), and an editor friend finally published it. Seuss's most famous book, *The Cat in the Hat* (1957), was written in reaction to the magazine article by John Hershey with the title "Why Johnny Can't Read" (1954), which linked growing illiteracy with the dull **primers** used to teach children. Seuss's editor sent him a list of 400 words that he felt were important and invited him to reduce it even further; the result was the hugely successful, zany picture book that uses only 236 distinct words and totally changed the face of **beginner books**. Seuss continued reducing vocabulary in *Green Eggs and Ham* (1960), where the infectious rhymes and wild story use 50 words only.

Other popular titles include *Horton Hears a Who!* (1954), released as a computer-animation film in 2008, and *How the Grinch Stole Christmas!* (1957). The subsequent television cartoon **adaptation**, narrated by Boris Karloff, has become a holiday classic. Live-action versions of *How the Grinch Stole Christmas!* (2000) and *The Cat in the Hat* (2003) were commercially successful but not popular among the writer's fans. Seuss resisted the commercial use of his famous characters throughout his career; after his death, his second wife founded Dr. Seuss Enterprises, which licenses their use. Since then his work has been available in various media, merchandising, and tie-in forms. His books have been **translated** into more than 15 languages, and more than 200 million copies have been sold worldwide. Seuss, one of the major contributors to **nonsense** literature in the 20th century, was awarded the Pulitzer Prize in 1984 "for his contribution over nearly half a century to the education and enjoyment of America's children and their parents."

SEVEN STORIES. Based near Newcastle, this major center for children's literature in Great Britain is dedicated to collecting, preserving, and making accessible the original work of British writers and **illustrators** for children, as well as organizing exhibitions and a range of creative activities. It opened to the public in August 2005.

SEWELL, ANNA (1820–1878). British author of *Black Beauty: The Autobiography of a Horse* (1877), one of the best-selling novels of all time. Written in the form of a fictional **animal** autobiography, it recounts Black Beauty's life as a working **horse**, from happy beginnings on a country estate, through times of mistreatment by successive owners, to a contented ending on green pastures. Sewell was lame because of an early accident, and could only get about in a pony cart. She wanted to write a book "to induce kindness, sympathy and understanding treatment of horses," and *Black Beauty* gives expression to these as well as to other Quaker values. Originally written as a didactic story for adults, it was immediately popular with children. It has been widely **translated** and **adapted** for other media.

SEXISM. *See* GENDER; COUNCIL ON INTERRACIAL BOOKS FOR CHILDREN.

SHEPARD, E. H. (ERNEST HOWARD) (1879–1976). British **illustrator** best known for his work accompanying **A. A. Milne**'s children's books and **Kenneth Grahame**'s *The Wind in the Willows*. Shepard was a master draftsman whose line drawings reveal a sure and light touch. His unframed illustrations for Milne's *When We Were Very Young* (1924), and their informal layout within and around the actual text, were unusual for that time. He breathed life into the stuffed animals in Milne's books, but in his illustrations for Grahame's *The Wind in the Willows* he showed that he could also handle **anthropomorphic** animals with great sensitivity, cleverly rigging the scale—as Grahame does implicitly in his text—to make the small animals coexist convincingly in their natural world and in the human one.

SHERWOOD, MARY MARTHA (1775–1851). English writer in the evangelical tradition who wrote close to 400 books, tracts, magazine articles, and essays. One of her most famous books is *The History of Little Henry and His Bearer* (1814), which tells how a young English **orphan** in India begins to convert the Hindu bearer who cares for him to Christianity, to save him from eternal death. The novel, which was hugely popular and reached its 30th edition by 1840, explicitly encourages children to follow Henry's example. The three-volume *History of the Fairchild Family* (1818, 1842, and 1847) tells the story of a family striving toward godliness by directing their souls toward Heaven and through the practice of morality on earth; it also incorporates prayers and hymns. A best seller that remained in print until 1913, the *Fairchild Family* is famous for a notorious scene in which the young children are brought by their father to look at the decomposed body of a man hanged for killing his brother. This served as a lesson on the evils of quarreling with one's siblings.

SHOCK-HEADED PETER. *See* HOFFMANN, HEINRICH.

SILVERSTEIN, SHEL (1930–1999). U.S. poet, cartoonist, playwright, and songwriter. Silverstein is one of the best-known contemporary authors of popular and **nonsense** verse for children, which he also **illustrated** with eccentric black-and-white line drawings. His prose and **poetry** can be outrageous, surreal, and hilarious; his comic excess and his opinion that children should be treated the same as anybody else led to Silverstein being one of the **American Library**

Association's **(ALA)** most challenged authors. He created the striking narrative persona of Uncle Shelby in his early children's books such as *Lafcadio: The Lion Who Shot Back* (1963), an exuberant **fable** about a lion who becomes civilized and famous. *The Giving Tree* (1964), one of his best-known titles, is a tale about the relationship between a female tree and a young boy who grows into adulthood. It has been **translated** into more than 30 languages. His anthologies of poetry include *Where the Sidewalk Ends* (1974) and *Falling Up: Poems and Drawings* (1996). In 1961, he published *Uncle Shelby's ABZ Book: A Primer for Tender Young Minds* (1961), a mock children's book whose subtitle was changed in later editions to "A Primer for Adults Only."

SIMMONDS, POSY (1945–). British cartoonist, **illustrator**, and author who created several popular comic strip series for the *Guardian* daily newspaper. She started writing for children in 1987 and carried into this work the witty and satirical view of the British middle class that characterized her comic strips. *Fred* (1987) is about a cat who slept all day but led an exciting double life as a pop star by night, a fact that is only revealed to his owners at Fred's funeral. In *Lulu and the Flying Babies* (1988), cherubs in an art gallery come to life; in *Lulu and the Chocolate Wedding* (1990), it is the figures on the wedding cake. Other best-selling **picture books** authored and illustrated by Simmonds include *F-freezing ABC* (1996) and *Lavender* (2003). In 1991 she illustrated **Hilaire Belloc**'s **cautionary tale** "Matilda, who told Lies, and was Burned to Death" with brightly colored and subversively humorous illustrations that ideally complement the text. In 1997, she illustrated the entire *Cautionary Tales, and Other Verses*. Simmonds was appointed MBE for services to the newspaper industry in 2002.

SINGER, ISAAC BASHEVIS (1902–1991). Polish-born U.S. journalist and author, and winner of the Nobel Prize for Literature in 1978. Singer, who came from a family of storytellers, wrote and published for adults and children in Yiddish, his first language, personally supervising later **translation** into English. His main subject was the traditional life of Eastern European Jews prior to the Holocaust, and its destruction therein. He started to write for children when he was in his sixties, following the suggestion of the English translator of his childhood memoirs for adults, *In My Father's Court* (English in 1966). His first book for children, illustrated by **Maurice Sendak**, was *Zlateh the Goat* (English in 1966), a collection of both original tales and stories based on **folktales** from his childhood. Many of his predominantly humorous stories for this age group are based on traditional tales, like those about the follies of the inhabitants of the legendary village of Chelm in *The Fools of Chelm and Their History* (English in 1973). *Stories for Children* (1984) brings together 47 of his published stories. Singer's **picture books** *Why Noah Chose the Dove* (English in 1974), with pictures by **Eric Carle**, and *The Golem* (1982), illustrated by Uri Shulevitz, also combine folklore and comedy.

SÍS, PETER (1949–). Czech-born **illustrator**, **picture-book** artist, author, and filmmaker who defected to the United States in 1984. Sís illustrated the work of many authors, including **Sid Fleischmann**, before authoring and illustrating his own picture books. He is a consummate draftsman who works with different techniques, such as washes and pointillism, and, especially in his more recent books, he plays with form by presenting frames within frames, playful cutouts and flaps, and inset maps. He has written **biographical** accounts of explorers such as Christopher Columbus (*Follow the Dream,* 1991), and scientists such as Galileo (*Starry Messenger: Galileo Galilei*, 1996) and Charles Darwin (*The Tree of Life,* 2003). He has authored a number of acclaimed personal books such as *The Three Golden Keys* (2001), a story set in his hometown Prague in the distant past, told by a father to his daughter; *The Wall: Growing Up Behind the Iron Curtain* (2007), a masterly blend of personal and political history; and the Madlenka books written for his daughter. *Madlenka* (2000) presents a city block in New York, home to the young girl and a huge variety of international inhabitants, and *Madlenka's Dog* (2002) revisits the girl and her neighborhood. Sís has been **translated** into many languages and has won numerous **awards** and honors.

SMITH, JESSIE WILCOX (1863–1935). U.S. **illustrator** famous for her portrayal of children at work and play. A pupil of **Howard Pyle**,

Smith was one of the most successful female illustrators of her day. She provided pictures for many leading magazines, such as *Collier's Weekly*, *Harper's*, and *Ladies' Home Journal*, and she painted the covers for one of America's most popular magazines, *Good Housekeeping*, for more than 15 years. Exploring the universe of the child in posters and portraits as well as in advertisements and calendars, Smith's confident, unsentimental portrayals changed the appreciation of children in American popular culture. The first children's book to appear with her pictures was *Rhymes for Real Children* (1903), and she illustrated **Robert Louis Stevenson**'s *A Child's Garden of Verses* in 1905. She produced acclaimed illustrations for a number of children's classics, including **Louisa May Alcott**'s *Little Women* (1914), **Charles Kingsley**'s *The Water-Babies* (1916), **George MacDonald**'s *At the Back of the North Wind* (1919), and **Johanna Spyri**'s *Heidi* (1922).

SMITH, LANE (1959–). U.S. author and **illustrator** who has created a number of humorous (e.g., *The Happy Hocky Family!* 1993) and **fantastic** (e.g., *The Big Pets*, 1991) **picture books**, but is perhaps best known for his partnership with **Jon Scieszka**. This has resulted in such remarkable postmodern picture books as *The True Story of the Three Little Pigs! by A. Wolf* (1989), *The Stinky Cheese Man* (1992), *Math Curse* (1995), and *Baloney (Henry P.)* (2001). He has also illustrated a number of volumes from Scieszka's The Time Warp Trio series. His art is striking for its distortions, quirky figures, collage effects, borrowings, and playful pastiches, and for the overall glossy sheen that has the effect of airbrushing but is actually created by thin layers of oil paint sealed with an acrylic spray varnish.

SNICKET, LEMONY (1970–). Pseudonym of U.S. author Daniel Handler and the name of a character in his A Series of Unfortunate Events (1999–2006), a comic-macabre series of 13 books—not counting later spin-offs—that follows the adventures of three siblings, Violet, Klaus, and Sunny Baudelaire, after their parents have died in a fire at the family mansion. It involves their distant cousin, Count Olaf, who wants to steal the **orphans**' fortune. The books are self-conscious and playful, and are infused with metafictional and metalinguistic reflections.

SOTO, GARY (1952–). U.S. poet, writer, and filmmaker who primarily draws on the daily realities of Mexican American life for his subject matter. He has published around 10 collections of **poetry** for adults and more than 30 books for children and teenagers. These include **picture books** such as *Chato's Kitchen* (1995); short stories, as in the collection *Baseball in April* (1990); poetry collections like *Fearless Fernie* (2003); and plays such as *Novio Boy* (1997). His semiautobiographical young adult novel *Jessie* (1994) is set during the Vietnam War and El Movimiento of the early 1970s. Soto explores the dilemmas and pleasures of Chicano life and culture in a language that is frequently poetic and is enriched by the inclusion of Spanish words. He has received numerous **awards** for his poetry, fiction, and films.

SOUTHALL, IVAN (1921–2008). Australian writer of fiction and nonfiction for both adults and children. One of the major figures in children's literature in Australia, Southall started his writing career with the Simon Black **adventure** series about a member of the Royal Australian Air Force, slightly reminiscent of **Captain W. E. Johns**'s Biggles series. He later moved on to write novels more concerned with character and development in a realistic mode, although many of them also contain an element of adventure. *Hill's End* (1962) tells of a group of adolescents struggling for survival against the forces of nature. It reveals Southall's interest in showing ordinary children facing physical and psychological dangers and demonstrating how, by coping with these, they learn, grow, and change. In *Ash Road* (1965), a bushfire isolates the young protagonists, while in *To the Wild Sky* (1967), they are stranded after a plane crash. Interpersonal relationships move to the foreground in titles such as *Bread and Honey* (1970; U.S. title *Walk a Mile and Get Nowhere*), which deals with a teenage boy's relationship with a younger girl; **Carnegie Medal**–winning *Josh* (1971) concentrates on the life of a clever adolescent boy alienated in a rural community. *Let the Balloon Go* (1968), made into a film in 1976, shows how a disabled boy's determination to climb a large tree enables him to show great courage while facing his inner fears. Southall's techniques of stream of consciousness, flashbacks, and different points of view were criticized by adult critics for being too complex for young readers; his themes for being too unpleasant; and the endings of his books as too ambiguous, but they show his respect for children as intellectuals, and his work has found many enthusiastic supporters. Southall was awarded an Order of Australia in 1981.

SPINELLI, JERRY (1941–). U.S. author of more than a dozen popular novels for middle-school readers as well as an autobiography, *Knots in My Yo-Yo String* (1998). Spinelli portrays, often humorously, the trials of adolescent life; frequent themes include bullying, peer pressure, **racism**, loyalty to friends, and nonconformity. His best-known novel, the **Newbery Medal**–winning *Maniac Magee* (1990), features a homeless boy with extraordinary athletic talent who becomes a hero for both blacks and whites in a small, racially divided town. *Stargirl* (2000) celebrates nonconformity, centering on an eccentric 10th-grade student; its sequel, *Love, Stargirl* (2007), is in the form of a journal. Spinelli also wrote a **school** series, School Daze, as well as *Tooter Pepperday* (1995) and a sequel, *Blue Ribbon Blues* (1998), for younger teenagers. A recent novel, *Milkweed* (2003), marks a departure; it is set in Nazi-occupied Warsaw during World War II.

SPYRI, JOHANNA (1827–1901). Swiss author of novels and stories for adults and children famous for her Heidi novels, *Heidis Lehr- und Wanderjahre* (1880; *Heidi's Early Experiences*, 1882) and *Heidi kann brauchen, was es gelernt hat* (1881; *Heidi's Further Experiences*, 1884). This two-volume bildungsroman in an Alpine setting focuses on events in the life of the title character, a young **orphan** who, at the age of 5, is brought to her social outcast grandfather in the mountains. Here she enjoys a Rousseauian natural education until the age of 8, when her aunt takes her to the city of Frankfurt. She learns to read and write there and so can further her own religious education. Heidi has a healing effect on her environment, most notably on the disabled Clara, but is deeply unhappy in the urban setting. Through her sleepwalking, she succeeds in fulfilling her regressive childish desire to return to the Alpine meadows. Here the child savior figure succeeds in bringing about the social integration of her grandfather, and later helps the disabled Clara to walk again in the Alpine air. The metaphoric expression that Spyri finds for depression and the trauma of a damaged child has been linked to the pious author's own crises of religious belief. This aspect is suppressed in modern **adaptations** and retellings that, especially in the popular 1975 Japanese animated version, show a jolly and bouncing girl who experiences endless adventures in the Alps. The children's classic is known in this form to readers and viewers throughout the world, and for many it epitomizes life in the Swiss mountains. Extensive merchandising of the book, its characters, and its setting includes an officially designated geographical region called Heidiland, now a major tourist spot in Switzerland. *See also* ROUSSEAU, JEAN-JACQUES.

STEIG, WILLIAM (1907–2003). U.S. cartoonist, sculptor, and **illustrator** and author for children. Steig was in his sixties when he wrote and illustrated his first **picture book**, *Roland the Minstrel Pig* (1968); *Sylvester and the Magic Pebble* (1969) won the **Caldecott Medal**. Many of its features recur in subsequent picture books: a small, usually intelligent, **anthropomorphic** creature overcomes a large obstacle in a tale furnished with lushly colored illustrations, told with much humor in rich and fresh language, with a happy ending. *Shrek!* (1990) served as the basis for the major movie by Dreamworks. Steig's narratives for older children, such as *Abel's Island* (1976), feature protagonists on a journey of self-discovery. His last book, *When Everybody Wore a Hat* (2003), is an autobiographical account of his childhood in the early 20th century. Steig's books have been published in more than a dozen languages, and he received a number of international **awards**.

STEVENSON, ROBERT LOUIS (1850–1894). Scottish writer who excelled in the genres of travel writing, **adventure novels**, **horror stories**, and **poetry**. Born into a family of engineers, Stevenson had decided by the age of 21 that he wanted to be a writer. He suffered poor health as a child and later developed tuberculosis, and much of his adult life was spent seeking a climate suitable for his health. In 1880, he began telling an adventure story about pirates to his young stepson Lloyd, a tale of "Buccaneers and buried gold" first serialized in the children's magazine *Young Folks* under the title *The Sea Cook, or Treasure Island* (1881–1882). It was published as *Treasure Island* in 1883. It tells the story of young Jim Hawkins's acquisition of a map to a treasure island, and his voyage there with his friends Doctor Livesey and Squire Trelawney, and a character that became the literary prototype of a pirate, the one-legged Long John Silver. Silver, the ship's quartermaster, serves as a mentor to Jim until it transpires that he is the ringleader of a mutiny against the boy and his friends. In the manner of a thriller that masterfully increases the tension in each episode, Jim finally triumphs over Silver. Stevenson skillfully portrays atmosphere, character, and action, and, unusually for a children's book, remains morally ambiguous while exploring contrasting sides of human nature.

Moral ambiguity is also at the center of *Kidnapped* (1886), a **historical** adventure story cum thriller set during the period after the 1795 Jacobite Rebellion in Scotland. The year 1886 also saw the publication of Stevenson's horror story for adults, *The Strange Case of Dr. Jekyll and Mr. Hyde*, a study of the divided nature of a doctor who, under the influence of drugs, becomes a violent murderer. This story and its title have become a metaphor for the duality of human nature. In a very different vein is his *A Child's Garden of Verses* (1885), a collection of 66 **poems** that describe childhood as seen by an adult from the outside, and attempt to recreate the sensations of the poet's own childhood. The poems are universally acknowledged in their attempt to capture the authenticity of the child's voice and vision, giving equal importance to the joys of play and to the loneliness of a child sick in bed. The collection has enjoyed numerous reprintings, with **illustrations** by a number of noted artists such as **Jessie Wilcox Smith**, **Brian Wildsmith**, and **Michael Foreman**.

ST. NICHOLAS MAGAZINE. *See* DODGE, MARY ELIZABETH MAPES.

STINE, R. L. (ROBERT LAWRENCE) (1943–). U.S. author of humor and **horror** books for children. Stine was editor of the children's magazine *Bananas* for 10 years and wrote several humor books for children during that time. In 1986, he wrote *Blind Date*, his first scary novel for teenagers; he created Fear Street, the first horror series for young adults, in 1989; and the Goosebumps series for readers from 8 to 12 followed in 1992. This scary but humorous series has become a global phenomenon; **translated** into more than 16 languages, it was certified the biggest-selling children's book series in the *Guinness Book of World Records 2001*. Stine, who has been called the Stephen King of children's literature, was the number one best-selling author in the United States from 1994 to 1996. The Goosebumps series was turned into a popular live-action children's television show on the Fox network. Other series by Stine include Rotten School, Mostly Ghostly, and The Nightmare Room. Many of the later volumes of Stine's series have been written by ghostwriters.

STORR, CATHERINE (1913–2001). British author, doctor, and psychiatrist, and reteller of classic **fairy tales** and **Bible** stories. Two of Storr's most popular books are early reversals of the classic version of "Little Red Riding Hood," *Clever Polly and the Stupid Wolf* (1955) and *The Adventures of Polly and the Wolf* (1957), in which a smart girl outwits the wolf. She is best known for her novel *Marianne Dreams* (1958), a psychological **fantasy** that was ahead of its time, in which a sick girl draws, with a magic pencil, a strange and menacing alternative world that she enters while asleep. It was made into a British television series, *Escape into Night*, in 1972 and a film, *Paperhouse*, in 1988. Storr was the author of more than 30 books for children covering a wide range of genres for different age groups.

STRASSER, TODD. *See* RHUE, MORTON.

STRATEMEYER SYNDICATE. *See* DIXON, FRANKLIN W.; THE HARDY BOYS; KEENE, CAROLYN; NANCY DREW.

STREATFEILD, NOEL (1895–1986). British author of plays, **nonfiction**, and fiction for adults and children. Streatfeild trained and worked as an actress and is mainly remembered for her novels that focus on child performers. She is considered one of the pioneers of the "career novel," writing about hard-working, money-conscious, and professional children who opt for careers on the stage, in the circus, on the tennis court, on the ice, or in the concert hall. Her first and possibly best-known novel is *Ballet Shoes: A Story of Three Children on the Stage* (1936); it was followed by *Tennis Shoes* (1937), and by the **Carnegie Medal**–winning *The Circus Is Coming* (1938; also published as *Circus Shoes*), about two runaway **orphans** and their circus clown uncle. Streatfeild also authored a number of nonfiction titles, many of which address the world portrayed in the novels, such as *A Young Person's Guide to Ballet* (1975). Several of her 58 books for children are still in print, and some of her novels have been **adapted** for film or television.

STRUWWELPETER. *See* HOFFMANN, HEINRICH.

SUTCLIFF, ROSEMARY (1920–1992). English author of **historical fiction** for children and young adults that also appeals to adult readers; she said herself that she wrote for "children of all ages from nine to 90." She set new standards in historical fiction and was instrumental in the development of the genre from the romantic, heroic, and glorifying historical fiction of the 19th century to one that examines the struggles of individuals—often from the lower classes—and the complexity of the decisions they faced, especially in times of war. In all, she wrote 45 historical novels and retellings of **legends**; many were **illustrated** by **Charles Keeping**. She retold the tale of King Arthur in three volumes (1979–1981), the Anglo-Saxon epic poem in *Beowulf: Dragonslayer* (1961), and parts of Irish heroic cycles in *The Hound of Ulster* (1963) and *The High Deeds of Finn Mac Cool* (1967). Her historical novels cover almost every era of British history; Viking settlers feature in the *The Shield Ring* (1956), Renaissance courtiers in *The Queen Elizabeth Story* (1950), Jacobites in *Bonnie Dundee* (1983), and 18th-century smugglers in *Flame-Colored Taffeta* (1986). She is best known for her portrayals of Roman Britain, which focus on the creation of British identity. Among them is the acclaimed saga of the Aquila family, four loosely linked novels starting with *The Eagle of the Ninth* (1954) and including *The Lantern Bearers* (1959), which won the **Carnegie Medal**. Many of her protagonists are physically disabled or outsiders, perhaps reflecting her own experience of childhood illness and later disability. Sutcliff was appointed OBE in 1975 for her services to literature.

SWIFT, JONATHAN (1667–1745). Irish cleric, satirist, and poet whose fame as a children's writer is based on his novel *Gulliver's Travels* (1726), an adult satire published under the full title *Travels into Several Remote Nations of the World, by Lemuel Gulliver, First* *a Surgeon, and Then a Captain of Several Ships*. Written, as Swift claimed, to vex the world rather than divert it, *Gulliver's Travels* purports to be a factual account of four voyages. The first is to Lilliput, a kingdom of beings no more than 6 inches tall; the second to Brobdingnag, a land of giants; the third to the flying island of Laputa, with its absurd inventers; and the last to the country of the Houyhnhnms, inhabited by rational horses and brutish human Yahoos. The book was instantly successful and reduced **chapbook** versions appeared in the late 18th century. In 1776, **John Newbery** published *The Adventures of Captain Gulliver, in a Voyage to the Islands of Lilliput and Brobdingnag*, and in most subsequent abridged versions for children, the voyage to Lilliput appears alone or with that to Brobdingnag. These versions emphasize the **adventure** or **fantasy** dimensions, and ignore the satire. Modern responses to Swift's Gulliver include **T. H. White**'s *Mistress Masham's Repose* (1946) and **Gary Crew**'s *Gulliver in the South Seas* (1994).

SWINDELLS, ROBERT (1939–). British author of fiction for children and young adults who gained experience in a number of professions before becoming a full-time writer in 1977. Swindells is a compelling storyteller and an uncompromisingly honest writer with strongly held political convictions. His fiction for teenagers blends realism with elements of **horror** and **science fiction** and addresses tough and controversial themes; he has said that his impetus to write has often been anger. *Brother in the Land* (1984), a postapocalyptic novel that follows a teenage boy fighting for survival following a nuclear attack on his home, won the Children's Book Award. He received the same award for *Room 13* (1989), a contemporary Dracula story. *Daz 4 Zoe* (1990) is a story of a socially mismatched pair set in a dystopian society in which the wealthy are socially segregated from the urban poor. It is presented in alternating narratives of the inner-city boy and the wealthy suburbanite girl, with their language embodying their class difference. Both controversial and acclaimed, his **Carnegie Medal**–winning *Stone Cold* (1993) addresses teenage homelessness; it was adapted for television in 1997. Fundamentalist religious sects are a focus in *Unbeliever* (1995), and asylum seeking in *Ruby Tanya* (2004). Swindells, whose books have been translated into more than 20 languages, has also written **picture books** for young readers, as well as the Outfit series of **adventure novels**. *The Last Bus* (1996) is an adventure story for less able readers about a nightmare bus journey.

THE SWISS FAMILY ROBINSON. *See* WYSS, JOHANN DAVID.

– T –

TAN, SHAUN (1974–). Australian **illustrator** and maker of **picture books**, and winner of multiple international and national **awards**. Tan's books demonstrate artistic sophistication in their broad range of intertextual references, their often surreal style, and their play with how the reader is positioned. His interest in social, political, and historical subjects, as well as in philosophical depth, is evident from his first books, starting with *The Viewer* (1997), created with **Gary Crew**, from which the reader looks out at the narrator. *The Rabbits* (1998), with John Marsden, is a fable about colonization, told from the viewpoint of the colonized. The notion of belonging is central to the work of Tan, who is himself half-Chinese: *The Lost Thing* (2000) is about a creature lost in a strange city, *The Red Tree* (2001) is about a girl wandering through shifting dreamscapes, and the wordless graphic novel *The Arrival* (2007), a migration story, is presented in a perspective that enables the viewer of the book to feel the immigrant's bewilderment at the incomprehensible new world. Tan's books are enjoyed by readers of all ages.

TAYLOR, ANN (1782–1866) and JANE (1783–1824). English sisters, writers, and engravers who authored, in collaboration, three collections of **poetry** that sold in large numbers and had an important influence on the development of child-centered children's poetry. The collections, *Original Poems for Infant Minds* (1804), *Rhymes for the Nursery* (1806), and *Hymns for Infant Minds* (1808), contain some of the most celebrated English children's poetry of the 19th century, including Ann's "My Mother" and Jane's "The Star" ("Twinkle, Twinkle Little Star"), later parodied in **Lewis Carroll**'s *Alice in Wonderland* as "Twinkle, Twinkle Little Bat." The Taylors were the first English writers of poetry exclusively for children.

TAYLOR, MILDRED D. (1943–). African American writer of **historical fiction** for young adults. Taylor's major work is a saga about the fictional Logan family. This started with *Song of the Trees* (1975), a novella set in Mississippi in the 1930s, which focuses on the eight-year-old African American girl Cassie Logan and her land-owning family during the Depression era. Taylor's next novel, the **Newbery Medal**–winning *Roll of Thunder, Hear My Cry* (1976), is her best known, and it was followed by two more sequels, *Let the Circle Be Unbroken* (1981) and *The Road to Memphis* (1990); all of these focus on Cassie's family and their community. The Logan family saga, narrated in a total of nine novels and story books, is a history of the American black experience with slave ancestors (*The Well: David's Story*, 1995), institutionalized **racism**, and injustice; it incorporates the oral history of Taylor's own family as told by her father, Wilbert Lee Taylor. Central themes include developing and maintaining self-respect, integrity, family bonds, and the importance of the black community. Apart from her ability to address the historical black experience, Taylor's stylistically accessible work features strong characterization, rich descriptions of nature, humor, and suspense.

THACKERAY, WILLIAM MAKEPEACE (1811–1863). English novelist and author of a single book for children, *The Rose and the Ring* (1855). Subtitled "A Fire-side Pantomime for Great or Small Children," it follows the **pantomimes** of the time in its arrangement of characters and scenes, incorporates plenty of satire and slapstick comedy, and provided amusement for both adults and children. The story follows the adventures of Prince Giglio of Paslagonia, who has been deposed by his uncle Bulbo, Prince of Crim Tartary, and the Princesses Rosalba and Angelica. The magic tokens that wreak **fairy-tale** havoc among the protagonists are the rose and the ring of the title.

THIELE, COLIN (1920–2006). Australian author of around 100 books for children, which include **historical novels**, **picture books**, and **biography**. Thiele's work is predominantly in the realistic mode, with a rural farming or wild coast-and-sea setting, and environmental and conservation issues are a central concern. His best-known work, *Storm Boy* (1963), is about a young boy who lives in a wild landscape; a local Aborigine, Fingerbone, who teaches him much about his traditional land; and a hand-reared pelican, "Mr. Percival," who is ultimately shot by hunters. It was made into a film in 1976, has been **translated** into several languages, won a major Dutch literary prize, and has remained in print since publication.

THOMAS THE TANK ENGINE. The most famous character in the Railway Series by the British Reverend W. Awdry, about a fictional railway system and the engines that serve it. Having begun in 1945, he had published 26 titles by 1972, and his son Christopher later continued the series. The **anthropomorphic** engines have names such as Edward the Blue Engine, Gordon the Big Engine, and Bill and Ben the Tank Engine Twins. Thomas the Tank Engine became the hero of a television series, and today appears on different types of merchandise with a permanent smile upon his face.

THOMPSON, KATE (1956–). English-born writer for children and adults who moved to Ireland in 1981. Between 1997 and 2008, Thompson authored more than a dozen novels for young readers, which have earned much critical acclaim and many **awards**. These are primarily in the **fantasy** mode and address such topics as genetic engineering, climatic crisis, and ecopolitics. One of her overriding concerns is the meaning of the word *human* and the rights and responsibilities incumbent on it. The Switchers trilogy (1997–1999), in which the young protagonists Tess and Kevin have the gift of being able to change into any creature at will, reflects on matters of transformation and mutation and on the issues involved in moving between human and nonhuman identities. *The Beguilers* (2001), set in a richly imagined world, is an allegorical treatment of a young woman's quest for independence. Irish legend and music are evident in many of Thompson's books; in *Annan Water* (2004), the words of a traditional folk song are merged into a contemporary story of adolescent romance that crosses over to the world of Irish **myth** and **legend**. *The New Policeman* (2005) uses music as the touchstone for communication between the fairy and the human domains.

TOLKIEN, J. R. R. (JOHN RONALD REUEL) (1892–1973). British scholar and translator of Anglo-Saxon and medieval literature, and major author of **fantasy** fiction. Tolkien's interest in languages, mythology, **legends**, and heroic epic **poetry** was a major force behind his creative writing. By 1917 he had already invented Middle-earth, the imaginary cosmos that was to become the setting of *The Hobbit* (1937), The Lord of the Rings trilogy (1954–1955), and his unfinished epic *The Silmarillion*, published posthumously by his son Christopher in 1977. A father of four, Tolkien told stories to his own children, many of which were published after his death—including the **picture book** *Mr. Bliss* (written in 1932, published in 1982).

In the early 1930s, Tolkien began to work on *The Hobbit,* a quest story with **fairy-tale** elements based on the encounters of the Hobbit Bilbo Baggins. It was written in a humorous tone, with an omniscient narrator, and deemed by Tolkien to be suitable for children. When it was issued in 1937 to enthusiastic reviews, publisher Stanley Unwin requested a sequel. Tolkien began work on what would become, by the time of its completion in 1949, a highly complex account of a negative quest that addresses central issues of a political and moral nature such as totalitarianism, the battle between good and evil, individual responsibility, and ecological exploitation. Set in a rich and credible secondary world that has its own complex history, geography, and languages and is populated by elves, dwarfs, magicians, and evil monsters, The Lord of the Rings is not a children's book sequel to *The Hobbit* but a work addressed to adults. Tolkien argued on a theoretical level that a taste for fantasy was legitimate, and his Lord of the Rings provided the model for modern fantasy fiction for adults: *heroic fantasy*, or *high fantasy*. The Lord of the Rings became a cult series among college students during the 1960s, and, while its popularity has remained constant, the film version directed by Peter Jackson (2001–2003) introduced Tolkien to an even wider audience.

TOM BROWN'S SCHOOL DAYS. *See* HUGHES, THOMAS.

TOURNIER, MICHEL (1924–). French essayist and novelist for adults and children. One of France's most acclaimed contemporary writers, Tournier came to fame with his first novel *Vendredi, ou Les limbes du Pacifique* (1967; *Friday*, 1969), a reworking of the classic

Robinson Crusoe theme, turning Friday into a mythical hero for the 20th century. Rewritten for children as *Vendredi, ou La vie sauvage* (1971; *Friday and Robinson*, 1972), the novel was widely **translated** and is a perennial best seller in France. In his novels Tournier often redrafts key **myths** and **legends**, such as those of St. Christopher, the Erl King, Castor and Pollux, and the Three Magi (in *Gaspard, Melchior et Balthazar*, 1980; translated as *The Four Wise Men*, 1982; refashioned for young readers as *Les rois mages* [The Wise Men], 1982). Many of his tales for children have also featured in adult collections. Tournier's practice of rewriting his own novels for children, as well as his publication of identical work for both adults and children, has made him one of the most prominent **crosswriters** and creative transgressors of literary boundaries.

TOWNSEND, JOHN ROWE (1922–). British novelist, critic, and author of the standard introduction *Written for Children: An Outline of English-Language Children's Literature*, first published in 1965. Townsend started writing fiction in response to the lack of books for children that addressed social problems such as poverty; *Grumble's Yard* (1961), which was followed by two sequels, was a book with a thriller plot involving children who lived in slums. Townsend has employed **science-fiction** elements in some of his narratives, such as *The Xanadu Manuscript* (1977), and has dealt with the topic of teenage love and sexuality in his young adult novels, such as the tragicomic *Goodnight, Prof. Love* (1970).

TOWNSEND, SUE (1946–). British playwright and novelist who, with *The Secret Diary of Adrian Mole, Aged 13¾* (1982) and the sequel *The Growing Pains of Adrian Mole* (1984), became one of the best-selling novelists of the 1980s. Written in diary form, these books combine comedy with social and political commentary, as well as recounting embarrassing adolescent experiences recognized by readers young and old. Four further volumes charted Adrian's development beyond adolescence into adulthood: *The True Confessions of Adrian Albert Mole* (1989), *Adrian Mole: The Wilderness Years* (1993), *Adrian Mole: The Cappuccino Years* (1999), and *Adrian Mole and the Weapons of Mass Destruction* (2004). Unlike the first two, these were of interest for adults only. The first three volumes were **adapted** for television.

TOY STORIES. *See* DOLL AND TOY STORIES.

TRAILL, CATHERINE PARR (1802–1899). English-born writer and naturalist, and one of Canada's most important 19th-century authors. She emigrated in 1832, and subsequently recorded and interpreted her experiences as a pioneer in the autobiographical *The Backwoods of Canada*, published in England in 1836. Before setting foot in Canada, she had written *The Young Emigrants, or Pictures of Canada* (1826), but her *Canadian Crusoes: A Tale of the Rice Lake Plains* (1852) was to become the first children's book produced by an author living in that country. A **robinsonade**, *Canadian Crusoes* tells the story of three children—two English Canadians and one French Canadian—lost in the wilderness. With the help of a young Mohawk woman, they survive for two years, providing an exemplary tale of how the different ethnic groups could survive in the new world of Canada and succeed in building a nation if they worked together. At the end of the novel they are paired off, English Canadian with native Canadian (who has been taught the Christian religion), and French Canadian with English Canadian. The novel is also remarkable because of the author's attention to the details of forest life.

TRANSLATION. The translation of works from other languages has been central to the development of children's literature everywhere. **Aesop**'s **fables**, **Comenius**'s *Orbis Sensualium Pictus*, *The Tales of **Mother Goose***, and the **Grimms**' **fairy tales** are examples of influential translations in the history of children's literature in English; and many of its classics, such as **Carlo Collodi**'s *The Adventures of Pinocchio*, **Johanna Spyri**'s *Heidi*, **Jean de Brunhoff**'s *Babar*, **Astrid Lindgren**'s *Pippi Longstocking*, and **Alf Prøysen**'s *Mrs. Pepperpot* were originally written in a language other than English. Today, Great Britain and the United States are the countries that "export" most (in other words, their literatures are the ones most translated); but they also import least, with translations into English accounting for only around 3 percent of books published annually in Great Britain, and only 1–2 percent in the United States. The exclusion of works translated from other languages is generally regarded to be a form of cultural poverty, as it is through translations that children become acquainted with other cultures. The **Mildred L. Batchelder Award** in the United States and the biennial Marsh **Award** in Great Britain, for children's literature in translation, work to raise the profile of translated children's literature. Heading the translation tables in Europe is Finland, with a proportion of about 80 percent, followed closely by the other Scandinavian countries; translations make up over 40 percent of the children's literature published in the Netherlands and in Italy, and in Germany around 30 percent. In most non-English-speaking countries, around 80 percent of all translated books are from English. *See also* ADAPTATION; ANDERSEN, HANS CHRISTIAN; BIERHORST, JOHN; CAXTON, WILLIAM; CROSSLEY-HOLLAND, KEVIN; CROSSOVER BOOKS; GÁG, WANDA; KRÜSS, JAMES; LANG, ANDREW; MONTEIRO LOBATO, JOSÉ; ORLEV, URI; POMBO, RAFAEL; PRESSLER, MIRJAM; VERNE, JULES.

TRAVERS, P. L. (PAMELA LYNDON) (1899–1996). Pseudonym of the Australian-born writer Helen Lyndon Goff, who immigrated to England at the age of 17. Her first publications were **poems**, but her real literary success came with the publication of *Mary Poppins* (1934), the first of six *Mary Poppins* titles issued between 1934 and 1988. The books center on a mysterious, vain, and acerbic English nanny with magical powers who comes and goes as she pleases, often blown in and away by the wind. As a character, she is not very attractive and she shows little affection toward the children in her care; nevertheless, everyone adores her, and this contributes to the air of mystery around her. Her constant props are her umbrella and her magical bag that can contain just about anything. In her presence, the line separating the real from the magical becomes blurred, statues come to life, paper stars become stars in the sky, and the children can float in the air. The stories became internationally famous through the 1964 **Walt Disney** musical film starring Julie Andrews and Dick Van Dyke, although in this film Mary Poppins has lost much of her ill temper, and full justice is not done to the psychological and existential dimensions of the books. Travers's other books for children include *I Go by Sea, I Go by Land* (1941), about the evacuation of two children to the United States during World War II. She was appointed OBE in 1977.

TREADGOLD, MARY (1910–2005). British author and editor. While working as an editor, Treadgold was shocked by the inferior quality of most **pony stories** submitted for publication and decided to write her own. Her most famous novel, *We Couldn't Leave Dinah* (1941), was one of the first children's books written about World War II. Set on a fictional Channel island during the summer of 1940, when some of the islands were already under Nazi occupation, the threat of invasion hangs over the usual holiday occupation of a group of children with their pony-club activities and explorations. The **Carnegie Medal**–winning novel skillfully blends the genres of pony story and war story and openly addresses such wartime issues as danger, fear, and ambiguous feelings of allegiance. Further novels that also combine suspense, adventure, and a sense of broader political issues include *No Ponies* (1946), set in France in 1944, which considers the consequences of collaboration; and *The 'Polly Harris'* (1949), which, in the form of an **adventure story**, addresses urban terrorism in postwar London.

TREASE, (ROBERT) GEOFFREY (1909–1998). English novelist, playwright, critic, and reviewer. The prolific author of some 120 books, which have been **translated** into 20 languages, Trease is best known for his pioneering work in **historical fiction**. In contrast to the romantic sentimentalism and jingoism of many of his predecessors, he concentrated on details of everyday life, the achievements of ordinary men and women, and the complexity and difficulty of decisions that individuals have to make in times of conflict and war. The first of his novels, *Bows Against the Barons* (1934), narrates the exploits of **Robin Hood**, emphasizing his proletarian origin and revolutionary character in the fight against injustice and oppression. His left-wing sympathies are evident in his choice and treatment of material; *Comrades for the Charter* (1934) deals with the Chartist movement, and *Follow My Black Plume* (1963) is the story of Giuseppe Garibaldi's struggle to unify Italy. *The Red Towers of Granada* (1966) is an **adventure** in medieval Spain and England, which features the treatment of Jews and lepers with great compassion. Avoiding archaic language and presenting characters that are powerful and vigorous in well-paced plots, Trease's books are accessible to contemporary readers. His work is notable for the fact that it features strong female protagonists who operate as equals with their male counterparts. He also wrote a series of five Bannermere **school stories** (1959–1966), about four children who attend a day school and who move up the school through the series. In 1949, he published *Tales Out of School*, the first critical overview of living British writers for children, which he revised in 1964. Trease was a Fellow of the Royal Society of Literature.

TREECE, HENRY (1911–1966). British **poet** and historical novelist. Treece worked as an English teacher and published a number of volumes of poetry before writing **historical novels** for adults. In 1954 he began to write historical novels for young readers, producing more than 20 in all, most of which are set in Roman or Viking times. He is best known for his two Viking trilogies: *Viking's Dawn* (1955), *The Road to Micklagard* (1957), and *Viking's Sunset* (1960), which trace the life of a Viking from a young oarsman to a leader; and the trilogy for younger children, *The Horned Helmet* (1963), *Last of the Vikings* (1964), and *The Broken Sword* (1966), all of which were **illustrated** by **Charles Keeping**. His novels are admired for the accuracy of their historical detail and their rational approach to history.

TRIER, WALTER (1890–1951). Czech-born German-Jewish **illustrator** whose economical style of illustration in satirical and humorous journals was influential in Germany during the 1920s. Forced by the Nazis into exile, Trier spent a few years in England before ultimately settling in Canada, where he produced his own **picture books**. The novels and poems of **Erich Kästner** stimulated his best work; his bright-yellow cover for *Emil und die Detektive* (1929; *Emil and the Detectives*, 1930), with its stylized figures and reduced forms, caused a sensation and introduced *Neue Sachlichkeit* (the New Objectivity) into children's illustration. Trier continued to work with Kästner during his exile and emigration; their styles are so complimentary that most **translations** of Kästner's works are adorned with Trier's illustrations. His lively line, intensive colors, and comical character portraits have had a marked influence on a number of contemporary German, Canadian, and British artists.

TRIMMER, SARAH (1741–1810). British author, educator, and editor whose books were inspired by the education of her own 12 children. Deeply suspicious of **fantasy**, she provided her own corrective in works such as *Fabulous Histories* (1786), later known as *The History of the Robins*, in which a family learns how to deal with **animals**. Editions of the book continued to appear until the beginning of the 20th century. An evangelist, Trimmer founded a Sunday school, produced a series of **biblical**, moral, and practical **primers**, wrote several books on education, and edited the periodical *The Guardian of Education* (1802–1806). It published highly critical reviews of **fairy tales** and praised books for children that encouraged intellectual instruction and Christian moral education.

TRIVIZAS, EUGENE (EUGENIOS) (1946–). Greek criminologist, author of more than 100 children's books and plays, and one of his country's leading writers for children. Trivizas achieved international fame with the publication, in English, of *The Three Little Wolves and the Big Bad Pig* (1993), illustrated by **Helen Oxenbury**. This witty and thought-provoking inversion of the classic tale was **translated** into 17 languages and sold more than a million copies in the United States alone. Humor, inventiveness, and creative use of language, as well as a concern for serious social issues, characterize his work, which includes **fairy tales**, **picture books**, **poems**, plays, and television series. One of his few other books that have been translated into English is *The Little Black Cat* (translation 2005), a novel written from the perspective of the **animal** protagonist about a ruthless hunt in a sinister and corrupted society. This poetic plea for an end to cruelty and persecution has also been translated into several European languages.

TURNER, ETHEL SIBYL MARY BURNWELL (1872–1958). English-born author who immigrated to Australia as a girl and is regarded as one of the founders of Australian children's literature. She authored some 44 books (published in London) but is most famous for *Seven Little Australians* (1894). Six of the little Australians of the title are the independent, energetic children of widower Captain Woolcot, who marries a young woman more than 20 years his junior; the seventh little Australian is their communal child. The six are "good bad" children—lively, natural, mischievous, and wary of authority—and this original feature, together with the novel's setting in suburban Sydney, contrasts strongly with previous Australian **adventure novels** for children set on sheep or cattle stations, which documented the successful struggle of British settlers with the Australian environment and the Aborigines. The novel's central figure, wild girl Judy, resembles Jo March in **Louisa May Alcott**'s *Little Women* in her quest for freedom from the constraints imposed upon her as a young female. Rather than choosing the conventional solution of having the girl rebel reform at the close of the narrative, Turner selects a dramatic plot device to prevent Judy from having to mend her ways: she is killed by a falling tree as she saves the life of her baby brother. Turner published three further novels based on the Woolcot family, *The Family at Misrule* (1895), *Little Mother Meg* (1902), and *Judy and Punch* (1928). *Seven Little Australians* is one of the classics of Australian children's literature; it has never been out of print and was made into a television series in 1973.

TWAIN, MARK (1835–1910). Pseudonym of Samuel Langhorne Clemens, U.S. novelist, satirist, and humorist. He is most famous for his classic **crossover** novels of boyhood, *The Adventures of Tom Sawyer* (1876), based on his memories of growing up in Hannibal, Missouri, and its sequel *Adventures of Huckleberry Finn* (1884). In *Tom Sawyer*, Twain presents a realistic and humorous account of antebellum American boyhood, with its adventures, games, and pranks. In contrast to conventional contemporary children's literature with its impossibly good or unacceptably bad children, Twain created a new type of "good bad boy" who plays pranks and tricks but is good at heart. *Adventures of Huckleberry Finn*, which has been called "the great American novel," is a coming-of-age quest featuring the uneducated, outcast **orphan** Huck, who, with the runaway slave Jim as his companion, journeys down the Mississippi purportedly toward freedom. With its first-person narrative in Huck's frontier dialect, its use of authentic vernacular, and its scathing satire of Southern society, the novel has variously been declared unsuitable for children and been the target of censorship, in recent times over use of the term "nigger." A fictional treatment of the controversies around the novel is Nat Hentoff's *The Day They Came to Arrest the Book* (1982).

Other children's books by Twain include *The Prince and the Pauper* (Great Britain 1881, United States 1882), a historical romance about two boys at the opposite ends of the social ladder exchanging identities; the derivative sequels *Tom Sawyer Abroad* (1894) and *Tom Sawyer, Detective* (1896); and the time-travel **fantasy** *A Connecticut Yankee in King Arthur's Court* (1889).

– U –

UNGERER, TOMI (JEAN THOMAS) (1931–). French **illustrator** and author for adults and children, whose books for adults are predominantly satirical and erotic. Born in Strasbourg in Alsace when it belonged to France, Ungerer's childhood was marked by the German occupation of the area; in 1945 he became French again. His *À la guerre comme à la guerre* (1991: *Tomi: A Childhood under the Nazis*, 1998) is an autobiographical account of these years. After immigrating to the United States in 1956, he produced his first children's books about a family of piglets, *Mellops Go Flying* (1957). Ungerer delights in the subversive in his children's books, starting with *Die drei Räuber* (1961; *The Three Robbers*, 1962), which reverses the classic **fairy-tale** model, making the baddies into the goodies. *No Kiss for Mother* (1973), both controversial and popular, is an attack on overpowering maternal love. In *Otto, Biography of a Teddybear* (1999), a teddy bear tells his life story beginning with his creation in Germany prior to World War II, and continuing through the war and on to America, where he is finally and miraculously reunited with his original owner. Tomi Ungerer received the **Hans Christian Andersen Award** in 1998 for his life's work.

UPTON, BERTHA (1849–1912) and FLORENCE K. (1873–1922). Anglo-American mother-and-daughter team who created the series of 13 Golliwogg books, starting with *The Adventures of Two Dutch Dolls—and a "Golliwogg"* (1895). Twelve books followed for the Christmas market; the final one was *Golliwogg in the African Jungle* (1909). Florence conceived and **illustrated** the story, and her mother, Bertha, wrote the verses. The stories tell the adventures of the dynamic and modern Golliwogg, who engages in exploration and is passionately interested in new technology (balloons, cars, bicycles). Upton's illustrations depict a figure with jet-black skin, bright red lips, and wild woolly hair, wearing red trousers, a shirt with a stiff collar, a red bow tie, and a blue jacket with tails. In recent times, the books have been accused of **racism**, especially in Great Britain. However, as some critics have pointed out, the books are surprisingly modern and even transgressive for their own time in their use of a black protagonist and in their gentle social satire, which even extends to criticism of war. The books were hugely popular, and countless imitations and unlicensed spin-off Golliwogg items flooded the market. The golliwog, whose final *g* was dropped in the course of time, changed from the kindly character in the Uptons' stories to a rascal figure or even a mean-spirited character in stories by authors such as **Enid Blyton**. "Golliwog" became the generic name for **dolls** of a similar type and was a popular children's doll throughout most of the 20th century.

URE, JEAN (1943–). British writer for both adults and children who has produced more than 100 titles for young readers. Especially popular are her novels that deal with all the normal interests of teenage girls—romance, rivalry, irritating siblings, and problems with parents—but do not shy away from tackling difficult themes. These include terminal illness in *One Green Leaf* (1987), homosexuality in *The Other Side of the Fence* (1986), and child abuse in *Bad Alice* (2003). In addition to her critical view of contemporary society, Ure's strengths are her humor and her empathy. Particularly popular is her Girlfriends series, with titles such as *Pink Knickers Aren't Cool!* (2002), *Girls Are Groovy!* (2002), and *Boys Are OK!* (2002). A vegan, Ure never shows any of her characters eating meat.

UTTLEY, ALISON (1884–1976). British author of more than 100 children's books in the mode of **Beatrix Potter**, which reveal her great love for, and knowledge of, the countryside. Among the most popular are the Little Grey Rabbit, Sam Pig, and Little Red Fox series, all of which were **illustrated** in watercolor by Margaret Tempest. In a different vein entirely is her time-shift **fantasy**, *A Traveller in Time* (1939), about a 20th-century girl transported back to the 16th century, where she becomes involved in a plot to free Mary, Queen of Scots. It unusually shows the negative effects of these experiences on the personality of the protagonist and ends tragically.

– V –

VAN ALLSBURG, CHRIS (1949–). U.S. artist (originally a sculptor) famous for his original **picture books**. Although most have a realistic setting, they combine surrealistic images with mythical plot lines and elements of **fantasy** to create dreamlike picture tales. *The Garden of Abdul Gasazi* (1979) is about an encounter between a boy and a magician who appears to have transformed a dog into a duck. A brother and sister find a mysterious jungle board game in *Jumanji* (1981), with the instruction to "finish the game"; this has dangerous consequences, as the events in the game also occur in their own home. It won Van Allsburg his first **Caldecott Medal**; his second was for the seasonal classic *The Polar Express* (1985), about a boy's miraculous train journey to the North Pole to visit Santa Claus. Van Allsburg often works in black and white, making use of light and shadow to generate an atmosphere of mystery; his use of perspective is another striking feature. Further important titles include the nearly wordless, fragmentary *The Mysteries of Harris Burdick* (1984); his **alphabet book**, *The Z Was Zapped* (1986); *Bad Day at Riverbend* (1995); and *Zathura* (2002), in which the board game featured in *Jumanji* reappears. Van Allsburg's work has been compared to that of M. C. Escher, and many of his books have been made into animated films. He has also **illustrated** some books by other authors and produced cover illustrations for new editions of children's classics such as **C. S. Lewis**'s *The Chronicles of Narnia* (1994).

VELTHUIJS, MAX (1923–2005). Dutch **picture-book** maker whose work is recognizable for its exuberant bright colors and bold outlines. Velthuijs, who started his career illustrating children's rhymes and **ABC books**, is one of the most famous **illustrators** for children in the Netherlands. He is best known for his plain, green, and instantly recognizable amphibious hero Frog. Curious, thoughtful, and innocent, Frog brings out the best in the co-inhabitants of his **animal**

cosmos. After having been rejected by Velthuijs's previous publishers, the first book, *Frog in Love* (1989), was published in English **translation** by Andersen Press, who ultimately published all 14 books, ending with *Frog Is Sad* (2003). The books are admired for their humanity and their gently humorous approach to life in all its facets, and have been translated into 20 languages. Velthuijs received the **Hans Christian Andersen Award** in 2002.

VERNE, JULES (1828–1905). French author and pioneer of **science fiction** who completed more than 100 novels. Verne's most famous works were part of a series entitled *Voyages extraordinaires* (Extraordinary Voyages), which included both terrestrial and extraterrestrial journeys, starting with *Cinq semaines en ballon* (1863; *Five Weeks in a Balloon*, 1869), followed by *Voyage au centre de la terre* (1864; *Journey to the Centre of the Earth*, 1871). The hugely popular *Vingt mille lieues sous les mers* (1870; *Twenty Thousand Leagues under the Sea*, 1876) contained detailed descriptions of underwater sea life and the emerging technology of submarines and diving suits. Although written for adults, Verne's novels have always appealed to young readers, and they have been **adapted** for **all ages**. He has been widely **translated** but was not served well by his English translators who, in translations fit "merely for boys," cut much of his original text, sometimes dramatically changing the meaning and undermining his humor in the process. It was not until the late 1970s that English readers could appreciate, in quality translations, Verne's political and social as well as his scientific prophecies. Several of his books have been made into films.

VIVAS, JULIE (1947–). Australian **illustrator** who was instantly successful with her illustrations for **Mem Fox**'s *Possum Magic* (1983), which contains a number of indigenous Australian animals, focusing especially on a family of possums. Vivas is a prolific illustrator in watercolor and ink, known for her humor, her lack of sentimentalism, and her originality. Acclaimed books include *The Nativity* (1986) and *Let the Celebrations Begin!* (1991), written by **Margaret Wild**. Set in the Nazi concentration camp in Belsen, it is narrated by a girl who, with the older women, is preparing a children's party for the time after liberation.

VOIGT, CYNTHIA (1942–). U.S. author of fiction for children and young adults, which includes **detective stories**, **fantasy** fiction, and realistic contemporary novels. Her young adult novels especially have received much critical acclaim. She addresses controversial issues in the family and school lives of teenagers, such as abuse, losing one's parents, serious economic challenges, and acute personal problems. Vivid and authentic settings, the development of her characters' inner lives, skillful plotting, and a poetic style are all features of Voigt's work. Her most ambitious and substantial novels are in the seven-book series about the Tillerman family and their friends. *Homecoming* (1981), the first, describes how 13-year-old Dicey Tillerman and her three younger siblings cover hundreds of miles on foot to their grandmother after their mentally disturbed mother abandons them in a parking lot. The subsequent novels follow the fortunes of different members of the family and their friends, with *Dicey's Song* (1982) winning a **Newbery Medal**. *A Solitary Blue* (1983) is a coming-of-age novel about a boy's growth to maturity and independence after rejecting his manipulative mother, and *When She Hollers* (1994) is a grim tale of sexual abuse. On a lighter note and written for younger readers, her three Bad Girl novels tell of two rebellious fifth-grade girls who join forces.

– W –

WADDELL, MARTIN (1941–). Northern Irish author of more than 100 books for babies, young adults, and readers in between. Waddell is especially known for his entertaining and often moving **picture books**, many of them created with well-known **illustrators**. With **Helen Oxenbury**, he produced *Farmer Duck* (1991), a hilarious children's version of George Orwell's *Animal Farm.* His Little Bear series, starting with the award-winning *Can't You Sleep, Little Bear?* (1988) and illustrated by Barbara Firth, has become world famous. It has several features of Waddell's successful books: an **animal** or human baby as protagonist, a strong sense of a cozy and secure home and family, safe excitement, such themes as growing up and the cycle of life and death, and writing that takes the form of simple prose. Under the pseudonym Catherine Sefton he has written thoughtful novels for older readers, including a trilogy set in Northern Ireland against the background of the troubles: *Starry Night* (1986), *Frankie's Story* (1988), and *The Beat of the Drum* (1989). Waddell received the **Hans Christian Andersen Award** in 2004.

WALL, DOROTHY (1894–1942). New Zealand–born author who moved to Australia in 1914. In *Blinky Bill, the Quaint Little Australian* (1933) she introduced a confident and cheeky character in the form of a koala, who became a symbol for the Australian republican movement. Wall published further volumes about Blinky's escapades; the character also appeared in an animated television series.

WALSH, JILL PATON (1937–). English author who began writing for children and adolescents in the 1960s and later started writing for adults. Her work for children and adolescents encompasses more than 20 titles and covers a wide range of genres and forms, from **picture books** to futuristic fiction and contemporary coming-of-age novels. Her **historical fiction**, which constitutes the largest group, is marked by her scholarly research. It includes periods from Anglo-Saxon England, in *Wordhoard* (1969), to the plague of 1665 in *A Parcel of Patterns* (1983) and World War II–era England in *The Dolphin Crossing* (1967) and *Fireweed* (1969). Characteristic of all Walsh's work are her evocative landscape, her attention to detail, and stories that deal with complex moral issues and values; a predominant theme is the survival of humanist values (*Wordhoard*, *A Parcel of Patterns*, and *Unleaving*, 1976). Other recurring themes include class difference and children's ability to survive in hostile environments (*The Huffler*, 1975; *Gaffer Samson's Luck*, 1984). A consummate stylist, Walsh makes skilled use of a number of narrative strategies, such as intertextuality, time-shift narratives that cross centuries or encompass several strands (*A Chance Child*, 1978), and multiple narrative voices and viewpoints. She was appointed CBE for her services to literature in 1996 and was elected a fellow of the Royal Society of Literature.

WARBURTON, NICK (1947–). English author and playwright for adults and children. Warburton is good at farce and slapstick, and stories such as *Normal Nesbitt: The Abnormally Average Boy* (1992) and *The Strange Case of Flora Young* (2002) are fast paced and funny; but serious issues involving the unremarkable child protagonists having to face challenging situations underlie the humor. His books for older readers mix **fantasy** and realism: *The Thirteenth Owl* (1993) is a story about a young girl's discovery of her own special power, while *Ackford's Monster* (1996) combines a realistic setting on the Suffolk coast in 1914 with the discovery of a fantastic sea creature. His **adventure story**, *Lost in Africa* (2000), is the story of a daughter-father conflict amid political intimidation and racial tensions on a 1960s trip to West Africa.

WARD, LYND (1905–1985). U.S. artist and **illustrator** who produced wordless graphic novels with woodcut illustrations for adults in the tradition of the Belgian Frans Masereel. Ward illustrated more than 200 books for adults and children; many of the latter, including his first, *Prince Bantam* (1929), were written by his wife, May McNee. His first authored and illustrated children's book, *The Biggest Bear* (1952), won the **Caldecott Medal**. He used a variety of techniques in his work for children, including watercolors and lithography. In 1973, Ward returned to the wordless story with *The Silver Pony* (1973), about a lonely boy and a flying horse.

WATTS, ISAAC (1674–1748). English Nonconformist minister and author of more than 600 hymns. His *Divine Songs, Attempted in Easy Language for the Use of Children* (1715) was a book of didactic songs and hymns in the Puritan tradition of stressing the wickedness of children, but it also displayed a gentleness and tolerance new for his time. The book was an immediate success and remained popular for more than 150 years. **Lewis Carroll** parodied two of the *Divine Songs* in *Alice's Adventures in Wonderland* (1865), "Against Idleness and Mischief" and "The Sluggard," which indicates that the originals were still widely known in nurseries in the 1860s.

WAUGH, SYLVIA (1935–). British author of the acclaimed Mennyms series of five **fantasy** novels (1993–1996), about a family of life-size rag **dolls** who magically come to life and have to develop strategies and complex games in order to make their way in the human world. They cannot eat or drink, and they never get older. One of them, Appleby, celebrates her 15th birthday every year for some

40 years and would seem to be condemned to the role of a surly adolescent for the rest of her days. However, in the third book in the series, *Mennyms under Siege* (1995), in which powers of destruction are unleashed upon the family, Appleby becomes the first rag doll to die. The series explores metaphysical questions of existence and, blending whimsy, imagination, psychology, and logic, is also highly entertaining. It has been **translated** into numerous languages and has enjoyed considerable international critical success.

WEBSTER, JEAN (1876–1916). U.S. novelist and grandniece of **Mark Twain**. Webster was keenly interested in social reform, and she supported the woman suffrage movement. Her best-known novel, *Daddy Long-Legs* (1912), is mainly in the form of letters written by an **orphan** to the anonymous benefactor who pays her college fees. She finally ends up marrying him. It was made into a British musical comedy, *Love from Judy* (1953), and into a Hollywood film starring Fred Astaire and Leslie Caron in 1954. *Dear Enemy* (1915), also concerned with women's interest in higher education, was filmed by the BBC in the early 1990s.

WEISGARD, LEONARD (1916–2000). U.S. **illustrator** who also used the pseudonym Adam Green for children's books he wrote and illustrated himself. Russian and other contemporary art movements influenced his style. He collaborated with **Margaret Wise Brown**, who was impressed by the modernism of his work. Together they produced *The Noisy Book* (1939) and its sequels, and *The Little Island* (1946), a **Caldecott Medal** winner. Weisgard illustrated more than 180 children's books, always using the medium—pencil, crayon, woodcuts, watercolor, or chalk—most suited to the project at hand.

WEISSE, CHRISTIAN FELIX (1726–1804). German author of the Enlightenment, generally credited with being one of the founders of German children's literature. His *Lieder für Kinder mit Melodien* [Songs for Children with Melodies] (1766) was the first collection of **poems** for children in German. *Der Kinderfreund* [The Child's Friend] (1776–1782), published in 24 volumes, was the first German children's magazine. Weisse's plays also made a significant contribution to children's drama.

WELLS, ROSEMARY (1943–). U.S. **illustrator** and author of books for all ages, from board books for babies to young adult fiction. She is best known for books for young children that deal with family conflict and sibling rivalry. Their protagonists are usually **animals** with markedly human behavior. The popular Max and Ruby books are about sibling rabbits, a younger brother and a bossy older sister; *Benjamin and Tulip* (1973) is a humorous story about a raccoon bully and her victim. Wells has also authored **mystery** novels for older readers, such as *Through the Hidden Door* (1987).

WESTALL, ROBERT (1929–1993). English author who lived on Tyneside, in the north of England, as a child and teen during World War II. His first novel, *The Machine Gunners* (1975), is set in wartime Tyneside, where a group of children tries to retrieve a machine gun from the turret of a felled German aircraft. It won the **Carnegie Medal**, and the BBC made it into a television serial in 1983. Children's need to establish their own moral code and the contradictions arising from war are recurrent themes in his stories. He wrote about war from different perspectives: in *Blackham's Wimpey* (1982) it is that of a young fighter pilot; a cat is the narrator in *Blitzcat* (1989); and a boy who loses his home and family in an air raid is at the center of *The Kingdom by the Sea* (1990). *Gulf* (1992) uses the supernatural device of merging the consciousness of an English boy with that of a young Iraqi soldier, which enables readers to see the war from the point of view of the Iraqi boy. Apart from war stories, Westall wrote a number of supernatural tales. In *The Scarecrows* (1981), a chilling tale about a boy's resentment of his mother's remarriage, three scarecrows slowly move toward the house in which the family is now living. For it, Westall received a second Carnegie Medal. His major works, including a large number of short stories, are included in the two-volume *Best of Robert Westall* (1998).

WHEATLEY, NADIA (1949–). Australian historian and author of children's and young adult novels, short stories, **picture books**, and scripts. Wheatley wrote her first book, *Five Times Dizzy* (1982), while living in Greece. This book and its sequel, *Dancing in the Anzac Deli* (1984), about a Greek girl and her family settling into urban Sydney, were among the first Australian children's books with multicultural subjects. They were subsequently made into a television series. Wheatley's concern for social justice and interest in history are also evident in her extensive picture book *My Place* (1987), which, moving backward in decades from 1988 to 1788 and starting and concluding with an Aboriginal girl, reveals how the same small area in Sydney changed over 200 years of white colonial history. The **historical fantasy** *The House That Was Eureka* (1985) tells of the Sydney eviction battles in the 1930s.

WHITE, E. B. (ELWYN BROOKS) (1899–1985). U.S. essayist, stylist, celebrated contributor to the *New Yorker*, and author of three popular and enduring children's novels, in which he blends the magical with the everyday world and explores such themes as tolerance, friendship, nature, and death. In *Stuart Little* (1945), a very small, independent, and adventurous child with the "shy, pleasant manner of a mouse" is born into a human family; Garth Williams's illustrations actually portray him as a mouse. The story was adapted into an animated television series and a film with two sequels, which combine live action with computer animation. *Charlotte's Web* (1952), an undisputed and much-loved children's classic, is about the friendship between a young pig, Wilbur, and a spider, Charlotte A. Cavatica, who craftily saves his life through weaving the message "Some Pig" in her web. Charlotte's solitary death is one of the saddest moments in a children's book. The book has sold more than 45 million copies and has been **translated** into more than 20 languages, and three different film **adaptations** have been made. In *The Trumpet of the Swan* (1970), a mute swan learns how to play the trumpet and becomes a celebrity. White won a Pulitzer Prize in 1978 for his entire body of work.

WHITE, T. H. (TERENCE HANBURY) (1906–1964). British author best known for his retelling of Sir Thomas Malory's *Morte d'Arthur* as the tetralogy *The Once and Future King*, starting with *The Sword in the Stone* (1938). *Mistress Masham's Repose* (1946) was inspired by **Jonathan Swift**'s *Gulliver's Travels*, and tells of a colony of descendents of Lilliputian captives brought to England in the 18th century.

WIESE, KURT (1887–1974). German-born, self-taught **illustrator** and author of children's fiction and **nonfiction**. Wiese lived and worked in China from 1909–1914, was a British prisoner of war in Hong Kong and later in Australia during World War I, and immigrated to the United States in 1927, where he became a successful and prolific illustrator of more than 300 books, 19 of which he wrote himself. He is acclaimed as a master of lithography and line drawing, and is particularly known for his Chinese illustrations. Among his best-known work are the illustrations for the first American edition of **Felix Salten**'s *Bambi* (1929), for Marjorie Flack's *The Story about Ping* (1933), and for Claire Huchet Bishop's **folktale** *The Five Chinese Brothers* (1938). Also popular are two books that he both illustrated and authored, *You Can Write Chinese* (1945) and *Fish in the Air* (1948).

WIESNER, DAVID (1956–). U.S. **illustrator** and author of innovative **picture books**. Among the books by other writers illustrated by Wiesner are **Laurence Yep**'s *Tongues of Jade* (1991), **Avi**'s *Man from the Sky* (1981), and **Eve Bunting**'s *Night of the Gargoyles* (1994). Wiesner is particularly acclaimed for his wordless and near-wordless picture books; in his *Free Fall* (1988), which includes references to **Lewis Carroll**'s *Alice in Wonderland*, the dreaming transformations are reminiscent of the metamorphoses of M. C. Escher. *Tuesday* (1991), which won Wiesner his first **Caldecott Medal**, is a humorous account of flying frogs. *The Three Pigs* (2001), which won him his second, breaks through the boundaries of the picture-book structure when the pigs are blown out of the tale and into a new, imaginative landscape. Wiesner's use of white space and perspective and his play with literary conventions invite the reader to explore the space outside the narrative and the images.

WIGGIN, KATE DOUGLAS (1856–1923). U.S. author and educator, and a pioneer in kindergarten education. Wiggin wrote or edited more than 60 books, but her most successful novel is *Rebecca of Sunnybrook Farm* (1903), which is still available today. This perennial best seller is a coming-of-age story about the education and tribulations of a lively girl from a fatherless family who comes to live in town with her repressive aunts; she ultimately triumphs over adversity to rescue her family from poverty. Later girls' books with a similar theme include **L. M. Montgomery**'s *Anne of Green Gables*

(1908) and Eleanor Porter's ***Pollyanna*** (1913). *Rebecca of Sunnybrook Farm* has been filmed three times, in 1917, 1932, and 1938; Mary Pickford starred in the first of these versions, Shirley Temple in the last.

WILD, MARGARET (1948–). South African–born writer who immigrated to Australia in 1973. Wild is the author of more than 30 **picture books**, mainly for younger children, some of them with controversial themes. *The Very Best of Friends* (1990), illustrated by **Julie Vivas** and winner of the Children's Book Council of Australia Picture Book of the Year Award, is a poignant tale about death and the need for friendship. *Let the Celebrations Begin!* (1991), also by Wild and Vivas, is set in a concentration camp and shows the power of the human spirit in the face of adversity. **Ron Brooks** has illustrated a number of her books, including *Old Pig* (1996) and *Fox* (2001).

WILDE, OSCAR (1854–1900). Irish playwright, novelist, and poet, and one of the greatest celebrities of his day, who suffered a dramatic downfall after his conviction for homosexuality. Wilde was the author of two collections of literary **fairy tales** in the tradition of **Hans Christian Andersen**, *The Happy Prince, and Other Tales* (1888) and *A House of Pomegranates* (1891). The stories explore such themes as self-sacrifice, salvation offered by selfless love, and the price paid in human suffering for beauty and art. They sometimes verge on the sentimental, and the endings are frequently unhappy or unresolved. Experimental in form and style, Wilde's tales subvert his readers' expectations; the "happy prince," for instance, is never actually happy. Wilde was ambivalent as to whether these tales were for children. They have been **illustrated** by such notable artists as **Walter Crane**, **P. J. Lynch**, and **Lisbeth Zwerger**.

WILDER, LAURA INGALLS (1867–1957). U.S. author whose pioneer childhood inspired her popular Little House series of eight children's novels. Starting with *Little House in the Big Woods* (1932) and concluding with *These Happy Golden Years* (1943), they describe the travels, work, and daily life of the Ingalls family as they move west to settle in different territories. *The Long Winter* (1940), regarded as one of the best novels in the series, describes the bitter hardship of the family having to survive 7 months cut off from supplies by a snowstorm. The protagonist Laura becomes a schoolteacher, marries Almanzo Wilder, and finally departs from the family home. Wilder was over 60 when she started writing her memoir novels at the suggestion of her daughter, Rose. The books' cheerfulness and their celebration of hard work, bravery, education, and family life have ensured their widespread popularity over the years. This popularity has also resulted in a multimillion-dollar franchise of mass marketing, several historical sites and museums, a spin-off book series, and a long-running television series. The novels have been **translated** into more than 40 languages. The Laura Ingalls Wilder Medal is awarded in her honor by the **American Library Association (ALA)** to U.S. writers who have made substantial and lasting contributions to children's literature.

WILDSMITH, BRIAN (1930–). British author and **illustrator** now resident in the south of France. Wildsmith's painterly art expresses his belief in the importance of beautiful **picture books** for the aesthetic development of a child. He has illustrated *Tales from the Arabian Nights* (1961), **poetry** anthologies such as *The Oxford Book of Poetry for Children* (1963) and **Robert Louis Stevenson**'s *A Child's Garden of Verses* (1966), **nursery rhymes** (*Mother Goose*, 1964), **Bible stories**, and **fairy tales**. He has also written a number of concept books, as well as authoring his own picture books. His *ABC* (1962) won the **Kate Greenaway Medal**. He is particularly popular in Japan, where the Brian Wildsmith Museum of Art opened in 1994.

WILLARD, NANCY (1936–). U.S. poet, novelist, writer, and **illustrator** of **picture books**, whose work often blends the ordinary with the extraordinary. *A Visit to William Blake's Inn: Poems for Innocent and Experienced Travelers* (1981), illustrated by Alice and Martin Provensen and the first book of **poetry** to win the **Newbery Medal**, evokes the spirit of Blake's writing while depicting the extraordinary life of an imaginary inn run by Willard's favorite poet. She has also worked successfully with illustrators **Leo** and **Diane Dillon**, whose playful and imaginative pictures in *Pish, Posh, Said Hieronymus Bosch* (1991) complement Willard's fantastic images in a poem about a housekeeper driven to distraction by the creatures that come to life under the painter's brush. In her **fantasy** trilogy reminiscent of **C. S. Lewis**'s Narnia series, *Sailing to Cythera* (1974), *The Island of the Grass King* (1979), and *Uncle Terrible* (1982), a small boy is tested against evil in fantasy worlds. Willard has written two books of poetry on angels, *An Alphabet of Angels* (1994) and *The Good-Night Blessing Book* (1996), which she illustrated with her own photographs.

WILLIAMS, GARTH (1912–1996). U.S. **illustrator** of more than 100 books, best known for his expressive line illustrations in modern children's classics such as **E. B. White**'s *Charlotte's Web* and the republished editions of **Laura Ingalls Wilder**'s Little House books, as well as books by **Margaret Wise Brown**, **Russell Hoban**, and Randall Jarrell. Williams also wrote books of his own, including *The Rabbits' Wedding* (1958), which stirred up unintended controversy in the Southern United States because it depicts the marriage of a black and a white rabbit.

WILLIAMS, JAY (1914–1978). U.S. author of **science-fiction** stories best known for his Danny Dunn series, written with Raymond Abrashkin between 1958 and 1977 and based on scientific fact. His collection *The Practical Princess, and Other Liberating Fairytales* (1978) subverts the stereotypes of traditional stories and became the model for many alternative **fairy-tale** versions.

WILLIAMS, MARGERY (1881–1944). English-born writer and translator of some 27 books in many genres who immigrated as a child to the United States. Her first and most famous book, *The Velveteen Rabbit, or How Toys Become Real* (1922), is the story of a toy rabbit that is transformed by a boy's love into a real one after escaping being burned in the wake of the boy's near-fatal illness. Many different **illustrators** have interpreted *The Velveteen Rabbit*, and it has been **adapted** into film and stage versions. It is still in print today.

WILSON, JACQUELINE (1945–). One of the most popular living British writers for children, dubbed "Queen of the Tweens." Wilson's comic and realistic novels of contemporary British childhood for preteens, especially girls, address challenging themes such as homelessness (*The Bed and Breakfast Star*, 1994), divorce (*The Suitcase Kid*, 1992), adoption, and parental depression (*The Illustrated Mum*, 1999). She has a sensitive understanding of modern children and always takes the side of her young protagonists, many of whom lead difficult lives. Her critical and popular breakthrough came with *The Story of Tracy Beaker* (1991), which remains one of her most popular titles. Both funny and moving, it is a first-person narrative about 10-year-old Tracy, who lives in a children's home and longs for a real family. Three sequels followed it: *The Dare Game* (2000), *Starring Tracy Beaker* (2006), and a story specially written for the Comic Relief Charity's Red Nose Day 2009, *Tracey Beaker's Thumping Heart* (2009). Wilson won the Smarties Prize, the first of many **awards**, for *Double Act* (1995), a story of identical twins with contrasting personalities. Her Girls series of four novels, starting with *Girls in Love* (1997) and ending with *Girls in Tears* (2002), addresses teenage topics such as first boyfriends, stepparents, drugs, and anorexia. More than 25 million copies of her books have been sold in Great Britain alone, and she has been voted the favorite author of English children in a number of polls. Several of her novels have been adapted for television. Wilson was appointed OBE for services to literacy in schools in 2002, was the fourth **children's laureate** from 2005–2007, and was appointed DBE in 2008. *See also* GENDER.

WINNIE-THE-POOH. *See* MILNE, A. A.

WITCHES. The Anglo-Saxon female term *wicce*, from which the word *witch* derives, means **wizard** or magician. Witches are traditionally female and were condemned by the Catholic Church from the Middle Ages onward; the later Salem witch trials in Puritan colonial Massachusetts in 1692 and 1693 are particularly notorious. The folklore of most countries features witches, usually as old women with magic powers. Examples include Russia's Baba Yaga, England's Morgan LeFay, and Germany's ogre witches, as in the story of "Hansel and Gretel," and good witches, such as the fairy godmother in "Snow White." Witches of all sorts people children's **fantasy**. Exclusively evil ones feature in **C. S. Lewis**'s The Chronicles of

Narnia (1950–1956) and in **Alan Garner**'s *The Weirdstone of Brisingamen* (1960), in the shape of the wicked sorceress the Morrigan. **Roald Dahl**'s *The Witches* (1983) has a boy and his grandmother fight female evil in the form of witches; it concludes with the boy transformed permanently into a mouse. In his *Wonderful Wizard of Oz* (1900), **L. Frank Baum** features two good witches as counterparts to the wicked ones; and in **J. K. Rowling**'s Harry Potter series, witches, who are the female equivalents of wizards, belong to both the light and the dark sides of magic. A comic strand is evident in books for younger children, which often depict young witches in the process of learning their skills. A classic of this type is **Otfried Preussler**'s *The Little Witch* (German original 1957, English translation 1961), and, more recently, Jill Murphy's successful series The Worst Witch (1974–2007), about Mildred Hubble, the worst student at Miss Cackle's Academy for Witches. As with books on **wizards**, books with witches have met with strong Christian opposition on the grounds that they propagate occult practices. *See also* DEPAOLA, TOMIE; MAGUIRE, GREGORY; MAHY, MARGARET; NAPOLI, DONNA JO; NAYLOR, PHYLLIS REYNOLDS; NORTON, ANDRE; PRATCHETT, TERRY; WIZARDS.

THE WIZARD OF OZ. *See* BAUM, L. FRANK.

WIZARDS. Traditionally a "wise man" or "sage," the term developed to denote a man skilled in occult arts. Arguably the most famous wizard is Merlin of the Arthurian Cycle, who features as a character in fiction for young readers in **T. H. White**'s *The Sword in the Stone* (1938) and in recent Merlin trilogies by **Jane Yolen** (1996–1997) and T. A. Barron (2008–2010). Merlin is also the inspiration behind the character Merriman in **Susan Cooper**'s **fantasy** sequence The Dark Is Rising (1965–1977). **J. R. R. Tolkien**'s The Lord of the Rings features the good, Merlin-like wizard Gandalf and the treacherous Saroman, and many later fantasy series, most notably **J. K. Rowling**'s Harry Potter novels, are based on the opposition between good and bad wizards, such as Dumbledore and Voldemort. The question of how wizards actually learn their art is at the fore in **Ursula K. Le Guin**'s *A Wizard of Earthsea* (1968), the first of her Earthsea series; in **Diana Wynne Jones**'s Chrestomanci series (1977–2006); and, of course, in the *Harry Potter* septet. One of the most famous wizards in children's fiction is in **L. Frank Baum**'s *The Wonderful Wizard of Oz* (1900), a figure unseen for most of the novel and held in great awe by his subjects; the novel culminates in the unmasking of the wizard as an ordinary American man. Wizards as characters and witchcraft as a topic have met with accusations from religious groups who claim that they lead children toward the occult. The Harry Potter series has been charged with promoting Satanism, and J. K. Rowling was the fourth most challenged author in the United States between 1990 and 2004. *See also* WITCHES.

WOOLSEY, SARAH CHAUNCEY. *See* COOLIDGE, SUSAN.

WORTIS, EDWARD IRVING. *See* AVI.

WRIGHTSON, PATRICIA (1921–2010). Australian writer for children who has won national and international acclaim and popularity for her evocation of the Australian countryside and for her use of Aboriginal traditions in the form of spirit creatures. This is especially evident in her award-winning Wirrun trilogy, comprising *The Ice Is Coming* (1977), *The Dark Bright Water* (1979), and *Behind the Wind* (1981), an epic heroic tale about a young Aboriginal man from the city and his journey back to his cultural heritage and spirituality. Wirrun is chosen as the hero required to restore order in the spiritual world. Wrightson has been criticized in recent years for her tendency toward appropriation of Aboriginal culture, but she defends her use of these traditions on the grounds that it enables the writing of genuine Australian **fantasy**. She received the **Hans Christian Andersen Award** in 1986.

WYNNE-JONES, TIM (1948–). British-born Canadian author of novels, short stories, and **picture books** for children as well as fiction for adults. Best known among his books for young readers is the Zoom series—*Zoom at Sea* (1983), *Zoom Away* (1985), and *Zoom Upstream* (1992)—about the adventures of a small, white cat and its friend Maria. Wynne-Jones has also produced picture-book retellings of Bram Stoker's *Dracula* and Victor Hugo's *The Hunchback of Notre Dame*. His short stories for adolescents are characterized by his dry humor (the title of one collection is *Lord of the Fries*, 1999), his creation of eccentric but believable characters, and his use of **fantasy** to resolve the problems confronting his young protagonists. Praised for their prose, his short stories, such as in the collection *Some of the Kinder Planets* (1995), have been widely anthologized. Wynne-Jones has won all of the major Canadian children's literature **awards**, including the Governor General's Award for Children's Literature for *The Maestro* (1995), a complex novel about an abused boy who runs away from home and encounters an eccentric, world-renowned pianist in the Canadian wilderness. Many of his books have been **translated** into other languages.

WYSS, JOHANN DAVID (1743–1818). Swiss army chaplain and author of *Der Schweizerische Robinson* (1812–1813; *The Swiss Family Robinson*, 1814), one of the most successful **robinsonades**. This **adventure story** about a Swiss family shipwrecked on an uninhabited island was subsequently enlarged by **translators** and editors; it inspired **Captain Frederick Marryat**'s sea novel *Masterman Ready*, as well as many imitations (including the U.S. **science-fiction** TV series of the 1960s, *Lost in Space*). Wyss's novel enjoyed a much wider reception in the English-speaking world than in his native Switzerland or in Germany.

– Y –

YEP, LAURENCE (1948–). Chinese American author of more than 40 novels and one of children's literature's leading Asian American writers. The search for identity by members of two cultural traditions, the need for tolerance by others, and the importance of family are key themes in his multicultural books. Yep has written realistic fiction and a **fantasy** series (beginning with *Dragon of the Lost Sea*, 1982), but is especially acclaimed for his **historical novels**. *The Star Fisher* (1992) is set among second-generation Asian Americans living in West Virginia; *Dragonwings* (1975) tells the story of Moon Shadow, who, at the age of 8, sailed from China to America to join his father; and *Dragon's Gate* (1993) is a survival adventure story about the immigration of a 14-year-old Chinese boy to California in 1865.

YOLEN, JANE (1939–). U.S. author of more than 200 books for children, young adults, and adults, encompassing **poetry**, folktales, songs, **fantasy**, and **science fiction**. Yolen's favored themes include Arthurian **legends**, dragon lore, and magical transformations. Her humorous **picture books** for beginning readers have been illustrated by such artists as **Ed Young** and **David Wiesner**, and she has written series such as the easy-to-read Commander Toad books. Her literary **fairy tales** helped start a revival of literary fairy tales in the late 20th century, and she was both criticized and praised for her daring use of fantasy in a novel about the Holocaust, *The Devil's Arithmetic* (1988), which presents her readers with an inside view of Nazi-concentration-camp existence. It was made into a film in 1999. Yolen's books have been **translated** into several languages, and she is the recipient of a number of major children's literature **awards**.

YONGE, CHARLOTTE M. (1823–1901). Prolific British writer of more than 250 works of fiction and **nonfiction**, credited with establishing the family story as a distinct genre. Yonge is regarded a pioneer writer of girls' books. She worked as a Sunday-school teacher and edited *The Monthly Packet*, a Church of England magazine for girls, from 1851 until 1890. *The Heir of Redclyffe* (1853) was one of the most widely read novels of the 19th century. Yonge's most famous and best-selling work was *The Daisy Chain* (1856), about the large, motherless May family; the self-sacrificing and virtuous heroine, Ethel May, was the idol of every female reader of her time. Yonge donated the revenue of all her books to charity.

YOUNG, ED (1931–). Chinese-born U.S. **illustrator** who immigrated to the United States in 1951. After studying architecture and art, he worked in advertising until the 1960s, when he received a contract for a children's **picture book**. Young's subjects often derive from **folklore**—from Chinese, Persian, and other cultural traditions. Traditional Chinese brushstroking is a technique he uses in many of his books, but he also draws inspiration from other styles. Elements borrowed from traditional Indian style feature in his illustration of **Jane Yolen**'s *The Girl Who Loved the Wind* (1972). Young uses Chinese paper-cut technique in *The Emperor and the Kite* (1967) and silhouette in *Seven Blind Mice* (1992), and his illustration of **Carlo Col-**

lodi's *The Adventures of Pinocchio* (1997) uses collage effectively. He received the **Caldecott Medal** for *Lon Po Po* (1989), a Chinese version of the "Little Red Riding Hood" story. Young has illustrated more than 70 books from a large range of genres by various authors, including **Aesop**, **Oscar Wilde**, and the poet Robert Frost.

– Z –

ZELINSKY, PAUL O. (1953–). U.S. **illustrator** and author who has illustrated work by such authors as **Beverly Cleary**, **E. Nesbit**, and **Carl Sandburg**. His style is eclectic, and he aims to create a specific, individual look for each book. Zelinsky has lushly illustrated a number of his own retellings of **fairy tales**, including *Hansel and Gretel* (1985), *Rumpelstiltskin* (1987), and the **Caldecott Medal** winner *Rapunzel* (1997). He has also created movable books based on popular children's songs, *The Wheels on the Bus* (1990) and *Knick-Knack Paddywhack!* (2002).

ZINDEL, PAUL (1936–2003). U.S. writer of young adult literature who was a chemistry teacher for several years before beginning his literary career, initially as a playwright. He won the Pulitzer Prize for his play *The Effect of Gamma Rays on Man-in-the-Moon Marigolds* (1965). Zindel's first book for adolescents was *The Pigman* (1968), a portrayal of the relationship between two teenagers and a lonely old man whom they befriend. After the success of this novel, today considered a classic of the genre, he went on to write novels such as *My Darling, My Hamburger* (1969), *The Amazing and Death-Defying Diary of Eugene Dingman* (1987), and *A Begonia for Miss Applebaum* (1989). In them, he discusses issues of central importance to young adults such as sexuality, love, death, and alcohol abuse. Zindel captures teenage life in a realistic fashion, and writes about it with honesty and humor.

ZOLOTOW, CHARLOTTE (1915–). U.S. author and editor of more than 70 **picture books**. Zolotow started working at Harper as assistant to Ursula Nordstrom, and went on to become editorial director of her own imprint from 1987. Most of her books for young children are in the realistic mode; examples include *The Storm Book* (1952), *William's Doll* (1972), and *The Hating Book* (1969). A rare example of **fantasy** is *Mister Rabbit and the Lovely Present* (1962), illustrated by **Maurice Sendak**, which was a **Caldecott** Honor Book. In 1998, the annual Charlotte Zolotow Lecture and Award for outstanding writing in a picture book was established at the University of Wisconsin, Madison, to honor her lifelong commitment to excellence in literature for children and young adults.

ZWERGER, LISBETH (1954–). Austrian artist who specializes in the **illustration** of classic texts, especially **fairy tales** and **fantasy**. Her first published work, in 1977, was *The Strange Child*, by **E. T. A. Hoffmann**. Her style is renowned for accuracy in detail, with the atmospheric pictures closely interpreting the text. Her watercolors with monochromic shades of brown and grayish blue are reminiscent of English illustrators of the 19th century, especially **Arthur Rackham**; over the years, her art has evolved to include more color. She has illustrated, among other things, the fairy tales of the **Grimm** brothers, **Hans Christian Andersen**, and **Oscar Wilde**, as well as **Lewis Carroll**'s *Alice in Wonderland* and the poems of Christian Morgenstern. Zwerger received the **Hans Christian Andersen Award** in 1990.

Appendix
Major Children's Literature Awards and Their Recipients

Astrid Lindgren Memorial Award

2003	Christine Nöstlinger (Austria) and Maurice Sendak (United States)
2004	Lygia Bojunga (Brazil)
2005	Ryôji Arai (Japan) and Philip Pullman (Great Britain)
2006	Katherine Paterson (United States)
2007	Banco del Libro (Venezuela)
2008	Sonya Hartnett (Australia)
2009	Tamer Institute for Community Education (Palestine)

Caldecott Medal

1938	Dorothy P. Lathrop: *Animals of the Bible* (text selected by Helen Dean Fish)
1939	Thomas Handforth: *Mei Li*
1940	Ingri and Edgar Parin D'Aulaire: *Abraham Lincoln*
1941	Robert Lawson: *They Were Strong and Good*
1942	Robert McCloskey: *Make Way for Ducklings*
1943	Virginia Lee Burton: *The Little House*
1944	Louis Slobodkin: *Many Moons* (text: James Thurber)
1945	Elizabeth Orton Jones: *Prayer for a Child* (text: Rachel Field)
1946	Maud and Miska Petersham: *The Rooster Crows*
1947	Leonard Weisgard: *The Little Island* (text: Golden MacDonald, pseud. Margaret Wise Brown)
1948	Roger Duvoisin: *White Snow, Bright Snow* (text: Alvin Tresselt)
1949	Berta and Elmer Hader: *The Big Snow*

1950	Leo Politi: *Song of the Swallows*
1951	Katherine Milhous: *The Egg Tree*
1952	Nicholas Mordvinoff: *Finders Keepers* (text: William Lipkind)
1953	Lynd Ward: *The Biggest Bear*
1954	Ludwig Bemelmans: *Madeline's Rescue*
1955	Marcia Brown: *Cinderella, or The Little Glass Slipper* (text: Charles Perrault, trans. by Marcia Brown)
1956	Feodor Rojankovsky: *Frog Went a-Courtin'* (text: John Langstaff)
1957	Marc Simont: *A Tree Is Nice* (text: Janice May Udry)
1958	Robert McCloskey: *Time of Wonder*
1959	Barbara Cooney: *Chanticleer and the Fox* (text adapted from Geoffrey Chaucer)
1960	Marie Hall Ets: *Nine Days to Christmas* (text: Marie Hall Ets and Aurora Labastida)
1961	Nicolas Sidjakov: *Baboushka and the Three Kings* (text: Ruth Robbins)
1962	Marcia Brown: *Once a Mouse . . .*
1963	Ezra Jack Keats: *The Snowy Day*
1964	Maurice Sendak: *Where the Wild Things Are*
1965	Beni Montresor: *May I Bring a Friend?* (text: Beatrice Schenk de Regniers)
1966	Nonny Hogrogian: *Always Room for One More* (text: Sorche Nic Leodhas)
1967	Evaline Ness: *Sam, Bangs and Moonshine*
1968	Ed Emberley: *Drummer Hoff* (text: Barbara Emberley)
1969	Uri Schulevitz: *The Fool of the World and the Flying Ship* (text: Arthur Ransome)
1970	William Steig: *Sylvester and the Magic Pebble*
1971	Gail E. Haley: *A Story, a Story*
1972	Nonny Hogrogian: *One Fine Day*
1973	Blair Lent: *The Funny Little Woman* (text: Arlene Mosel)
1974	Margot Zemach: *Duffy and the Devil* (text: Harve Zemach)
1975	Gerald McDermott: *Arrow to the Sun: A Pueblo Indian Tale*

1976	Leo and Diane Dillon: *Why Mosquitoes Buzz in People's Ears: A West African Tale* (text: Verna Aardema)
1977	Leo and Diane Dillon: *Ashanti to Zulu: African Traditions* (text: Margaret Musgrove)
1978	Peter Spier: *Noah's Ark*
1979	Paul Goble: *The Girl Who Loved Wild Horses*
1980	Barbara Cooney: *Ox-Cart Man* (text: Donald Hall)
1981	Arnold Lobel: *Fables*
1982	Chris van Allsburg: *Jumanji*
1983	Marcia Brown: *Shadow* (text: Blaise Cendrars)
1984	Alice and Martin Provensen: *The Glorious Flight: Across the Channel with Louis Blériot*
1985	Trina Schart Hyman: *Saint George and the Dragon* (text: Margaret Hodges)
1986	Chris van Allsburg: *The Polar Express*
1987	Richard Egielski: *Hey, Al* (text: Arthur Yorinks)
1988	John Schoenherr: *Owl Moon* (text: Jane Yolen)
1989	Stephen Gammell: *Song and Dance Man* (text: Karen Ackerman)
1990	Ed Young: *Lon Po Po: A Red-Riding Hood Story from China*
1991	David Macaulay: *Black and White*
1992	David Wiesner: *Tuesday*
1993	Emily Arnold McCully: *Mirette on the High Wire*
1994	Allen Say: *Grandfather's Journey* (text edited by Walter Lorraine)
1995	David Diaz: *Smoky Night* (text: Eve Bunting)
1996	Peggy Rathmann: *Officer Buckle and Gloria*
1997	David Wisniewski: *Golem*
1998	Paul O. Zelinsky: *Rapunzel*
1999	Mary Azarian: *Snowflake Bentley* (text: Jacqueline Briggs Martin)
2000	Simms Taback: *Joseph Had a Little Overcoat*
2001	David Small: *So You Want to Be President?* (text: Judith St. George)
2002	David Wiesner: *The Three Pigs*
2003	Eric Rohmann: *My Friend Rabbit*

2004	Mordicai Gerstein: *The Man Who Walked between the Towers*
2005	Kevin Henkes: *Kitten's First Full Moon*
2006	Chris Raschka: *The Hello, Goodbye Window* (text: Norton Juster)
2007	David Wiesner: *Flotsam*
2008	Brian Selznick: *The Invention of Hugo Cabret*
2009	Beth Krommes: *The House in the Night* (text: Susan Marie Swanson)

Carnegie Medal

Note: Before 2007, the year refers to the publication rather than the award.

1936	Arthur Ransome: *Pigeon Post*
1937	Eve Garnett: *The Family from One End Street*
1938	Noel Streatfeild: *The Circus Is Coming*
1939	Eleanor Doorly: *The Radium Woman*
1940	Kitty Barne: *Visitors from London*
1941	Mary Treadgold: *We Couldn't Leave Dinah*
1942	"BB" [Denys J. Watkins-Pitchford]: *The Little Grey Men*
1943	No award
1944	Eric Linklater: *The Wind on the Moon*
1945	No award
1946	Elizabeth Goudge: *The Little White Horse*
1947	Walter de la Mare: *Collected Stories for Children*
1948	Richard Armstrong: *Sea Change*
1949	Agnes Allen: *The Story of Your Home*
1950	Elfrida Vipont Foulds: *The Lark on the Wing*
1951	Cynthia Harnett: *The Wool-Pack*
1952	Mary Norton: *The Borrowers*
1953	Edward Osmond: *A Valley Grows Up*
1954	Ronald Welch: *Knight Crusader*
1955	Eleanor Farjeon: *The Little Bookroom*
1956	C. S. Lewis: *The Last Battle*
1957	William Mayne: *A Grass Rope*
1958	Philippa Pearce: *Tom's Midnight Garden*
1959	Rosemary Sutcliff: *The Lantern Bearers*

1960 I. W. Cornwall: *The Making of Man*
1961 Lucy M. Boston: *A Stranger at Green Knowe*
1962 Pauline Clarke: *The Twelve and the Genii*
1963 Hester Burton: *Time of Trial*
1964 Sheena Porter: *Nordy Bank*
1965 Philip Turner: *The Grange at High Force*
1966 No award
1967 Alan Garner: *The Owl Service*
1968 Rosemary Harris: *The Moon in the Cloud*
1969 K. M. Peyton: *The Edge of the Cloud*
1970 Leon Garfield and Edward Blishen: *The God beneath the Sea*
1971 Ivan Southall: *Josh*
1972 Richard Adams: *Watership Down*
1973 Penelope Lively: *The Ghost of Thomas Kempe*
1974 Mollie Hunter: *The Stronghold*
1975 Robert Westall: *The Machine-Gunners*
1976 Jan Mark: *Thunder and Lightnings*
1977 Gene Kemp: *The Turbulent Term of Tyke Tiler*
1978 David Rees: *The Exeter Blitz*
1979 Peter Dickinson: *Tulku*
1980 Peter Dickinson: *City of Gold*
1981 Robert Westall: *The Scarecrows*
1982 Margaret Mahy: *The Haunting*
1983 Jan Mark: *Handles*
1984 Margaret Mahy: *The Changeover*
1985 Kevin Crossley-Holland: *Storm*
1986 Berlie Doherty: *Granny Was a Buffer Girl*
1987 Susan Price: *The Ghost Drum*
1988 Geraldine McCaughrean: *A Pack of Lies*
1989 Anne Fine: *Goggle-Eyes*
1990 Gillian Cross: *Wolf*
1991 Berlie Doherty: *Dear Nobody*
1992 Anne Fine: *Flour Babies*
1993 Robert Swindells: *Stone Cold*
1994 Theresa Breslin: *Whispers in the Graveyard*
1995 Philip Pullman: *Northern Lights* (*His Dark Materials*, book 1)

1996	Melvin Burgess: *Junk*
1997	Tim Bowler: *River Boy*
1998	David Almond: *Skellig*
1999	Aidan Chambers: *Postcards from No Man's Land*
2000	Beverley Naidoo: *The Other Side of Truth*
2001	Terry Pratchett: *The Amazing Maurice and His Educated Rodents*
2002	Sharon Creech: *Ruby Holler*
2003	Jennifer Donnelly: *A Gathering Light*
2004	Frank Cottrell Boyce: *Millions*
2005	Mal Peet: *Tamar*
2007	Meg Rosoff: *Just in Case*
2008	Philip Reeve: *Here Lies Arthur*
2009	Siobhan Dowd: *Bog Child*
2010	Neil Gaiman: *The Graveyard Book*

Hans Christian Andersen Award

1956	Author: Eleanor Farjeon (UK)
1958	Author: Astrid Lindgren (Sweden)
1960	Author: Erich Kästner (West Germany)
1962	Author: Meindert DeJong (United States)
1964	Author: René Guillot (France)
1966	Author: Tove Jansson (Finland) Illustrator: Alois Carigiet (Switzerland)
1968	Authors: James Krüss (West Germany) and José Maria Sanchez-Silva (Spain) Illustrator: Jirí Trnka (Czechoslovakia)
1970	Author: Gianni Rodari (Italy) Illustrator: Maurice Sendak (United States)
1972	Author: Scott O'Dell (United States) Illustrator: Ib Spang Olsen (Denmark)
1974	Author: Maria Gripe (Sweden) Illustrator: Farshid Mesghali (Iran)
1976	Author: Cecil Bødker (Denmark) Illustrator: Tatjana Mawrina (Soviet Union)
1978	Author: Paula Fox (United States) Illustrator: Svend Otto Sorensen (Denmark)

1980	Author: Bohumil Ríha (Czechoslovakia)
	Illustrator: Suekichi Akaba (Japan)
1982	Author: Lygia Bojunga Nunes (Brazil)
	Illustrator: Zbigniew Rychlicki (Poland)
1984	Author: Christine Nöstlinger (Austria)
	Illustrator: Mistumasa Anno (Japan)
1986	Author: Patricia Wrightson (Australia)
	Illustrator: Robert Ingpen (Australia)
1988	Author: Annie M. G. Schmidt (Netherlands)
	Illustrator: Dusan Kállay (Czechoslovakia)
1990	Author: Tormod Haugen (Norway)
	Illustrator: Lisbeth Zwerger (Austria)
1992	Author: Virginia Hamilton (United States)
	Illustrator: Kveta Pacovská (Czech Republic)
1994	Author: Michio Mado (Japan)
	Illustrator: Jörg Müller (Switzerland)
1996	Author: Uri Orlev (Israel)
	Illustrator: Klaus Ensikat (Germany)
1998	Author: Katherine Paterson (United States)
	Illustrator: Tomi Ungerer (France)
2000	Author: Ana Maria Machado (Brazil)
	Illustrator: Anthony Browne (Great Britain)
2002	Author: Aidan Chambers (Great Britain)
	Illustrator: Quentin Blake (Great Britain)
2004	Author: Martin Waddell (Ireland)
	Illustrator: Max Velthuijs (Netherlands)
2006	Author: Margaret Mahy (New Zealand)
	Illustrator: Wolf Erlbruch (Germany)
2008	Author: Jürg Schubiger (Switzerland)
	Illustrator: Roberto Innocenti (Italy)

Kate Greenaway Medal

Note: Before 2007, the year refers to the publication rather than the award.

1956	Edward Ardizzone: *Tim All Alone*
1957	V. H. Drummond: *Mrs Easter and the Storks*

1958	No award
1959	William Stobbs: *Kashtanka* (text: Anton Chekov) and *A Bundle of Ballads* (compiled by Ruth Manning-Sanders)
1960	Gerald Rose: *Old Winkle and the Seagulls* (text: Elizabeth Rose)
1961	Antony Maitland: *Mrs. Cockle's Cat* (text: Philippa Pearce)
1962	Brian Wildsmith: *A.B.C.*
1963	John Burningham: *Borka: The Adventures of a Goose with No Feathers*
1964	C. W. Hodges: *Shakespeare's Theatre*
1965	Victor Ambrus: *The Three Poor Tailors*
1966	Raymond Briggs: *Mother Goose Treasury*
1967	Charles Keeping: *Charley, Charlotte and the Golden Canary*
1968	Pauline Baynes: *Dictionary of Chivalry* (text: Grant Uden)
1969	Helen Oxenbury: *The Quangle-Wangle's Hat* (text: Edward Lear) and *The Dragon of an Ordinary Family* (text: Margaret Mahy)
1970	John Burningham: *Mr. Gumpy's Outing*
1971	Jan Pienkowski: *The Kingdom under the Sea*
1972	Krystyna Turska: *The Woodcutter's Duck*
1973	Raymond Briggs: *Father Christmas*
1974	Pat Hutchins: *The Wind Blew*
1975	Victor Ambrus: *Horses in Battle* and *Mishka*
1976	Gail E. Haley: *The Post Office Cat*
1977	Shirley Hughes: *Dogger*
1978	Janet Ahlberg: *Each Peach Pear Plum* (text: Allan Ahlberg)
1979	Jan Pienkowski: *The Haunted House*
1980	Quentin Blake: *Mr. Magnolia*
1981	Charles Keeping: *The Highwayman* (text: Alfred Noyes)
1982	Michael Foreman: *Long Neck and Thunder Foot* (text: Helen Piers) and *Sleeping Beauty, and Other Favourite Fairy Tales* (text: Angela Carter)
1983	Anthony Browne: *Gorilla*
1984	Errol Le Cain: *Hiawatha's Childhood*

1985	Juan Wijngaard: *Sir Gawain and the Loathly Lady* (text: Selina Hastings)
1986	Fiona French: *Snow White in New York*
1987	Adrienne Kennaway: *Crafty Chameleon* (text: Mwenye Hadithi)
1988	Barbara Firth: *Can't You Sleep, Little Bear?* (text: Martin Waddel)
1989	Michael Foreman: *War Boy: A Country Childhood*
1990	Gary Blythe: *The Whales' Song* (text: Dyan Sheldon)
1991	Janet Ahlberg: *The Jolly Christmas Postman* (text: Allan Ahlberg)
1992	Anthony Browne: *Zoo*
1993	Alan Lee: *Black Ships before Troy* (text: Rosemary Sutcliff)
1994	Gregory Rogers: *Way Home* (text: Libby Hathorn)
1995	P. J. Lynch: *The Christmas Miracle of Jonathan Toomey* (text: Susan Wojciechowski)
1996	Helen Cooper: *The Baby Who Wouldn't Go to Bed*
1997	P. J. Lynch: *When Jessie Came across the Sea* (text: Amy Hest)
1998	Helen Cooper: *Pumpkin Soup*
1999	Helen Oxenbury: *Alice's Adventures in Wonderland* (text: Lewis Carroll)
2000	Lauren Child: *I Will Not Ever Never Eat a Tomato*
2001	Chris Riddell: *Pirate Diary* (text: Richard Platt)
2002	Bob Graham: *Jethro Byrde, Fairy Child*
2003	Shirley Hughes: *Ella's Big Chance*
2004	Chris Riddell: *Jonathan Swift's Gulliver*
2005	Emily Gravett: *Wolves*
2007	Mini Grey: *The Adventures of the Dish and the Spoon*
2008	Emily Gravett: *Little Mouse's Big Book of Fears*
2009	Catherine Rayner: *Harris Finds His Feet*

Marsh Award for Children's Literature in Translation

1990–1996	Anthea Bell, for *A Dog's Life* by Christine Nöstlinger
1996	Anthea Bell, for *The Penny Mark* by Gert Loschutz
1999	Patricia Crampton, for *The Final Journey* by Gudrun Pausewang

2001	Betsy Rosenberg, for *Duel* by David Grossmann
2003	Anthea Bell, for *Where Were You Robert?* by Hans Magnus Enzensberger
2005	Sarah Adams, for *Eye of the Wolf* by Daniel Pennac
2007	Anthea Bell, for *The Flowing Queen* by Kai Meyer
2009	Sarah Ardizzone, for *Toby Alone* by Timothée de Fombelle

Mildred L. Batchelder Award

1968	Alfred A. Knopf, for *The Little Man*, by Erich Kästner; trans. from German by James Kirkup
1969	Charles Scribner's Sons, for *Don't Take Teddy*, by Babbis Friis-Baastad; trans. from Norwegian by Lise Sømme McKinnon
1970	Holt, Rinehart and Winston, for *Wildcat under Glass*, by Aliki Zei; trans. from Greek by Edward Fenton
1971	Pantheon Books, for *In the Land of Ur: The Discovery of Ancient Mesopotamia*, by Hans Baumann; trans. from German by Stella Humphries
1972	Holt, Rinehart and Winston, for *Friedrich*, by Hans Peter Richter; trans. from German by Edite Kroll
1973	William Morrow, for *Pulga*, by S. R. Van Iterson; trans. from Dutch by Alexander and Alison Gode
1974	E. P. Dutton, for *Petros' War*, by Aliki Zei; trans. from Greek by Edward Fenton
1975	Crown, for *An Old Tale Carved Out of Stone*, by A. Linevskii; trans. from Russian by Maria Polushkin
1976	Henry Z. Walck, for *The Cat and Mouse Who Shared a House*, by Ruth Hürlimann; trans. from German by Anthea Bell
1977	Atheneum, for *The Leopard*, by Cecil Bødker; trans. from Danish by Gunnar Poulsen
1978	No award
1979	Two awards granted: Harcourt Brace Jovanovich, for *Rabbit Island*, by Jörg Steiner; trans. from German by Ann Conrad Lammers Franklin Watts, for *Konrad*, by Christine Nöstlinger; trans. from German by Anthea Bell

1980 E. P. Dutton, for *The Sound of the Dragon's Feet*, by Aliki Zei; trans. from Greek by Edward Fenton

1981 William Morrow, for *The Winter When Time Was Frozen*, by Els Pelgrom; trans. from Dutch by Maryka and Raphael Rudnik

1982 Bradbury Press, for *The Battle Horse*, by Harry Kullman; trans. from Swedish by George Blecher and Lone Thygesen Blecher

1983 Lothrop, Lee and Shepard, for *Hiroshima No Pika*, by Toshi Maruki; trans. from Japanese through Kurita-Bando Literary Agency

1984 Viking Press, for *Ronia, the Robber's Daughter*, by Astrid Lindgren; trans. from Swedish by Patricia Crampton

1985 Houghton Mifflin, for *The Island on Bird Street*, by Uri Orlev; trans. from Hebrew by Hillel Halkin

1986 Creative Education, for *Rose Blanche*, by Christophe Gallaz and Roberto Innocenti; trans. from Italian by Martha Coventry and Richard Craglia

1987 Lothrop, Lee and Shepard, for *No Hero for the Kaiser*, by Rudolph Frank; trans. from German by Patricia Crampton

1988 McElderry Books, for *If You Didn't Have Me*, by Ulf Nilsson; trans. from Swedish by Lone Thygesen Blecher and George Blecher

1989 Lothrop, Lee and Shepard, for *Crutches*, by Peter Härtling; trans. from German by Elizabeth D. Crawford

1990 E. P. Dutton, for *Buster's World*, by Bjarne Reuter; trans. from Danish by Anthea Bell

1991 E. P. Dutton, for *A Hand Full of Stars*, by Rafik Schami; trans. from German by Rika Lesser

1992 Houghton Mifflin, for *The Man from the Other Side*, by Uri Orlev; trans. from Hebrew by Hillel Halkin

1993 No award

1994 Farrar, Straus and Giroux, for *The Apprentice*, by Pilar Molina Llorente; trans. from Spanish by Robin Longshaw

1995 E. P. Dutton, for *The Boys from St. Petri*, by Bjarne Reuter; trans. from Danish by Anthea Bell

1996 Houghton Mifflin, for *The Lady with the Hat*, by Uri Orlev; trans. from Hebrew by Hillel Halkin

1997	Farrar, Straus and Giroux, for *The Friends*, by Kazumi Yumoto; trans. from Japanese by Cathy Hirano
1998	Henry Holt, for *The Robber and Me*, by Josef Holub. Edited by Mark Aronson and trans. from German by Elizabeth D. Crawford
1999	Dial, for *Thanks to My Mother*, by Schoschana Rabinovici; trans. from German by James Skofield
2000	Walker, for *The Baboon King* by Anton Quintana; trans. from Dutch by John Nieuwenhuizen
2001	Arthur A. Levine/Scholastic, for *Samir and Yonatan*, by Daniella Carmi; trans. from Hebrew by Yael Lotan
2002	Cricket Books/Carus, for *How I Became an American*, by Karin Gündisch; trans. from German by James Skofield
2003	The Chicken House/Scholastic, for *The Thief Lord*, by Cornelia Funke; trans. from German by Oliver Latsch
2004	Walter Lorraine Books/Houghton Mifflin, for *Run, Boy, Run*, by Uri Orlev; trans. from Hebrew by Hillel Halkin
2005	Delacorte Press/Random House Children's Books, for *The Shadows of Ghadames*, by Joëlle Stolz; trans. from French by Catherine Temerson
2006	Arthur A. Levine Books, for *An Innocent Soldier*, by Josef Holub; trans. from German by Michael Hofmann
2007	Delacorte Press, for *The Pull of the Ocean*, by Jean-Claude Mourlevat; trans. from French by Y. Maudet
2008	VIZ Media, for *Brave Story*, by Miyuki Miyabe, trans. from Japanese by Alexander O. Smith
2009	Arthur A. Levine Books/Scholastic, for *Moribito: Guardian of the Spirit*, by Nahoko Uehashi; trans. from Japanese by Cathy Hirano

Newbery Medal

1922	Hendrik Willem van Loon: *The Story of Mankind*
1923	Hugh Lofting: *The Voyages of Doctor Dolittle*
1924	Charles Hawes: *The Dark Frigate*
1925	Charles Finger: *Tales from Silver Lands*
1926	Arthur Bowie Chrisman: *Shen of the Sea*
1927	Will James: *Smoky, the Cowhorse*
1928	Dhan Gopal Mukerji: *Gay-Neck, the Story of a Pigeon*

1929 Eric P. Kelly: *The Trumpeter of Krakow: A Tale of the Fifteenth Century*
1930 Rachel Field: *Hitty, Her First Hundred Years*
1931 Elizabeth Coatsworth: *The Cat Who Went to Heaven*
1932 Laura Adams Armer: *Waterless Mountain*
1933 Elizabeth Lewis: *Young Fu of the Upper Yangtze*
1934 Cornelia Meigs: *Invincible Louisa: The Story of the Author of* Little Women
1935 Monica Shannon: *Dobry*
1936 Carol Ryrie Brink: *Caddie Woodlawn*
1937 Ruth Sawyer: *Roller Skates*
1938 Kate Seredy: *The White Stag*
1939 Elizabeth Enright: *Thimble Summer*
1940 James Daugherty: *Daniel Boone*
1941 Armstrong Sperry: *Call It Courage*
1942 Walter D. Edmonds: *The Matchlock Gun*
1943 Elizabeth Janet Gray: *Adam of the Road*
1944 Esther Forbes: *Johnny Tremain*
1945 Robert Lawson: *Rabbit Hill*
1946 Lois Lenski: *Strawberry Girl*
1947 Carolyn Sherwin Bailey: *Miss Hickory*
1948 William Pène du Bois: *The Twenty-One Balloons*
1949 Marguerite Henry: *King of the Wind*
1950 Marguerite de Angeli: *The Door in the Wall*
1951 Elizabeth Yates: *Amos Fortune, Free Man*
1952 Eleanor Estes: *Ginger Pye*
1953 Ann Nolan Clark: *Secret of the Andes*
1954 Joseph Krumgold: *. . . And Now Miguel*
1955 Meindert DeJong: *The Wheel on the School*
1956 Jean Lee Latham: *Carry On, Mr. Bowditch*
1957 Virginia Sorensen: *Miracles on Maple Hill*
1958 Harold Keith: *Rifles for Watie*
1959 Elizabeth George Speare: *The Witch of Blackbird Pond*
1960 Joseph Krumgold: *Onion John*
1961 Scott O'Dell: *Island of the Blue Dolphins*
1962 Elizabeth George Speare: *The Bronze Bow*
1963 Madeleine L'Engle: *A Wrinkle in Time*
1964 Emily C. Neville: *It's Like This, Cat*
1965 Maia Wojciechowska: *Shadow of a Bull*

1966	Elizabeth Borton de Treviño: *I, Juan de Pareja*
1967	Irene Hunt: *Up a Road Slowly*
1968	E. L. Konigsburg: *From the Mixed-Up Files of Mrs. Basil E. Frankweiler*
1969	Lloyd Alexander: *The High King*
1970	William H. Armstrong: *Sounder*
1971	Betsy Byars: *The Summer of the Swans*
1972	Robert C. O'Brien: *Mrs. Frisby and the Rats of NIMH*
1973	Jean Craighead George: *Julie of the Wolves*
1974	Paula Fox: *The Slave Dancer*
1975	Virginia Hamilton: *M. C. Higgins, the Great*
1976	Susan Cooper: *The Grey King*
1977	Mildred D. Taylor: *Roll of Thunder, Hear My Cry*
1978	Katherine Paterson: *Bridge to Terabithia*
1979	Ellen Raskin: *The Westing Game*
1980	Joan W. Blos: *A Gathering of Days: A New England Girl's Journal, 1830–1832*
1981	Katherine Paterson: *Jacob Have I Loved*
1982	Nancy Willard: *A Visit to William Blake's Inn: Poems for Innocent and Experienced Travelers*
1983	Cynthia Voigt: *Dicey's Song*
1984	Beverly Cleary: *Dear Mr. Henshaw*
1985	Robin McKinley: *The Hero and the Crown*
1986	Patricia MacLachlan: *Sarah, Plain and Tall*
1987	Sid Fleischman: *The Whipping Boy*
1988	Russell Freedman: *Lincoln: A Photobiography*
1989	Paul Fleischman: *Joyful Noise: Poems for Two Voices*
1990	Lois Lowry: *Number the Stars*
1991	Jerry Spinelli: *Maniac Magee*
1992	Phyllis Reynolds Naylor: *Shiloh*
1993	Cynthia Rylant: *Missing May*
1994	Lois Lowry: *The Giver*
1995	Sharon Creech: *Walk Two Moons*
1996	Karen Cushman: *The Midwife's Apprentice*
1997	E. L. Konigsburg: *The View from Saturday*
1998	Karen Hesse: *Out of the Dust*
1999	Louis Sachar: *Holes*
2000	Christopher Paul Curtis: *Bud, Not Buddy*

2001	Richard Peck: *A Year Down Yonder*
2002	Linda Sue Park: *A Single Shard*
2003	Avi: *Crispin: The Cross of Lead*
2004	Kate DiCamillo: *The Tale of Despereaux: Being the Story of a Mouse, a Princess, Some Soup, and a Spool of Thread*
2005	Cynthia Kadohata: *Kira-Kira*
2006	Lynne Rae Perkins: *Criss Cross*
2007	Susan Patron: *The Higher Power of Lucky*
2008	Laura Amy Schlitz: *Good Masters! Sweet Ladies! Voices from a Medieval Village*
2009	Neil Gaiman: *The Graveyard Book*
2010	Rebecca Stead: *When You Reach Me*

Bibliography

CONTENTS

INTRODUCTION

Children's literature has featured on the curricula in education, teacher training, and library-studies departments in universities and colleges since the early 20th century, but its establishment as an academic discipline only started after the 1960s, when it gradually gained entry into the literature departments. In 1964 the first chair for children's literature was established at the University of Frankfurt in Germany, and its incumbent, Klaus Doderer, edited children's literature's first encyclopedia: the four-volume, comprehensive, and international *Lexikon der Kinder- und Jugendliteratur* [Encyclopedia of Children's Literature] (1975–1982). The first English reference book, Humphrey Carpenter and Mari Prichard's *Oxford Companion to Children's Literature* (1984), was on a smaller scale. It was of great value to teachers, parents, librarians, and critics, for whom it was a welcome first port of call, and it was rereleased, unchanged, as a paperback in 1999.

The last decade and a half has seen the publication of a number of major reference works in English. In 1996, Peter Hunt's *International Companion Encyclopedia of Children's Literature* featured over 80 lengthy articles that "demonstrate the evolution of a discipline fit for academic recognition and institutionalized research" in sections on theory and critical approaches, on the different genres, on contexts and applications, and on children's literature in 21 different countries and regions. It was completely revised, updated, and expanded to appear as a two-volume second edition in 2004. Two single-volume, A–Z encyclopedias were published in 2001, in the United States and Great Britain respectively: *The Continuum Encyclopedia of Children's Literature* (Cullinan and Person 2001) in the United States, and the British *Cambridge Guide to Children's Books in English* (Watson 2001). These were followed by the extensive, scholarly, and authoritative four-volume encyclopedia, *Oxford Encyclopedia of Children's Literature* (Zipes 2006), an explicit and worthy English-language successor to Doderer's *Lexikon*. Although the academic mainstream is slow to accept children's literature, and the subject still meets with resistance from some established quarters today, the recent encyclopedias and other publications reflect its maturity and increased respectability.

A further crucial aspect influencing publications has to do with the popularity and increasing number of courses on children's literature in U.S., British, and international universities over the past two decades. Anthologies of primary texts (*Children's Literature: An Anthology, 1801–1902*, Hunt 2004; *The Norton Anthology of Children's Literature*, Zipes et al. 2005), ones that offer both primary and secondary sources (*Crosscurrents of Children's Literature*, Stahl, Hanlon, and Lennox Keyser 2006), and readers that collate critical contributions from a variety of subject areas (*Considering Children's Literature*, Wyile and Rosenberg 2008) or focus on a specific issue (*The Translation of Children's Literature*, Lathey 2006), all suitable for use as course material, reflect this development, as well as a new apparent salability of children's literature studies.

The aim of this bibliography is to document resources directly relevant for the study and use of children's literature, from catalogs to histories, from theoretical aspects through research on international issues to pragmatic aspects of reading and literacy. The first section, "General Reference," contains details of encyclopedias, dictionaries, surveys of children's literature, anthologies, and introductions. The second, "Bibliographies, Catalogs, and Guides," lists bibliographies of primary literature on a variety of themes, catalogs of the most important collections (such as the Cotsen Children's Library in Princeton), and guides to resources. The monographs in the third section, "Historical Studies," attest to the huge interest generated by this aspect in recent years, interest especially in the beginnings of children's literature, with work on medieval literature for children (Kline 2003) and on *Childhood and Children's Books in Early Modern Europe, 1550–1800* (Immel and Witmore 2005). As titles such as *The Making of the Modern Child: Children's Literature and Childhood in the Late Eighteenth Century* (O'Malley 2003) indicate, much contemporary historical research on children's literature is situated within the broad context of childhood studies, which is interested in the "invention" (Philippe Ariès), construction, or conditions of childhood in history. Most publications in this section relate to English-language children's literature, especially from Britain and the United States, and a few panoramic histories and collective histories are also included. Historical accounts of children's literature from other countries are otherwise listed in the section "Continents and Regions."

The work in the "Theoretical Aspects" section documents children's literature's engagement with different fields of literary and cultural studies, such as subjectivity (McCallum 1999), psychoanalysis (Rose 1984; Coats 2004), or systems theory (Shavit 1986; Ewers 2000). Some of these works explore how ideological assumptions are encoded in children's literature (Stephens 1992; Zornado 2001); attempt to define children's literature by identifying characteristic features (Nodelman 2008); or explore book production and mediational structures (Paul 2008), while the question of how children's literature contributes to the social and aesthetic formation of culture is at the center of others (Dusinberre 1987; Reynolds 2007). Theoretical work on individual genres can be found in the section "Genres and Forms," with research on feminism and gender studies featured in the subsection "Gender-Specific Literature," and studies in comparative children's literature in the section "Comparative and Intercultural Aspects."

While some of the titles listed in the section "Thematic Aspects" also have a strong theoretical underpinning (for instance *Reading Race: Aboriginality in Australian Children's Literature*, Bradford 2001), their focus on clearly identifiable themes led to their inclusion in this section. The themes range from the representation of individual countries or continents (such as Africa in Yenika-Agbaw 2007), to historical events (such as the Holocaust in Bosmajian 2001; Kertzer 2002; Kokkola 2002), to religion, war, and imperialism. The extensive sixth section, "Genres and Forms," is devoted to the major categories of children's literature, from picture books to poetry to biography.

Although the original plan to include articles on children's literature in various countries of the world in the A–Z section could not be realized within a dictionary of this scope, the section "Continents and Regions" provides bibliographical details of works on the literatures of the different countries and continents. Many of these works come from the areas concerned, and some of them are written in their languages. This section concerns literature *from* these different countries rather than how these countries are portrayed in children's literature in English. Bibliographies of books on the representation of eastern Europe in children's literature, or of children's books on Africa, for instance, are listed in the section "Bibliographies, Catalogs, and Guides," while analyses of the representation of nations and races in literature are detailed in "Comparative and Intercultural Aspects." In addition, this latter section includes works on internationalism and studies with an international, intercultural or transcultural focus—a focus that is also at the heart of the following section, "Translation." The important and flourishing fields documented in these two sections constitute a vital element in children's literature studies, counterbalancing the almost exclusively monolingual focus in the United States and Britain.

A brief section, "Media," lists some important works on film and Internet presentations of children's literature, and their reception. Then "Reading and Literacy" includes theoretical, psychological, biographical, and practical approaches to children's reading, and works about how the changing conditions of children's literature and media influence literacy development. The "Journals" section is devoted to periodicals from the United States, Canada, Britain, Australia, and Ireland, from publications that exclusively review primary texts to those with a more theoretical focus. Numerous websites in operation at the time of publication are listed in the final section. The range is wide and includes professional organizations such as the Association for Library Service to Children (ALSC), research societies such as the International Research Society for Children's Literature (IRSCL), and databases and online bibliographies of children's literature, as well as special sites for teachers that provide educational materials and links to reading organizations and so on. The list also includes a number of metasites and sites with annotated lists of links to author and illustrator sites and to sites associated with awards, organizations, journals, academic programs, and scholarly resources.

GENERAL REFERENCE

Allen, Ruth. *Winning Books: An Evaluation and History of Major Awards for Children's Books in the English-Speaking World*. New ed. Shenstone, UK: Pied Piper, 2005.

Avery, Gillian, and Julia Briggs. *Children and Their Books: A Celebration of the Work of Iona and Peter Opie*. Oxford: Clarendon Press, 1989.

Beckett, Sandra L., and Maria Nikolajeva, eds. *Beyond Babar: The European Tradition in Children's Literature*. Lanham, Md.: Scarecrow Press, 2006.

Bingham, Jane M., ed. *Writers for Children*. New York: Scribner's, 1988.

Blishen, Edward, ed. *The Thorny Paradise. Writers on Writing for Children*. Harmondsworth, UK: Kestrel, 1975.

Bradford, Clare, and Valerie Coghlan, eds. *Expectations and Experiences: Children, Childhood, and Children's Literature*. Shenstone, UK: Pied Piper, 2007.

Butler, Charles, ed. *Teaching Children's Fiction*. Basingstoke, UK: Palgrave Macmillan, 2006.

Carpenter, Humphrey, and Mari Prichard. *The Oxford Companion to Children's Literature*. Oxford: Oxford University Press, 1984.

Cart, Michael. *From Romance to Realism: 50 Years of Growth and Change in Young Adult Literature*. New York: HarperCollins, 1996.

Chambers, Aidan. *Booktalk: Occasional Writing on Literature and Children*. London: Bodley Head, 1985.

Chevalier, Tracy, ed. *Twentieth-Century Children's Writers*. 3rd ed. Chicago: St. James Press, 1989.

Coillie, Jan van, et al., eds. *Encyclopedie van de jeugdliteratuur*. Baarn, The Netherlands: De Fontein, 2004.

Cullinan, Bernice E., and Diane Goetz Person, eds. *The Continuum Encyclopedia of Children's Literature*. New York: Continuum, 2001.

Cullinan, Bernice E., Bonnie Kunzel, and Deb Wooten. *The Continuum Encyclopedia of Young Adult Literature*. New York: Continuum, 2005.

Doderer, Klaus, ed. *Lexikon der Kinder- und Jugendliteratur. Personen-, Länder- und Sachartikel zu Geschichte und Gegenwart der Kinder- und Jugendliteratur*. 4 vols. Weinheim, Germany: Beltz, 1975–1982.

Doyle, Brian. *The Who's Who of Children's Literature*. London: Hugh Evelyn, 1968.

Egoff, Sheila, Gordon Stubbs, Ralph Ashley, and Wendy Sutton, eds. *Only Connect: Readings on Children's Literature*. 3rd ed. Toronto: Oxford University Press, 1996 (1st ed. 1969).

Frey, Charles, and John Griffith. *The Literary Heritage of Childhood: An Appraisal of Children's Classics in the Western Tradition*. Westport, Conn.: Greenwood Press, 1987.

Goldthwaite, John. *The Natural History of Make-Believe: A Guide to the Principal Works of Britain, Europe, and America*. New York: Oxford University Press, 1996.

Grenby, M. O. *Children's Literature*. Edinburgh: Edinburgh University Press, 2008.

Hearne, Betsy, and Marilyn Kaye, eds. *Celebrating Children's Books: Essays on Children's Literature in Honor of Zena Sutherland*. New York: Lothrop, Lee and Shepard, 1981.

Helbig, Alethea K., and Agnes Perkins. *Dictionary of Children's Fiction from Australia, Canada, India, New Zealand, and Selected African Countries*. Westport, Conn.: Greenwood Press, 1992.

Hunt, Peter, ed. *Children's Literature: An Anthology, 1801–1902*. Oxford: Blackwell, 2001.

——, ed. *International Companion Encyclopedia of Children's Literature*. 2nd ed. London: Routledge, 2004.

Kümmerling-Meibauer, Bettina. *Klassiker der Kinder- und Jugendliteratur. Ein internationales Lexikon*. 2 vols. Stuttgart: J. B. Metzler, 1999.

Murphy, Barbara Thrash, and Deborah L. Murphy. *Black Authors and Illustrators of Books for Children and Young Adults*. 4th ed. New York: Routledge, 2006.

Nodelman, Perry, ed. *Touchstones: Reflections on the Best in Children's Literature*. 4 vols. West Lafayette, Ind.: Children's Literature Association Publishers, 1985–1989.

Pellowski, Anne. *The World of Children's Literature*. New York: Bowker, 1968.

——. *Made to Measure: Children's Books in Developing Countries*. Paris: UNESCO, 1980.

Reynolds, Kimberley, ed. *Modern Children's Literature: An Introduction*. Basingstoke, UK: Palgrave Macmillan, 2005.

Rollock, Barbara. *Black Authors and Illustrators of Children's Books: A Biographical Dictionary*. New York: Garland, 1992.

Sale, Roger. *Fairy Tales and After: From Snow White to E. B. White*. Cambridge, Mass.: Harvard University Press, 1978.

Silvey, Anita, ed. *Children's Books and Their Creators*. Boston: Houghton Mifflin, 1995.

Stahl, J. D., Tina L. Hanlon, and Elizabeth Lennox Keyser, eds. *Crosscurrents of Children's Literature: An Anthology of Texts and Criticism*. New York: Oxford University Press, 2006.

Thacker, Deborah Cogan, and Jean Webb. *Introducing Children's Literature: From Romanticism to Postmodernism*. London: Routledge, 2002.

Townsend, John Rowe. *Written for Children: An Outline of English-Language Children's Literature*. 6th ed. London: Bodley Head, 1995.

Vandergrift, Kay E. *Child and Story: The Literary Connection*. New York: Neal-Schuman, 1980.

Watson, Victor, ed. *The Cambridge Guide to Children's Books in English*. Cambridge: Cambridge University Press, 2001.

Wyile, Andrea Schwenke, and Teya Rosenberg, eds. *Considering Children's Literature: A Reader*. Guelph, ON: Broadview Press, 2008.

Zipes, Jack, ed. *The Oxford Encyclopedia of Children's Literature*. 4 vols. Oxford: Oxford University Press, 2006.

Zipes, Jack, et al., eds. *The Norton Anthology of Children's Literature: The Traditions in English*. New York: Norton, 2005.

Zoughebi, Henriette, ed. *Guide européen du livre de jeunesse*. Paris: Editions du Cercle de la Librairie, 1994.

BIBLIOGRAPHIES, CATALOGS, AND GUIDES

Appelsoff, Marilyn Fain. *They Wrote for Children Too: An Annotated Bibliography of Children's Literature by Famous Writers for Adults*. Westport, Conn.: Greenwood Press, 1989.

Barr, Catherine, ed. *From Biography to History: Best Books for Children's Entertainment and Education*. New Providence, N.J.: Bowker, 1998.

Barron, Neil. *Fantasy and Horror: A Critical and Historical Guide to Literature, Illustration, Film, TV, Radio, and the Internet*. Lanham, Md.: Scarecrow Press, 1999.

Blanck, Jacob. *Peter Parley to Penrod: A Bibliographical Description of the Best-Loved American Juvenile Books*. New York: Bowker, 1956.

Brazouski, Antoinette, and Mary J. Klatt. *Children's Books on Ancient Greek and Roman Mythology: An Annotated Bibliography*. Westport, Conn.: Greenwood Press, 1994.

Cotsen Collection. *A Catalogue of the Cotsen Children's Library*. Vol. 1, *The Twentieth Century, A–L*. Princeton: Princeton University Library, 2000.

——. *A Catalogue of the Cotsen Children's Library*. Vol. 2, *The Twentieth Century, M–Z*. Princeton: Princeton University Library, 2003.

Crew, Hilary S. *Women Engaged in War in Literature for Youth: A Guide to Resources for Children and Young Adults*. Lanham, Md.: Scarecrow Press, 2007.

Day, Frances Ann. *Lesbian and Gay Voices: An Annotated Bibliography and Guide to Literature for Children and Young Adults*. Westport, Conn.: Greenwood Press, 2000.

Dole, Patricia Pearl. *Children's Religious Books: An Annotated Bibliography*. New York: Garland, 1988.

——. *Children's Books about Religion*. Englewood, Colo.: Libraries Unlimited, 1999.

Eiss, Harry Edwin. *Literature for Young People on War and Peace: An Annotated Bibliography*. Westport, Conn.: Greenwood Press, 1989.

Gilton, Donna L. *Multicultural and Ethnic Children's Literature in the United States*. Lanham, Md.: Scarecrow Press, 2007.

Haviland, Virginia. *Children's Literature: A Guide to Reference Sources*. Washington, D.C.: Library of Congress, 1966. (First supplement 1972, second supplement 1977, both with M. N. Coughlan.)

Holsinger, M. Paul. *The Ways of War: The Era of World War II in Children's and Young Adult Fiction; An Annotated Bibliography*. Metuchen, N.J.: Scarecrow Press, 1995.

Jones, Dolores Blythe. *Special Collections in Children's Literature: An International Directory*. 3rd ed. Chicago: American Library Association, 1995.

Khorana, Meena. *The Indian Subcontinent in Literature for Children and Young Adults: An Annotated Bibliography of English-Language Books*. Westport, Conn.: Greenwood Press, 1991.

——. *Africa in Literature for Children and Young Adults: An Annotated Bibliography of English-Language Books*. Westport, Conn.: Greenwood Press, 1994.

Kinderbuchfonds Baobab, ed. *Fremde Welten. Kinder- und Jugendbücher zu den Themen: Afrika, Asien, Lateinamerika, ethnische Minderheiten und Rassismus, empfohlen von den Lesegruppen des Kinderbuchfonds Baobab*. 17th ed. Basel, Switzerland: Editor, 2007.

Kuipers, Barbara J. *American Indian Reference and Resource Books for Children and Young Adults*. 2nd ed. Englewood, Colo.: Libraries Unlimited, 1995.

Kutzer, Daphne, ed. *Writers of Multicultural Fiction for Young Adults: A Bio-Critical Sourcebook*. Westport, Conn.: Greenwood, 1996.

Lynn, Ruth Nadelman. *Fantasy Literature for Children and Young Adults: An Annotated Bibliography*. New York: Bowker, 1995.

MacCann, Donnarae, and Gloria Woodard. *The Black American in Books for Children: Reading in Racism*. Metuchen, N.J.: Scarecrow Press, 1985.
Magness, Patricia Philipps, and Joyce Elizabeth Potter. *A Guide to Children's Bible Story Books in Twentieth-Century America: To Hold and to Have*. New York: Peter Lang, 2001.
Miller-Lachmann, Lyn. *Our Family, Our Friends, Our World: An Annotated Guide to Significant Multicultural Books for Children and Teenagers*. New Providence, N.J.: Bowker, 1992.
Povsic, Frances. *Eastern Europe in Children's Literature: An Annotated Bibliography of English-Language Books*. Westport, Conn.: Greenwood Press, 1986.
———. *The Soviet Union in Literature for Children and Young Adults: An Annotated Bibliography of English-Language Books*. Westport, Conn.: Greenwood Press, 1991.
Reetz, Marianne. *International Periodicals: The IYL Guide to Professional Periodicals in Children's Literature*. 2nd rev. ed. Munich: International Youth Library, 1990.
Roscoe, Sydney. *John Newbery and His Successors, 1740–1814: A Bibliography*. Wormley, UK: Five Owls Press, 1973.
Rühle, Reiner. *"Böse Kinder." Kommentierte Bibliographie von Struwwelpetriaden und Max-und-Moritziaden mit biographischen Daten zu Verfassern und Illustratoren*. Osnabrück, Germany: Wenner, 1999.
Schmidt, Nancy J. *Children's Books on Africa and Their Authors: An Annotated Bibliography*. New York: Africana Publishing, 1975.
Schon, Isabel. *A Hispanic Heritage: A Guide to Juvenile Books about Hispanic People and Cultures*. Metuchen, N.J.: Scarecrow Press, 1980.
———. *Spanish-Speaking Writers and Illustrators for Children and Young Adults: A Biographical Dictionary*. Westport, Conn.: Greenwood Press, 1994.
Stan, Susan, ed. *The World through Children's Books*. Lanham, Md.: Scarecrow Press, 2002.
Tomlinson, Carl. *Children's Books from Other Countries*. Lanham, Md.: Scarecrow Press, 1998.

HISTORICAL STUDIES

Arzipe, Evelyne, Morag Styles, and Shirley Brice Heath, eds. *Reading Lessons from the Eighteenth Century: Mothers, Children, Texts*. Shenstone, UK: Pied Piper, 2006.

Avery, Gillian. *Childhood's Pattern: A Study of the Heroes and Heroines of Children's Fiction, 1770–1950.* London: Hodder and Stoughton, 1975.

——. *Behold the Child: American Children and Their Books, 1621–1922.* London: Bodley Head, 1994.

Barney, Richard. *Plots of Enlightenment: Education and the Novel in Eighteenth Century England.* Stanford: Stanford University Press, 1999.

Classen, Albrecht, ed. *Childhood in the Middle Ages and the Renaissance: The Results of a Paradigm Shift in the History of Mentality.* New York: Walter de Gruyter, 2005.

Cunningham, Hugh. *Children and Childhood in Western Society since 1500.* London: Longman, 1996.

Cutt, Margaret Nancy. *Ministering Angels: A Study of Nineteenth-Century Evangelical Writing for Children.* Wormley, UK: Five Owls Press, 1979.

Daniels, Morna. *The Firm of Blackie and Son and Some of Their Children's Books.* Hoddesdon, UK: Children's Books History Society, 1999.

Darton, Frederick Joseph Harvey. *Children's Books in England: Five Centuries of Social Life.* 3rd ed., rev. Brian Alderson. Cambridge: Cambridge University Press, 1982 (1st ed. 1932).

Demers, Patricia. *Heaven upon Earth. The Form of Moral and Religious Children's Literature to 1850.* Knoxville: University of Tennessee Press, 1993.

Deschamps, J.-G. *The History of French Children's Books, 1750–1900: From the Collection of J.-G. Deschamps.* Boston: Bookshop for Boys and Girls, 1934.

Elbert, Monika, ed. *Enterprising Youth: Social Values and Acculturation in Nineteenth-Century American Children's Literature.* New York: Routledge, 2008.

Ellis, Alec. *Educating Our Masters: Influences on the Growth of Literacy in Victorian Working Class Children.* Aldershot, UK: Gower, 1985.

Galbraith, Gretchen. *Reading Lives: Reconstructing Childhood, Books, and Schools in Britain, 1870–1920.* New York: St. Martin's, 1997.

Gottlieb, Gerald. *Early Children's Books and Their Illustrators.* New York: Pierpont Morgan Library, 1975.

Hilton, Mary, Morag Styles, and Victor Watson, eds. *Opening the Nursery Door: Reading, Writing and Childhood, 1600–1900.* London: Routledge, 1997.

Hürlimann, Bettina. *Europäische Kinderbücher aus drei Jahrhunderten.* Zurich: Atlantis, 1963.

——. *Three Centuries of Children's Books in Europe.* Trans. Brian Alderson. London: Oxford University Press, 1967.

Immel, Andrea, and Michael Witmore, eds. *Childhood and Children's Books in Early Modern Europe, 1550–1800.* London: Routledge, 2005.

Jackson, Mary V. *Engines of Instruction, Mischief and Magic: Children's Literature in England from Its Beginning to 1839*. Aldershot, UK: Scolar Press, 1989.

Kline, Daniel T., ed. *Medieval Literature for Children*. New York: Routledge, 2003.

MacDonald, Ruth. *Literature for Children in England and America from 1646 to 1774*. Troy, N.Y.: Whitston, 1982.

MacLeod, Anne Scott. *A Moral Tale: Children's Fiction and American Culture, 1829–1860*. Hamden, Conn.: Archon Books, 1975.

——. *American Childhood. Essays on Children's Literature of the Nineteenth and Twentieth Centuries*. Athens: University of Georgia Press, 1994.

McGavran, James Holt, ed. *Romanticism and Children's Literature in Nineteenth Century England*. Athens: University of Georgia Press, 1991.

Meigs, Cornelia, et al., eds. *A Critical History of Children's Literature: A Survey of Children's Books in English from Earliest Times to the Present*. Rev. ed. New York: Macmillan, 1969.

Muir, Percy. *English Children's Books, 1600–1900*. London: Batsford, 1954.

Novaes Coelho, Nelly. *Panorama histórico da literatura infantil y juvenil*. São Paulo: Quíron, 1991.

O'Malley, Andrew. *The Making of the Modern Child: Children's Literature and Childhood in the Late Eighteenth Century*. London: Routledge, 2003.

Ottevaere van Praag, Ganna. *La littérature pour la jeunesse en Europe occidentale (1750–1925). Histoire sociale et courants d'idées Angleterre, France, Pays-Bas, Allemagne, Italie*. Bern: Peter Lang, 1987.

Pickering, Samuel. *John Locke and Children's Books in Eighteenth Century England*. Knoxville: University of Tennessee Press, 1981.

——. *Moral Instruction and Fiction for Children, 1749–1820*. Athens: University of Georgia Press, 1993.

Ray, Gordon N. *The Illustrator and the Book in England from 1790 to 1914*. New York: Pierpont Morgan Library, 1976.

Smith, Karen Patricia. *The Fabulous Realm: A Literary-Historical Approach to British Fantasy, 1780–1990*. Metuchen, N. J.: Scarecrow Press, 1993.

Sommerville, John C. *The Discovery of Childhood in Puritan England*. Athens: University of Georgia Press, 1992.

Spufford, Margaret. *Small Books and Pleasant Histories: Popular Fiction and Its Readership in Seventeenth Century England*. Cambridge: Cambridge University Press, 1981.

Styles, Morag. *From the Garden to the Street: An Introduction to 300 Years of Poetry for Children*. London: Cassell, 1998.

Summerfield, Geoffrey. *Fantasy and Reason: Children's Literature in the Eighteenth Century*. London: Methuen, 1984.

Thwaite, Mary F. *From Primer to Pleasure in Reading*. 2nd ed. London: Library Association, 1972 (1st ed. 1963).

Townsend, John Rowe. *Trade and Plumb-Cake For Ever, Huzza! The Life and Work of John Newbery, 1713–1767*. Cambridge: Colt Books, 1994.

Whalley, Joyce Irene. *Cobwebs to Catch Flies: Illustrated Books for the Nursery and Schoolroom, 1700–1900*. London: Elek, 1974.

Whalley, Joyce Irene, and Tessa R. Chester. *A History of Children's Book Illustration*. London: John Murray with the Victoria and Albert Museum, 1988.

THEORETICAL ASPECTS

Alberghene, Janice M., and Beverly Lyon Clark, eds. *Little Women and the Feminist Imagination: Criticism, Controversy, Personal Essays*. New York: Garland, 1999.

Armstrong, Frances. "The Dollhouse as Ludic Space, 1690–1920." *Children's Literature* 24 (1996): 23–54.

Beckett, Sandra L., ed. *Transcending Boundaries: Writing for a Dual Audience of Children and Adults*. New York: Garland, 1999.

———. *Crossover Fiction: Global and Historical Perspectives*. New York: Routledge, 2008.

Bradford, Clare, and Valerie Coghlan, eds. *Expectations and Experiences: Children, Childhood and Children's Literature*. Shenstone, UK: Pied Piper, 2007.

Butts, Dennis, ed. *Stories and Society: Children's Literature in Its Social Context*. Basingstoke, UK: Macmillan, 1992.

Chapleau, Sebastien, ed. *New Voices in Children's Literature Criticism*. Shenstone, UK: Pied Piper, 2004.

Clark, Beverly Lyon. *Kiddie Lit: The Cultural Construction of Children's Literature in America*. Baltimore: Johns Hopkins University Press, 2003.

Coats, Karen. *Looking Glasses and Neverlands: Lacan, Desire, and Subjectivity in Children's Literature*. Iowa City: University of Iowa Press, 2004.

Cott, Jonathan. *Pipers at the Gates of Dawn: The Wisdom of Children's Literature*. New York: Random House, 1983.

Dresang, Eliza. *Radical Change: Books for Youth in a Digital Age*. New York: H. Wilson, 1999.

Dusinberre, Juliet. *Alice to the Lighthouse. Children's Books and Radical Experiments in Art*. Basingstoke, UK: Macmillan, 1987.

Ewers, Hans-Heino. *Literatur für Kinder und Jugendliche. Eine Einführung in grundlegende Aspekte des Handlungs- und Symbolsystems Kinder- und Jugendliteratur*. Munich: Fink, 2000.

Falconer, Rachel. *The Crossover Novel: Contemporary Children's Fiction and Its Adult Readership*. New York: Routledge, 2008.

Goodenough, Elizabeth, Mark A. Heberle, and Naomi Sokoloff, eds. *Infant Tongues: The Voice of the Child in Literature*. Detroit: Wayne State University Press, 1994.

Goodenough, Elizabeth, and Andrea Immel, eds. *Under Fire: Childhood in the Shadow of War*. Detroit: Wayne State University Press, 2008.

Greenway, Betty, ed. *Twice-Told Children's Tales: The Influence of Childhood Reading on Writers for Adults*. London: Routledge, 2005.

Hollindale, Peter. *Signs of Childness in Children's Books*. South Woodchester, UK: Thimble Press, 1997.

Hourihan, Margery. *Deconstructing the Hero: Literary Theory and Children's Literature*. London: Routledge, 1997.

Hunt, Peter. *Criticism, Theory, and Children's Literature*. Oxford: Blackwell, 1991.

——, *An Introduction to Children's Literature*. Oxford: Oxford University Press, 1994.

——, ed. *Children's Literature: The Development of Criticism*. London: Routledge, 1990.

——, ed. *Literature for Children: Contemporary Criticism*. London: Routledge, 1992.

——, ed. *Understanding Children's Literature*. London: Routledge, 2005.

——, ed. *Children's Literature: Critical Concepts in Literary and Cultural Studies*. 4 vols. London: Routledge, 2006.

Inglis, Fred. *The Promise of Happiness: Value and Meaning in Children's Fiction*. Cambridge: Cambridge University Press, 1981.

Jenkins, Henry, ed. *The Children's Culture Reader*. New York: New York University Press, 1998.

Jones, Dudley, and Tony Watkins, eds. *A Necessary Fantasy? The Heroic Figure in Children's Popular Culture*. New York: Garland, 2000.

Joosen, Vanessa, and Katrien Vloeberghs, eds. *Changing Concepts of Childhood and Children's Literature*. Newcastle, UK: Cambridge Scholars Publishing, 2006.

Knowles, Murray, and Kirsten Malmkjaer. *Language and Control in Children's Literature*. London: Routledge, 1996.

Kohl, Herbert. *Should We Burn Babar? Essays on Children's Literature and the Power of Story*. New York: New Press, 1995.

Lassén-Seger, Maria: *Adventures into Otherness: Child Metaphors in Late Twentieth-Century Literature*. Abo, Finland: Abo Akademi University Press, 2007.

Lesnik-Oberstein, Karin. *Children's Literature: Criticism and the Fictional Child*. Oxford: Clarendon Press, 1994.

——, ed. *Children in Culture: Approaches to Childhood.* Basingstoke, UK: Macmillan, 1998.

——, ed. *Children's Literature: New Approaches.* Basingstoke, UK: Palgrave Macmillan, 2004.

Lundin, Anne H. *Constructing the Canon of Children's Literature: Beyond Library Walls and Ivory Towers.* New York: Routledge, 2004.

Lurie, Alison. *Don't Tell the Grownups: Subversive Children's Literature.* Boston: Little Brown, 1990.

——. *Boys and Girls Forever: Children's Classics from Cinderella to Harry Potter.* New York: Penguin Books, 2003.

Mackey, Margaret. *The Case of Peter Rabbit: Changing Conditions of Literature for Children.* New York: Garland, 1998.

McCallum, Robyn. *Ideologies of Identity in Adolescent Fiction: The Dialogic Construction of Subjectivity.* New York: Garland, 1999.

McGavran, James Holt. *Literature and the Child: Romantic Continuations, Postmodern Contestations.* Iowa City: University of Iowa Press, 1999.

McGillis, Roderick. *The Nimble Reader: Literary Theory and Children's Literature.* New York: Twayne, 1996.

Meek, Margaret, Aidan Warlow, and Griselda Barton, eds. *The Cool Web: The Pattern of Children's Reading.* London: Bodley Head, 1977.

Myers, Mitzi. "Missed Opportunities and Critical Malpractice: New Historicism and Children's Literature." *Children's Literature Association Quarterly* 13, no. 1 (1988): 41–3.

Natov, Roni. *The Poetics of Childhood.* New York: Routledge, 2003.

Nikolajeva, Maria. *Children's Literature Comes of Age: Towards a New Aesthetic.* New York: Garland, 1996.

——. *From Mythic to Linear: Time in Children's Literature.* Lanham, Md.: Scarecrow Press, 2000.

——. *The Rhetoric of Character in Children's Literature.* Lanham, Md.: Scarecrow Press, 2002.

——. *Aesthetic Approaches to Children's Literature: An Introduction.* Lanham, Md.: Scarecrow Press, 2005.

Nodelman, Perry. "The Other: Orientalism, Colonialism, and Children's Literature." *Children's Literature Association Quarterly* 17, no. 1 (1992): 29–35.

——. *The Hidden Adult: Defining Children's Literature.* Baltimore: Johns Hopkins University Press, 2008.

Nodelman, Perry, and Mavis Reimer. *The Pleasures of Children's Literature.* 3rd ed. Boston: Allyn and Bacon, 2003 (1st ed. 1991).

Ord, Priscilla, ed. *The Child and the Story: An Exploration of Narrative Forms.* Boston: Children's Literary Association, 1983.

Otten, Charlotte, and Gary D. Schmidt, eds. *The Voice of the Narrator in Children's Literature: Insights from Writers and Critics*. New York: Greenwood Press, 1989.

Paul, Lissa. *The Children's Book Business*. New York: Routledge, 2008.

Perrot, Jean. *Art baroque, art d'enfance*. Nancy, France: Universitaires de Nancy, 1991.

Reimer, Mavis, ed. *Home Words: Discourses of Children's Literature in Canada*. Waterloo, ON: Wilfrid Laurier University Press, 2008.

Reynolds, Kimberley. *Radical Children's Literature: Future Visions and Aesthetic Transformations in Juvenile Fiction*. London: Palgrave Macmillan, 2007.

Rose, Jacqueline. *The Case of Peter Pan, or The Impossibility of Children's Fiction*. Rev. ed. London: Macmillan, 1994 (1st ed. 1984).

Rudd, David. *Culture Matters: A Communication Studies Approach to Children's Literature*. Sheffield, UK: Hallam University, 1992.

———. *Enid Blyton and the Mystery of Children's Literature*. Houndmills, UK: Macmillan, 2000.

Rustin, Margaret, and Michael Rustin. *Narratives of Love and Loss: Studies in Modern Children's Fiction*. Rev. ed. London: Karnac, 2001.

Rutherford, Jonathan. *Forever England: Reflections on Race, Masculinity and Empire*. London: Lawrence and Wishart, 1997.

Salem, Linda. *Children's Literature Studies: Cases and Discussions*. Westport, Conn.: Libraries Unlimited, 2006.

Scheper-Hughes, Nancy, and Carolyn Sargent, eds. *Small Wars: The Cultural Politics of Childhood*. Berkeley: University of California Press, 1998.

Shavit, Zohar. *Poetics of Children's Literature*. Athens: University of Georgia Press, 1986.

Steedman, Carolyn. *Strange Dislocations: Childhood and the Idea of Human Interiority, 1780–1930*. London: Virago Press, 1995.

Stephens, John. *Language and Ideology in Children's Fiction*. London: Longman, 1992.

Stephens, John, and Robyn McCallum. *Retelling Stories, Framing Culture: Traditional Story and Metanarratives in Children's Literature*. New York: Garland, 1998.

Trites, Roberta Seelinger. *Waking Sleeping Beauty: Feminist Voices in Children's Novels*. Iowa City: University of Iowa Press, 1997.

Wall, Barbara. *The Narrator's Voice: The Dilemma of Children's Fiction*. London: Macmillan, 1991.

Wallace, Jo-Ann. "De-Scribing *The Water-Babies*: 'The Child' in Post-colonial Theory." In *De-Scribing Empire: Post-colonialism and Textuality*, ed. Chris Tiffin and Alan Lawson, 171–84. London: Routledge, 1994.

Waller, Alison. *Constructing Adolescence in Fantastic Realism.* New York: Routledge, 2008.
Weinreich, Torben. *Children's Literature: Art or Pedagogy.* Frederiksberg, Denmark: Roskilde University Press, 2000.
Zipes, Jack. *Happily Ever After: Fairy Tales, Children and the Culture Industry.* New York: Routledge, 1997.
——. *Sticks and Stones: The Troublesome Success of Children's Literature from Slovenly Peter to Harry Potter.* New York: Routledge, 2001.
Zornado, Joseph. *Inventing the Child: Culture, Ideology, and the Story of Childhood.* New York: Garland, 2001.

THEMATIC ASPECTS

Agnew, Kate, and Geoff Fox. *Children at War: From the First World War to the Gulf.* New York: Continuum, 2001.
Alston, Ann. *The Family in English Children's Literature.* New York: Routledge, 2008.
Bosmajian, Hamida. *Sparing the Child: Grief and the Unspeakable in Youth Literature about Nazism and the Holocaust.* New York: Routledge, 2001.
Bradford, Clare. *Reading Race: Aboriginality in Australian Children's Literature.* Carlton, Australia: Melbourne University Press, 2001.
Daniel, Carolyn. *Voracious Children: Who Eats Whom in Children's Literature.* New York: Routledge, 2006.
De Maeyer, Jan, et al., eds. *Religion, Children's Literature and Modernity in Western Europe, 1750–2000.* Leuven, Belgium: Leuvense Universitaire Press, 2003.
Dobrin, Sidney I., and Kenneth B. Kidd, eds. *Wild Things: Children's Culture and Ecocriticism.* Detroit: Wayne State University Press, 2004.
Griswold, Jerry. *Audacious Kids: Coming of Age in America's Classic Children's Books.* New York: Oxford University Press, 1992.
——. *Feeling Like a Kid: Five Essential Themes in Children's Literature.* Baltimore: Johns Hopkins University Press, 2006.
Hintz, Carrie, and Elaine Ostry, eds. *Utopian and Dystopian Writing for Children and Young Adults.* New York: Routledge, 2002.
Kertzer, Adrienne. *My Mother's Voice: Children's Literature and the Holocaust.* Toronto: Broadview, 2002.
Kincaid, James R. *Child-Loving: The Erotic Child and Victorian Culture.* New York: Routledge, 1992.

Kokkola, Lydia. *Representing the Holocaust in Children's Literature*. New York: Routledge, 2002.

Krips, Valerie. *The Presence of the Past: Memory, Heritage and Childhood in Postwar Britain*. New York: Garland, 2000.

Kutzer, M. Daphne. *Empire's Children: Empire and Imperialism in Classic British Children's Books*. New York: Garland, 2000.

Kuznets, Lois R. *When Toys Come Alive: Narratives of Animation, Metamorphosis and Development*. New Haven, Conn.: Yale University Press, 1994.

Lenz, Millicent. *Nuclear Age Literature for Youth: The Quest for a Life-Affirming Ethic*. Chicago: American Library Association, 1990.

Levy, Michael M. *Refugees and Immigrants: The Southeast Asian Experience as Depicted in Recent American Children's Books*. Lewiston, N.Y.: Edwin Mellen, 2000.

Logan, Mawuena Kossi. *Narrating Africa: George Henty and the Fiction of Empire*. New York: Garland, 1999.

MacCann, Donnarae. *White Supremacy in Children's Literature: Characterizations of African-Americans, 1830–1900*. New York: Garland, 1998.

MacCann, Donnarae, and Yulisa Amadu Maddy. *Apartheid and Racism in South African Children's Literature, 1985–1995*. New York: Routledge, 2001.

Meek, Margaret, and Victor Watson. *Coming of Age in Children's Literature: Growth and Maturity in the Work of Philippa Pearce, Cynthia Voigt and Jan Mark*. London: Continuum, 2002.

Mickenberg, Julia L. *Learning from the Left: Children's Literature, the Cold War, and Radical Politics in the United States*. New York: Oxford University Press, 2006.

Nelson, Claudia. *Little Strangers: Portrayals of Adoption and Foster Care in America, 1850–1929*. Bloomington: Indiana University Press, 2003.

Pinsent, Pat. *Children's Literature and the Politics of Equality*. London: David Fulton, 1997.

Richards, Jeffrey, ed. *Imperialism and Juvenile Literature*. Manchester: Manchester University Press, 1989.

Sands-O'Connor, Karen. *Soon Come Home to This Island: West Indians in British Children's Literature*. London: Routledge, 2007.

Stewart, Susan. *On Longing: Narratives of the Miniature, the Gigantic, the Souvenir, the Collection*. Baltimore: Johns Hopkins University Press, 1984.

Watkins, Tony, ed. *A Necessary Fantasy? The Heroic Figure in Children's Popular Culture*. New York: Garland, 2000.

Yenika-Agbaw, Vivian. *Representing Africa in Children's Literature: Old and New Ways of Seeing*. New York: Routledge, 2007.

GENRES AND FORMS

Picture Books and Illustration

Alderson, Brian. *Sing a Song for Sixpence: The English Picture Book Tradition and Randolph Caldecott*. Cambridge: Cambridge University Press, 1986.

Anstey, Michèle, and Geoff Bull. *Reading the Visual: Written and Illustrated Children's Literature*. Sydney: Harcourt, 2000.

Bader, Barbara. *American Picture Books from Noah's Ark to the Beast Within*. New York: Macmillan, 1976.

Doderer, Klaus, and Helmut Müller, eds. *Das Bilderbuch. Geschichte und Entwicklung des Bilderbuchs in Deutschland von den Anfängen bis zur Gegenwart*. Weinheim, Germany: Beltz, 1973.

Doonan, Jane. *Looking at Pictures in Picture Books*. South Woodchester, UK: Thimble Press, 1993.

Gottlieb, Gerald. *Early Children's Books and Their Illustration*. New York: Pierpont Morgan Library, 1975.

Horne, Alan. *The Dictionary of 20th Century British Book Illustrators*. Woodbridge, UK: Antique Collectors' Club, 1994.

Kiefer, Barbara Zulandt. *The Potential of Picture Books: From Visual Literacy to Aesthetic Understanding*. Englewood Cliffs, N.J.: Merrill, 1995.

Kirk, Ann. *Companion to American Children's Picture Books*. Westport, Conn.: Greenwood Press, 2005.

Lewis, David. "The Picture Book: A Form Awaiting Its History." *Signal* 77 (1995): 99–112.

——. "The Jolly Postman's Long Ride, or Sketching a Picture-Book History." *Signal* 78 (1995): 178–92.

——. "Going Along with Mr. Gumpy: Polysystemy and Play in the Modern Picture Book." *Signal* 80 (1996): 105–19.

——. *Reading Contemporary Picturebooks: Picturing Text*. London: RoutledgeFalmer, 2001.

Martin, Michelle H. *Brown Gold: Milestones of African-American Children's Picture Books, 1845–2002*. New York: Routledge, 2004.

Moebius, William. "Introduction to Picturebook Codes." *Word and Image* 2, no. 2 (1986): 141–58.

Muir, Marcie. *A History of Australian Children's Book Illustration*. Melbourne: Oxford University Press, 1982.

Nikolajeva, Maria, and Carole Scott. *How Picturebooks Work*. New York: Garland, 2001.

Nodelman, Perry. *Words about Pictures: The Narrative Art of Children's Picture Books*. Athens: University of Georgia Press, 1988.

Ray, Gordon N. *The Illustrator and the Book in England from 1790 to 1914.* New York: Pierpont Morgan Library, 1976.

Ries, Hans. *Illustration und Illustratoren des Kinder- und Jugendbuchs im deutschsprachigen Raum 1871–1914.* Osnabrück, Germany: Wenner, 1992.

Schwarcz, Joseph H. *Ways of the Illustrator: Visual Communication in Children's Literature.* Chicago: American Library Association, 1982.

Schwarcz, Joseph H., and Chava Schwarcz. *The Picturebook Comes of Age: Looking at Childhood through the Art of Illustration.* Chicago: American Library Association, 1991.

Schweizerisches Jugendbuch-Institut, ed. *Siehst Du das? Die Wahrnehmung von Bildern in Kinderbüchern—Visual Literacy.* Zürich: Chronos, 1997.

Sendak, Maurice. *Caldecott and Co.: Notes on Books and Pictures.* New York: Farrar, Straus and Giroux, 1988.

Sipe, Lawrence R., and Sylvia Pantaleo, eds. *Postmodern Picturebooks: Play, Parody, and Self-Referentiality.* New York: Routledge. 2008.

Stanton, Joseph. *The Important Books: Children's Picture Books as Art and Literature.* Lanham, Md.: Scarecrow Press, 2005.

Stephens, John, Ken Watson, and Judith Parker. *From Picture Book to Literary Theory.* Sydney: St. Clair Press, 2003.

Styles, Morag, and Eve Bearne, eds. *Art, Narrative and Childhood.* Stoke on Trent, UK: Trentham Books, 2003.

Watson, Victor, and Morag Styles, eds. *Talking Pictures: Pictorial Texts and Young Readers.* London: Hodder and Stoughton, 1996.

Whalley, Joyce Irene. *Cobwebs to Catch Flies: Illustrated Books for the Nursery and Schoolroom, 1700–1900.* London: Elek, 1974.

Whalley, Joyce Irene, and Tessa R. Chester. *A History of Children's Book Illustration.* London: John Murray with the Victoria and Albert Museum, 1988.

Poetry

Abrahams, Roger D., and Lois Rankin. *Counting-Out Rhymes: A Dictionary.* London: University of Texas Press, 1980.

Bottum, Joseph. "What Children's Poetry Is For." *American Educator*, 1997, at www.aft.org/pubs-reports/american_educator/fall97/index.html (accessed July 2, 2007).

Despringre, André-Marie, ed. *Chants enfantins d'Europe. Systèmes poético-musiciaux de jeux chantés (France, Espange, Chypre, Italie).* Paris: L'Harmattan, 1997.

Flynn, Richard. "Can Children's Poetry Matter?" *Lion and the Unicorn* 17, no.1 (1993): 37–44.

Hall, Donald. *The Oxford Book of Children's Verse in America.* Oxford: Oxford University Press, 1985.

McVitty, Walter, ed. *Word Magic: Poetry as a Shared Adventure.* Rosebery, Australia: PETA, 1986.

Opie, Iona, and Peter Opie. *The Oxford Dictionary of Nursery Rhymes.* Oxford: Oxford University Press, 1951.

——. *Three Centuries of Nursery Rhymes and Poetry for Children.* Oxford: Oxford University Press, 1977.

Rollin, Lucy. *Cradle and All: A Cultural and Psychoanalytic Reading of Nursery Rhymes.* Jackson: University Press of Mississippi, 1992.

Rosen, Michael, and Susanna Steele. *Inky, Pinky, Ponky: Children's Playground Rhymes.* London: Granada, 1982.

Sloan, Glenna. "But Is It Poetry?" *Children's Literature in Education* 32, no.1 (2001): 45–56.

Styles, Morag. *From the Garden to the Street: An Introduction to 300 Years of Poetry for Children.* London: Cassell, 1998.

Thomas, Joseph T., Jr. *Poetry's Playground: The Culture of Contemporary American Children's Poetry.* Detroit: Wayne State University Press, 2007.

Wade, Barrie. *A Guide to Children's Poetry for Teachers and Librarians.* Aldershot, UK: Scolar Press, 1996.

Fairy Tales and Folktales

Anderson, Graham. *Fairytales in the Ancient World.* London: Routledge, 2000.

Auerbach, Nina, and Ulrich. C. Knoepflmacher. *Forbidden Journeys: Fairy Tales and Fantasies by Victorian Women Writers.* Chicago: University of Chicago Press, 1992.

Beckett, Sandra. *Recycling Red Riding Hood.* New York: Routledge, 2002.

Bettelheim, Bruno. *The Uses of Enchantment: The Meaning and Importance of Fairy Tales.* New York: Knopf, 1976.

Bottigheimer, Ruth. *Grimms' Bad Girls and Bold Boys: The Moral and Social Visions of the Tales.* New Haven, Conn.: Yale University Press, 1987.

Haase, Donald, ed. *Reception of Grimms' Fairy Tales: Responses, Reactions, Revisions.* Detroit: Wayne State University Press, 1993.

Harries, Elizabeth Wanning. *Twice upon a Time: Women Writers and the History of the Fairy Tale.* Princeton: Princeton University Press, 2001.

Knoepflmacher, Ulrich C. *Ventures into Childland: Victorians, Fairy Tales, and Femininity.* Chicago: University of Chicago Press, 1998.

Leverato, Alessandra. *Language and Gender in the Fairy Tale Tradition.* London: Routledge, 2003.

Lüthi, Max, and Heinz Rölleke. *Märchen.* 9th rev. ed. Stuttgart: Metzler, 1997.

Opie, Peter, and Iona Opie. *The Classic Fairy Tales*. Oxford: Oxford University Press, 1974.

Sale, Roger. *Fairy Tales and After: From Snow White to E. B. White*. Cambridge, Mass.: Harvard University Press, 1978.

Scherf, Walter. *Das Märchenlexikon*. 2 vols. Munich: Beck, 1995.

Swann Jones, Stephen. *The Fairy Tale: The Magic Mirror of the Imagination*. New York: Routledge, 2002.

Tatar, Maria. *Hard Facts of the Grimms' Fairy Tales*. Princeton: Princeton University Press, 1987.

——. *Off with Their Heads! Fairy Tales and the Culture of Childhood*. Princeton, N.J.: Princeton University Press, 1992.

Warner, Marina. *From the Beast to the Blonde: On Fairytales and Their Tellers*. New York: Farrar, Straus and Giroux, 1995.

——. *No Go the Bogeyman: Lulling, Scaring and Making Mock*. London: Vintage Press, 2000.

Zipes, Jack. *Breaking the Magic Spell: Radical Theories of Folk and Fairy Tales*. London: Heinemann, 1979.

——. *The Brothers Grimm: From Enchanted Forests to the Modern World*. New York: Routledge, 1988.

——. *Victorian Fairy Tales: The Revolt of the Fairies and Elves*. New York: Routledge, 1989.

——. *The Trials and Tribulations of Little Red Riding Hood*. 2nd ed. New York: Routledge, 1993.

——. *Fairy Tale as Myth / Myth as Fairy Tale*. Lexington: University Press of Kentucky, 1994.

——. *When Dreams Came True: Classical Fairy Tales and Their Tradition*. New York: Routledge, 1999.

——. *The Oxford Companion to Fairy Tales*. Oxford: Oxford University Press, 2000.

——. *Hans Christian Andersen: The Misunderstood Storyteller*. New York: Routledge, 2005.

——. *Fairy Tales and the Art of Subversion*. 2nd rev. ed. New York: Routledge, 2006.

——. *Why Fairy Tales Stick*. New York: Routledge, 2006.

Fantasy

Attebery, Brian. *The Fantasy Tradition in American Literature: From Irving to Le Guin*. Bloomington: Indiana University Press, 1982.

Barron, Neil. *Fantasy and Horror: A Critical and Historical Guide to Literature, Illustration, Film, TV, Radio, and the Internet*. Lanham, Md.: Scarecrow Press, 1999.

Eccleshare, Julia. *A Guide to the Harry Potter Novels*. London: Continuum, 2002.

Heilman, Elizabeth E., ed. *Harry Potter's World: Multidisciplinary Critical Perspectives*. New York: RoutledgeFalmer, 2002.

Hunt, Peter, and Millicent Lenz. *Alternative Worlds in Fantasy Fiction*. London: Continuum, 2002.

Kuznets, Lois Rostow. *When Toys Come Alive*. New Haven, Conn.: Yale University Press, 1994.

Lynn, Ruth Nadelman. *Fantasy Literature for Children and Young Adults: An Annotated Bibliography*. New York: Bowker, 1995.

Manlove, Colin Nicholas. *The Impulse of Fantasy Literature*. Kent, Ohio: Kent State University Press, 1983.

Mendlesohn, Farah. *Diana Wynne Jones: The Fantastic Tradition and Children's Literature*. New York: Routledge, 2005.

Molson, Francis J. *Children's Fantasy*. San Bernardino, Calif.: Borgo Press, 1989.

Nikolajeva, Maria. *The Magic Code: The Use of Magical Patterns in Fantasy for Children*. Stockholm: Almqvist and Wiksell International, 1988.

Pflieger, Pat. *A Reference Guide to Modern Fantasy for Children*. Westport, Conn.: Greenwood Press, 1984.

Phillips, Robert S., ed. *Aspects of Alice: Lewis Carroll's* Dreamchild *as Seen through the Critics' Looking-Glasses, 1865–1971*. New York: Vanguard Press, 1971.

Schlobin, Roger C., ed. *The Aesthetics of Fantasy Literature and Art*. Notre Dame: University of Notre Dame Press, 1982.

Scott, Carole, and Millicent Lenz. *His Dark Materials Illuminated: Critical Essays on Philip Pullman's Trilogy*. Detroit: Wayne State University Press, 2005.

Smith, Karen Patricia. *The Fabulous Realm: A Literary-Historical Approach to British Fantasy, 1780–1990*. Metuchen, N.J.: Scarecrow Press, 1993.

Thompson, Raymond Henry. *The Return from Avalon*. Westport, Conn.: Greenwood, 1985.

Science Fiction

Antczak, Janice. *Science Fiction: The Mythos of a New Romance*. New York: Neal-Schuman, 1985.

Beetz, Kirk H., and Suzanne Niedermeyer, eds. *Beacham's Guide to Literature for Young Adults*. Vol. 4, *Science Fiction, Mystery, Adventure, and Mythology*. Washington, D.C.: Beacham, 1993.

Cadden, Mike. *Ursula K. Le Guin beyond Genre: Fiction for Children and Adults*. New York: Routledge, 2005.

Clute, John, and Peter Nicholls. *The Encyclopedia of Science Fiction*. New York: St. Martin's, 1993.

Esmonde, Margaret. "Children's Science Fiction." In *Signposts to Criticism of Children's Literature*, ed. Robert Bator. Chicago: American Library Association, 1983.

Foundation: The International Review of Science Fiction 70 (Summer 1997): 1–82.

Lenz, Millicent. *Nuclear Age Literature for Youth: The Quest for a Life-Affirming Ethic*. Chicago: American Library Association, 1990.

Molson, Francis J., and Susan G. Miles. "Young Adult Science Fiction." In *Anatomy of Wonder: A Critical Guide to Science Fiction*, 4th ed., ed. Neil Barron. New Providence, N.J.: Bowker, 1995.

Reid, Suzanne Elizabeth. *Presenting Young Adult Science Fiction*. New York: Twayne, 1998.

Sands, Karen, and Marietta Frank. *Back in the Spaceship Again: Juvenile Science Fiction Series since 1945*. Westport, Conn.: Greenwood Press, 1999.

Sullivan, Charles William, III, ed. *Science Fiction for Young Readers*. Westport, Conn.: Greenwood Press, 1993.

——, ed. *Young Adult Science Fiction*. Westport, Conn.: Greenwood Press, 1999.

Lion and the Unicorn 28, no. 2 (2004): 171–313.

Westfahl, Gary. *Science Fiction, Children's Literature, and Popular Culture: Coming of Age in Fantasyland*. Westport, Conn.: Greenwood Press, 2000.

Adventure Stories

Bristow, Joseph. *Empire Boys: Adventures in a Man's World*. London: HarperCollins Academic, 1991.

Butts, Dennis. "The Adventure Story." In *Stories and Society: Children's Literature in a Social Context*, ed. Dennis Butts, 65–83. Basingstoke, UK: Macmillan, 1992.

——. "Shaping Boyhood: Empire Builders and Adventurers." In *International Companion Encyclopedia of Children's Literature*, 2nd ed., ed. Peter Hunt, 340–51. London: Routledge, 2004.

Green, Martin. *Dreams of Adventure, Deeds of Empire*. London: Routledge and Kegan Paul, 1980.

——. *The Robinson Crusoe Story*. University Park: Pennsylvania State University Press, 1990.

——. *Seven Types of Adventure Tale: An Etiology of a Major Genre*. University Park: Pennsylvania University Press, 1991.

Howarth, Patrick. *Play Up and Play the Game: The Heroes of Popular Fiction*. London: Eyre Methuen, 1973.

Jones, Dudley, and Tony Watkins, eds. *A Necessary Fantasy? The Heroic Figure in Popular Children's Fiction*. New York: Garland, 2000.

Kutzer, M. D. *Empire Children: Empire and Imperialism in Classic British Children's Literature*. New York: Routledge, 2000.

Horror

Barron, Neil. *Fantasy and Horror: A Critical and Historical Guide to Literature, Illustration, Film, TV, Radio, and the Internet*. Lanham, Md.: Scarecrow Press, 1999.

Gavin, Adrienne, and Christopher Routledge, eds. *Mystery in Children's Literature: From the Rational to the Supernatural*. Basingstoke, UK: Palgrave, 2001.

Jackson, Anna, Roderick McGillis, and Karen Coats, eds. *The Gothic in Children's Literature: Haunting the Borders*. New York: Routledge, 2007.

Overstreet, Deborah Wilson. *Not Your Mother's Vampire: Vampires in Young Adult Fiction*. Lanham, Md.: Scarecrow Press, 2006.

Reynolds, Kimberley, ed. *Frightening Fiction*. London: Continuum, 2001.

Warner, Marina. *No Go the Bogeyman: Scaring, Lulling and Making Mock*. London: Vintage, 2000.

School Stories

Auchmuty, Rosemary. *The World of Girls: The Appeal of the Girls' School Story*. London: The Women's Press, 1992.

——. *A World of Women: Growing Up in the Girls' School Story*. London: Women's Press, 1999.

Cadogan, Mary, and Patricia Craig. *You're a Brick, Angela: The Girls' Story, 1839–1985*. Rev. ed. London: Gollancz, 1986.

Cadogan, Mary, and Norman Wright, comps. *A Treasury of Enid Blyton's School Stories*. London: Hodder Headline, 2002.

Clark, Beverly. *Regendering the School Story: Sassy Sissies and Tattling Tomboys*. New York: Garland, 1996.

Kirkpatrick, Robert J. *The Encyclopedia of Boys' School Stories*. Aldershot, UK: Ashgate, 2000.

——. *Bullies, Beaks and Flannelled Fools: An Annotated Bibliography of Boys' School Fiction, 1742–1990*. New ed. London: Author, 2001.

Musgrave, Peter William. *From Brown to Bunter: The Life and Death of the School Story*. London: Routledge and Kegan Paul, 1985.

Quigly, Isabel. *The Heirs of Tom Brown: The English School Story*. London: Chatto and Windus, 1982.

Richard, Jeffery. *Happiest Days: The Public Schools in English Fiction*. Manchester: Manchester University Press, 1988.

Sims, Sue, and Hilary Clare, eds. *The Encyclopaedia of Girls' School Stories*. Aldershot, UK: Ashgate, 2000.

Walkerdine, Valerie. *Schoolgirl Fictions*. London: Verso, 1990.

Gender-Specific Literature

Auchmuty, Rosemary. *The World of Girls: The Appeal of the Girls' School Story*. London: The Women's Press, 1992.

———. *A World of Women: Growing Up in the Girls' School Story*. London: Women's Press, 1999.

Boyd, Kelly. *Manliness and the Boys' Story Paper in Britain: A Cultural History, 1855–1940*. Basingstoke, UK: Palgrave Macmillan, 2003.

Bristow, Joseph. *Empire Boys: Adventures in a Man's World*. London: HarperCollins, 1991.

Butts, Dennis. "Shaping Boyhood: Empire Builders and Adventurers." In *International Companion Encyclopedia of Children's Literature*, 2nd ed., ed. Peter Hunt, 340–51. London: Routledge, 2004.

Cadogan, Mary, and Patricia Craig. *You're a Brick, Angela: The Girls' Story, 1839–1985*. Rev. ed. London: Gollancz, 1986.

Clark, Beverly. *Regendering the School Story: Sassy Sissies and Tattling Tomboys*. New York: Garland, 1996.

Cohoon, Lorinda. *Serialized Citizenships: Periodicals, Books, and American Boys, 1840–1911*. Lanham, Md.: Scarecrow Press, 2006.

Doyle, Brian. *Who's Who of Boys' Writers and Illustrators*. London: Hugh Evelyn, 1964.

Flanagan, Victoria. *Into the Closet: Cross-Dressing and the Gendered Body in Children's Literature and Film*. New York: Routledge, 2007.

Foster, Shirley, and Judy Simons. *What Katy Read: Feminist Re-readings of 'Classic' Stories for Girls*. Basingstoke, UK: Macmillan, 1995.

Grenz, Dagmar, and Gisela Wilkending, eds. *Geschichte der Mädchenlektüre. Mädchenliteratur und die gesellschaftliche Situation der Frauen vom 18. Jahrhundert bis zur Gegenwart*. Weinheim, Germany: Juventa, 1997.

Kirkpatrick, Robert J. *The Encyclopedia of Boys' School Stories*. Aldershot, UK: Ashgate, 2000.

Lehr, Susan, ed. *Beauty, Brains, and Brawn: The Construction of Gender in Children's Literature*. Portsmouth, N.H.: Heinemann, 2001.

Lofts, Wiliam O. G., and Derek J. Adley. *The Men behind Boy's Fiction: A Collective Biography of All British Authors Who Ever Wrote for Boys*. London: Howard Baker, 1970.

Lyon Clark, Beverly, and Margaret R. Higgonet, eds. *Girls, Boys, Books, Toys: Gender in Children's Literature*. Baltimore, Md.: Johns Hopkins University Press, 1999.

Nelson, Claudia. *Boys Will Be Girls: The Feminine Ethic and British Children's Fiction, 1857–1917*. New Brunswick, N.J.: Rutgers University Press, 1991.

Paul, Lissa. *Reading Otherways*. South Woodchester, UK: Thimble Press, 1997.

Reynolds, Kimberley. *Girls Only? Gender and Popular Children's Fiction in Britain, 1880–1910*. Hemel Hempstead, UK: Harvester, 1990.

Romines, Ann. *Constructing the Little House: Gender, Culture, and Laura Ingalls Wilder*. Amherst: University of Massachusetts Press, 1997.

Sims, Sue, and Hilary Clare. *The Encyclopaedia of Girls' School Stories*. Aldershot, UK: Ashgate, 2000.

Stephens, John. "Gender, Genre and Children's Literature." *Signal* 79 (1996): 17–30.

——, ed. *Ways of Being Male: Representing Masculinities in Children's Literature and Film*. New York: Routledge, 2002.

Vallone, Lynne M. "Laughing with the Boys and Learning with the Girls: Humor in Nineteenth Century American Juvenile Fiction." *Children's Literature Association Quarterly* 15, no. 3 (1990): 127–35.

——. *Disciplines of Virtue: Girls' Culture in the Eighteenth and Nineteenth Centuries*. New Haven, Conn.: Yale University Press, 1995.

Wannamaker, Annette. *Boys in Children's Literature and Popular Culture: Masculinity, Abjection, and the Fictional Child*. New York: Routledge, 2008.

Wilkie-Stibbs, Christine. *The Feminine Subject in Children's Literature*. New York: Routledge, 2002.

Adolescent Novels

Cart, Michael. *From Romance to Realism: 50 Years of Growth and Change in Young Adult Literature*. New York: HarperCollins, 1996.

Grotzer, Peter. *Die zweite Geburt. Figuren des Jugendlichen in der Literatur des 20. Jahrhunderts*. 2 vols. Zürich: Ammann, 1991.

McCallum, Robyn. *Ideologies of Identity in Adolescent Fiction: The Dialogic Construction of Subjectivity*. New York: Garland, 1999.

Neubauer, John. *The Fin-de-Siècle Culture of Adolescence*. New Haven, Conn.: Yale University Press, 1991.

Randall, Don. *Kipling's Imperial Boy: Adolescence and Cultural Hybridity*. Basingstoke, UK: Palgrave, 2000.

Soter, Anna O. *Young Adult Literature and the New Literary Theories: Developing Critical Readers in Middle School*. New York: Teachers College Press, 1999.

Trites, Roberta Seelinger. *Disturbing the Universe: Power and Repression in Adolescent Literature*. Iowa City: University of Iowa Press, 2000.

Historical Fiction

Barnhouse, Rebecca. *Recasting the Past: The Middle Ages in Young Adult Literature*. Portsmouth, UK: Boynton/Cook, 2000.

Casement, Rose. *Black History in the Pages of Children's Literature*. Lanham, Md.: Scarecrow Press, 2007.

Collins, Fiona M., and Judith Graham, eds. *Historical Fiction for Children: Capturing the Past*. London: David Fulton, 2001.

Galway, Elizabeth. "Fact, Fiction, and the Tradition of Historical Narratives in Nineteenth-Century Canadian Children's Literature." *Canadian Children's Literature* 102 (2001): 20–32.

Lathey, Gillian. *The Impossible Legacy: Identity and Purpose in Autobiographical Children's Literature set in the Third Reich and the Second World War*. Bern: Peter Lang, 1999.

McGillis, Roderick. "The Opportunity to Choose a Past: Remembering History." *Children's Literature Association Quarterly* 25, no. 1 (2000): 49–55.

McLeod, Anne Scott. "Writing Backward: Modern Models in Historical Fiction." *Horn Book Magazine* 74, no. 1 (1998): 26–33.

Moffat, Mary S. *Historical Fiction for Children: A Bibliography*. Darlington, UK: Castle of Dreams Books, 2000.

Shavit, Zohar. *A Past Without Shadow: Constructing the Past in German Books for Children*. New York: Routledge, 2005.

Youngerman, Miriam Miller. "In Days of Old: The Middle Ages in Children's Non-fiction." *Children's Literature Association Quarterly* 12, no. 4 (1987): 167–72.

Zornado, Joseph. "A Poetics of History: Karen Cushman's Medieval World." *Lion and the Unicorn* 21, no. 2 (1997): 251–66.

Nonfiction and Biography

Barr, Catherine, ed. *From Biography to History: Best Books for Children's Entertainment and Education*. New Providence, N.J.: Bowker, 1998.

Carr, Jo. *Beyond Fact: Nonfiction for Children and Young People*. Chicago: American Library Association, 1982.

Casement, Rose. *Black History in the Pages of Children's Literature*. Lanham, Md.: Scarecrow Press, 2007.

Fisher, Margery. *Matters of Fact: Aspects of Non-fiction for Children*. New York: Crowell, 1972.

Hannabuss, Stuart, and Rita Marcella. *Biography and Children: A Study of Biography for Children and Children in Biography*. London: Library Association, 1993.

Harvey, Stephanie. *Nonfiction Matters*. Portland, Maine: Stenhouse, 1998.

Kuipers, Barbara J. *American Indian Reference and Resource Books for Children and Young Adults*. 2nd ed. Englewood, Colo.: Libraries Unlimited, 1995.

Mallet, Margaret. *Young Researchers: Informational Reading in the Early and Primary Years*. London: Routledge, 1999.

——. *Early Years Nonfiction: A Guide to Helping Young Researchers Use and Enjoy Information Texts*. London: Routledge, 2003.

——. "Children's Information Texts." In *International Companion Encyclopedia of Children's Literature*, 2nd ed., ed. Peter Hunt, 622–31. London: Routledge, 2004.

Meek, Margaret. *Information and Book Learning*. South Woodchester, UK: Thimble Press, 1996.

Wray, David, and Maureen Lewis. *Extending Literacy: Children Reading and Writing Non-fiction*. London: Routledge, 1997.

Other Genres and Forms

Bedard, Roger L., ed. *Dramatic Literature for Children: A Century in Review*. New Orleans: Anchorage Press, 1984.

Bottigheimer, Ruth B. *The Bible for Children: From the Age of Gutenberg to the Present*. New Haven, Conn.: Yale University Press, 1996.

Davidoff, Leonore, et al., eds. *The Family Story: Blood, Contract and Intimacy*. Harlow, UK: Addison Wesley Longman, 1999.

Davis, Jed Horace, and Mary Jane Evans, eds. *Theatre, Children, and Youth*. New Orleans: Anchorage Press, 1987.

Deane, Paul. *Mirrors of American Culture: Children's Fiction Series in the Twentieth Century*. Metuchen, N.J.: Scarecrow Press, 1991.

England, Alan. *Theatre for the Young*. Basingstoke, UK: Macmillan, 1990.
McCaslin, Nellie. *Historical Guide to Children's Theatre in America*. New York: Greenwood Press, 1987.
Swortzell, Lowell, ed. *International Guide to Children's Theatre and Educational Drama*. Westport, Conn.: Greenwood Press, 1995.
Thiel, Elizabeth. *The Fantasy of Family: Nineteenth-Century Children's Literature and the Myth of the Domestic Ideal*. New York: Routledge, 2008.
Tucker, Nicholas, and Nikki Gamble. *Family Fictions*. London: Continuum, 2001.
Watson, Victor. *Reading Series Fiction. from Arthur Ransome to Gene Kemp*. New York: Routledge, 2000.

CONTINENTS AND REGIONS

North America

Avery, Gillian. *Behold the Child: American Children and Their Books, 1621–1922*. London: Bodley Head, 1994.
Bronner, Simon J. *American Children's Folklore*. Annotated ed. Little Rock, Ark.: August House, 1988.
Egoff, Sheila, and Judith Saltman. *The New Republic of Childhood: A Critical Guide to Canadian Children's Literature in English*. Toronto: Oxford University Press, 1990.
Egoff, Sheila, Gordon Stubbs, Ralph Ashley, and Wendy Sutton, eds. *Only Connect: Readings on Children's Literature*. 3rd ed. Toronto: Oxford University Press, 1996 (1st ed. 1969).
Galway, Elizabeth. *From Nursery Rhymes to Nationhood: Children's Literature and the Construction of Canadian Identity*. New York: Routledge, 2008.
Gammel, Irene, and Elizabeth Epperly, eds. *L. M. Montgomery and Canadian Culture*. Toronto: University of Toronto Press, 1999.
Griswold, Jerry. "The USA: A Historical Overview." In *International Companion Encyclopedia of Children's Literature*, 2nd ed., ed. Peter Hunt, 1271–79. London: Routledge, 2004.
Johnson, Dianne. *Telling Tales: The Pedagogy and the Promise of African-American Literature for Youth*. Westport, Conn.: Greenwood Press, 1990.
Jones, Raymond, and Jon C. Stott. *Canadian Children's Books: A Critical Guide to Authors and Illustrators*. Don Mills, ON: Oxford University Press, 2000.
Lepage, Françoise. *Histoire de la littérature pour la jeunesse. Québec et francophonies due Canada, suivie d'un dictionnaire des auteurs et des illustrateurs*. Orléans: Les Éditions David, 2000.

Lester, Neal A. *Once upon a Time in a Different World: Issues and Ideas in African American Children's Literature*. New York: Routledge, 2007.

Lystad, Mary. *From Dr. Mather to Dr. Seuss: Two Hundred Years of American Books for Children*. Boston: G. K. Hall, 1980.

MacDonald, Ruth. *Christian's Children: The Influence of John Bunyan's* The Pilgrim's Progress *on American Children's Literature*. New York: Peter Lang, 1989.

MacLeod, Anne Scott. *A Moral Tale: Children's Fiction and American Culture, 1829–1860*. Hamden, Conn.: Archon Books, 1975.

———. *American Childhood: Essays on Children's Literature of the Nineteenth and Twentieth Centuries*. Athens: University of Georgia Press, 1994.

Madore, Edith. *La littérature pour la jeunesse en Québec*. Montréal: Boréal, 1994.

Marcus, Leonard S. *Minders of Make-Believe: Idealists, Entrepreneurs, and the Shaping of American Children's Literature*. New York: Houghton Mifflin, 2008.

Murray, Gail Schmunk. *American Children's Literature and the Construction of Childhood*. New York: Twayne, 1998.

Nodelman, Perry. "Where We've Come From, Where We Are Now, Where We're Going." *Canadian Children's Literature* 31, no. 1 (2005): 1–18.

Osa, Osayimwense, ed. *The All-White World of Children's Books and African American Children's Literature*. Trenton, N.J.: Africa World Press, 1995.

Potvin, Claude. *La littérature de jeunesse au Canada français*. Moncton: CRP, 1981.

Pouliot, Suzanne. "Children's Literature in Quebec and French-Speaking Canada." In *International Companion Encyclopedia of Children's Literature*, 2nd ed., ed. Peter Hunt, 1019–24. London: Routledge, 2004.

Reimer, Mavis. "Canada: Canadian Children's Literature in English." In *International Companion Encyclopedia of Children's Literature*, 2nd ed., ed. Peter Hunt, 1011–19. London: Routledge, 2004.

Saltman, Judith. *Modern Canadian Children's Books*. Toronto: Oxford University Press, 1987.

Smith, Katharine Capshaw. *Children's Literature of the Harlem Renaissance*. Bloomington: Indiana University Press, 2004.

Waterston, Elizabeth. *Children's Literature in Canada*. New York: Twayne, 1992.

Central America, South America, and Caribbean Countries

Arizpe, Evelyn. "Mexico and Central America." In *International Companion Encyclopedia of Children's Literature*, 2nd ed., ed. Peter Hunt, 1132–37. London: Routledge, 2004.

Arroyo, Leonardo. *Literatura infantil brasileira.* São Paulo: Melhoramento, 1968.

Bravo-Villasante, Carmen. *Historia y antologia de la literatura infantile iberoamericana.* 2 vols. Madrid: Ministerio de Cultura, 1966.

Delgado, Francisco. *Ecuador y su literatura infantil.* Quito: Subsecretaría de Cultura del Ministerio de Educación, 1987.

Donnet, Beatrice, and Guillermo Murray Prisant. *Palabra de juguete; una historia y una antología de la literatura infantil y juvenil en México.* México City: Lectorum, 1999.

IBBY. *Se hace camino . . . Escritores e ilustradores latinoamericanos del libro infantil y juvenil.* Bogata: Secciones Latinoamericanas de IBBY, Fundalectura, 2000.

Lajolo, Marisa, and Regina Zilberman. *Literatura infantil brasileira. História & Histórias.* São Paulo: Ática, 1984.

Medina, Maria Beatriz, and Olga García Larralde. "South American and Spanish-Speaking Caribbean Countries." In *International Companion Encyclopedia of Children's Literature,* 2nd ed., ed. Peter Hunt, 1194–1206. London: Routledge, 2004.

Mehl, Ruth. *Con este sí, con este no. Mas de 500 fichas de literature infantile argentina.* Buenos Aires: Ediciones Colihue, 1993.

Muñoz, Manuel Peña. *Había una vez—en América. Literatura infantil de America Latina.* Santiago, Chile: Dolmen Estudio, 1997.

Novaes Coelho, Nelly. *Dicionario critico da literatura infantil/juvenil brasileira 1882–1982.* São Paulo: Quiron, 1983.

Peñez Muñoz, Manuel. "La literatura infantil en Centroamérica." *Educacion y Biblioteca* 11, no. 102 (1999): 54–64.

Penteado, Jose Roberto Whitaker. *Os Filhos e Lobato.* Rio de Janeiro: Dunya, 1997.

Ray, Sheila. "The Caribbean (English-Speaking)." In *International Companion Encyclopedia of Children's Literature,* 2nd ed., ed. Peter Hunt, 1025–28. London: Routledge, 2004.

Rey, Mario. *Historia y muestra de la literatura infantil mexicana.* Mexico City: Consejo Nacional para la Cultura y las Artes/SM des Ediciones, 2000.

Rodriguez, Antonio Orlando. *Literatura infantil de América Latina.* San José, Costa Rica: Oficina Subregional de Educación de la UNESCO para Centroamérica y Panamá, 1993.

Sandroni, Laura. *De Lobato a Bojunga, as reinações renovadas.* Rio de Janeiro: Livraria Agir Editora, 1987.

———. *Minha memória de Monteiro Lobato.* São Paulo: Companhia das Lenrinhas, 1997.

———. "Brazil." In *International Companion Encyclopedia of Children's Literature,* 2nd ed., ed. Peter Hunt, 1004–10. London: Routledge, 2004.

Vallejo, E., and V. Sanchez. *Experiencas de motivación lectora y produccion de textos en Paraguay*. Asuncion: Cámara Paraguaya de Editores, Liberos y Asociados, 2002.

Northern and Western Europe

Birkeland, Tone, Gunvor Risa, and Karin Beate Vold. *Norsk barnelitteraturhistorie*. Oslo: Norske samlaget, 1997.

Blinnika, Vuokko, Kaija Salonen, and Kari Vaijärvi. *Barn- och ungdomsförfattare in Finland*. 3 vols. Helsinki: Finlands biblioteksförening, 1983.

Bratton, Jacqueline S. *The Impact of Victorian Children's Fiction*. London: Croom Helm, 1981.

Breen, Else. *Slik skrev de. Verdi og virkelighet i barnebøker, 1968–1990*. Oslo: Aschehoug, 1995.

Brown, Penelope E. *A Critical History of French Children's Literature*. Vol. 1, *1600–1830*. Routledge, 2007.

———. *A Critical History of French Children's Literature*. Vol. 2, *1830–Present*. Routledge, 2007.

Brüggemann, Theodor, and Otto Brunken, eds. *Handbuch zur Kinder- und Jugendliteratur. Vom Beginn des Buchdrucks bis 1570*. Stuttgart: Metzler, 1987.

———, eds. *Handbuch zur Kinder- und Jugendliteratur. Von 1570–1750*. Stuttgart: Metzler, 1991.

Brüggemann, Theodor, and Hans-Heino Ewers, eds. *Handbuch zur Kinder- und Jugendliteratur. Von 1750–1800*. Stuttgart: Metzler, 1982.

Brunken, Otto, Bettina Hurrelmann, and Klaus-Ulrich Pech, eds. *Handbuch zur Kinder- und Jugendliteratur. Von 1800 bis 1850*. Stuttgart: Metzler, 1998.

Buijnsters, Piet J., and Leontine Buijnsters-Smets. *Bibliografie van Nederlandse school - en kinderboeken 1700–1800*. Zwolle, The Netherlands: Waanders Uitgev, 1997.

———. *Lust en leering. Geschiedenis van het Nederlandse kinderboek in de negentiende eeuw*. Zwolle, The Netherlands: Waanders, 2001.

Caradec, François. *Histoire de la littérature enfantine en France*. Paris: Albin Michel, 1977.

Carpenter, Humphrey. *The Secret Gardens: A Study of the Golden Age of Children's Literature*. London: Allen and Unwin, 1985.

Coghlan, Valerie. "Ireland." In *International Companion Encyclopedia of Children's Literature*, 2nd ed., ed. Peter Hunt, 1099–1103. London: Routledge, 2004.

Coghlan, Valerie, and Celia Keenan, eds. *The Big Guide to Irish Children's Books*. Dublin: Irish Children's Book Trust, 1996.

Darton, Frederick Joseph Harvey. *Children's Books in England: Five Centuries of Social Life*. 3rd ed., rev. Brian Alderson. Cambridge: Cambridge University Press, 1982 (1st ed. 1932).

De Vries, Anne. "The Netherlands." In *International Companion Encyclopedia of Children's Literature*, 2nd ed., ed. Peter Hunt, 1140–48. London: Routledge, 2004.

Deschamps, J.-G. *The History of French Children's Books, 1750–1900: From the Collection of J.-G. Deschamps*. Boston: Bookshop for Boys and Girls, 1934.

Diament, Nic, ed. *Dictionnaire des écrivains français pour la jeunesse*. Paris: Ecole des Loisirs, 1993.

Dolle-Weinkauff, Bernd. "The German Democratic Republic." In *International Companion Encyclopedia of Children's Literature*, 2nd ed., ed. Peter Hunt, 1063–66. London: Routledge, 2004.

Duijx, Toin, ed. *More Than Just Windmills! Children's Literature in the Netherlands*. The Hague: NBLC, 1992.

Dunbar, Robert. "Rarely Pure and Never Simple: The World of Irish Children's Literature." *Lion and the Unicorn* 21, no. 3 (1997): 309–21.

Ewers, Hans-Heino. "Germany." In *International Companion Encyclopedia of Children's Literature*, 2nd ed., ed. Peter Hunt, 1055–62. London: Routledge, 2004.

Ewers, Hans-Heino, and Ernst Seibert, eds. *Geschichte der österreichischen Kinder- und Jugendliteratur. Vom 18. Jahrhundert bis zur Gegenwart*. Vienna: Buchkultur, 1997.

Fielitz, Sonja. "Austria." In *The Oxford Encyclopedia of Children's Literature*, ed. Jack Zipes, 1:100–102. Oxford: Oxford University Press, 2006.

Fraser, Lindsey. "Scotland." In *International Companion Encyclopedia of Children's Literature*, 2nd ed., ed. Peter Hunt, 1263–66. London: Routledge, 2004.

Glasenapp, Gabriele von, and Michael Nagel. *Das jüdische Jugendbuch. Von der Aufklärung bis zum Dritten Reich*. Stuttgart: Metzler, 1996.

Haller, Karin. "Austria." In *International Companion Encyclopedia of Children's Literature*, 2nd ed., ed. Peter Hunt, 984–89. London: Routledge, 2004.

Heimerisken, Nettie, and Willem van Toorn. *De hele Bibelebontse berg. De geschiedenis van het kinderboek in Nederland and Vlaanderen von de middeleeuwen to heden*. Amsterdam: Querido, 1990.

Hunt, Peter, ed. *Children's Literature: An Illustrated History*. Oxford: Oxford University Press, 1995.

Jaasko, Andres. *A Guide to Estonian Children's Literature*. Tallinn: Eesti Raamat, 1984.

Joosen, Vanessa. "Belgium." In *International Companion Encyclopedia of Children's Literature*, 2nd ed., ed. Peter Hunt, 998–1003. London: Routledge, 2004.

Klingberg, Göte. *Svensk barn- och ungdomslitteratur 1591–1839. En pedagogisk och bibliografisk översik*. Stockholm: Natur och Kultur, 1964.

Klingberg, Göte, and Ingar Bratt. *Barnböcker utgivna i Sverige 1840–1889. En kommenterad bibliografi*. Lund, Sweden: Lund University Press, 1988.

Kuivasmäki, Riitta. *Some Facts about Children's Literature in Finland*. 4th rev. ed. Tampere, Finland: Soun nuorisokirjallisuuden Institutti, 1998.

Linders, Joke, and Marita de Sterck, eds. *Behind the Story: Children's Book Authors in Flanders and the Netherlands*. Amsterdam: ONUB, 1996.

Niekus-Moore, Cornelia. *The Maiden's Mirror: Reading Material for German Girls in the Sixteenth and Seventeenth Centuries*. Wiesbaden, Germany: Harassowitz, 1987.

Noesen, Paul. *Geschichte der Luxemburger Jugendliteratur*. Luxembourg: Verlag der L.K.A., 1951.

Ottevaere van Praag, Ganna. *La littérature pour la jeunesse en Europe occidentale (1750–1925). Histoire sociale et courants d'idées Angleterre, France, Pays-Bas, Allemagne, Italie*. Bern: Peter Lang, 1987.

Perrot, Jean. "France." In *International Companion Encyclopedia of Children's Literature*, 2nd ed., ed. Peter Hunt, 1043–54. London: Routledge, 2004.

Reynolds, Kimberley. *Children's Literature in the 1890s and the 1990s*. Plymouth: Northcote, 1994.

Rutschmann, Verena, ed. *Nebenan. Der Anteil der Schweiz an der deutschsprachigen Kinder- und Jugendliteratur*. Zurich: Chronos, 1999.

———. "Switzerland." In *International Companion Encyclopedia of Children's Literature*, 2nd ed., ed. Peter Hunt, 1236–40. London: Routledge, 2004.

Shavit, Zohar, Hans-Heino Ewers, Annegret Völpel, Ran HaCohen, and Dieter Richter. *Deutsch-jüdische Kinder- und Jugendliteratur von der Haskala bis 1945. Die deutsch- und hebräischsprachigen Schriften des deutschsprachigen Raumes. Ein bibliographisches Handbuch*. 2 vols. Stuttgart: Metzler, 1996.

Sønsthagen, Kari, and Lena Eilstrup, eds. *Dansk børnelitteratur historie*. Copenhagen: Host & Son, 1992.

Springman, Luke. *Carpe Mundum: German Youth Culture of the Weimar Republic*. Frankfurt: Peter Lang, 2007.

Townsend, John Rowe. "United Kingdom: British Children's Literature; A Historical Overview." In *International Companion Encyclopedia of Children's Literature*, 2nd ed., ed. Peter Hunt, 1252–63. London: Routledge, 2004.

Völpel, Annegret, and Zohar Shavit. *Deutsch-Jüdische Kinder- und Jugendliteratur. Ein literaturgeschichtlicher Grundriß*. Stuttgart: Metzler, 2002.

Weilenmann, Claudia, and Josiane Cetlin. *Annotierte Bibliographie der Schweizer Kinder- und Jugendliteratur von 1750 bis 1900. Bibliographie annotée de livres suisses pour l'enfance et la jeunesse de 1750 à 1900*. Stuttgart: Metzler, 1993.

Westin, Birgitta. *Children's Literature in Sweden*. New ed. Stockholm: Swedish Institute, 1996.

Westin, Boel. "The Nordic Countries." In *International Companion Encyclopedia of Children's Literature*, 2nd ed., ed. Peter Hunt, 1156–67. London: Routledge, 2004.

Wild, Reiner, ed. *Geschichte der deutschen Kinder- und Jugendliteratur*. 3rd rev. ed. Stuttgart: Metzler, 2007.

Williams, Menna Lloyd. "Wales." In *International Companion Encyclopedia of Children's Literature*, 2nd ed., ed. Peter Hunt, 1266–69. London: Routledge, 2004.

Eastern and Southern Europe

Anagnostopoulos, Vassilis D. "Greece: From the Beginnings to 1945." In *International Companion Encyclopedia of Children's Literature*, 2nd ed., ed. Peter Hunt, 1067–69. London: Routledge, 2004.

Balina, Marina, and Larissa Rudova, eds. *Russian Children's Literature and Culture*. New York: Routledge, 2007.

Baptista, Dulce Maria Pires. *História da literatura infantil em Portugal*. Lisbon: Vega, 1990.

Barreto, António Garcia. *Literatura para crianças e jovens em Portugal*. Oporto: Campo das Letras, 1998.

Battistelli, Vincenzina. *Il libro del fanciullo: La letteratura per l'infanzia*. 2nd ed. Florence: La Nuova Italia, 1962.

Blazic, Milena Mileva. "Slovenia." In *International Companion Encyclopedia of Children's Literature*, 2nd ed., ed. Peter Hunt, 1190–93. London: Routledge, 2004.

———. "South East Europe." In *International Companion Encyclopedia of Children's Literature*, 2nd ed., ed. Peter Hunt, 1213–25. London: Routledge, 2004.

Blockeel, Francesca, and José António Gomes. "Portugal." In *International Companion Encyclopedia of Children's Literature*, 2nd ed., ed. Peter Hunt, 1168–73. London: Routledge, 2004.

Bravo-Villasante, Carmen. *Historia de la literatura infantil española*. Madrid: Ministerio de Cultura, 1985 (1st ed. 1972).

Cano, Isabel, and Pablo Barrena. *Autores españoles de literatura infantil y juvenil*. Valencia: Asociación Española de Amigos del Libro Infantil y Juvenil, 1991.

Giakos, Demetres. *Historia tes hellenikes paidikes logotechnicas*. Athens: Deēm. N. Papadeēmas, 1990.

Gomes, José António. *Towards a History of Portuguese Children's and Youth Literature*. Lisbon: Ministério da Cultura, 1997.

Hawkes, Louise Restiaux. *Before and after Pinocchio: A Study of Italian Children's Books*. Paris: The Puppet Press, 1933.

Hellman, Ben. "Russia." In *International Companion Encyclopedia of Children's Literature*, 2nd ed., ed. Peter Hunt, 1174–83. London: Routledge, 2004.

Kreyder, Laura. "Italy." In *International Companion Encyclopedia of Children's Literature*, 2nd ed., ed. Peter Hunt, 1104–7. London: Routledge, 2004.

Nun, Katalin. "Hungary." In *International Companion Encyclopedia of Children's Literature*, 2nd ed., ed. Peter Hunt, 1072–75. London: Routledge, 2004.

Ray, Sheila. "Eastern Europe: Bulgaria, Poland, Romania." In *International Companion Encyclopedia of Children's Literature*, 2nd ed., ed. Peter Hunt, 1042–44. London: Routledge, 2004.

Rocha, Natércia. *Breve história da literatura para crianças em Portugal*. Lisbon: Instituto de Cultura e Língua Portuguesa, Ministério da Educaçã, 1984.

Schiaffino, Gualtiero, ed. *Andersen Archivio: Gli scrittori italiani per ragazzi*. 3rd ed. Geneva: Feguagiskia' Studios, 1995.

Sieglova, Nadezda. "Czech Republic." In *International Companion Encyclopedia of Children's Literature*, 2nd ed., ed. Peter Hunt, 1039–41. London: Routledge, 2004.

Sokol, Elena. *Russian Poetry for Children*. Knoxville: University of Tennessee Press, 1994.

Stanislavová, Zuzana. "Slovak Republic." In *International Companion Encyclopedia of Children's Literature*, 2nd ed., ed. Peter Hunt, 1184–89. London: Routledge, 2004.

Steiner, Evgeny. *Stories for Little Comrades: Revolutionary Artists and the Making of Early Soviet Children's Books*. Trans. Jane Ann Miller. Seattle: University of Washington Press, 1999.

Surrallés, Carmen García, and Antonio Moreno Verdulla. "Spain." In *International Companion Encyclopedia of Children's Literature*, 2nd ed., ed. Peter Hunt, 1227–35. London: Routledge, 2004.

Tsilimeni, Tassoula. "Greece: From 1945 to the Present." In *International Companion Encyclopedia of Children's Literature*, 2nd ed., ed. Peter Hunt, 1069–71. London: Routledge, 2004.

Urba, Kestutis. "The Baltic Countries." In *International Companion Encyclopedia of Children's Literature*, 2nd ed., ed. Peter Hunt, 990–97. London: Routledge, 2004.

Africa

Cassiau, Christophe, Véronique Botte, and Paul Tête. "L'Edition de jeunesse au Kenya et au Congo Démocratique." *Takam Tikou* 10 (2003): 21–25.

Dillsworth, Gloria. "Children's and Youth Literature in Sierra Leone." In *African Youth Literature Today and Tomorrow*. Bonn: Deutsche UNESCO Kommission, 1988.

Fayose, Philomena Osazee. *Nigerian Children's Literature in English*. Ibadan: AENL Educational Publishers, 1995.

——. "Africa." In *International Companion Encyclopedia of Children's Literature*, 2nd ed., ed. Peter Hunt, 927–35. London: Routledge, 2004.

Gazza, Sophia. *Les habitudes de lecture en Afrique Subsaharienne et les apprentissages traditionnels*. London: Association for the Development of Education in Africa, 1997.

Heale, Jay. "English-Speaking Africa." In *International Companion Encyclopedia of Children's Literature*, 2nd ed., ed. Peter Hunt, 945–53. London: Routledge, 2004.

Ikonné, Chidi, et al., eds. *Children and Literature in Africa*. Ibadan: Heinemann Educational (Nigeria), 1992.

Jenkins, Elwyn. *Children of the Sun: Selected Writers and Themes in South African Children's Literature*. Johannesburg: Ravan Press, 1993.

——. *National Character in South African English Children's Literature*. New York: Routledge, 2006.

Kaye, Jaqueline, and Abdelhamid Zoubir. *The Ambiguous Compromise: Language, Literature and National Identity in Algeria and Morocco*. London: Routledge, 1990.

Khorana, Meena, ed. *Critical Perspectives on Postcolonial African Children's and Young Adult Literature*. Westport, Conn.: Greenwood, 1991.

Konaté, Sie. *La littérature d'enfance et de jeunesse en Afrique noire francophone. Burkina Faso, Côte d'Ivoire et Sénégal. L'impérialisme culturel à travers la production et la distribution du livre pour enfants*. Quebec: IEPF, 1993.

——. *La littérature d'enfance et de jeunesse au Côte d'Ivoire. Structures de production et de distribution du livre pour enfants*. Paris: L'Harmattan, 1996.

Kruger, Johann A., ed. *Kinderkeur. 'n Gids Tot Bekroonde Suid-Afrikaanse kleuker-, kinder- en jeugdliteratuur tot 1989*. Pretoria: University of South Africa, 1991.

Laurentin, Marie. "French-Speaking Africa." In *International Companion Encyclopedia of Children's Literature*, 2nd ed., ed. Peter Hunt, 935–45. London: Routledge, 2004.

Laurentin, Marie, Vivana Quiñones, and Hasmig Chahinian. *L'Edition africaine en français pour la jeunesse*. Clamart, France: La Joie par les Livres, 2001.

Lebon, C. "Le roman africain français pour la jeunesse." *Takam Tikou* 10 (2003): 30–35.

MacCann, Donnarae, and Yulisa Amadu Maddy. *Apartheid and Racism in South African Children's Literature, 1985–1995.* New York: Routledge, 2001.

Odaga, Asenath Bole. *Literature for Children and Young People in Kenya.* Nairobi: Kenya Literature Bureau, 1985.

Odiase, J. O. U. *African Books for Children and Young Adults.* Benin City, Nigeria: Nationwide Publication Bureau, 1986.

Osa, Osayimwense. *Nigerian Youth Literature.* Benin City, Nigeria: Paramount Publishers, 1987.

———. *African Children's and Youth Literature.* New York: Twayne, 1995.

Rubio, Mary et al. "Children's Literature." In *Encyclopedia of Post-Colonial Literatures in English*, ed. Eugene Benson and Leonard W. Conolly, 1:228–47. London: Routledge, 1994.

Traoré, R. *La littérature d'enfance et de jeunesse en Afrique. L'exemple de la Côte d'Ivoire.* Abidjan, Ivory Coast: Cerav, 1987.

Wahdan, Nadra Abd el-Halim. *Literatura infantil en Egipto.* Madrid: Insituto Hispano-Arabe de Cultura, 1972.

Middle East

Alqudsi-Ghabra, Taghreed. "Arabic Children's Literature." In *International Companion Encyclopedia of Children's Literature*, 2nd ed., ed. Peter Hunt, 954–59. London: Routledge, 2004.

Darr, Yael, and Zohar Shavit. "Jewish-Hebrew, Hebrew and Israeli Children's Literature." In *International Companion Encyclopedia of Children's Literature*, 2nd ed., ed. Peter Hunt, 1115–23. London: Routledge, 2004.

El Kholy, Nadia. "Arab World." In *The Oxford Encyclopedia of Children's Literature*, ed. Jack Zipes, 1:74–78. Oxford: Oxford University Press, 2006.

Khosronejad, Morteza. "Iran." In *International Companion Encyclopedia of Children's Literature*, 2nd ed., ed. Peter Hunt, 1095–98. London: Routledge, 2004.

Ofek, Uriel. *Hebrew Children's Literature: The Beginnings.* Tel Aviv: Porter Institute for Poetics and Semiotics, 1979.

Asia

Asian Cultural Centre for UNESCO. *Bibliography of Children's Books from Asia.* Tokyo: Author, 1980.

Association of Writers and Illustrators for Children. *Creators of Children's Literature in India*. New Delhi: Author, 2003.

Children's Book Trust. *Children's Literature in India*. New Delhi: Author, 1999.

Dasgupta, Amit, ed. *Telling Tales in India*. New Delhi: New Age International, 1995.

Dashondog, Jambyn. "Children's Literature in Mongolia Needs Renovation." *Asian-Pacific Book Development* 32, no. 1 (2003).

Desmet, Mieke, and Ming Cherng Duh. "Taiwan." In *International Companion Encyclopedia of Children's Literature*, 2nd ed., ed. Peter Hunt, 1241–45. London: Routledge, 2004.

Devsare, Hari Krishna, ed. *Who's Who of Indian Children's Writers*. New Delhi: Communication Publications, 1980.

Erdogan, Fatih. "Turkey." In *International Companion Encyclopedia of Children's Literature*, 2nd ed., ed. Peter Hunt, 1246–51. London: Routledge, 2004.

Farquhar, Mary Ann. *Children's Literature in China: From Lu Xun to Mao Zedong*. Armonk, N.Y.: M. E. Sharpe, 1999.

Ho, L. "Of Morals, Misguided Writing and Commercialism: The Essence of Children's Literature in Singapore." *International Review of Children's Literature and Librarianship* 8, no. 3 (1993): 181–89.

——. "Chinese Children's Literature—Then and Now." *The New Review of Children's Literature and Librarianship* 3 (1997): 127–38.

——. "China." In *International Companion Encyclopedia of Children's Literature*, 2nd ed., ed. Peter Hunt, 1029–38. London: Routledge, 2004.

Hoang, Nguyen. "Literature for Young People in Vietnam." *Bookbird* 1 (1984): 24–26.

Jafa, Manorama. "Children's Literature and Research in India, Bangladesh, Sri Lanka and Nepal." In *Children's Literature Research, International Resources and Exchange, First International Conference, 5–7 April 1988*, ed. International Youth Library. Munich: K. G. Saur, 1991.

——. "The Indian Sub-Continent." In *International Companion Encyclopedia of Children's Literature*, 2nd ed., ed. Peter Hunt, 1076–94. London: Routledge, 2004.

Jamuna, K. A., ed. *Children's Literature in Indian Languages*. New Delhi: Publications Division, 1982.

Jinguh, Teruo. "Japan." In *International Companion Encyclopedia of Children's Literature*, 2nd ed., ed. Peter Hunt, 1108–14. London: Routledge, 2004.

Kim, Ho-Kyung. "Korea." In *International Companion Encyclopedia of Children's Literature*, 2nd ed., ed. Peter Hunt, 1124–31. London: Routledge, 2004.

Knuth, Rebecca. "Japan and Malaysia: How Two Countries Promote the Reading Habit." *International Review of Children's Literature and Librarianship* 8, no. 3 (1993): 108–80.

Mughal, Raees-Ahmed. "Five Decades of Children's Literature in Pakistan." *Bookbird* 38, no. 4 (2000): 10–15.

Ray, Sheila. "Mongolia." In *International Companion Encyclopedia of Children's Literature*, 2nd ed., ed. Peter Hunt, 1138–39. London: Routledge, 2004.

———. "South East Asia: Indonesia, Malaysia, Singapore, Thailand, Vietnam." In *International Companion Encyclopedia of Children's Literature*, 2nd ed., ed. Peter Hunt, 1207–12. London: Routledge, 2004.

Scott, Dorothea Hayward. *Chinese Popular Literature and the Child*. Chicago: American Library Association, 1980.

Seriña, Loreto M., and Fe Aldave Yap. *Children's Literature in the Philippines: An Annotated Bibliography of Pilipino and English Works, 1901–1979*. Manila: National Book Store, 1980.

Shima, Tayo. *Japanese Children's Books at the Library of Congress: A Bibliography of Books from the Postwar Years, 1946–1985*. Washington, D.C.: Library of Congress, 1987.

Shu-Jy Duan. "Text and Context: Factors in the Development of Children's Literature in Taiwan, 1945–1995, and the Emergence of Young Adult Literature." In *Reflections of Change: Children's Literature since 1945*, ed. Sandra L. Beckett. Westport, Conn.: Greenwood Press, 1997.

Sunindyo. "Publishing and Translating in Indonesia." In *A Track to Unknown Water: Pacific Rim Conference on Children's Literature*, ed. Stella Lees. Carlton, Australia: Melbourne State College, 1980.

Australia and New Zealand

Authors and Illustrators Scrapbook: Featuring 24 Creators of Australian Children's Books. Norwood, Australia: Omnibus Books, 1991.

Factor, June. *Captain Cook Chased a Chook: Children's Folklore in Australia*. Ringwood, Australia: Penguin, 1988.

Fitzgibbon, Tom, with Barbara Spiers. *Beneath Southern Skies: New Zealand Children's Book Authors and Illustrators*. Auckland: Ashton Scholastic, 1993.

Foster, John E., Ern J. Finnis, and Maureen Nimon. *Australian Children's Literature: An Exploration of Genre and Theme*. Wagga Wagga, Australia: Centre for Information Studies, 1995.

———. *Bush, City, Cyberspace: The Development of Australian Children's Literature into the 21st Century*. Wagga Wagga, Australia: Centre for Information Studies, 2006.

Gilderdale, Betty. *A Sea Change: One Hundred Forty-Five Years of New Zealand Junior Fiction*. Auckland: Longman Paul, 1982.

——. *Introducing Twenty-One New Zealand Children's Writers*. Auckland: Hodder and Stoughton, 1991.

——. "New Zealand." In *International Companion Encyclopedia of Children's Literature*, 2nd ed., ed. Peter Hunt, 1149–55. London: Routledge, 2004.

Hebley, Diane. *The Power of Place: Landscape in New Zealand Children's Fiction*. Dunedin, New Zealand: University of Ortago Press, 1998.

Johnston, Rosemary Ross. "Australia." In *International Companion Encyclopedia of Children's Literature*, 2nd ed., ed. Peter Hunt, 960–83. London: Routledge, 2004.

Lees, Stella, and Pam Macintyre. *The Oxford Companion to Australian Children's Literature*. Melbourne: Oxford University Press, 1993.

McVitty, Walter, ed. *Authors and Illustrators of Australian Children's Books*. Sydney: Hodder and Stoughton, 1990.

Muir, Marcie. *A History of Australian Children's Book Illustration*. Melbourne: Oxford University Press, 1982.

——. *Australian Children's Books: A Bibliography*. Vol. 1, *1774–1972*. Carlton, Australia: Melbourne University Press, 1992.

Niall, Brenda. *Australia through the Looking-Glass: Children's Fiction, 1830–1980*. Carlton, Australia: Melbourne University Press, 1984.

O'Neill, Terence, and Frances O'Neill. *Australian Children's Books to 1980*. Canberra: National Library of Australia, 1989.

Saxby, Maurice. *The Proof of the Puddin': Australian Children's Literature, 1970–1990*. Sydney: Ashton Scholastic, 1993.

——. *Offered to Children: A History of Australian Children's Literature, 1841–1941*. Sydney: Scholastic Australia, 1998.

——. *Images of Australia: Australian Children's Literature, 1941–1970*. Lindfield, Australia: Scholastic, 2002.

The Second Authors and Illustrators Scrapbook: Featuring 25 More Creators of Australian Children's Books. Norwood, Australia: Omnibus Books, 1992.

White, Kerry. *Australian Children's Books: A Bibliography*. Vol. 2, *1973–1988*. Carlton, Australia: Melbourne University Press, 1992.

——. *Australian Children's Books: A Bibliography*. Vol. 3, *1989–2000*. Carlton, Australia: Melbourne University Press, 2004.

COMPARATIVE AND INTERCULTURAL ASPECTS

Bradford, Clare. *Reading Race: Aboriginality in Australian Children's Literature*. Carlton, Australia: Melbourne University Press, 2001.

Chen, Lai Nam. *Images of South East Asia in Children's Books*. Singapore: Singapore University Press, 1981.

Colin, Mariella. "Children's Literature in France and Italy in the Nineteenth Century: Influences and Exchanges." In *Aspects and Issues in the History of Children's Literature*, ed. Maria Nikolajeva. Westport, Conn.: Greenwood Press, 1995.

Current Trends in Comparative Children's Literature Research: Compar(a) ison; An International Journal of Comparative Literature II (1995).

Ewers, Hans-Heino, Gertrud Lehnert, and Emer O'Sullivan, eds. *Kinderliteratur im interkulturellen Prozess. Studien zur Allgemeinen und Vergleichenden Kinderliteraturwissenschaft.* Stuttgart: Metzler, 1994.

Freeman, Evelyn B., and Barbara A. Lehman. *Global Perspectives in Children's Literature.* Boston: Allyn and Bacon, 2001.

Gebel, Doris, ed. *Crossing Boundaries with Children's Books.* Lanham, Md.: Scarecrow Press, 2006.

Hazard, Paul. *Books, Children and Men.* Trans. Marguerite Mitchell. Boston: Horn Book, 1944.

Johnston, Rosemary Rose. "Summer Holidays and Landscapes of Fear: Towards a Comparative Study of 'Mainstream' Canadian and Australian Children's Books." *Canadian Children's Literature* 109–10 (2003): 87–104.

Klingberg, Göte. *Das deutsche Kinder- und Jugendbuch im schwedischen Raum. Ein Beitrag zum Studium der Verbreitungswege der Kinder- und Jugendliteratur.* Weinheim, Germany: Beltz, 1973.

Kuivasmäki, Riitta. "International Influence on the Nineteenth Century Finnish Children's Literature." In *Aspects and Issues in the History of Children's Literature*, ed. Maria Nikolajeva, 97–102. Westport, Conn.: Greenwood Press, 1995.

Lathey, Gillian. *The Impossible Legacy: Identity and Purpose in Autobiographical Children's Literature Set in the Third Reich and the Second World War.* Bern: Peter Lang, 1999.

Levy, Michael M. *Refugees and Immigrants: The Southeast Asian Experience as Depicted in Recent American Children's Books.* Lewiston, N.Y.: Edwin Mellen, 2000.

Lowery, Ruth McKoy. *Immigrants in Children's Literature.* New York: Peter Lang, 2000.

Maddy, Yulisa Amadu, and Donnarae MacCann. *Neo-Imperialism in Children's Literature about Africa: A Study of Contemporary Fiction.* New York: Routledge, 2008.

McGillis, Roderick, ed. *Voices of the Other: Children's Literature and the Postcolonial Context.* New York: Garland, 1999.

Meek, Margaret, ed. *Children's Literature and National Identity.* London: Trentham, 2001.

Mingshui, Cai. *Multicultural Literature for Children and Young Adults: Reflections on Critical Issues.* Westport, Conn.: Greenwood, 2002.

Müller, Heidy Margrit, ed. *Migration, Minderheiten und kulturelle Vielfalt in der europäischen Jugendliteratur. Migration, Minorities and Multiculturalism in European Youth Literature*. Bern: Peter Lang, 2001.

Nodelman, Perry. "The Other: Orientalism, Colonialism, and Children's Literature." *Children's Literature Association Quarterly* 17 (1992): 29–35.

O'Sullivan, Emer. *Friend and Foe: The Image of Germany and the Germans in British Children's Fiction from 1870 to the Present*. Tübingen, Germany: Narr, 1990.

———. *Comparative Children's Literature*. London: Routledge, 2005.

Pellowski, Anne. *Made to Measure: Children's Books in Developing Countries*. Paris: UNESCO, 1980.

———. *The World of Children's Literature*. New York: Bowker, 1968.

———. "Story in Orature and Literature: Why and How We Make It Available to Children in Different Cultures." In International Board on Books for Young People, *Proceedings, 25th Congress, 12–16 August 1996: Telling the Tale*. Amsterdam: Dutch Section of IBBY, 1997.

———. "Culture and Developing Countries." In *International Companion Encyclopedia of Children's Literature*, 2nd ed., ed. Peter Hunt, 663–75. London: Routledge, 2004.

Pratt, Linda, and Janice J. Beaty. *Transcultural Children's Literature*. Columbus, Ohio: Prentice-Hall, 1999.

Randall, Don. *Kipling's Imperial Boy: Adolescence and Cultural Hybridity*. Basingstoke, UK: Palgrave, 2000.

Sands-O'Connor, Karen. *Soon Come Home to This Island: West Indians in British Children's Literature*. New York: Routledge, 2007.

Stan, Susan, ed. *The World through Children's Books*. Lanham, Md.: Scarecrow Press, 2002.

Webb, Jean, ed. *Text, Culture and National Identity in Children's Literature*. Helsinki: Nordinfo, 2000.

TRANSLATION

Bell, Anthea. "Translating Verse for Children." *Signal* 85 (1998): 3–14.

Ben-Ari, Nitsa. "Didactic and Pedagogic Tendencies in the Norms Dictating the Translation of Children's Literature: The Case of Postwar German-Hebrew Translations." *Poetics Today* 13, no. 1 (1992): 221–30.

Coillie, Jan van, and Walter P. Verschueren, eds. *Children's Literature in Translation: Challenges and Strategies*. Manchester: St. Jerome Press, 2006.

Craig, Ian. *Children's Classics under Franco: Censorship of the William Books and the Adventures of Tom Sawyer*. Oxford: Peter Lang, 2001.

Desmet, Mieke K. T. "Intertextuality/Intervisuality in Translation: *The Jolly Postman*'s Intercultural Journey from Britain to the Netherlands." *Children's Literature in Education* 32, no. 1 (2001): 31–43.

——. *Babysitting the Reader: Translating Narrative Fiction for Girls from English to Dutch (1946–1995)*. Bern: Peter Lang, 2007.

Even-Zohar, Basmat. "Translation Policy in Hebrew Children's Literature: The Case of Astrid Lindgren." *Poetics Today* 13, no. 1 (1992): 231–45.

Fernández López, Marisa. *Traducción y literatura juvenil. Narrativa anglosajona contemporánea en España*. León, Spain: Universidad de León, 1996.

——. "Translation Studies in Contemporary Children's Literature: A Comparison of Intercultural Ideological Factors." *Children's Literature Association Quarterly* 25, no. 1 (2000): 29–37.

Flugge, Klaus. "Crossing the Divide: Publishing Children's Books in the European Context." *Signal* 75 (1994): 209–14.

Hagfors, Irma. "The Translation of Culture-Bound Elements into Finnish in the Post War Period." *Meta* 48 (2003): 115–27.

Klingberg, Göte. *Children's Fiction in the Hands of the Translator*. Lund, Sweden: Gleerup, 1986.

Klingberg, Göte, Mary Ørvig, and Stuart Amor, eds. *Children's Books in Translation*. Stockholm: Almqvist and Wiksell International, 1978.

Kreller, Susan: *Englischsprachige Kinderlyrik: Deutsche Übersetzungen im 20. Jahrhundert*. Frankfurt: Peter Lang, 2007.

Lathey, Gillian. "Time, Narrative Intimacy and the Child: Implications of the Transition from the Present to the Past Tense in the Translation into English of Children's Texts." *Meta* 48 (2003): 233–40.

——, ed. *The Translation of Children's Literature: A Reader*. Clevendon, UK: Multilingual Matters, 2006.

Marcus, Kendra. "Buying and Selling International Children's Books Rights: A Literary Agent's Perspective." *Publishing Research Quarterly* 19, no. 2 (2003): 52–56.

Oittinen, Rita. *Translating for Children*. New York: Garland, 2000.

O'Sullivan, Emer. "Narratology Meets Translation Studies, or The Voice of the Translator in Children's Literature." In *Meta* 48, nos. 1–2 (2003): 197–207.

——. "*Rose Blanche, Rosa Weiss, Rosa Blanca*. A Comparative View of a Controversial Picture Book." *Lion and the Unicorn* 29 (2005): 152–70.

——. "Translating Pictures." In *Considering Children's Literature: A Reader*, ed. Andrea Schwenke Wyile and Teya Rosenberg, 117–26. Guelph, ON: Broadview Press, 2008.

Pincent, Pat, ed. *No Child Is an Island: The Case for Children's Literature in Translation*. Shenstone, UK: Pied Piper, 2006.

Tabbert, Reinbert. "Approaches to the Translation of Children's Literature: A Review of Critical Studies since 1960." *Target* 14, no. 2 (2002): 303–51.
Thomson-Wohlgemuth, Gabriele. *Translation Under State Control: Books for Young People in the German Democratic Republic*. New York: Routledge, 2009.
Webb Joels, Rosie. "Weaving World Understanding: The Importance of Translations in International Children's Literature." *Children's Literature in Education* 30, no. 1 (1999): 65–83.
White, Maureen. "Children's Books from Other Languages: A Study of Successful Translations." *Journal of Youth Services in Libraries* 5, no. 3 (1992): 261–75.
Wunderlich, Richard, and Thomas J. Morrissey. *Pinocchio Goes Postmodern: Perils of a Puppet in the United States*. 2nd ed. New York: Routledge, 2008.

MEDIA

Collins, Fiona M., and Jeremy Ridgman, eds. *Turning the Page: Children's Literature in Performance and the Media*. Oxford: Peter Lang, 2006.
Home, Anna. *Into the Box of Delights: A History of Children's Television*. London: BBC Books, 1993.
Mackey, Margaret. "The Survival of Engaged Reading in the Internet Age: New Media, Old Media, and the Book." *Children's Literature in Education* 32, no. 3 (2001): 167–89.
———. *Literacies across Media: Playing the Text*. London: Routledge, 2002.
McCallum, Robyn. "The Past Reshaping the Present: Film Versions of *Little Women*." *Lion and the Unicorn* 24, no. 1 (2000): 81–96.
Morris, Tim. *You're Only Young Twice: Children's Literature and Film*. Urbana: University of Illinois Press, 2000.
Rollin, Lucy, ed. *Antic Art: Enhancing Children's Literary Experiences through Films and Video*. Fort Atkinson, Wis.: Highsmith, 1993.
Stephens, John, ed. *Ways of Being Male. Representing Masculinities in Children's Literature and Film*. 2nd ed. New York: Routledge, 2008.
Street, Douglas, ed. *Children's Novels and the Movies*. New York: Ungar, 1983.
Wojik-Andrews, Ian. *Children's Films: History, Ideology, Pedagogy, Theory*. New York: Garland, 2000.
Zipes, Jack. *Happily Ever After: Fairy Tales, Children and the Culture Industry*. New York: Routledge, 1997.

READING AND LITERACY

Appleyard, J. A. *Becoming a Reader: The Experience of Fiction from Childhood to Adulthood.* Cambridge: Cambridge University Press, 1990.

Chambers, Aidan. *The Reading Environment.* South Woodchester, UK: Thimble Press, 1991.

Crago, Hugh, and Maureen Crago. *Prelude to Literacy: A Pre-School Child's Encounter with Picture and Story.* Carbondale: Southern Illinois University Press, 1983.

Fox, Carol. *At the Very Edge of the Forest: The Influence of Literature on Storytelling by Children.* London: Cassell, 1993.

Fry, Donald. *Children Talk about Books: Seeing Themselves as Readers.* Milton Keynes, UK: Open University Press, 1985.

Hade, Daniel. "Storytelling: Are Publishers Changing the Way Children Read?" *Horn Book Magazine* 78 (2002): 509–17.

Kimberley, Keith, Margaret Meek, and Jane Miller, eds. *New Readings: Contributions to an Understanding of Literacy.* London: A. and C. Black, 1992.

Lowe, Virginia. *Stories, Pictures and Reality: Young Children's Understanding of Reality and Pretence.* London: Routledge, 2007.

Mackey, Margaret. *The Case of Peter Rabbit: Changing Conditions of Literature for Children.* New York: Garland, 1998.

Many, Joyce, and Carol Cox, eds. *Reader Stance and Literary Understanding: Exploring the Theories, Research and Practice.* Norwood, N.J.: Ablex, 1992.

Meek, Margaret. *How Texts Teach What Readers Learn.* South Woodchester, UK: Thimble Press, 1988.

Paul, Lissa. *Reading Otherways.* South Woodchester, UK: Thimble Press, 1997.

Sarland, Charles. *Young People Reading: Culture and Response.* Milton Keynes, UK: Open University Press, 1991.

Scholes, Robert E. *Protocols of Reading.* New Haven, Conn.: Yale University Press, 1989.

Soter, Anna O. *Young Adult Literature and the New Literary Theories: Developing Critical Readers in Middle School.* New York: Teachers College Press, 1999.

Spufford, Francis. *The Child That Books Built.* London: Faber and Faber, 2002.

Styles, Morag, Eve Bearne, and Victor Watson, eds. *The Prose and the Passion: Children and Their Reading.* London: Cassell, 1994.

Tucker, Nicholas. *The Child and the Book: A Psychological and Literary Exploration.* Cambridge: Cambridge University Press, 1981.

Watson, Victor, and Morag Styles, eds. *Talking Pictures: Pictorial Texts and Young Readers.* London: Hodder and Stoughton, 1996.

Wolf, Shirley Anne, and Shirley Brice Heath. *The Braid of Literature: Children's Worlds of Reading*. Cambridge, Mass.: Harvard University Press, 1992.

JOURNALS

ALAN Review. National Council of Teachers of English. 1979ff. scholar.lib.vt.edu/ejournals/ALAN/

Bookbird: A Journal of International Children's Literature. International Board on Books for Young People (IBBY). 1962ff. www.ibby.org

Booklist. The Library Association. 1969ff. www.ala.org/ala/aboutala/offices/publishing/booklist_publications/booklist/booklist.cfm

Books for Keeps. www.booksforkeeps.co.uk

Bulletin of the Center for Children's Books. The Center for Children's Books. 1947ff. bccb.lis.uiuc.edu/

Canadian Children's Literature (CCL) / Littérature canadienne pour la jeunesse. Canadian Children's Literature Association. 1975ff. ccl.uwinnipeg.ca

Children's Literature (CL). Annual of the Modern Language Association Division on Children's Literature and the Children's Literature Association. 1972ff. www.childlitassn.org/childrens_literature_journal.html

Children's Literature Association Quarterly (ChLAQ). 1974ff. www.childlitassn.org/chla_quarterly_journal.html

Children's Literature in Education: An International Quarterly (CLE). 1970ff.

Children's Literature Review (CLR). 1976ff.

Horn Book Magazine. 1924ff. www.hbook.com

Inis: The Children's Books Ireland Magazine (formerly *Children's Books in Ireland*). 1989ff. www.childrensbooksireland.com

International Research in Children's Literature (IRCL). 2008ff. www.eupjournals.com/journal/ircl

Journal of Children's Literature Studies. 2004ff.

The Lion and the Unicorn: A Critical Journal of Children's Literature (L&U). 1977ff. www.press.jhu.edu/journals/lion_and_the_unicorn/

The Looking Glass: New Perspectives on Children's Books; An On-Line Children's Literature Journal. 1997ff. www.the-looking-glass.net

Magpies. 1986ff. www.magpies.net.au

New Review of Children's Literature and Librarianship (NRCLL). 1995ff. www.tandf.co.uk/journals/titles/13614541.asp

Papers: Explorations into Children's Literature. 1990ff.

Phaedrus: An International Annual of Children's Literature Research. 1973–1988.

The School Librarian: The Journal of the School Library Association. 1937ff. www.sla.org.uk/school-librarian.php

School Library Journal (SLJ). 1975ff. www.schoollibraryjournal.com

Signal: Approaches to Children's Books. 1970–2003.

Through the Looking Glass: An Online Children's Book Review Journal (TTLG). 2003ff. www.lookingglassreview.com/

WEBSITES

ABC-Lit: An Index to Children's Literature Scholarship www.abc-lit.com/

About.com: Children's Books (book reviews; linked list of awards; links to author and illustrator sites; reading lists) childrensbooks.about.com

Association for Library Service to Children (ALSC; American Library Association; publications; conferences; links to awards and scholarships) www.ala.org/ala/alsc

Books'n'Bytes (links to author sites) www.booksnbytes.com/authors/allauths_a.html

BUBL LINK Catalogue of Internet Resources (Strathclyde University, UK; annotated collection of links to children's literature sites) bubl.ac.uk/LINK/linkbrowse.cfm?menuid=10950

Canadian Children's Book Centre (professional and student resources; list of Canadian awards; links to Canadian author and illustrator sites; programs and publications) www.bookcentre.ca/

Carol Hurst's Children's Literature Site (reviews; teaching ideas; children's books in various curriculum areas; information about topics, authors, and illustrators) www.carolhurst.com

Children's and Young Adult Books (links to institutional, publisher, and agent sites) www.sharyn.org/children.html

The Children's Book Council (CBC; links to author websites; reading lists; criteria for choosing books for different ages; resources for writers and artists) www.cbcbooks.org

Children's Literature (La Trobe University, Australia; comprehensive links) latrobe.libguides.com/Childrens_Literature

Children's Literature Association (ChLA; awards; links to academic programs; scholarly resources) www.childlitassn.org/

Children's Literature Center (Library of Congress; catalog of children's literature of the Library of Congress) www.loc.gov/rr/child/

Children's Literature Network (links to author and illustrator sites; reading lists) www.childrensliteraturenetwork.org/

Children's Literature Webguide (University of Calgary, Canada; metasite) www.acs.ucalgary.ca/~dkbrown/
Children's Picture Book Database (Miami University, Ohio; abstracts of over 5,000 children's picture books) www.lib.muohio.edu/pictbks/
The Clearinghouse on Reading, English, and Communication (Indiana University; educational materials; lesson plans; links to reading organizations; links to children's literature; links to review and award sites) reading.indiana.edu/
The Database of Award-Winning Children's Literature (over 7,000 records from 84 awards across six English-speaking countries) www.dawcl.com/
The Digital Librarian: Children's Literature (metasite) www.digital-librarian .com/childlit.html
The Educator's Reference Desk (Information Institute of Syracuse, New York; annotated list of links to sites related to children's literature in general, teaching ideas, and organizations) www.eduref.org/cgi-bin/print.cgi/Resources/Subjects/Language_Arts/Literature/Childrens_Literature.html
General Children's Literature Resources (annotated list of links to sites related to children's literature, awards, organizations, and journals; reading lists) frankrogers.home.mindspring.com/general.html
The Hockliffe Project (De Montfort University, UK; database, including digitized images, of the books in the Hockliffe Collection of early British children's literature; critical essays) www.cts.dmu.ac.uk/hockliffe/
International Board on Books for Young People (IBBY; information on activities of the organization, the Hans Christian Andersen Award, etc.) www .ibby.org
International Children's Digital Library (free online access to some 4,000 children's books in 51 languages) www.childrenslibrary.org/
International Research Society for Children's Literature (congresses; reviews of academic literature; links to national research societies and international academic journals) www.irscl.com
Internet Public Library Author Page (author biographies; links to author sites) www.ipl.org/div/askauthor/
Kay Vandergrift's Special Interest Page (Rutgers State University of New Jersey; history of children's literature; links to author sites; information on biography and autobiography; videos of authors) www.scils.rutgers.edu/professional-development/childlit/
Kerlan Collection (University of Minnesota; database of online collections of children's literature) special.lib.umn.edu/clrc/kerlan/othercollections
The Parents' Choice Foundation (award program; reading lists) www .parentschoice.org/
Philip Nel's Literary Links (Kansas State University; metasite; links to sites related to authors, awards, scholars, journals, organizations, etc.) www.k-state.edu/english/nelp/weblinks/literary/childrens.html

Picturing Books (information about picture books; glossary; database; reviews; comprehensive list of links to author and illustrator sites, institutions, journals etc.) www.imaginarylands.org/

Teacher Oz's Literature and Drama (links to various genres, including Australian children's literature) www.teacheroz.com/literature.htm

Teachers at Random Authors and Illustrators www.randomhouse.com/teachers/authors/

Women Children's Book Illustrators (database of female illustrators; biographies; bibliographies) www.ortakales.com/Illustrators/index.html

Young Adult Library Services Association (YALSA; American Library Association; linked list of books and awards; grants; publications) www.ala.org/ala/yalsa/yalsa.htm

About the Author

Emer O'Sullivan, originally from Ireland, is professor of English literature at Leuphana University in Lüneburg, Germany. She has published widely in both German and English on comparative literature, image studies, children's literature, and translation, and has received international recognition for her pioneering work in comparative children's literature studies. Her first two scholarly publications, *Das ästhetische Potential nationaler Stereotypen in literarischen Texten* [The Aesthetic Potential of National Stereotypes in Literature] (1989) and *Friend and Foe: The Image of Germany and the Germans in British Children's Fiction from 1870 to the Present* (1990), were the first imagological studies of children's literature. *Kinderliterarische Komparatistik* won the biennial International Research Society for Children's Literature (IRSCL) Award for outstanding research in 2001, and *Comparative Children's Literature* won the Children's Literature Association 2007 Book Award. She worked at the Institut für Jugendbuchforschung (Institute for Children's Literature Research) at Frankfurt University from 1990 to 2004 and served as vice president of the IRSCL from 2003 to 2005. She has also coauthored, with Dietmar Rösler, eight genuinely bilingual (English-German) children's novels.

Lightning Source UK Ltd.
Milton Keynes UK
171993UK00001B/6/P